FOND DU LAC PUBLIC LIBRARY

WITHDRAWN

Yamaha FZR600, 750 & 1000 Fours
Service and Repair Manual

by Alan Ahlstrand
and John H Haynes Member of the Guild of Motoring Writers

Models covered

UK:
Yamaha FZR600. 599cc. 1989 through 1993
Yamaha FZR750R (OW01). 749cc. 1989 through 1992
Yamaha FZR1000. 989cc. 1987 through 1988
Yamaha FZR1000 EXUP. 1002cc. 1989 through 1996

US:
Yamaha FZR600/600R. 599cc. 1989 through 1996
Yamaha FZR750R. 750cc. 1987 and 1988
Yamaha FZR1000. 989cc. 1987 and 1988
Yamaha FZR1000. 1002cc. 1989 through 1995

(2056-320-6Z5)

ABCDE
FGHIJ
KLM

© Haynes Publishing 2000

A book in the Haynes Service and Repair Manual Series

All rights reserved. No part of this book may be reproduced or transmitted in any form or by any means, electronic or mechanical, including photocopying, recording or by any information storage or retrieval system, without permission in writing from the copyright holder.

ISBN 1 85960 370 X

Library of Congress Catalog Card Number 97-74469

British Library Cataloguing in Publication Data
A catalogue record for this book is available from the British Library.

Printed in the USA

Haynes Publishing
Sparkford, Yeovil, Somerset BA22 7JJ, England

Haynes North America, Inc
861 Lawrence Drive, Newbury Park, California 91320, USA

Editions Haynes
4, Rue de l'Abreuvoir
92415 COURBEVOIE CEDEX, France

Haynes Publishing Nordiska AB
Box 1504, 751 45 UPPSALA, Sweden

Contents

LIVING WITH YOUR YAMAHA FZR

Introduction

Yamaha – Musical Instruments to Motorcycles	Page	0•4
Acknowledgements	Page	0•7
About this manual	Page	0•7
Safety first!	Page	0•8
Identification numbers	Page	0•9
Buying spare parts	Page	0•9

Daily (pre-ride) checks

Engine/transmission oil level	Page	0•10
Coolant level	Page	0•10
Cable clutch check	Page	0•10
Brake and hydraulic clutch fluid levels	Page	0•11
Suspension, steering and drive chain	Page	0•11
Legal and safety checks	Page	0•11
Tires	Page	0•12

MAINTENANCE

Routine maintenance and servicing

Specifications	Page	1•1, 1•3
Recommended lubricants and fluids	Page	1•2, 1•3
Component locations	Page	1•6
Maintenance schedule	Page	1•8
Maintenance procedures	Page	1•9

Contents

REPAIRS AND OVERHAUL

Engine, transmission and associated systems

FZR600 engine, clutch and transmission	Page	2•1
FZR750/1000 engine, clutch and transmission	Page	3•1
Cooling system	Page	4•1
Fuel and exhaust systems	Page	5•1
Ignition system	Page	6•1

Chassis components

Frame, suspension and final drive	Page	7•1
Brakes	Page	8•1
Wheels	Page	8•15
Tyres	Page	8•24
Fairing and bodywork	Page	9•1

Electrical system

Page 10•1

Wiring diagrams

Page 10•21

REFERENCE

Dimensions and Weights	Page	REF•1
Conversion Factors	Page	REF•3
Tools and Workshop Tips	Page	REF•4
MOT Test Checks	Page	REF•22
Storage	Page	REF•26
Motorcycle Chemicals and Lubricants	Page	REF•28
Fault Finding	Page	REF•29
Fault Finding Equipment	Page	REF•37
Technical Terms Explained	Page	REF•41

Index

Page REF•45

Introduction

Yamaha
Musical instruments to Motorcycles

The Yamaha Motor Company

The Yamaha name can be traced back to 1889, when Torakusu Yamaha founded the Yamaha Organ Manufacturing Company. Such was the success of the company, that in 1897 it became Nippon Gakki Limited and manufactured a wide range of reed organs and pianos.

During World War II, Nippon Gakki's manufacturing base was utilised by the Japanese authorities to produce propellers and fuel tanks for their aviation industry. The end of the war brought about a huge public demand for low cost transport and many firms decided to utilise their obsolete aircraft tooling for the production of motorcycles. Nippon Gakki's first motorcycle went on sale in February 1955 and was named the 125 YA-1 Red Dragonfly. This machine was a copy of the German DKW RT125 motorcycle, featuring a single cylinder two-stroke engine with a four-speed gearbox. Due to the outstanding success of this model the motorcycle operation was separated from Nippon Gakki in July 1955 and the Yamaha Motor Company was formed.

The YA-1 also received acclaim by winning two of Japan's biggest road races, the Mt. Fuji Climbing race and the Asama Volcano race. The high level of public demand for the YA-1 led to the development of a whole series of two-stroke singles and twins.

Having made a large impact on their home market, Yamahas were exported to the USA in 1958 and to the UK in 1962. In the UK the signing of an Anglo-Japanese trade agreement during 1962 enabled the sale of Japanese lightweight motorcycles and scooters in Britain. At that time, competition between the many motorcycle producers in Japan had reduced numbers significantly and by the end of the sixties, only the big-four which are familiar with today remained.

Yamaha Europe was founded in 1968 and based in Holland. Although originally set up to market marine products, the Dutch base is now the official European Headquarters and distribution centre. Yamaha motorcycles are built at factories in Holland, Denmark, Norway, Italy, France, Spain and Portugal. Yamahas are imported into the UK by Yamaha Motor UK Ltd, formerly Mitsui Machinery Sales (UK) Ltd. Mitsui and Co. were originally a trading house, handling the shipping, distribution and marketing of Japanese products into western countries. Ultimately Mitsui Machinery Sales was formed to handle Yamaha motorcycles and outboard motors.

Based on the technology derived from its motorcycle operation, Yamaha have produced many other products, such as automobile and lightweight aircraft engines, marine engines and boats, generators, pumps, ATVs, snowmobiles, golf cars, industrial robots, lawnmowers, swimming pools and archery equipment.

Two-strokes first

Part of Yamaha's success was a whole string of innovations in the two-stroke world. Autolube engine lubrication, pressed steel monocoque frame, electric starting, torque induction, multi-ported engines, reed valves and power valves kept their two-strokes at the forefront of technology.

In the 1960s and 70s the two-stroke engined YAS3 125, YDS1 to YDS7 250 and YR5 350 formed the core of Yamaha's range. By the mid-70s they had been superseded by the RD (Race-Developed) 125, 250, and 350 range of two-stroke twins, featuring improved 7 port engines with reed valve induction. Braking was improved by the use of an hydraulic brake on the front wheel of DX models, instead of the drum arrangement used previously, and cast alloy wheels were available as an option on later RD models. The RD350 was replaced by the RD400 in 1976.

The FS1-E - first bike of many sixteen year olds in the UK

Introduction

Running parallel with the RD twins was a range of single-cylinder two-strokes. Used in a variety of chassis types, the engine was used in the popular 50 cc FS1-E moped, the V50 to 90 step-thrus, RS100 and 125, YB100 and the DT trail range.

The air-cooled single and twin cylinder RD models were eventually replaced by the LC series in 1980, featuring liquid-cooled engines, radical new styling, spiral pattern cast wheels and cantilever rear suspension (Yamaha's Monoshock). Of all the LC models, the RD350LC, or RD350R as it was later known, has made the most impact in the market. Later models had YPVS (Yamaha Power Valve System) engines, another first for Yamaha - this was essentially a valve located in the exhaust ports which was electronically operated to alter port timing to achieve maximum power output. The RD500LC was the largest two-stroke made by Yamaha and differed from the other LCs by the use of its vee-four cylinder engine.

With the exception of the RD350R, now manufactured in Brazil, the LC range has been discontinued. Two-stroke engined models have given way to environmental pressure, and thus with a few exceptions, such as the TZR125 and TZR250, are used only in scooters and small capacity bikes.

The Four-strokes

Yamaha concentrated solely on two-stroke models until 1970 when the XS1 was produced, their first four-stroke motorcycle. It was perhaps Yamaha's success with two-strokes that postponed an earlier move into the four-stroke motorcycle market, although their work with Toyota during the 1960s had given them a sound base in four-stroke technology.

The XS1 had a 650 cc twin-cylinder SOHC engine and was later to become known as the XS650, appearing also in the popular SE custom form. Yamaha introduced a three cylinder 750 cc engine in 1976, fitted in a sport-tourer frame and called the XS750, TX750 in the USA. The XS750 established itself well in the sport tourer class and remained in production with very few changes until uprated to 850 cc in 1980.

Other four-strokes followed in 1976, with the introduction of the XS250/360/400 series twins. The XS range was strengthened in 1978 by the four-cylinder XS1100.

The 1980s saw a new family of four-strokes, the XJ550, 650, 750 and 900 Fours. Improvements over the XS range amounted to a slimmer DOHC engine unit due to the relocation of the alternator behind the cylinders, electronic ignition and uprated braking and suspension systems. Models were available mainly in standard trim, although custom-styled Maxims were produced especially for the US market. The XJ650T was the first model from Yamaha to have a turbo-charged engine. Although these early XJ models have now been discontinued, their roots live on in the XJ600S and XJ900S Diversion (Seca II) models.

The FZR prefix encompasses the pure sports Yamaha models. With the exception of the 16-valve FZR400 and FZR600 models, the FZ/FZR750 and FZR1000 used 20-valve engines, two exhaust valves and three inlet valves per cylinder. This concept was called Genesis and gave improved gas flow to the combustion chambers. Other features of the new engine were the use of down-draught carburetors and the engine's inclined angle in the frame, plus the change to liquid-cooling.

The distinctive paintwork and trim of the RD models

The XS650 led the way for Yamaha's four-stroke range

Introduction

Yamaha's XS750 was produced from 1976 to 1982 and then uprated to 850 cc

A new family of four-strokes was released in 1980 with the introduction of the XJ range

Lightweight Deltabox design aluminium frames and uprated suspension improved the bikes's handling. The Genesis engine lives on in the YZF750 and 1000 models.

The vee-twin engine has been the mainstay of the XV Virago range. Since 1981 XVs have been produced in 535, 700, 750, 920, 1000 and 1100 engine sizes, all using the same basic air-cooled sohc vee-twin engine. Other uses of vee engines have been in the XZ550 of the early 1980s, the XVZ12 Venture and the mighty VMX-12 V-Max.

Anti-lock braking, engine management, catalytic converters and hub center steering are all features found on present-day models, ensuring that Yamaha remain at the forefront of technology.

The FZRs

The air-cooled FZ600 produced from 1986 to 1988 was no match for the 16-valve engined CBR600, GSX600 and ZX600 competition, and was eventually replaced by the FZR600 in 1989. The new FZR used a 16-valve, liquid-cooled engine, inclined 45° in the frame to allow the use of downdraught carburettors. In keeping with the Genesis concept of the larger FZRs, the engine was housed in a Deltabox frame, although the frame was made of steel instead of aluminium. To allow a lower centre of gravity and provide space for the airbox directly above the carburettors, the fuel tank was nestled between the frame top tubes and covered by a dummy plastic fuel tank cover.

As a sign of getting it right first time, there have been very few changes to the FZR600 during its model run. In 1991 a wedge-shaped single headlight was fitted although customer preference for the twin headlights saw a new fairing and return to dual headlights in 1993. The FZR600 was superseded by the FZR600R and thence the YZF600 Thundercat in the UK, but continues to run alongside the YZF600 in the US.

The 20-valve engine of the FZR750 and 1000 models can be traced back to the 1985 FZ750. Each cylinder has 5 valves, three intake and two exhaust, and the cylinders are angled forwards 45°, lowering the engine's weight in the frame and allowing the use of downdraught carburettors.

New to the first FZR750 and 1000 models, was the Deltabox aluminium frame. The frame spars run straight from the headstock to the swingarm pivot, bulging out slightly to accommodate the carburettors. Box-section steel tube was used to support the engine in the frame and to support the seat and rear mudguard components.

For 1989 the FZR1000's engine was angled just 35° in the frame, making it slightly more upright and taller than its predecessor. Improvements were made to the engine by strengthening the big-end bearings and piston pin, and altering the valve angle and lifter arrangement. Engine displacement increased from 989 cc to 1002 cc. Increased power was obtained by larger bore carburettors (up to 38 mm) and Yamaha's EXUP (Exhaust Ultimate Power Valve) system. The EXUP device is located in the exhaust system, between the header pipes and silencer. Triggered by electronic signals from the ignitor unit, the EXUP servo motor uses cables to operate the internal valves in the exhaust.

The 1989 FZR1000 received a modified, stiffer, Deltabox frame and a new style Deltabox swingarm with modified rear suspension linkage.

For 1991 the FZR1000 received a new fairing, with single headlight, redesigned side covers and tail piece. Front suspension was via a pair of upside down forks, with a new style wrap-around front fender to protect the exposed fork tubes. Engine changes were few; hoses from the cooling system routed coolant around the new spin-on type oil filter and an electric fuel pump was fitted.

The next change to the FZR1000 came in 1994, with a new fairing and twin fox-eye headlights. Ohlins front forks replaced the Kayaba forks of the previous models. Braking was improved with six-piston calipers at the front.

Production of the FZR1000 came to an end in 1996, and the YZF1000 Thunderace took over as Yamaha's Superbike.

Only a limited number of FZR750R models (OW01 in the UK) were introduced, their purpose being as homologation specials for Formula One and Superbike race requirements that race bikes must start life as production road bikes. Although using the 20-valve engine of the earlier FZ750 and FZR1000, numerous components were uprated to ensure its suitability for the race track.

The FZR600

Acknowledgements

Our thanks are due to Mitsui Machinery Sales (UK) Ltd for permission to reproduce certain illustrations used in this manual. We would also like to thank the Avon Rubber Company, who kindly supplied information and technical assistance on tyre fitting, and NGK Spark plugs (UK) Ltd for information on spark plug maintenance and electrode conditions.

Special thanks to Grand Prix Kawasaki/Yamaha, Santa Clara, California, for providing the motorcycles used in these photographs ; to Pete Sirett, service manager, for arranging the facilities and fitting the mechanical work into his shop's busy schedule; and to Chris Campbell, service technician, for doing the mechanical work and providing valuable technical information.

Thanks are also due to Yamaha Motor (UK) Ltd and Kel Edge for supplying colour transparencies.

About this Manual

The The aim of this manual is to help you get the best value from your motorcycle. It can do so in several ways. It can help you decide what work must be done, even if you choose to have it done by a dealer; it provides information and procedures for routine maintenance and servicing; and it offers diagnostic and repair procedures to follow when trouble occurs.

We hope you use the manual to tackle the work yourself. For many simpler jobs, doing it yourself may be quicker than arranging an appointment to get the motorcycle into a dealer and making the trips to leave it and pick it up. More importantly, a lot of money can be saved by avoiding the expense the shop must pass on to you to cover its labour and overhead costs. An added benefit is the sense of satisfaction and accomplishment that you feel after doing the job yourself.

References to the left or right side of the motorcycle assume you are sitting on the seat, facing forward.

We take great pride in the accuracy of information given in this manual, but motorcycle manufacturers make alterations and design changes during the production run of a particular motorcycle of which they do not inform us. No liability can be accepted by the authors or publishers for loss, damage or injury caused by any errors in, or omissions from, the information given.

0•8 Safety first!

Professional mechanics are trained in safe working procedures. However enthusiastic you may be about getting on with the job at hand, take the time to ensure that your safety is not put at risk. A moment's lack of attention can result in an accident, as can failure to observe simple precautions.

There will always be new ways of having accidents, and the following is not a comprehensive list of all dangers; it is intended rather to make you aware of the risks and to encourage a safe approach to all work you carry out on your bike.

Asbestos

● Certain friction, insulating, sealing and other products - such as brake pads, clutch linings, gaskets, etc. - contain asbestos. Extreme care must be taken to avoid inhalation of dust from such products since it is hazardous to health. If in doubt, assume that they do contain asbestos.

Fire

● Remember at all times that petrol is highly flammable. Never smoke or have any kind of naked flame around, when working on the vehicle. But the risk does not end there - a spark caused by an electrical short-circuit, by two metal surfaces contacting each other, by careless use of tools, or even by static electricity built up in your body under certain conditions, can ignite petrol vapour, which in a confined space is highly explosive. Never use petrol as a cleaning solvent. Use an approved safety solvent.

● Always disconnect the battery earth terminal before working on any part of the fuel or electrical system, and never risk spilling fuel on to a hot engine or exhaust.

● It is recommended that a fire extinguisher of a type suitable for fuel and electrical fires is kept handy in the garage or workplace at all times. Never try to extinguish a fuel or electrical fire with water.

Fumes

● Certain fumes are highly toxic and can quickly cause unconsciousness and even death if inhaled to any extent. Petrol vapour comes into this category, as do the vapours from certain solvents such as trichloro-ethylene. Any draining or pouring of such volatile fluids should be done in a well ventilated area.

● When using cleaning fluids and solvents, read the instructions carefully. Never use materials from unmarked containers - they may give off poisonous vapours.

● Never run the engine of a motor vehicle in an enclosed space such as a garage. Exhaust fumes contain carbon monoxide which is extremely poisonous; if you need to run the engine, always do so in the open air or at least have the rear of the vehicle outside the workplace.

The battery

● Never cause a spark, or allow a naked light near the vehicle's battery. It will normally be giving off a certain amount of hydrogen gas, which is highly explosive.

● Always disconnect the battery ground (earth) terminal before working on the fuel or electrical systems (except where noted).

● If possible, loosen the filler plugs or cover when charging the battery from an external source. Do not charge at an excessive rate or the battery may burst.

● Take care when topping up, cleaning or carrying the battery. The acid electrolyte, evenwhen diluted, is very corrosive and should not be allowed to contact the eyes or skin. Always wear rubber gloves and goggles or a face shield. If you ever need to prepare electrolyte yourself, always add the acid slowly to the water; never add the water to the acid.

Electricity

● When using an electric power tool, inspection light etc., always ensure that the appliance is correctly connected to its plug and that, where necessary, it is properly grounded (earthed). Do not use such appliances in damp conditions and, again, beware of creating a spark or applying excessive heat in the vicinity of fuel or fuel vapour. Also ensure that the appliances meet national safety standards.

● A severe electric shock can result from touching certain parts of the electrical system, such as the spark plug wires (HT leads), when the engine is running or being cranked, particularly if components are damp or the insulation is defective. Where an electronic ignition system is used, the secondary (HT) voltage is much higher and could prove fatal.

Remember...

✗ **Don't** start the engine without first ascertaining that the transmission is in neutral.

✗ **Don't** suddenly remove the pressure cap from a hot cooling system - cover it with a cloth and release the pressure gradually first, or you may get scalded by escaping coolant.

✗ **Don't** attempt to drain oil until you are sure it has cooled sufficiently to avoid scalding you.

✗ **Don't** grasp any part of the engine or exhaust system without first ascertaining that it is cool enough not to burn you.

✗ **Don't** allow brake fluid or antifreeze to contact the machine's paintwork or plastic components.

✗ **Don't** siphon toxic liquids such as fuel, hydraulic fluid or antifreeze by mouth, or allow them to remain on your skin.

✗ **Don't** inhale dust - it may be injurious to health (see Asbestos heading).

✗ **Don't** allow any spilled oil or grease to remain on the floor - wipe it up right away, before someone slips on it.

✗ **Don't** use ill-fitting spanners or other tools which may slip and cause injury.

✗ **Don't** lift a heavy component which may be beyond your capability - get assistance.

✗ **Don't** rush to finish a job or take unverified short cuts.

✗ **Don't** allow children or animals in or around an unattended vehicle.

✗ **Don't** inflate a tyre above the recommended pressure. Apart from overstressing the carcass, in extreme cases the tyre may blow off forcibly.

✔ **Do** ensure that the machine is supported securely at all times. This is especially important when the machine is blocked up to aid wheel or fork removal.

✔ **Do** take care when attempting to loosen a stubborn nut or bolt. It is generally better to pull on a spanner, rather than push, so that if you slip, you fall away from the machine rather than onto it.

✔ **Do** wear eye protection when using power tools such as drill, sander, bench grinder etc.

✔ **Do** use a barrier cream on your hands prior to undertaking dirty jobs - it will protect your skin from infection as well as making the dirt easier to remove afterwards; but make sure your hands aren't left slippery. Note that long-term contact with used engine oil can be a health hazard.

✔ **Do** keep loose clothing (cuffs, ties etc. and long hair) well out of the way of moving mechanical parts.

✔ **Do** remove rings, wristwatch etc., before working on the vehicle - especially the electrical system.

✔ **Do** keep your work area tidy - it is only too easy to fall over articles left lying around.

✔ **Do** exercise caution when compressing springs for removal or installation. Ensure that the tension is applied and released in a controlled manner, using suitable tools which preclude the possibility of the spring escaping violently.

✔ **Do** ensure that any lifting tackle used has a safe working load rating adequate for the job.

✔ **Do** get someone to check periodically that all is well, when working alone on the vehicle.

✔ **Do** carry out work in a logical sequence and check that everything is correctly assembled and tightened afterwards.

✔ **Do** remember that your vehicle's safety affects that of yourself and others. If in doubt on any point, get professional advice.

● If in spite of following these precautions, you are unfortunate enough to injure yourself, seek medical attention as soon as possible.

Identification numbers 0•9

Frame and engine numbers

The frame serial number is stamped into the right side of the frame and printed on a label affixed to the frame. The engine number is stamped into the right upper side of the crankcase. Both of these numbers should be recorded and kept in a safe place so they can be furnished to law enforcement officials in the event of a theft.

The frame serial number, engine serial number and carburetor identification number should also be kept in a handy place (such as with your driver's license) so they are always available when purchasing or ordering parts for your machine.

The models covered by this manual are as follows:

FZR600/600R, 1989 through 1994*
FZR750R, 1987 and 1988 (US), 1989 through 1992 (UK)
FZR1000, 1987 through 1995 (US), 1987 through 1996 (UK)

*Not including 1994-on UK FZR600R models.

Identifying model years

The procedures in this manual identify the bikes by model year. To determine which model year a given machine is, look for the identification codes in the engine and frame numbers. The initial frame/engine no. is given in parentheses for UK models. Refer to the accompanying table for details.

Buying spare parts

Once you have found all the identification numbers, record them for reference when buying parts. Since the manufacturers change specifications, parts and vendors (companies that manufacture various components on the machine), providing the ID numbers is the only way to be reasonably sure that you are buying the correct parts.

Whenever possible, take the worn part to the dealer so direct comparison with the new component can be made. Along the trail from the manufacturer to the parts shelf, there are numerous places that the part can end up with the wrong number or be listed incorrectly.

The two places to purchase new parts for your motorcycle - the accessory store and the franchised dealer - differ in the type of parts they carry. While dealers can obtain virtually every part for your motorcycle, the accessory store is usually limited to normal high wear items such as shock absorbers, tune-up parts, various engine gaskets, cables, chains, brake parts, etc. Rarely will an accessory outlet have major suspension components, cylinders, transmission gears, or cases.

Used parts can be obtained for roughly half the price of new ones, but you can't always be sure of what you're getting. Once again, take your worn part to the wrecking yard (breaker) for direct comparison.

Whether buying new, used or rebuilt parts, the best course is to deal directly with someone who specializes in parts for your particular make.

FZR600 models

Year	Code
1989	3HH1 - US except California
	3HW1 - California
	3HE1 - UK (3HE-000101)
1990	3HH4 - US except California
	3HW2 - California
	3HE3 - UK (3HE-026101)
1991	3HH6 - US except California
	3UU2 - California
	3HE7 - UK (3HE-054101)
1992	3HH8 - US except California
	3UU3 - California
	3HE8 - UK (3HE-088101)
1993	3HHA - US except California
	Not available - California
	3HEE - UK (3HE-106101)
1994	3HHC - US except California
	3UU5 - California
1995	3HHE - US except California
	3UU6 - California
1996	3HHG - US except California
	3UU7 - California

FZR750 models

Year	Code
1987	2NK - US
1988	3CS1 - US
1989	3SG1 - UK (3PK-001101)
1990	3SG2 - UK (3PK-003101)
1991/2	As 1989 model - UK

FZR1000 models

Year	Code
1987	2LH - US except California
	2LJ - California
	2RG - UK (2RG-000101)
1988	3DU1 - US except California
	3CA1 - California
	2RG - UK
1989	3LK1 - US except California
	3LK2 - California
	3LG1 - UK (3LG-000101)
1990	3LK4 - US except California
	3LK5 - California
	3LG2 - UK (3LG-004101)
1991	3LK7 - US except California
	3LK8 - California
	3LG3 - UK (3LG-009101)
1992	3LKA - US except California
	3LKB - California
	3LG4 - UK (LG6-012101)
1993	3LKD - US except California
	3LKE - California
	3LG5 - UK (LG5-017101)
1994	3LKG - US except California
	3LKH - 3LKH - California
	3LG6 - UK (3LH-019101)
1995	3LKK - US except California
	3LKL - California
	3LG7 - UK (3LH-022101)
1996	3LG7 - UK

The frame number is stamped in the right side of the frame and is also displayed on a decal

The engine number is stamped in the right side of the crankcase

0•10 Daily (pre-ride) checks

1 Engine/transmission oil level

Before you start:

✔ Start the engine and allow it to reach normal operating temperature.

Caution: Do not run the engine in an enclosed space such as a garage or shop.

✔ Stop the engine and allow the machine to sit undisturbed for about five minutes.
✔ Hold the motorcycle level.

Bike care:

● If you have to add oil frequently, you should check whether you have any oil leaks. If there is no sign of oil leakage from the joints and gaskets the engine could be burning oil (see *Fault Finding*).

The correct oil

● Modern, high-revving engines place great demands on their oil. It is very important that the correct oil for your bike is used.
● Always top up with a good quality oil of the specified type and viscosity and do not overfill the engine.

Oil type	API grade SE or SF (minimum)
Oil viscosity - below 15°C (60°F)	SAE 10W30
Oil viscosity - above 5°C (40°F)	SAE 20W40

1 Check the oil level in the window located at the lower part of the right crankcase cover. The oil level should be between the Maximum and Minimum level marks next to the window.

2 If the level is below the Minimum mark, remove the oil filler cap from the right crankcase and add enough oil of the recommended grade and type to bring the level up to the Maximum mark. Do not overfill.

2 Coolant level

Before you start:

✔ The engine must be cold for the results to be accurate, so always perform this check before starting the engine for the first time each day.
✔ Make sure the motorcycle is level.

1 The reservoir is located on the right side of the motorcycle below the seat. The coolant level can be viewed from underneath the rear fender.

2 If the level is at or below the Low mark, remove the reservoir cap and add the recommended coolant mixture (see Chapter 1 Specifications) until the Full level is reached.

Bike care:

● Use only the specified coolant mixture. It is important that antifreeze is used in the cooling system all year round, not just during the winter months. Don't top-up with water alone, as the antifreeze will become too diluted.

● Do not overfill the coolant reservoir. The coolant level is satisfactory if it is between the Low and Full marks on the reservoir.

● If the coolant level seems to be consistently low, check the entire cooling system for leaks.

● If you're working on an FZR600, remove the seat (see Chapter 9). The level marks are on the inboard side of the reservoir. The marks on FZR750/1000 models are visible without removing the seat, but you'll need to remove it if it's necessary to add coolant.

3 Cable clutch check

Bike care:

● Correct clutch freeplay is necessary to ensure proper clutch operation and reasonable clutch service life. Freeplay normally changes because of cable stretch and clutch wear, so it should be checked and adjusted periodically.
● Too little freeplay might result in the clutch not engaging completely. If there is too much freeplay, the clutch might not release fully.

● If the lever is stiff to operate and doesn't return quickly, lubricate the cable (see Chapter 1).
● If adjustment is required, refer to Chapter 1 for details.

Daily (pre-ride) checks 0•11

4 Brake and hydraulic clutch fluid levels

> **Warning:** *Brake hydraulic fluid can harm your eyes and damage painted surfaces, so use extreme caution when handling and pouring it and cover surrounding surfaces with rag. Do not use fluid that has been standing open for some time, as it absorbs moisture from the air which can cause a dangerous loss of braking/clutch effectiveness.*

Before you start:
✔ Make sure you have the correct hydraulic fluid - DOT 4.
✔ Remove the right side cover for access to the rear brake reservoir (see Chapter 9).
✔ With the motorcycle held level, turn the handlebars until the top of the master cylinder is as level as possible.

Bike care:
● In order to ensure proper operation of the hydraulic disc brake and clutch, the fluid level in the master cylinder reservoir must be properly maintained. If the fluid level was low, inspect the brake system for leaks.
● The fluid in the brake master cylinder reservoir will drop slightly as the brake pads wear down.
● Check the operation of the brakes before taking the machine on the road; if there is evidence of air in the system (spongy feel to lever), it must be bled as described in Chapter 8.
● Before removing the master cylinder cap, protect the motorcycle from fluid spills (which will damage the paint) and remove all dust and dirt from the area around the cap.

1 Look closely at the inspection window in the master cylinder reservoir (front brake and clutch). Make sure that the fluid level is above the LOWER line on the reservoir. If the level is low, the fluid must be replenished.

2 To top up front brake or clutch fluid, remove the screws and lift off the cap and rubber diaphragm. Top up with new DOT 4 hydraulic fluid until the level is above the LOWER mark - install the diaphragm and cap.

3 Check the rear brake fluid level through the translucent body of the reservoir. The fluid level should be above the LOWER line.

4 To top up the rear brake fluid, remove the seat and unscrew the reservoir cap, then lift out the rubber diaphragm. Top up with new DOT 4 hydraulic fluid until the level is above the LOWER mark. Install the diaphragm, cap, seat and side cover.

5 Suspension, steering and drive chain

Suspension and steering:
● Make sure the steering operates smoothly, without looseness and without binding.
● Check front and rear suspension for smooth operation.

Drive chain:
● Make sure the drive chain isn't out of adjustment (Chapter 1).

6 Legal and safety checks

Lighting and signalling:
● Take a minute to check that the headlight, taillight, brake light and turn signals all work correctly.
● Check that the horn sounds when the switch is operated.
● A working speedometer is a statutory requirement in the UK.

Safety:
● Check that the throttle grip rotates smoothly and snaps shut when released, in all steering positions.
● Check that the engine shuts off when the kill switch is operated.
● Check that sidestand return spring holds the stand securely up when retracted. The same applies to the centerstand (where fitted).
● Following the procedure in your owner's manual, check the operation of the sidestand switch.

Fuel:
● This may seem obvious, but check that you have enough fuel to complete your journey. If you notice signs of fuel leakage - rectify the cause immediately.
● Ensure you use the correct grade fuel.

Daily (pre-ride) checks

7 Tires

The correct pressures:
- The tires must be checked when **cold**, not immediately after riding. Note that low tire pressures may cause the tire to slip on the rim or come off. High tire pressures will cause abnormal tread wear and unsafe handling.
- Use an accurate pressure gauge.
- Proper air pressure will increase tire life and provide maximum stability and ride comfort.

Tire pressures	Front	Rear
FZR600		
Up to 90 kg (198 lbs)	2.27 bar (33 psi)	2.48 bar (36 psi)
Above 90 kg (198 lbs) or high speed riding	2.48 bar (36 psi)	2.89 bar (42 psi)
FZR750/1000		
Up to 90 kg (198 lbs)	2.48 bar (36 psi)	2.48 bar (36 psi)
Above 90 kg (198 lbs) or high speed riding	2.48 bar (36 psi)	2.89 bar (42 psi)

Tire care:
- Check the tires carefully for cuts, tears, embedded nails or other sharp objects and excessive wear. Operation of the motorcycle with excessively worn tires is extremely hazardous, as traction and handling are directly affected.
- Check the condition of the tire valve and ensure the dust cap is in place.
- Pick out any stones or nails which may have become embedded in the tire tread. If left, they will eventually penetrate through the casing and cause a puncture.
- If tire damage is apparent, or unexplained loss of pressure is experienced, seek the advice of a tire fitting specialist without delay.

Tire tread depth:
- At the time of writing UK law requires that tread depth must be at least 1 mm over 3/4 of the tread breadth all the way around the tire, with no bald patches. Many riders, however, consider 2 mm tread depth minimum to be a safer limit.
- Many tires now incorporate wear indicators in the tread. Identify the triangular pointer on the tire sidewall to locate the indicator bar and replace the tire if the tread has worn down to the bar.

1 Check the tire pressures when the tires are **cold** and keep them properly inflated.

2 Measure the tread depth at the center of the tire using a tread depth gauge.

3 Tire tread wear indicator bar and its location marking on the sidewall (usually an arrow, a triangle, or the letters TWI).

Chapter 1
Routine maintenance and servicing

Contents

Air filter element - servicing	3
Alternator brushes (FZR750/1000 models) - renewal	30
Battery electrolyte level/specific gravity - check	14
Brake system - check	9
Brake/clutch fluid - renewal	25
Brake/clutch hoses - renewal	33
Brake/clutch system seals - renewal	32
Carburetors - check and adjustment	7
Clutch - check and adjustment	8
Cooling system - draining, flushing and refilling	31
Cooling system - inspection	4
Crankcase ventilation system - inspection	17
Cylinder compression - check	23
Drive chain and sprockets - check, adjustment and lubrication	1
Engine oil and oil filter - renewal	20
Engine oil/filter - change	2
Exhaust system - check	15
Fasteners - check	19
Fuel filter - renewal	28
Fuel system - check and filter replacement	16
Lubrication - general	10
Sidestand switch - check	18
Spark plugs - renewal	21
Spark plugs - replacement	5
Steering head bearings - check, adjustment and repacking	11
Steering head bearings - clean and repack	26
Suspension - check	12
Suspension operation and swingarm play - check	22
Swingarm bearings and rear suspension pivot points - lubrication	27
Throttle operation/grip freeplay - check and adjustment	6
Tires, wheels and wheel bearings - check	13
Valve clearances (FZR600 models) - check and adjustment	24
Valve clearances (FZR750/1000 models) - check and adjustment	29

Degrees of difficulty

Easy, suitable for novice with little experience	**Fairly easy,** suitable for beginner with some experience	**Fairly difficult,** suitable for competent DIY mechanic	**Difficult,** suitable for experienced DIY mechanic	**Very difficult,** suitable for expert DIY or professional

Specifications

FZR600

Engine

Spark plugs
- Type .... NGK CR9E or CR8E, ND U27ESR-N or U24ESR-N
- Gap .... 0.7 to 0.8 mm (0.028 to 0.032 inch)

Valve clearances (COLD engine)
- Intake .... 0.11 to 0.20 mm (0.004 to 0.008 inch)
- Exhaust .... 0.21 to 0.30 mm (0.008 to 0.012 inch)

Engine idle speed
- Except California .... 1150 to 1250 rpm
- California .... 1250 to 1350 rpm

Cylinder compression pressure (at sea level)
- Standard .... 11.02 bar (160 psi)
- Maximum .... 11.29 bar (164 psi)
- Minimum .... 9.99 bar (145 psi)

Specifications

FZR600 (continued)

Engine (continued)
Carburetor synchronization
    Vacuum at idle speed .... 155 to 165 mm Hg (6.1 to 6.5 inch Hg)
    Maximum vacuum difference between cylinders .... 10 mm Hg (0.39 inch Hg)
Cylinder numbering (from left side to right side of bike) 1-2-3-4

Miscellaneous
Brake pad material minimum thickness .... 0.5 mm (0.02 inch) - see text
Brake pedal position .... 44 mm (1.7 inch) below the top of the footpeg
Freeplay adjustments
    Throttle grip .... 3 to 7 mm (0.12 to 0.28 inch)
    Clutch lever .... 2 to 3 mm (0.08 to 0.12 inch)
    Front brake lever .... 2 to 5 mm (0.08 to 0.20 inch)
Drive chain
    Slack .... 20 to 30 mm (0.8 to 1.2 inch)
    10-link length .... 150.1 mm (5.91 inch)
Battery electrolyte specific gravity .... 1.280 at 20-degrees C (68 degrees F)
Minimum tire tread depth* .... 1 mm (0.04 inch)
Tire pressures (cold)
    Front
        Up to 90 kg (198 lbs) .... 2.27 bar (33 psi)
        Above 90 kg (198 lbs) or high speed riding .... 2.48 bar (36 psi)
    Rear
        Up to 90 kg (198 lbs) .... 2.48 bar (36 psi)
        Above 90 kg (198 lbs or high speed riding) .... 2.89 bar (42 psi)

*In the UK, tread depth must be at least 1 mm over 3/4 of the tread breadth all the way around the tire, with no bald patches.

Recommended lubricants and fluids
Engine/transmission oil
    Type .... API grade SE or SF (minimum)
    Viscosity
        Consistently below 15 degrees C (60 degrees F) .... SAE 10W30
        Consistently above 5 degrees C (40 degrees F) .... SAE 20W40
    Capacity (without oil cooler)
        With filter change .... 2.5 liters (2.6 US qt, 4.4 Imperial pt)
        Oil change only .... 2.2 liters (2.3 US qt, 3.8 Imperial pt)
Coolant type .... 50/50 mixture of water and ethylene glycol antifreeze containing corrosion inhibitors for aluminum engines
Coolant capacity .... 2.2 liters (2.3 US qt, 3.8 Imperial pt)
Brake fluid .... DOT 4 (DOT 3 may be used in the rear, but not the front, if DOT 4 is unavailable)
Fork oil
    Type .... SAE 10W - fork oil
    Amount .... 435 cc (14.7 US fl oz, 15.3 Imperial fl oz)
    Oil level (fully compressed with spring removed) .... 101 mm (3.98 inch)
Drive chain .... SAE 30 to 50W engine oil
Wheel bearings .... Medium weight, lithium-based multi-purpose grease
Swingarm pivot bearings .... Medium weight, lithium-based multi-purpose grease
Cables and lever pivots .... Chain and cable lubricant or 10W30 motor oil
Sidestand/centerstand pivots .... Medium-weight, lithium-based multi-purpose grease
Brake pedal/shift lever pivots .... Chain and cable lubricant or 10W30 motor oil
Throttle grip .... Multi-purpose grease or dry film lubricant

Torque specifications
Oil drain plug .... 43 Nm (31 ft-lbs)
Oil filter bolt - cartridge type .... 15 Nm (11 ft-lbs)
Oil filter - spin-on type .... 17 Nm (12.5 ft-lbs)
Coolant drain plug in water pump .... 7 Nm (5.1 ft-lbs)
Coolant drain plug in coolant tube .... 10 Nm (7.2 ft-lbs)
Coolant drain plugs in cylinder block .... 7 Nm (5.1 ft-lbs)
Spark plugs .... 12.5 Nm (9 ft-lbs)
Steering head bearing lower ring nut
    Initial torque .... 52 Nm (37 ft-lbs)
    Final torque .... 3 Nm (2.2 ft-lbs)
Valve cover bolts .... See Chapter 2

Specifications

FZR750/1000

Engine
Spark plugs
  US .... NGK DP8EA-9, ND X24EP-U9
  UK
    1989 through 1993 .... NGK DR8ES-L, ND X24ESR-U
    1994-on .... NGK DR8EA-L, ND X24ESR-U
  Gap
    1989 through 1993 US .... 0.8 to 0.9 mm (0.031 to 0.035 inch)
    1994-on US, all UK .... 0.6 to 0.7 mm (0.024 to 0.028 inch)
Valve clearances (COLD engine)
  Intake .... 0.11 to 0.20 mm (0.004 to 0.008 inch)
  Exhaust .... 0.21 to 0.30 mm (0.008 to 0.012 inch)
Engine idle speed .... 950 to 1050 rpm
Cylinder compression pressure (at sea level)
  1987 and 1988 models
    Standard .... 11.02 bar (160 psi)
    Maximum .... 11.29 bar (164 psi)
    Minimum .... 9.99 bar (145 psi)
    Maximum variation .... 0.96 bar (14 psi)
  1989-on models
    Standard .... 13.71 bar (199 psi)
    Maximum .... 14.47 bar (210 psi)
    Minimum .... 13.37 bar (194 psi)
    Maximum variation .... 0.96 bar (14 psi)
Carburetor synchronization
  Vacuum at idle speed .... 195 to 205 mm Hg (7.67 to 8.07 inch Hg)
  Maximum vacuum difference between cylinders .... 10 mm Hg (0.39 inch Hg)
Cylinder numbering (from left side to right side of bike) 1-2-3-4

Miscellaneous
Brake pad material minimum thickness
  1989-on (UK) FZR750 .... 1.0 mm (0.04 inch) front; 0.5 mm (0.02 inch) rear
  1987 and 1988 FZR750, 1987 through 1993 FZR1000 .... 1.0 mm (0.04 inch) - see text
  1994-on FZR1000 .... 0.5 mm (0.02 inch) front and rear
Brake pedal position
  FZR750 and 1987/1988 FZR1000 .... 50 mm (1.97 inch) below top of footpeg
  1989-on FZR1000 .... 60 mm (2.36 inch) below top of footpeg
Freeplay adjustments
  Throttle grip .... 3 to 7 mm (0.12 to 0.28 inch)
  Front brake lever .... 2 to 5 mm (0.08 to 0.20 inch)
  Clutch lever (UK FZR750) .... 2 to 3 mm (0.08 to 0.12 inch)
Drive chain
  Slack .... 15 to 20 mm (0.6 to 0.8 inch)
  10-link length .... 150.1 mm (5.91 inch)
Battery electrolyte specific gravity .... 1.280 at 20-degrees C (68-degrees F)
Minimum tire tread depth* .... 1 mm (0.04 inch)
Tire pressures (cold)
  Front (all loads and conditions) .... 2.48 bar (36 psi)
  Rear
    Up to 90 kg (198 lbs) .... 2.48 bar (36 psi)
    Above 90 kg (198 lbs) or high speed riding .... 2.89 bar (42 psi)

*In the UK, tread depth must be at least 1 mm over 3/4 of the tread breadth all the way around the tire, with no bald patches.

Recommended lubricants and fluids
Engine/transmission oil
  Type .... API grade SE or SF (minimum)
  Viscosity
    Consistently below 15 degrees C (60 degrees F) .... SAE 10W30
    Consistently above 5 degrees C (40 degrees F) .... SAE 20W40
  Capacity (without oil cooler)
    All except 1989-on UK FZR750
      With filter change .... 3.0 liters (3.2 US qt, 5.2 Imperial pt)
      Oil change only .... 2.7 liters (2.9 US qt, 4.8 Imperial pt)
    1989-on UK FZR750
      With filter change .... 3.2 liters (3.4 US qt, 5.6 Imperial pt)
      Oil change only .... 2.8 liters (2.6 US qt, 4.6 Imperial pt)

Specifications

FZR750/1000 (continued)

Recommended lubricants and fluids (continued)

Coolant type	Same as FZR600
Coolant capacity (US FZR750)	Not available
Coolant capacity (UK FZR750)	2.7 liters (2.9 US qt, 4.8 Imperial pt)
Coolant capacity (FZR1000)	
1987 through 1990	2.1 liters (2.2 US qt, 3.8 Imperial pt)
1991 through 1993	2.8 liters (3.0 US qt, 5.0 Imperial pt)
1994 on	2.4 liters (2.54 US qt, 4.22 Imperial pt)
Brake fluid	DOT 4
Fork oil	
Type	
1987 through 1990 (except UK FZR750)	SAE 10W - fork oil
UK FZR750 and 1991 through 1993 FZR1000	SAE 5W - fork oil
1994-on FZR1000	Suspension oil 01 or equivalent
Amount	
1987 and 1988 FZR750	434 cc (14.7 US fl oz, 15.3 Imperial fl oz)
1989-on (UK) FZR750	437 cc (14.8 US fl oz, 15.4 Imperial fl oz)
1987 and 1988 FZR1000	425 cc (14.4 US fl oz, 15.0 Imperial fl oz)
1989 and 1990 FZR1000	535 cc (18.1 US fl oz, 18.9 Imperial fl oz)
1991 through 1993 FZR1000	462 cc (15.6 US fl oz, 16.3 Imperial fl oz)
1994-on FZR1000	470 cc (15.9 US fl oz, 16.5 Imperial fl oz)
Oil level (fully compressed with spring removed)	
1987 and 1988 FZR750	138 mm (5.43 inches)
1989-on (UK) FZR750	131 mm (5.16 inches)
1987 and 1988 FZR1000	143 mm (5.64 inches)
1989 and 1990 FZR1000	116 mm (4.57 inches)
1991 through 1993 FZR1000	124 mm (4.88 inches)
1994-on FZR1000	78 mm (3.07 inches)
Drive chain	SAE 30 to 50W engine oil
Wheel bearings	Medium weight, lithium-based multi-purpose grease
Swingarm pivot bearings	Medium weight, lithium-based multi-purpose grease
Cables and lever pivots	Chain and cable lubricant or 10W30 motor oil
Sidestand/centerstand pivots	Medium-weight, lithium-based multi-purpose grease
Brake pedal/shift lever pivots	Chain and cable lubricant or 10W30 motor oil
Throttle grip	Multi-purpose grease or dry film lubricant

Torque specifications

Oil drain plug	43 Nm (31 ft-lbs)
Oil filter bolt - cartridge type	15 Nm (11 ft-lbs)
Oil filter - spin-on type	17 Nm (12.5 ft-lbs)
Coolant drain plugs in water pump and cylinder	
1987 and 1988 FZR750/1000	8 Nm (5.8 ft-lbs)
1989-on FZR750/1000	10 Nm (7.2 ft-lbs)
Spark plugs	17.5 Nm (12.5 ft-lbs)
Steering head bearing lower ring nut	
All except 1989-on UK FZR750	
Initial torque	52 Nm (37 ft-lbs)
Final torque	3 Nm (2.2 ft-lbs)
1989-on UK FZR750	
Initial torque	48 Nm (35 ft-lbs)
Final torque	16 Nm (11 ft-lbs)
Valve cover bolts	See Chapter 3

Routine maintenance and servicing 1•5

Introduction

This Chapter covers in detail the checks and procedures necessary for the tune-up and routine maintenance of your motorcycle. The routine maintenance schedule is designed to keep the machine in proper running condition and prevent possible problems. The remaining Sections contain detailed procedures for carrying out the items listed on the maintenance schedule, as well as additional maintenance information designed to increase reliability.

Since routine maintenance plays such an important role in the safe and efficient operation of your motorcycle, it is presented here as a comprehensive check list. For the rider who does all his own maintenance, these lists outline the procedures and checks that should be done on a routine basis.

Maintenance information is printed on labels attached to the motorcycle (see illustrations). If the information on the labels differs from that included here, use the information on the label.

Deciding where to start or plug into the routine maintenance schedule depends on several factors. If you have a motorcycle whose warranty has recently expired, and if it has been maintained according to the warranty standards, you may want to pick up routine maintenance as it coincides with the next mileage or calendar interval. If you have owned the machine for some time but have never performed any maintenance on it, then you may want to start at the nearest interval and include some additional procedures to ensure that nothing important is overlooked. If you have just had a major engine overhaul, then you may want to start the maintenance routine from the beginning. If you have a used machine and have no knowledge of its history or maintenance record, you may desire to combine all the checks into one large service initially and then settle into the maintenance schedule prescribed.

The Sections which outline the inspection and maintenance procedures are written as step-by-step comprehensive guides to the performance of the work. They explain in detail each of the routine inspections and maintenance procedures on the check list. References to additional information in applicable Chapters is also included and should not be overlooked.

Before beginning any maintenance or repair, the machine should be cleaned thoroughly, especially around the oil filter, spark plugs, cylinder head covers, side covers, carburetors, etc. Cleaning will help ensure that dirt does not contaminate the engine and will allow you to detect wear and damage that could otherwise easily go unnoticed.

Maintenance information printed on decals includes tune-up data . . .

. . . tire pressure specifications (1994 FZR600 shown) . . .

. . . and vacuum hose routing information

1•6 Component locations

Component locations on right side

1 Coolant reservoir
2 Rear brake fluid reservoir
3 Spark plugs and valves
4 Air filter
5 Front brake fluid reservoir
6 Front brake lever position adjuster
7 Throttle cable upper adjusters
8 Fork seals
9 Brake pads
10 Engine oil level window
11 Engine oil filler cap
12 Rear brake light switch and pedal height adjuster

Component locations 1•7

Component locations on left side

1 Clutch fluid reservoir (US FZR750, all FZR1000)
2 Clutch cable adjuster (all FZR600, UK FZR750)
3 Steering head bearings
4 Engine idle speed adjuster
5 Alternator brushes (FZR750/1000)
6 Battery
7 Drive chain adjusters
8 Drive chain
9 Engine oil drain plug
10 Coolant drain bolt
11 Engine oil filter
12 Front brake pads

Maintenance schedule

Note: *The pre-ride inspection outlined in the owner's manual covers checks and maintenance that should be carried out on a daily basis. Always perform the pre-ride inspection (given in greater detail in 'Daily (pre-ride) checks' at the beginning of this Manual) at every maintenance interval (in addition to the procedures listed). The intervals listed below are the shortest intervals recommended by the manufacturer for each particular operation during the model years covered in this manual. Your owner's manual may have different intervals for your model.*

Daily or before riding
- [ ] See *'Daily (pre-ride) checks'* at the beginning of this Manual

After the initial 600 miles/1000 km
Note: *This check is usually performed by a Yamaha dealer after the first 600 miles from new. Thereafter, maintenance is carried out acccording to the following intervals of the schedule.*

Every 300 miles/500 km
- [ ] Check/adjust the drive chain slack (Section 1)
- [ ] Lubricate the drive chain (Section 1)

Every 4000 miles/6000 km or 6 months
- [ ] Change the engine oil (Section 2)
- [ ] Clean the air filter element and replace it if necessary (Section 3)
- [ ] Inspect the cooling system hoses (Section 4)
- [ ] Clean and gap the spark plugs (Section 5)
- [ ] Check/adjust throttle cable free play (Section 6)
- [ ] Check/adjust the idle speed (Section 7)
- [ ] Check/adjust the carburetor synchronization (Section 7)
- [ ] Check/adjust the carburetor (Section 8)
- [ ] Check the brake discs and pads (Section 9)
- [ ] Check/adjust the brake pedal position (Section 9)
- [ ] Check the operation of the brake light (Section 9)
- [ ] Lubricate the clutch and front brake lever pivots (Section 10)
- [ ] Lubricate the shift/brake pedal pivots and the sidestand pivots (Section 10)
- [ ] Lubricate the clutch cable (if equipped), throttle cables and speedometer cable (Section 10)
- [ ] Check the steering for looseness or binding (Section 11)
- [ ] Check the front forks for proper operation and fluid leaks (Section 12)
- [ ] Check the tires, wheels and wheel bearings (Section 13)
- [ ] Check the battery electrolyte level and specific gravity; inspect the breather tube (Section 14)
- [ ] Check the exhaust system for leaks and check the tightness of the fasteners (Section 15)
- [ ] Check the cleanliness of the fuel system and the condition of the fuel lines and vacuum hoses (Section 16)

- [ ] Inspect the crankcase ventilation system (Section 17)
- [ ] Check the operation of the sidestand switch (Section 18)
- [ ] Check the tightness of all fasteners (Section 19)

Every 8000 miles/12,000 km or 12 months
- [ ] Change the engine oil and oil filter (Section 20)
- [ ] Replace the spark plugs (Section 21)
- [ ] Check rear suspension operation and swingarm play (Section 22)
- [ ] Check cylinder compression (Section 23)

Every 16,000 miles/24,000 km or two years
- [ ] Adjust the valve clearances (FZR600) (Section 24)
- [ ] Change the brake/clutch fluid (Section 25)
- [ ] Clean and repack the steering head bearings (Section 26)
- [ ] Lubricate the swingarm bearings and rear suspension pivot points (Section 27)

Every 18,000 miles/30,000 km
- [ ] Replace the fuel filter (Section 28)

Every 26,000 miles/42,000 km
- [ ] Adjust the valve clearances (FZR750/1000) (Section 29)

Every 60,000 miles/100,000 km
- [ ] Replace the alternator brushes (FZR750/1000) (Section 30)

Every two years
- [ ] Change the coolant (Section 31)
- [ ] Replace the brake/clutch master cylinder seals and caliper/release cylinder seals (Section 32)

Every four years
- [ ] Replace the brake/clutch hoses (Section 33)

Every 300 miles / 500 km 1•9

1.3 Push up on the lower run - if the deflection is not within the specified limits, adjust the slack

1.4 The chain guard is held on by two screws (arrowed)

1.5 Check the sprockets in the areas indicated to see if they are worn excessively

Every 300 miles/500 km

1 Drive chain and sprockets - check, adjustment and lubrication

Check

1 A neglected drive chain won't last long and can quickly damage the sprockets. Routine chain adjustment and lubrication isn't difficult and will ensure maximum chain and sprocket life.

2 To check the chain, support the bike securely so it can't be knocked over and shift the transmission into Neutral. Make sure the ignition switch is off.

3 Push up on the bottom run of the chain and measure the slack midway between the two sprockets **(see illustration)**, then compare your measurements to the value listed in this Chapter's Specifications. As wear occurs, the chain will actually stretch, which means adjustment usually involves removing some slack from the chain. In some cases where lubrication has been neglected, corrosion and galling may cause the links to bind and kink, which effectively shortens the chain's length. If the chain is tight between the sprockets, rusty or kinked, it's time to replace it with a new one. **Note:** *Repeat the chain slack measurement along the length of the chain -* ideally, every inch or so. If you find a tight area, mark it with felt pen or paint and repeat the measurement after the bike has been ridden. If the chain's still tight in the same area, it may be damaged or worn. Because a tight or kinked chain can damage the transmission output shaft bearing, it's a good idea to replace it.

4 Remove the chain guard **(see illustration)**. Check the entire length of the chain for damaged rollers, loose links and pins. Hang a 20-lb (9 kg) weight on the bottom run of the chain and measure the length of 10 links along the top run. Rotate the wheel and repeat this check at several places on the chain, since it may wear unevenly. Compare your measurements with the maximum 10-link length listed in this Chapter's Specifications. If any of your measurements exceed the maximum, replace the chain. **Note:** *Never install a new chain on old sprockets, and never use the old chain if you install new sprockets - replace the chain and sprockets as a set.*

5 Remove the engine sprocket cover (see Chapter 7). Check the teeth on the engine sprocket and the rear sprocket for wear **(see illustration)**.

Adjustment

6 Rotate the rear wheel until the chain is positioned with the least amount of slack present.

1.7a On FZR600 models, remove the cotter pin (lower arrow); the marks are used to adjust the chain

FZR600 and early FZR750/1000 models

7 Remove the cotter pin from the axle nut and loosen the nut **(see illustrations)**.

8 Loosen and back-off the locknuts on the adjuster bolts **(see illustration)**.

9 Turn the axle adjusting nut on both sides of the swingarm until the proper chain tension is obtained (get the adjuster on the chain side close, then set the adjuster on the opposite side). Be sure to turn the adjusting nuts evenly to keep the rear wheel in alignment. If the adjusting nuts reach the end of their travel, the chain is excessively worn and should be replaced with a new one (see Chapter 7).

10 When the chain has the correct amount of slack, make sure the marks on the adjusters correspond to the same relative marks on each side of the swingarm **(see illustration 1.7a)**. Tighten the axle nut to the torque listed in the Chapter 6 Specifications, then install a new cotter pin and bend it properly **(see illustration)**. If necessary, turn the nut an

1.7b Loosen the axle nut with a socket or box wrench (ring spanner)

1.8 Loosen the locknut on each chain adjuster so the adjuster can be turned

1.10 Always use a new cotter pin whenever the old one is removed. This is the correct way to bend it

1 Cotter pin

1•10 Every 300 miles / 500 km

1.11a On UK FZR750 and all later FZR1000 models, pull out the cotter pin (arrowed) . . .

1.11b . . . and loosen the axle nut with a socket or box wrench (ring spanner)

1.12 Loosen the locknut (arrowed), then turn the adjusting bolt to change position of the chain adjuster

1.14 The marks on the swingarm on each side of the bike (arrowed) are used to adjust the chain evenly

additional amount to line up the cotter pin hole with the castellations in the nut - don't loosen the nut to do this.

Later FZR750/1000 models

11 Remove the cotter pin from the axle nut and loosen the nut **(see illustrations)**.
12 Loosen and back-off the locknuts on the adjuster bolts, then back-off the bolts **(see illustration)**.

13 Turn the axle adjusting bolts on both sides of the swingarm until the proper chain tension is obtained (get the adjuster on the chain side close, then set the adjuster on the opposite side). Be sure to turn the adjusting bolts evenly to keep the rear wheel in alignment. If the adjusting bolts reach the end of their travel, the chain is excessively worn and should be replaced with a new one (see Chapter 7).

14 When the chain has the correct amount of slack, make sure the marks on the adjusters correspond to the same relative marks on each side of the swingarm **(see illustration)**. Tighten the axle nut to the torque listed in the Chapter 8 Specifications, then install a new cotter pin and bend it properly **(see illustration 1.10)**. If necessary, turn the nut an additional amount to line up the cotter pin hole with the castellations in the nut - don't loosen the nut to do this.

All models

15 Tighten the chain adjuster locknuts securely.

Lubrication

Note: *If the chain is extremely dirty, it should be removed and cleaned before it's lubricated (see Chapter 7).*

16 The best time to lubricate the chain is after the motorcycle has been ridden. When the chain is warm, the lubricant will penetrate the joints between the side plates more easily.
Note: *If the chain is dirty, remove and clean it (see Chapter 7). Yamaha specifies SAE 30 to SAE 50 engine oil; only use aerosol chain lube if it is marked as being suitable for O-ring chains.*

> **HAYNES HiNT** *Apply the oil to the area where the side plates overlap - not the middle of the rollers. Apply the oil to the top of the lower chain run, so centrifugal force will work the oil into the chain when the bike is moving. After applying the lubricant, let it soak in a few minutes before wiping off any excess.*

Every 4000 miles/6000 km or 6 months

Note: *Engine oil change should be carried out every 4000 miles (6000 km) and oil and filter change every 8000 miles (12,000 km)*

2 Engine oil/filter - change

1 Consistent routine oil and filter changes are the single most important maintenance procedure you can perform on a motorcycle. The oil not only lubricates the internal parts of the engine, transmission and clutch, but it also acts as a coolant, a cleaner, a sealant, and a protectant. Because of these demands,

> **HAYNES HiNT** *Saving a little money on the difference in cost between a good oil and a cheap oil won't pay off if the engine is damaged.*

the oil takes a terrific amount of abuse and should be replaced often with new oil of the recommended grade and type.

2 Before changing the oil and filter, warm up the engine so the oil will drain easily. Be careful when draining the oil, as the exhaust pipes, the engine, and the oil itself can cause severe burns.

3 Remove the oil filler cap to vent the crankcase and act as a reminder that there is no oil in the engine. Remove fairing panels as necessary for access (see Chapter 9). On FZR600 models with a cartridge filter, remove the exhaust pipes (see Chapter 5).

4 Support the motorcycle securely over a clean drain pan. Remove the drain plug from the engine **(see illustrations)** and allow the oil to drain into the pan **(see illustration)**. Discard the sealing washer on the drain plug;

it should be replaced whenever the plug is removed.

2.4a Remove the oil pan drain plug (this is an FZR600) . . .

Every 4000 miles / 6000 km

2.4b ... and this is an FZR1000 (arrowed) - FZR750 similar

2.4c Let the oil drain completely

2.5 Remove the oil filter cover bolt (circled) ...

2.6 ... and take off the cover - the filter element, washer and spring are inside

A Filter bolt
B Cover
C Spring
D Washer

2.7 Remove the O-ring (upper arrow) - the washer tends to stick to the filter, so be sure not to discard it

2.11 Position the tab on the filter cover in the slot (arrowed)

Cartridge filter models

5 Remove the oil filter bolt and take off the filter cover (see illustration).

6 Remove the filter element, washer and spring from the cover (see illustration).

7 Remove the O-ring from its groove in the cover (see illustration).

8 Clean the filter cover and housing with solvent or clean rags. Make sure the holes in the filter bolt are clear. Wipe any remaining oil off the filter sealing area of the crankcase.

9 Clean the components and check them for damage - especially, be sure to check the spring for distortion. If any damage is found, replace the damaged part(s).

10 Check the condition of the drain plug threads and the sealing washer.

11 Install a new O-ring in the cover groove and make sure it's positioned securely (see illustration 2.7). Install the spring, washer and filter element in the cover. Install the cover on the engine with the adjusting tab in the slot (see illustration) and tighten the bolt to the torque listed in this Chapter's Specifications.

Spin-on filter models

12 Unscrew the filter element with a ratchet and filter wrench (Yamaha tool no. J-37140A/part no. 90890-04126 or equivalent) (see illustrations). Let the oil drain from the filter adapter.

13 Apply a film of oil to the gasket on the new filter (see illustration). Thread the filter onto the adapter and tighten it to the torque listed in this Chapter's Specifications.

All models

14 Slip a new sealing washer over the oil drain plug, then install and tighten it to the torque listed in this Chapter's Specifications. Avoid overtightening, as damage to the engine case will result.

2.12a This tool is used to remove spin-on oil filters ...

2.12b ... you'll need an extension to reach between the exhaust pipes

2.13 Apply a film of clean engine oil to the filter gasket (arrowed)

1•12 Every 4000 miles / 6000 km

> **HAYNES HiNT**
> Before refilling the engine, check the old oil carefully. If the oil was drained into a clean pan, small pieces of metal or other material can be easily detected. If the oil is very metallic colored, then the engine is experiencing wear from break-in (new engine) or from insufficient lubrication. If there are flakes or chips of metal in the oil, then something is drastically wrong internally and the engine will have to be disassembled for inspection and repair. If there are pieces of fiber-like material in the oil, the clutch is experiencing excessive wear and should be checked.

15 If the inspection of the oil turns up nothing unusual, refill the crankcase to the proper level with the recommended oil and install the filler cap. Start the engine and let it run. If you're working on an FZR750/1000, slightly loosen (DO NOT remove) the oil gallery bolt at the upper corner of the cylinder head, just below and behind the rear cam tower. Oil should seep out within one minute; if not, shut the engine off immediately so it won't seize. Shut it off, wait a few minutes, then check the oil level. If necessary, add more oil to bring the level up to the Maximum mark. Check around the drain plug and filter housing for leaks.

16 The old oil drained from the engine cannot be reused in its present state and should be disposed of. Check with your local refuse disposal company, disposal facility or environmental agency to see whether they will accept the used oil for recycling. Don't pour used oil into drains or onto the ground. After the oil has cooled, it can be drained into a suitable container (capped plastic jugs, topped bottles, etc.) for transport to one of these disposal sites.

3 Air filter element - servicing

1 Remove the seat.
2 If you're working on an FZR600, remove the top cover (see Chapter 9).
3 If you're working on a 1987 or 1988 model, remove the side covers (see Chapter 9) and fuel tank (see Chapter 5).
4 If you're working on a 1989 or later FZR750/1000, remove the fuel tank (see Chapter 5).
5 Remove the cover screw(s) and lift off the housing cover **(see illustrations)**. Inspect the cover O-ring and replace it if it's damaged or deteriorated.
6 Lift out the filter and tap the element on a hard surface to shake out any dirt. If compressed air is available, use it to clean the element by blowing from the outside in. If the element is extremely dirty or torn, replace it with a new one.
7 Reinstall the filter by reversing the removal procedure. Make sure the element is seated properly in the filter housing before installing the cover.
8 Install all components removed for access.

4 Cooling system - inspection

> ⚠ **Warning:** The engine must be cool before beginning this procedure.

Note: *Refer to 'Daily (pre-ride) checks' at the beginning of this Manual and check the coolant level before performing this check.*

1 The entire cooling system should be checked carefully at the recommended intervals. Look for evidence of leaks, check the condition of the coolant, check the radiator for clogged fins and damage and make sure the fan operates when required.
2 Remove fairing panels as necessary for access to the cooling system components (see Chapter 9).
3 Examine each of the rubber coolant hoses along its entire length. Look for cracks, abrasions and other damage. Squeeze each hose at various points. They should feel firm, yet pliable, and return to their original shape when released. If they are dried out or hard, replace them with new ones.
4 Check for evidence of leaks at each cooling system joint. Tighten the hose clamps careful to prevent future leaks. If coolant has been leaking from the joints of steel or aluminum coolant tubes, remove the tubes and replace the O-rings (see Chapter 4).
5 Check the radiator for evidence of leaks and other damage. Leaks in the radiator leave telltale scale deposits or coolant stains on the outside of the core below the leak. If leaks are noted, remove the radiator (see Chapter 4) and have it repaired by a radiator shop or replace it with a new one.

Caution: *Do not use a liquid leak stopping compound to try to repair leaks.*

6 Check the radiator fins for mud, dirt and insects, which may impede the flow of air through the radiator. If the fins are dirty, force water or low pressure compressed air through the fins from the backside. If the fins are bent or distorted, straighten them carefully with a screwdriver.
7 Remove the pressure cap by turning it counterclockwise (anti-clockwise) until it reaches a stop. If you hear a hissing sound (indicating there is still pressure in the system), wait until it stops. Now, press down on the cap with the palm of your hand and continue turning the cap counterclockwise

3.5a Remove the four cover screws (arrowed) on FZR600 and UK 750 models . . .

3.5b . . . or the single screw (US 750 and all 1000 models)

3.5c . . . and lift out the element; this is an FZR600 (UK 750 similar) . . .

3.5d . . . and this is an FZR1000 (US 750 similar)

Every 4000 miles / 6000 km

4.7a Be sure to let all cooling system pressure escape before removing the pressure cap completely

4.7b Inspect both cap gaskets (arrowed)

4.8 An antifreeze hydrometer is helpful in determining the condition of the coolant

(anti-clockwise) until it can be removed **(see illustration)**. Check the condition of the coolant in the system. If it is rust colored or if accumulations of scale are visible, drain, flush and refill the system with new coolant. Check the cap gaskets for cracks and other damage **(see illustration)**. Have the cap tested by a dealer service department or replace it with a new one. Install the cap by turning it clockwise until it reaches the first stop, then push down on the cap and continue turning until it can turn no further.

8 Check the antifreeze content of the coolant with an antifreeze hydrometer **(see illustration)**. Sometimes coolant may look like it's in good condition, but might be too weak to offer adequate protection. If the hydrometer indicates a weak mixture, drain, flush and refill the cooling system (see Section 31).

9 Start the engine and let it reach normal operating temperature, then check for leaks again. As the coolant temperature increases, the fan should come on automatically and the temperature should begin to drop. If it doesn't, refer to Chapter 4 and check the fan and fan circuit carefully.

10 If the coolant level is consistently low, and no evidence of leaks can be found, have the entire system pressure checked by a Yamaha dealer service department, motorcycle repair shop or service station.

5 Spark plugs - replacement

1 Make sure your spark plug socket is the correct size before attempting to remove the plugs.
2 Remove fairing components as necessary for access to the plugs (see Chapter 9).
3 Disconnect the spark plug caps from the spark plugs **(see illustration)**. If available, use compressed air to blow any accumulated debris from around the spark plugs. Remove the plugs **(see illustration)**.
4 Inspect the electrodes for wear. Both the center and side electrodes should have square edges and the side electrode should be of uniform thickness. Look for excessive deposits and evidence of a cracked or chipped insulator around the center electrode. Compare your spark plugs to the color spark plug reading chart. Check the threads, the washer and the ceramic insulator body for cracks and other damage.
5 If the electrodes are not excessively worn, and if the deposits can be easily removed with a wire brush, the plugs can be regapped and reused (if no cracks or chips are visible in the insulator). If in doubt concerning the condition of the plugs, replace them with new ones, as the expense is minimal.

6 Cleaning spark plugs by sandblasting is permitted, provided you clean the plugs with a high flash-point solvent afterwards.
7 Before installing new plugs, make sure they are the correct type and heat range. Check the gap between the electrodes, as they are not preset. For best results, use a wire-type gauge rather than a flat gauge to check the gap **(see illustration)**. If the gap must be adjusted, bend the side electrode only and be very careful not to chip or crack the insulator nose **(see illustration)**. Make sure the washer is in place before installing each plug.
8 Since the cylinder head is made of aluminum, which is soft and easily damaged, thread the plugs into the heads by hand.

5.3a Rotate the caps back and forth to loosen them, pull them off and check for brittleness and cracking

5.3b Use an extension and a deep socket to remove the spark plugs

5.7a If the wire gauge doesn't slide between the electrodes with a slight drag, adjustment is required

5.7b Bend the side electrode only; be careful not to crack or chip the center insulator

1•14 Every 4000 miles / 6000 km

6.2 Twist the throttle grip lightly and check freeplay

6.6 On most models, there's an adjuster at the handlebar; the 1994-on FZR1000 has an adjuster mounted in the upper section of the cable

6.8 Initial adjustments are made at the carburetor throttle cable adjuster(s)

> **HAYNES HINT** *Since the plugs are recessed, slip a short length of hose over the end of the plug to use as a tool to thread it into place. The hose will grip the plug well enough to turn it, but will start to slip if the plug begins to cross-thread in the hole - this will prevent damaged threads and the accompanying repair costs.*

9 Once the plugs are finger-tight, the job can be finished with a socket. If a torque wrench is available, tighten the spark plugs to the torque listed in this Chapter's Specifications. If you do not have a torque wrench, tighten the plugs finger-tight (until the washers bottom on the cylinder head) then use a wrench to tighten them an additional 1/4 turn. Regardless of the method used, do not over-tighten them.
10 Reconnect the spark plug caps and reinstall all removed components.

6 Throttle operation/grip freeplay - check and adjustment

Throttle check

1 Make sure the throttle grip rotates easily from fully closed to fully open with the front wheel turned at various angles. The grip should return automatically from fully open to fully closed when released. If the throttle sticks, check the throttle cables for cracks or kinks in the housings. Also, make sure the inner cables are clean and well-lubricated.
2 Check for a small amount of freeplay at the grip and compare the freeplay to the value listed in this Chapter's Specifications **(see illustration)**. If adjustment is necessary, adjust idle speed first (see Section 7).

Throttle cable adjustment

Note: *Some models use two throttle cables - an accelerator cable and a decelerator cable.*
3 Initial freeplay adjustments are made at the carburetor end of the cable.
4 Remove the seat and side covers (see Chapter 9).

5 Remove the fuel tank cover (FZR600), fuel tank (all others) and air filter case (see Chapter 5).
6 Make sure the locknuts at the handlebar throttle cable adjusters are tight **(see illustration)**.
7 On early UK models with adjusters at the carburetor ends of both cables, loosen the locknuts on the decelerator cable (the one that closes the throttle). Turn the adjuster to eliminate throttle grip freeplay, then tighten the locknuts.
8 Loosen the cable locknuts at the carburetor (the accelerator cable locknut on early UK models) **(see illustration)**. Turn the adjuster nuts to change freeplay, then tighten the locknuts.
9 To make fine adjustments, loosen the locknut on the handlebar cable adjuster **(see illustration 6.6)**. Turn the adjuster until the desired freeplay is obtained, then retighten the lockwheel.
10 Make sure the throttle grip is in the fully closed position.
11 Make sure the throttle linkage lever contacts the idle adjusting screw when the throttle grip is in the closed throttle position.

⚠ **Warning:** *Turn the handlebars all the way through their travel with the engine idling. Idle speed should not change. If it does, the cables may be routed incorrectly. Correct this condition before riding the bike.*

7 Carburetors - check and adjustment

Idle speed

1 The idle speed should be checked and adjusted before and after the carburetors are synchronized and when it is obviously too high or too low. Before adjusting the idle speed, make sure the valve clearances and spark plug gaps are correct. Also, turn the handlebars back-and-forth and see if the idle speed changes as this is done. If it does, the accelerator cable may not be routed correctly, or it may be worn out. This is a dangerous condition that can cause loss of control of the bike. Be sure to correct this problem before proceeding.
2 The engine should be at normal operating temperature, which is usually reached after 10 to 15 minutes of stop and go riding. Support the motorcycle securely and make sure the transmission is in Neutral.
3 Turn the throttle stop screw **(see illustrations)**, until the idle speed listed in this Chapter's Specifications is obtained.
4 Snap the throttle open and shut a few times, then recheck the idle speed. If necessary, repeat the adjustment procedure.
5 If a smooth, steady idle can't be achieved, the fuel/air mixture may be incorrect. Refer to Chapter 5 for additional carburetor information.

7.3a Turn the throttle stop screw (arrowed) until the correct idle speed is obtained (this is an FZR600) . . .

7.3b . . . and this is an FZR1000 (FZR750 similar) (arrowed)

Every 4000 miles / 6000 km

7.14a Remove the vacuum hoses or screws and install fittings like this one . . .

7.14b . . . so a test gauge setup like this can be installed

7.17 Turn this screw (arrowed) to synchronize carburetors no. 1 and 2 to each other

Carburetor synchronization

Warning: Gasoline (petrol) is extremely flammable, so take extra precautions when you work on any part of the fuel system. Don't smoke or allow open flames or bare light bulbs near the work area, and don't work in a garage where a natural gas-type appliance (such as a water heater or clothes dryer) is present. If you spill any fuel on your skin, rinse it off immediately with soap and water.
When you perform any kind of work on the fuel system, wear safety glasses and have a class B type fire extinguisher on hand.

6 Carburetor synchronization is simply the process of adjusting the carburetors so they pass the same amount of fuel/air mixture to each cylinder. This is done by measuring the vacuum produced in each cylinder. Carburetors that are out of synchronization will result in decreased fuel mileage, increased engine temperature, less than ideal throttle response and higher vibration levels.

7 To properly synchronize the carburetors, you will need some sort of vacuum gauge setup, preferably with a gauge for each cylinder, or a mercury manometer, which is a calibrated tube arrangement that utilizes columns of mercury to indicate engine vacuum. You'll also need an auxiliary fuel tank, since the bike's fuel tank must be removed for access to the vacuum fittings and synchronizing screws.

8 A manometer can be purchased from a motorcycle dealer or accessory shop and should have the necessary rubber hoses supplied with it for hooking into the vacuum hose fittings on the carburetors.

9 A vacuum gauge setup can also be purchased from a dealer or fabricated from commonly available hardware and automotive vacuum gauges.

10 The manometer is the more reliable and accurate instrument, and for that reason is preferred over the vacuum gauge setup; however, since the mercury used in the manometer is a liquid, and extremely toxic, extra precautions must be taken during use and storage of the instrument.

11 Because of the nature of the synchronization procedure and the need for special instruments, most owners leave the task to a dealer service department or a reputable motorcycle repair shop.

12 Remove the side covers, seat and fuel tank (see Chapters 9 and 5).

13 Start the engine and let it run until it reaches normal operating temperature, then shut it off.

14 Remove the screws from the vacuum ports on the carburetors and install vacuum fittings **(see illustration)**, then hook up the vacuum gauge set or the manometer according to the manufacturer's instructions **(see illustration)**. Make sure there are no leaks in the setup, as false readings will result.

15 Start the engine and make sure the idle speed is correct. If it isn't, adjust it.

16 The vacuum readings for all of the cylinders should be the same, or at least within the tolerance listed in this Chapter's Specifications. If the vacuum readings vary, adjust as necessary.

17 To perform the adjustment, synchronize the carburetors for no. 1 and no. 2 cylinders by turning the synchronizing screw, as needed, until the vacuum is identical or nearly identical for both cylinders **(see illustration)**. Snap the throttle open and shut 2 or 3 times, then recheck the adjustment and readjust as necessary.

18 Next synchronize the carburetors for no. 3 and no. 4 cylinders to each other by turning the synchronizing screw for those two carburetors **(see illustration)**. As with the no. 1 and no. 2 carburetors, snap the throttle open and shut 2 or 3 times, then recheck the adjustment and readjust as necessary.

19 Finally, turn the center synchronizing screw to synchronize the two pairs of carburetors to each other **(see illustration)**.

20 When the adjustment is complete, recheck the vacuum readings and idle speed, then stop the engine. Remove the vacuum gauge or manometer and install the screws or carburetor vacuum hoses.

8 Clutch - check and adjustment

Cable clutch

1 Correct clutch freeplay is necessary to ensure proper clutch operation and reasonable clutch service life. Freeplay normally changes because of cable stretch and clutch wear, so it should be checked and adjusted periodically.

2 Clutch cable freeplay is checked at the lever on the handlebar. Slowly pull in on the lever until resistance is felt, then note how big the gap is between the lever but end and its pivot bracket. Compare this distance with the value listed in this Chapter's Specifications.

7.18 Turn this screw (arrowed) to synchronize carburetors no. 3 and 4 to each other

7.19 Turn this screw (arrowed) to synchronize the two pairs of carburetors to each other

1•16 Every 4000 miles / 6000 km

8.3 Adjustments are made at the handlebar - loosen the lockwheel (left arrow) and turn the adjuster (right arrow)

8.4a Initial FZR600 clutch cable adjustments are made at the engine; pry off the cover . . .

8.4b . . . loosen the locknut and turn the screw in until it bottoms lightly, then back it out 1/4 turn and tighten the locknut

8.7 Follow the hydraulic line and check for fluid leaks at the fitting (arrowed)

Too little freeplay might result in the clutch not engaging completely. If there is too much freeplay, the clutch might not release fully.

3 Normal freeplay adjustments are made at the clutch lever by loosening the lockwheel and turning the adjuster until the desired freeplay is obtained **(see illustration)**. Always retighten the lockwheel once the adjustment is complete.

4 If freeplay can't be adjusted at the handlebar, check the initial adjustment at the engine. On FZR600 models, remove the adjuster cover from the engine sprocket cover **(see illustration)**. Loosen the locknut on the adjuster, turn the screw in until it bottoms lightly and back it out 1/4 turn **(see illustration)**. Retighten the locknut. On UK FZR750 models, loosen the locknut at the engine end of the cable, turn the adjuster as needed and tighten the locknut.

5 Recheck freeplay at the clutch lever and make further adjustments (if necessary) with the adjuster at the lever. If freeplay still can't be adjusted within the Specifications, the cable may be stretched or the clutch may be worn. Refer to Chapter 2 or Chapter 3 for inspection and repair procedures.

Hydraulic clutch

6 The hydraulic clutch release mechanism eliminates the need for freeplay adjustment. No means of manual adjustment is provided.

7 Check the fluid level (see Section 3). Check for fluid leaks around the master cylinder, at the fluid line connections and at the release cylinder on the left side of the engine **(see illustration)**. If leaks are found, refer to Chapter 3 for repair procedures.

8 Start the bike, release the clutch and ride off, noting the position of the clutch lever when the clutch begins to engage. If it's too close to the handlebar, there may be air in the clutch fluid (the air compresses, rather than transmitting lever force to the release mechanism). Refer to Chapter 3 and bleed the system.

9 Brake system - check

General

1 A routine general check of the brakes will ensure that any problems are discovered and remedied before the rider's safety is jeopardized.

2 Check the brake lever and pedal for loose connections, excessive play, bends, and other damage. Replace any damaged parts with new ones (see Chapter 8).

3 Make sure all brake fasteners are tight.

9.6a If you're working on an FZR600, remove two bolts (arrows and take off the protective cover

Check the brake pads for wear (see Section 9) and make sure the fluid level in the reservoirs is correct (see 'Daily (pre-ride) checks' at the beginning of this Manual). Look for leaks at the hose connections and check for cracks in the hoses. If the lever or pedal is spongy, bleed the brakes as described in Chapter 8.

4 Make sure the brake light operates when the brake lever is depressed.

5 Make sure the brake light is activated just before the rear brake takes effect.

6 If adjustment is necessary, remove the aluminum protective cover (if equipped) **(see illustration)**. Hold the switch and turn the adjusting nut on the switch body **(see illustration)** until the brake light is activated when required. If the switch doesn't operate the brake lights, check it as described in Chapter 10.

7 The front brake light switch is not adjustable. If it fails to operate properly, replace it with a new one (see Chapter 10).

Brake pads wear check

8 The front and rear brake pads should be checked at the recommended intervals and replaced with new ones when worn beyond the limit listed in this Chapter's Specifications.

9 To check the front brake pads, remove the

9.6b Hold the switch body and turn the nut (arrowed) to adjust the switch

Every 4000 miles / 6000 km 1•17

9.9a Lift off the front pad cover to expose the pads . . .

9.9b . . . and check to see if the raised corner of the backing metal (arrowed) is close to the disc

9.10 Lift off the rear pad cover to inspect the rear pads

pad covers (if equipped) **(see illustration)**. Reach up and operate the brake lever while you look at the back of each caliper. On all except UK FZR750 models, if the pad wear indicator is close to the disc **(see illustration)**, the pads are worn excessively and must be replaced with new ones (see Chapter 8). On UK FZR750 models, replace the pads if the friction material is worn to the minimum.

10 To check the brake pads, remove the pad cover (if equipped) **(see illustration)**. Press the brake pedal firmly while you look at the wear indicators on the pads **(see illustration 9.9b)**. If the indicators are close to the disc, replace the pads (see Chapter 8).

11 If the pads are in good condition, reinstall the covers. The words "Uncover for pad service" stamped in the front pad covers may be upside down when the cover is installed. This doesn't mean the cover is upside down.

Brake lever play and pedal position check and adjustment

Front brakes

12 The front brake lever on models without a span adjuster must have the amount of freeplay listed in this Chapter's Specifications to prevent brake drag.

13 Operate the lever and check freeplay at the ball end of the lever. If it's not correct, loosen the adjuster locknut, turn the adjuster to bring freeplay within the Specifications and tighten the locknut **(see illustration)**.

9.13 To adjust the freeplay, loosen the locknut (arrowed) and turn the screw

Rear brakes

14 The rear brake pedal should be positioned below the top of the footpeg the distance listed in this Chapter's Specifications.

15 To adjust the position of the pedal, loosen the locknut on the adjuster, turn the adjuster to set the pedal position and tighten the locknut **(see illustration)**.

16 If necessary, adjust the brake light switch (see Section 9).

10 Lubrication - general

1 Since the controls, cables and various other components of a motorcycle are exposed to

9.15 To adjust the height, loosen the locknut (upper arrow) and turn the bolt. The end of the adjusting bolt must be visible in the hole (lower arrow) after adjustment

the elements, they should be lubricated periodically to ensure safe and trouble-free operation.

2 The footpegs, clutch and brake lever, brake pedal, shift lever and sidestand pivots should be lubricated frequently **(see illustrations)**. In order for the lubricant to be applied where it will do the most good, the component should be disassembled. However, if chain and cable lubricant is being used, it can be applied to the pivot joint gaps and will usually work its way into the areas where friction occurs. If motor oil or light grease is being used, apply it sparingly as it may attract dirt (which could cause the controls to bind or wear at an

10.2a Lubricate the front footpegs and the brake pedal at their pivot points . . .

10.2b . . . to lubricate the brake pedal, remove the retaining bolt (arrowed)

10.2c Lubricate the rear footpegs at their pivot points

1•18 Every 4000 miles / 6000 km

10.2d Lubricate the front brake lever at its pivot point, then lubricate the clutch lever in the same way

10.2e Lubricate the sidestand pivot point (arrowed)

10.3 Lubricating a cable with a pressure lube adapter (make sure the tool seats around the inner cable)

11.4 Grasp the wheel and pull it back and forth; if it moves, the bearings are in need of adjustment

11.5a Loosen the lower triple clamp bolt or bolts on each fork; this is an FZR600 . . .

11.5b . . . and this is an FZR1000

accelerated rate). **Note**: *One of the best lubricants for the control lever pivots is a dry-film lubricant (available from many sources by different names).*

3 To lubricate the throttle and choke cables, disconnect the cable(s) at the lower end, then lubricate the cable with a pressure lube adapter **(see illustration)**. See Chapter 3 for the choke cable removal procedure. **Note**: *Yamaha recommends that the throttle twist grip be disassembled and lubricated whenever the throttle cables are lubricated. Refer to the handlebars section of Chapter 7.*

4 The speedometer cable should be removed from its housing and lubricated with motor oil or cable lubricant.

5 Refer to Chapter 7 for the swingarm needle bearing and rear suspension linkage lubrication procedures.

11 Steering head bearings - check, adjustment and repacking

1 This vehicle is equipped with tapered roller type steering head bearings which can become dented, rough or loose during normal use of the machine. In extreme cases, worn or loose steering head bearings can cause steering wobble that is potentially dangerous.

Check

2 To check the bearings, support the motorcycle securely and block the machine so the front wheel is in the air.

3 Point the wheel straight ahead and slowly move the handlebars from side-to-side. Dents or roughness in the bearing races will be felt and the bars will not move smoothly.

4 Next, grasp the wheel and try to move it forward and backward **(see illustration)**. Any looseness in the steering head bearings will be felt as front-to-rear movement of the fork legs. If play is felt in the bearings, adjust the steering head as follows:

Adjustment

5 Loosen the lower triple clamp bolts **(see illustrations)**. This allows the necessary vertical movement of the steering stem in relation to the fork tubes.

6 Remove the handlebars and upper triple clamp (see Chapter 7).

7 Remove the lockwasher from the ring nuts **(see illustration)**.

8 Use a ring nut wrench (Yamaha tool no. YU-33975/part no. 90890-01430 or equivalent) to remove the upper ring nut and rubber washer **(see illustrations)**.

9 Carefully tighten the lower ring nut to the initial torque listed in this Chapter's

11.7 Remove the lockwasher from the ring nuts

11.8a Use a ring nut wrench like this one to loosen the upper ring nut . . .

11.8b . . . then unscrew the upper ring nut and remove the washer from beneath it (arrowed)

Every 4000 miles / 6000 km

Specifications, then loosen it all the way and retighten to the final torque listed in this Chapter's Specifications.

10 Turn the steering from lock to lock and check for binding. If there is any, remove the bearings for inspection (see Chapter 7).

11 If the steering operates properly, install the rubber washer and upper ring nut. Tighten the upper ring nut so its slots align with those of the lower ring nut (don't allow the lower ring nut to turn). If necessary, use the ring nut wrench to keep the lower ring nut from turning while you tighten the upper ring nut.

12 Install the lockwasher with its tabs in the ring nut slots.

13 Recheck the steering head bearings for play as described above. If necessary, repeat the adjustment procedure. Reinstall all parts previously removed. Tighten the steering stem nut, triple clamp bolts and handlebar bolts to the torques listed in the Chapter 7 Specifications.

Lubrication

14 Periodic cleaning and repacking of the steering head bearings is recommended by the manufacturer. Refer to Chapter 7 for steering head bearing lubrication and replacement procedures.

12 Suspension - check

1 The suspension components must be maintained in top operating condition to ensure rider safety. Loose, worn or damaged suspension parts decrease the vehicle's stability and control.

2 While standing alongside the motorcycle, lock the front brake and push on the handlebars to compress the forks several times. See if they move up-and-down smoothly without binding. If binding is felt, the forks should be disassembled and inspected as described in Chapter 7.

3 Carefully inspect the area around the fork seals for any signs of fork oil leakage **(see illustration)**. If leakage is evident, the seals must be replaced as described in Chapter 7.

12.3 Check above and below the fork seals (arrowed) for signs of oil leakage

4 Check the tightness of all suspension nuts and bolts to be sure none have worked loose.

5 Inspect the rear shock for fluid leakage and tightness of the mounting nuts. If leakage is found, the shock should be replaced.

6 Support the bike securely so it can't be knocked over during this procedure. Grab the swingarm on each side, just ahead of the axle. Rock the swingarm from side to side - there should be no discernible movement at the rear. If there's a little movement or a slight clicking can be heard, make sure the pivot shaft nuts are tight. If the pivot nuts are tight but movement is still noticeable, the swingarm will have to be removed and the bearings replaced as described in Chapter 7.

7 Inspect the tightness of the rear suspension nuts and bolts.

13 Tires, wheels and wheel bearings - check

Tires

Refer to 'Daily (pre-ride) checks' at the begining of this Manual.

Wheels

1 The cast wheels used on this machine are virtually maintenance free, but they should be kept clean and checked periodically for cracks and other damage. Never attempt to repair damaged cast wheels; they must be replaced with new ones.

2 Check the valve stem locknuts to make sure they are tight. Also, make sure the valve stem cap is in place and tight. If it is missing, install a new one made of metal or hard plastic.

Wheel bearings

3 Refer to Chapter 8, Section 13.

14 Battery electrolyte level/specific gravity - check

Warning: Be extremely careful when handling or working around the battery. The electrolyte is very caustic and an explosive gas (hydrogen) is given off when the battery is charging.

Note: *The first Steps describe battery removal. If the electrolyte level is known to be sufficient it won't be necessary to remove the battery.*

1 This procedure applies to batteries that have removable filler caps, which can be removed to add water to the battery. The sealed maintenance-free batteries used on some models can't be topped up.

2 Remove the seat (see Chapter 9).

3 If necessary for access to remove the battery, remove the side covers (see Chapter 9).

4 Remove the screws securing the battery cables to the battery terminals (remove the negative cable first, positive cable last) **(see illustration)**. Remove the battery retaining strap and pull the battery straight up to remove it **(see illustration)**. The electrolyte level will now be visible through the translucent battery case - it should be between the Upper and Lower level marks.

5 If the electrolyte is low, remove the cell caps and fill each cell to the upper level mark with distilled water **(see illustration)**. Do not use tap water (except in an emergency), and do not overfill.

14.4a Detach the negative cable (left arrow) first, then detach the positive cable (right arrow)

14.4b Unhook the retaining strap and lift out the battery

14.5 Remove the filler caps with a screwdriver

1•20 Every 4000 miles / 6000 km

14.7 Check the specific gravity with a hydrometer

> **HAYNES HiNT** *The battery cell holes are quite small, so it may help to use a plastic squeeze bottle with a small spout to add the water.*

6 Next, check the specific gravity of the electrolyte in each cell with a small hydrometer made especially for motorcycle batteries. These are available from most dealer parts departments or motorcycle accessory stores.

7 Remove the caps, draw some electrolyte from the first cell into the hydrometer **(see illustration)** and note the specific gravity. Compare the reading to the Specifications listed in this Chapter. **Note:** *Add 0.004 points to the reading for every 10-degrees F above 20-degrees C (68-degrees F) - subtract 0.004 points from the reading for every 10-degrees below 20-degrees C (68-degrees F). Return the electrolyte to the appropriate cell and repeat the check for the remaining cells. When the check is complete, rinse the hydrometer thoroughly with clean water.*

14.11a Pull the retaining strap over the battery and hook its end

8 If the specific gravity of the electrolyte in each cell is as specified, the battery is in good condition and is apparently being charged by the machine's charging system.

9 If the specific gravity is low, the battery is not fully charged. This may be due to corroded battery terminals, a dirty battery case, a malfunctioning charging system, or loose or corroded wiring connections. On the other hand, it may be that the battery is worn out, especially if the machine is old, or that infrequent use of the motorcycle prevents normal charging from taking place.

10 Be sure to correct any problems and charge the battery if necessary. Refer to Chapter 10 for additional battery maintenance and charging procedures.

11 Install the battery cell caps, tightening them securely. Secure the battery with the strap **(see illustration)**. Reconnect the cables to the battery, attaching the positive cable first and the negative cable last. Make sure to install the insulating boot over the positive terminal. Install the side cover (if removed) and the seat. Be very careful not to pinch or otherwise restrict the battery vent tube **(see illustrations)**, as the battery may build up enough internal pressure during normal charging system operation to explode.

15 Exhaust system - check

1 Periodically check all of the exhaust system joints for leaks and loose fasteners. The lower fairing(s) will have to be removed to do this properly (see Chapter 9). If tightening the clamp bolts fails to stop any leaks, replace the gaskets with new ones (a procedure which requires disassembly of the system - see Chapter 5).

2 The exhaust pipe flange nuts at the cylinder heads are especially prone to loosening, which could cause damage to the head. Check them frequently and keep them tight.

16 Fuel system - check and filter replacement

> ⚠ **Warning:** *Gasoline (petrol) is extremely flammable, so take extra precautions when you work on any part of the fuel system. Don't smoke or allow open flames or bare light bulbs near the work area, and don't work in a garage where a natural gas-type appliance (such as a water heater or clothes dryer) is present. If you spill any fuel on your skin, rinse it off*

14.11b Be sure the vent tube is routed correctly, with no kinking or obstruction; this is an FZR600 . . .
1. Vent tube
2. Hose guide on swingarm

14.11c . . . this is an early FZR750/1000 vent tube . . .
1. Vent tube

14.11d . . . and this is a 1989 and later FZR1000 vent tube
1. Vent tube
2. Tube holder
3. Tube guide
4. Carburetor overflow hose
5. Fuel tank vent hose
6. Air filter housing vent hose
7. Coolant reservoir tank breather hose

Every 4000 miles / 6000 km

16.6 Fuel filter details (FZR600 shown; others similar)

immediately with soap and water. When you perform any kind of work on the fuel system, wear safety glasses and have a class B type fire extinguisher on hand.

Check

1 Check the fuel tank, the tank breather hose, the fuel tap, the lines and the carburetors for leaks and evidence of damage.
2 If carburetor gaskets are leaking, the carburetors should be disassembled and rebuilt (see Chapter 5).
3 If the fuel tap is leaking, tightening the screws may help. If leakage persists, the tap should be disassembled and repaired or replaced with a new one.
4 If the fuel lines are cracked or otherwise deteriorated, replace them with new ones.

Filter replacement

5 Remove the fuel tank (see Chapter 5).
6 Disconnect the lines from the filter and remove it from its bracket **(see illustration)**.
7 Install a new filter and reconnect the lines.

17 Crankcase ventilation system - inspection

Inspect the hose that runs from the ventilation fitting on the top of the engine to the air filter case. Make sure it's securely attached. Replace the hose if it's cracked or deteriorated.

18 Sidestand switch - check

Refer to Chapter 10, Section 21.

19 Fasteners - check

1 Since vibration of the machine tends to loosen fasteners, all nuts, bolts, screws, etc. should be periodically checked for proper tightness.
2 Pay particular attention to the following:
   Spark plugs
   Engine oil drain plug
   Oil filter cover bolt and drain plug
   Gearshift lever
   Footpegs, sidestand and centerstand
   Engine mount bolts
   Shock absorber mount bolts
   Rear suspension linkage bolts
   Front axle and clamp bolt
   Rear axle nut
3 If a torque wrench is available, use it along with the torque specifications at the beginning of this, or other, Chapters.

Every 8000 miles/12,000 km or 12 months

20 Engine oil and oil filter - renewal

Refer to Section 2.

21 Spark plugs - renewal

Refer to Section 5.

22 Suspension operation and swingarm play - check

Refer to Section 12.

23 Cylinder compression - check

1 Among other things, poor engine performance may be caused by leaking valves, incorrect valve clearances, a leaking head gasket, or worn pistons, rings and/or cylinder walls. A cylinder compression check will help pinpoint these conditions and can also indicate the presence of excessive carbon deposits in the cylinder heads.
2 The only tools required are a compression gauge and a spark plug wrench. Depending on the outcome of the initial test, a squirt-type oil can may also be needed.
3 Start the engine and allow it to reach normal operating temperature.
4 Support the bike securely so it can't be knocked over during this procedure.
5 Remove fairing panels as necessary for access to the spark plug holes (see Chapter 9).
6 Remove the spark plugs (see Section 5, if necessary). Work carefully - don't strip the spark plug hole threads and don't burn your hands.
7 Disable the ignition by unplugging the primary wires from the coils (see Chapter 6). Be sure to mark the locations of the wires before detaching them.
8 Install the compression gauge in one of the spark plug holes **(see illustration)**.
9 Hold or block the throttle wide open **(see illustration)**.
10 Crank the engine over a minimum of four or five revolutions (or until the gauge reading stops increasing) and observe the initial movement of the compression gauge needle as well as the final total gauge reading. Repeat the procedure for the other cylinders and compare the results to the value listed in this Chapter's Specifications.

23.8 A gauge with a threaded fitting is preferred over one that requires hand pressure to seal it

23.9 Twist the throttle wide open while you crank the engine

1•22 Every 8000 miles / 12,000 km

11 If the compression in all four cylinders built up quickly and evenly to the specified amount, you can assume the engine upper end is in reasonably good mechanical condition. Worn or sticking piston rings and worn cylinders will produce very little initial movement of the gauge needle, but compression will tend to build up gradually as the engine spins over. Valve and valve seat leakage, or head gasket leakage, is indicated by low initial compression which does not tend to build up.

12 To further confirm your findings, add a small amount of engine oil to each cylinder by inserting the nozzle of a squirt-type oil can through the spark plug holes. The oil will tend to seal the piston rings if they are leaking. Repeat the test for the other cylinders.

13 If the compression increases significantly after the addition of the oil, the piston rings and/or cylinders are definitely worn. If the compression does not increase, the pressure is leaking past the valves or the head gasket. Leakage past the valves may be due to insufficient valve clearances, burned, warped or cracked valves or valve seats or valves that are hanging up in the guides.

14 If compression readings are considerably higher than specified, the combustion chambers are probably coated with excessive carbon deposits. It is possible (but not very likely) for carbon deposits to raise the compression enough to compensate for the effects of leakage past rings or valves. Remove the cylinder head and carefully decarbonize the combustion chambers (see Chapter 2 or 3).

Every 16,000 miles/24,000 km or two years

24 Valve clearances (FZR600 models) - check and adjustment

1 The engine must be completely cool for this maintenance procedure, so let the machine sit overnight before beginning.
2 Disconnect the cable from the negative terminal of the battery.
3 Refer to Chapter 9 and remove the seat. Remove fairing panels as necessary for access.
4 Remove the air filter housing (see Chapter 5).

24.9a The line next to the T mark must be exactly aligned with the crankcase seam (arrowed) . . .

24.9b . . . and the punch marks on the camshafts must be exactly aligned with the cast marks on the bearing caps (arrowed); if the camshaft marks aren't lined up, turn the crankshaft exactly one full turn

5 If you're working on an FZR600, remove the top covers, unbolt the fuel tank, lift it up enough to provide access and support it in that position. If you're working on an FZR750/1000, remove the fuel tank.
6 Remove the radiator (see Chapter 4).
7 Remove the oil cooler (if equipped) and the valve cover (see Chapter 2 or Chapter 3).

FZR600 models

8 Remove the alternator cover from the left side of the engine (see Chapter 10).
9 Position the number 1 piston (on the left side of the engine) at Top Dead Center (TDC) on the compression stroke. Do this by turning the crankshaft, with a socket placed on the alternator rotor bolt, until the line next to the T mark on the rotor is aligned with the crankcase seam and the punch marks on the camshafts align with the marks on the cam bearing caps (see illustrations). Now, check the position of the no. 1 cylinder cam lobes - they should be pointing away from each other (see illustration). Piston number 1 is now at TDC compression. **Note:** *Turn the engine in the normal direction of rotation (counterclockwise (anti-clockwise), viewed from the signal generator end).*
10 With the engine in this position, all of the valves for cylinder no. 1 can be checked.
11 Start with the no. 1 intake valve clearance. Insert a feeler gauge of the thickness listed in

24.9c Make sure the cam lobes for no. 1 cylinder point away from each other - if the cam lobes aren't in this position, turn the crankshaft exactly one full turn to bring no. 1 cylinder to TDC

this Chapter's Specifications between each cam lobe and its lifter (see illustration). Pull the feeler gauge out slowly - you should feel a slight drag. If there's no drag, the clearance is too loose. If there's a heavy drag, the clearance is too tight.
12 If the clearance is incorrect, write down the actual measured clearance. You'll need this information later to select a new valve adjusting shim.
13 Now measure the no. 1 exhaust valves, following the same procedure you used for the intake valves. Make sure to use a feeler gauge of the specified thickness and write down the actual clearances of any valves that aren't within the Specifications.
14 Rotate the crankshaft exactly one-half turn to place piston no. 2 at TDC compression. The cam lobes for no. 2 cylinder should now point away from each other (see illustration 24.9c).
15 Measure the clearances of all four valves on cylinder no. 2 and write down any that aren't within the Specifications.
16 Turn the engine exactly one-half turn again to place cylinder no. 4 at TDC. The alternator rotor mark will align with the crankcase seam (see illustration 24.9a) and the no. 4 cam lobes will be pointing away from each other (see illustration 24.9c). The punch marks on the camshafts will be straight down, so they won't be visible. Measure the valve clearances for all four valves on no. 4 cylinder and write them down.

24.11 Slip a feeler gauge between the cam lobe and valve lifter - it should pull out with a very light drag

Every 16,000 miles / 24,000 km

24.21a Pull the lifter out with a magnet (use a suction cup if it's stuck) . . .

24.21b . . . and remove the adjusting shim . . .

24.21c . . . the shim may be held on the underside of the lifter by the magnet . . .

17 Turn the engine exactly one-half turn again to place cylinder no. 3 at TDC (its cam lobes facing away from each other) and measure its valve clearances.

18 If any of the clearances need to be adjusted, go to Step 19. If all the clearances were within the Specifications, no adjustment is necessary; reinstall all removed components and be sure to refill the cooling system.

19 Remove the camshafts (see Chapter 2). *Caution: Follow the procedure in Chapter 2 carefully to prevent breaking a cam bearing cap. If a cap breaks, it may be necessary to replace the entire cylinder head. Be sure to wire the cam chain up so it doesn't fall down off the crankshaft sprocket. Also, pack clean shop rags into the timing chain cavity so the valve lifters don't fall into the crankcase when they're removed.*

20 Make a holder to keep the lifters in order so they can be returned to their original bores.

21 Remove the lifter for each valve to be adjusted with a magnet **(see illustrations)**.

22 Determine the thickness of the shim you removed. It should be marked on the top of the shim **(see illustration 24.21d)**. The number indicates the shim thickness in hundredths of a millimeter. For example, the shim marked 170 in **illustration 24.21d** is 1.70 mm thick. The ideal way to judge shim thickness is to measure it with a micrometer.

24.21d . . . there's a thickness mark on the top of each valve shim

INTAKE

MEASURED CLEARANCE [B]	\[A\] INSTALLED PAD NUMBER																								
	120	125	130	135	140	145	150	155	160	165	170	175	180	185	190	195	200	205	210	215	220	225	230	235	240
0.00~0.02			120	125	130	135	140	145	150	155	160	165	170	175	180	185	190	195	200	205	210	215	220	225	
0.03~0.07		120	125	130	135	140	145	150	155	160	165	170	175	180	185	190	195	200	205	210	215	220	225	230	
0.08~0.10	120	125	130	135	140	145	150	155	160	165	170	175	180	185	190	195	200	205	210	215	220	225	230	235	
0.11~0.20	RECOMMENDED CLEARANCE																								
0.21~0.22	125	130	135	140	145	150	155	160	165	170	175	180	185	190	195	200	205	210	215	220	225	230	235	240	
0.23~0.27	130	135	140	145	150	155	160	165	170	175	180	185	190	195	200	205	210	215	220	225	230	235	240		
0.28~0.32	135	140	145	150	155	160	165	170	175	180	185	190	195	200	205	210	215	220	225	230	235	240			
0.33~0.37	140	145	150	155	160	165	170	175	180	185	190	195	200	205	210	215	220	225	230	235	240				
0.38~0.42	145	150	155	160	165	170	175	180	185	190	195	200	205	210	215	220	225	230	235	240					
0.43~0.47	150	155	160	165	170	175	180	185	190	195	200	205	210	215	220	225	230	235	240						
0.48~0.52	155	160	165	170	175	180	185	190	195	200	205	210	215	220	225	230	235	240							
0.53~0.57	160	165	170	175	180	185	190	195	200	205	210	215	220	225	230	235	240								
0.58~0.62	165	170	175	180	185	190	195	200	205	210	215	220	225	230	235	240									
0.63~0.67	170	175	180	185	190	195	200	205	210	215	220	225	230	235	240										
0.68~0.72	175	180	185	190	195	200	205	210	215	220	225	230	235	240											
0.73~0.77	180	185	190	195	200	205	210	215	220	225	230	235	240												
0.78~0.82	185	190	195	200	205	210	215	220	225	230	235	240													
0.83~0.87	190	195	200	205	210	215	220	225	230	235	240														
0.88~0.92	195	200	205	210	215	220	225	230	235	240															
0.93~0.97	200	205	210	215	220	225	230	235	240																
0.98~1.02	205	210	215	220	225	230	235	240																	
1.03~1.07	210	215	220	225	230	235	240																		
1.08~1.12	215	220	225	230	235	240																			
1.13~1.17	220	225	230	235	240																				
1.18~1.22	225	230	235	240																					
1.23~1.27	230	235	240																						
1.28~1.32	235	240																							
1.33~1.37	240																								

EXAMPLE:

VALVE CLEARANCE (cold):
 0.11 ~ 0.20 mm (0.004 ~ 0.008 in)
Installed is 148 (Rounded off number is 150)
Measured clearance is 0.24 mm (0.009 in)
Replace 148 pad with 160 pad

24.23a Intake valve shim selection chart

1•24 Every 16,000 miles / 24,000 km

EXHAUST

[B] MEASURED CLEARANCE	[A] INSTALLED PAD NUMBER																								
	120	125	130	135	140	145	150	155	160	165	170	175	180	185	190	195	200	205	210	215	220	225	230	235	240
0.00~0.02							120	125	130	135	140	145	150	155	160	165	170	175	180	185	190	195	200	205	210	215
0.03~0.07						120	125	130	135	140	145	150	155	160	165	170	175	180	185	190	195	200	205	210	215	220
0.08~0.12					120	125	130	135	140	145	150	155	160	165	170	175	180	185	190	195	200	205	210	215	220	225
0.13~0.17				120	125	130	135	140	145	150	155	160	165	170	175	180	185	190	195	200	205	210	215	220	225	230
0.18~0.20			120	125	130	135	140	145	150	155	160	165	170	175	180	185	190	195	200	205	210	215	220	225	230	235
0.21~0.30	RECOMMENDED CLEARANCE																								
0.31~0.32	125	130	135	140	145	150	155	160	165	170	175	180	185	190	195	200	205	210	215	220	225	230	235	240	
0.33~0.37	130	135	140	145	150	155	160	165	170	175	180	185	190	195	200	205	210	215	220	225	230	235	240		
0.38~0.42	135	140	145	150	155	160	165	170	175	180	185	190	195	200	205	210	215	220	225	230	235	240			
0.43~0.47	140	145	150	155	160	165	170	175	180	185	190	195	200	205	210	215	220	225	230	235	240				
0.48~0.52	145	150	155	160	165	170	175	180	185	190	195	200	205	210	215	220	225	230	235	240					
0.53~0.57	150	155	160	165	170	175	180	185	190	195	200	205	210	215	220	225	230	235	240						
0.58~0.62	155	160	165	170	175	180	185	190	195	200	205	210	215	220	225	230	235	240							
0.63~0.67	160	165	170	175	180	185	190	195	200	205	210	215	220	225	230	235	240								
0.68~0.72	165	170	175	180	185	190	195	200	205	210	215	220	225	230	235	240									
0.73~0.77	170	175	180	185	190	195	200	205	210	215	220	225	230	235	240										
0.78~0.82	175	180	185	190	195	200	205	210	215	220	225	230	235	240											
0.83~0.87	180	185	190	195	200	205	210	215	220	225	230	235	240												
0.88~0.92	185	190	195	200	205	210	215	220	225	230	235	240													
0.93~0.97	190	195	200	205	210	215	220	225	230	235	240														
0.98~1.02	195	200	205	210	215	220	225	230	235	240															
1.03~1.07	200	205	210	215	220	225	230	235	240																
1.08~1.12	205	210	215	220	225	230	235	240																	
1.13~1.17	210	215	220	225	230	235	240																		
1.18~1.22	215	220	225	230	235	240																			
1.23~1.27	220	225	230	235	240																				
1.28~1.32	225	230	235	240																					
1.33~1.37	230	235	240																						
1.38~1.42	235	240																							
1.43~1.47	240																								

EXAMPLE:

VALVE CLEARANCE (cold):
0.21 ~ 0.30 mm (0.008 ~ 0.012 in)
Installed is 175
Measured clearance is 0.35 mm (0.014 in)
Replace 175 pad with 185 pad

24.23b Exhaust valve shim selection chart

Note: *If the number on the shim does not end in 0 or 5, round it off to the nearest zero or 5. For example, if the number on the shim is 179,* round it off to 180. If it's 234, round it off to 235.

23 If the measured clearance was too large, you need a thicker shim. If the clearance was too small, you need a thinner shim. Calculate the thickness of the replacement shim by referring to the accompanying charts **(see illustrations)**.
24 Install the new shims and recheck the clearance. If they're within the Specifications, the valves are properly adjusted.

> **HAYNES HINT** *It is worthwhile noting down all the valve shim thicknesses to save time and expense when the valve clearances are next adjusted; provided they are not worn or damaged, the shims can be moved to other locations.*

FZR750/1000 models

25 Remove the timing window cover and crankshaft end cover from the left side of the engine **(see illustrations)**.
26 Install a timing rotor and dowel on the end of the crankshaft **(see illustration)**. This special tool consists of three parts:
 a) Timing rotor (part no. 33M-81673-10)
 b) Dowel pin (part no. 93604-08071)
 c) 8 mm bolt (part no. 91316-08030)
The timing rotor isn't used to indicate crankshaft position; it's simply a means of turning the engine by hand.
27 Position the number 1 piston (on the left side of the engine) at Top Dead Center (TDC) on the compression stroke. Do this by turning

24.25a Remove the cover from the timing window . . .

24.25b . . . remove the screws that secure the left crankshaft end cover . . .

24.25c . . . and lift the cover off

24.26 This tool provides a way to turn the engine in its normal direction of rotation; place a wrench on the square section (DO NOT use the timing marks on the timing plate)

Every 16,000 miles / 24,000 km

24.27a This pointer inside the timing window (arrowed) must be aligned with the line next to the T mark on the crankshaft web ...

24.27b ... and the cam lobes for no. 1 cylinder must be pointing away from each other like this; if the cam lobes are in a different position, turn the crankshaft one full turn

the crankshaft, with a wrench placed on the timing rotor flats, until the pointer inside the timing window is aligned with the line next to the T mark on the crankshaft web and the cam lobes for no. 1 cylinder point away from each other **(see illustrations)**. Piston number 1 is now at TDC compression. **Note:** *Turn the engine in the normal direction of rotation (counterclockwise (anti-clockwise), viewed from the left end).*

28 With the engine in this position, all of the valves for cylinder no. 1 can be checked.

29 Start with the no. 1 intake valve clearance. Insert a tapered feeler gauge of the thickness listed in this Chapter's Specifications between each cam lobe and its lifter **(see illustrations)**. Pull the feeler gauge out slowly - you should feel a slight drag. If there's no drag, the clearance is too loose. If there's a heavy drag, the clearance is too tight.

30 If the clearance is incorrect, write down the actual measured clearance. You'll need this information later to select a new valve adjusting shim.

31 Now measure the no. 1 exhaust valves, following the same procedure you used for the intake valves. Make sure to use a feeler gauge of the specified thickness and write down the actual clearances of any valves that aren't within the Specifications.

32 Rotate the crankshaft exactly one-half turn to place piston no. 2 at TDC compression. The cam lobes for no. 2 cylinder should now point away from each other **(see illustration 24.9c)**.

33 Measure the clearances of all five valves on cylinder no. 2 and write down any that aren't within the Specifications.

34 Turn the engine exactly one-half turn again to place cylinder no. 4 at TDC. The T mark line will align with the timing window pointer **(see illustration 24.27a)** and the no. 4 cam lobes will be pointing away from each other **(see illustration 24.9c)**. Measure the valve clearances for all five valves on no. 4 cylinder and write them down.

35 Turn the engine exactly one-half turn again to place cylinder no. 3 at TDC (its cam lobes facing away from each other) and measure its valve clearances.

36 If any of the clearances need to be adjusted, go to Step 37. If all the clearances were within the Specifications, no adjustment is necessary; reinstall all removed components and be sure to refill the cooling system.

37 Remove the camshafts (see Chapter 3). **Caution:** *Follow the procedure in Chapter 3 carefully to prevent breaking a cam bearing cap. If a cap breaks, it may be necessary to replace the entire cylinder head. Be sure to wire the cam chain up so it doesn't fall down off the crankshaft sprocket. Also, pack clean shop rags into the timing chain cavity so the valve lifters don't fall into the crankcase when they're removed.*

38 Make a holder to keep the lifters in order so they can be returned to their original bores.

39 Remove the lifter for each valve to be adjusted with a magnet **(see illustrations 24.21a, 24.21b, 24.21c and 24.21d)**.

40 Determine the thickness of the shim you removed. It should be marked on the top of the shim **(see illustration 24.21d)**. The number indicates the shim thickness in hundredths of a millimeter. For example, the shim marked 170 in illustration 24.21d is 1.70 mm thick. The ideal way to judge shim thickness is to measure it with a micrometer. **Note:** *If the number on the shim does not end in 0 or 5, round it off to the nearest zero or 5. For example, if the number on the shim is 179, round it off to 180. If it's 234, round it off to 235.*

41 If the measured clearance was too large, you need a thicker shim. If the clearance was too small, you need a thinner shim. Calculate the thickness of the replacement shim by referring to the accompanying charts **(see illustrations 24.23a and 24.23b)**.

42 Install the new shims and recheck the clearance. If they're within the Specifications, the valves are properly adjusted. Reinstall all removed components and refill the cooling system.

> **HAYNES HiNT** *It is worthwhile noting down all the valve shim thicknesses to save time and expense when the valve clearances are next adjusted; provided they are not worn or damaged, the shims can be moved to other locations.*

25 Brake/clutch fluid - renewal

Refer to Chapter 8, Section 8 and Chapter 3, Section 20.

26 Steering head bearings - clean and repack

Refer to Section 11.

27 Swingarm bearings and rear suspension pivot points - lubrication

Refer to Section 12.

24.29a You'll need tapered feeler gauges to fit between the bolt bosses on the cam bearing caps

24.29b Insert the feeler gauge blade between the camshaft and lifter to measure the clearance

Every 18,000 miles/30,000 km

28 Fuel filter - renewal

Refer to Section 16.

Every 26,000 miles/42,000 km

29 Valve clearances (FZR750/1000 models) - check and adjustment

Refer to Section 24.

Every 60,000 miles/100,000 km

30 Alternator brushes (FZR750/1000 models) - renewal

Refer to Chapter 10, Section 32.

Every two years

31 Cooling system - draining, flushing and refilling

Warning: *Allow the engine to cool completely before performing this maintenance operation. Also, don't allow antifreeze to come into contact with your skin or painted surfaces of the motorcycle. Rinse off spills immediately with plenty of water. Antifreeze is highly toxic if ingested. Never leave antifreeze lying around in an open container or in puddles on the floor; children and pets are attracted by its sweet smell and may drink it. Check with local authorities (councils) about disposing of used antifreeze. Many communities have collection centers which will see that antifreeze is disposed of safely. Antifreeze is also combustible, so don't store or use it near open flames.*

Draining

1 Place a large, clean drain pan under the left side of the engine.
2 Remove the drain bolt from the bottom of the coolant tube or water pump cover **(see illustrations)** and allow the coolant to drain into the pan. After removing the drain bolt, remove the pressure cap **(see illustration 4.7a)** to ensure that all of the coolant can drain. **Note**: *The coolant will rush out with considerable force as soon as the cap is removed, so position the drain pan accordingly* **(see illustration)**. Remove the drain plugs from the front of the cylinder block **(see illustration)**.
3 Drain the coolant reservoir. Refer to Chapter 4 for the reservoir removal procedure. Wash the reservoir out with water.

31.2a Later models have a drain bolt on the water pump; this is an FZR600 . . .

31.2b . . . and this is an FZR750/1000

31.2c The coolant will shoot out of the drain hole, so position the pan accordingly

31.2d In addition to the lower drain bolt, there's a screw on each front corner or side of the block

Every two years

Flushing

4 Flush the system with clean tap water by inserting a garden hose in the radiator filler neck. Allow the water to run through the system until it is clear when it exits the drain bolt holes. If the radiator is extremely corroded, remove it (see Chapter 4) and have it cleaned at a radiator shop.

5 Check the drain bolt gaskets. Replace them with new ones if necessary.

6 Clean the holes, then install the drain bolts and tighten them to the torque listed in this Chapter's Specifications.

7 Fill the cooling system with clean water mixed with a flushing compound. Make sure the flushing compound is compatible with aluminum components, and follow the manufacturer's instructions carefully.

8 Start the engine and allow it to reach normal operating temperature. Let it run for about ten minutes.

9 Stop the engine. Let the machine cool for a while, then cover the pressure cap with a heavy rag and turn it counterclockwise (anti-clockwise) to the first stop, releasing any pressure that may be present in the system. Once the hissing stops, push down on the cap and remove it completely.

10 Drain the system once again.

11 Fill the system with clean water, then repeat Steps 8, 9 and 10.

Refilling

12 Fill the system with the proper coolant mixture (see this Chapter's Specifications). When the system is full (all the way up to the top of the radiator cap filler neck), start the engine. Watch the coolant and level as the engine runs, and add coolant when the level drops. When the coolant level stabilizes, shut the engine off.

13 Fill the system with coolant to the top of the filler neck.

14 Allow the engine to cool, then check the coolant level in the reservoir (see 'Daily (pre-ride) checks' at the beginning of this Manual). If the coolant level is low, add the specified mixture until it reaches the Full mark in the reservoir.

15 Check the system for leaks.

16 Do not dispose of the old coolant by pouring it down a drain. Instead, pour it into a heavy plastic container, cap it tightly and take it to an authorized disposal site or a service station.

32 Brake/clutch system seals - renewal

Refer to Chapter 8, Sections 3, 5 and 6, and Chapter 3, Section 20.

Every four years

33 Brake/clutch hoses - renewal

Refer to Chapter 8, Section 7, and Chapter 3, Section 20.

1•28 Routine maintenance and servicing

Notes

Chapter 2
FZR600 engine, clutch and transmission

Contents

Camshaft chain and guides - removal, inspection and installation ... 27
Camshaft chain tensioner - removal and installation 8
Camshafts and lifters - removal, inspection and installation 9
Clutch cable - removal and installation 20
Clutch - removal, inspection and installation 19
Compression test .... See Chapter 1
Connecting rods and bearings - removal, inspection, bearing selection and installation 26
Crankcase components - inspection and servicing 23
Crankcase - disassembly and reassembly 22
Crankshaft and main bearings - removal, inspection, main bearing selection and installation 25
Cylinder block - removal, inspection and installation 13
Cylinder head and valves - disassembly, inspection and reassembly 12
Cylinder head - removal and installation 10
Engine disassembly and reassembly - general information 6
Engine - removal and installation 5
External shift mechanism - removal, inspection and installation ... 21
General information 1
Initial start-up after overhaul 32
Main and connecting rod bearings - general note 24
Major engine repair - general note 4
Oil and filter change .... See Chapter 1
Oil cooler (UK models) - removal and installation 31
Oil pan and relief valve - removal, relief valve inspection and installation 16
Oil pump - oil pressure check, removal, inspection and installation 17
Operations possible with the engine in the frame 2
Operations requiring engine removal 3
Piston rings - installation 15
Pistons - removal, inspection and installation 14
Recommended break-in procedure 33
Shift cam and forks - removal, inspection and installation 30
Spark plug replacement .... See Chapter 1
Starter clutch - removal, inspection and installation 18
Transmission shafts - disassembly, inspection and reassembly ... 29
Transmission shafts - removal and installation 28
Valve cover - removal and installation 7
Valves/valve seats/valve guides - servicing 11

Degrees of difficulty

Easy, suitable for novice with little experience	Fairly easy, suitable for beginner with some experience	Fairly difficult, suitable for competent DIY mechanic	Difficult, suitable for experienced DIY mechanic	Very difficult, suitable for expert DIY or professional

Specifications

General
Bore .... 59 mm (2.323 inches)
Stroke .... 54.8 mm (2.158 inches)
Displacement .... 599 cc
Compression ratio .... 12 to 1

Camshafts
Intake camshaft
  Lobe height
    Standard .... 32.75 to 32.85 mm (1.2894 to 1.2933 inch)
    Minimum .... 32.7 mm (1.287 inch)
  Base circle
    Standard .... 24.998 to 25.098 mm (0.9842 to 0.9881 inch)
    Minimum .... 24.95 mm (0.982 inch)
Exhaust camshaft
  Lobe height
    Standard .... 32.55 to 32.65 mm (1.2815 to 1.2854 inch)
    Minimum .... 32.5 mm (1.280 inch)
  Base circle
    Standard .... 24.998 to 25.098 mm (0.9842 to 0.9881 inch)
    Minimum .... 24.95 mm (0.982 inch)
Bearing oil clearance
  Standard .... 0.020 to 0.054 mm (0.0008 to 0.0021 inch)
  Maximum .... 0.08 mm (0.0031 inch)
Journal diameter .... 22.967 to 22.980 mm (0.9042 to 0.9047 inch)
Bearing bore .... 23.000 to 23.021 mm (0.9055 to 0.9063 inch)
Camshaft runout limit .... 0.06 mm (0.0024 inch)

Cylinder head, valves and valve springs

Cylinder head warpage limit	0.05 mm (0.002 inch)
Valve stem bend limit	0.04 mm (0.0016 inch)
Valve head diameter	
Intake	23.9 to 24.1 mm (0.941 to 0.949 inch)
Exhaust	20.9 to 21.1 mm (0.823 to 0.831 inch)
Valve margin thickness (minimum)	0.7 mm (0.0276 inch)
Valve stem diameter	
Standard	
Intake	4.475 to 4.490 mm (0.1762 to 0.1768 inch)
Exhaust	4.460 to 4.475 mm (0.1756 to 0.1762 inch)
Minimum	
Intake	4.45 mm (0.1752 inch)
Exhaust	4.435 mm (0.1746 inch)
Valve head thickness (intake and exhaust)	
Standard	0.6 to 0.8 mm (0.236 to 0.0315 inch)
Minimum	0.5 mm (0.020 inch)
Valve guide inside diameter (intake and exhaust)	
Standard	4.500 to 4.512 mm (0.1772 to 0.1776 inch)
Maximum	4.542 mm (0.179 inch)
Stem-to-guide clearance limit	
Intake	0.08 mm (0.0031 inch)
Exhaust	0.10 mm (0.0039 inch)
Valve seat width (intake and exhaust)	0.9 to 1.1 mm (0.0354 to 0.0433 inch)
Valve face width (intake and exhaust)	1.56 to 2.40 mm (0.061 to 0.095 inch)
Valve spring free length (intake and exhaust)	
Standard	43.15 mm (1.70 inch)
Minimum	41.2 mm (1.62 inch)
Valve spring installed length (intake and exhaust)	37.5 mm (1.48 inch)
Compressed pressure at installed length	11.6 to 13.4 kg (25.9 to 29.6 lbs)
Valve spring bend limit	1.9 mm (0.075 inch)

Cylinder block

Bore diameter	
Standard	59.00 to 59.01 mm (2.3228 to 2.3232 inch)
Maximum	59.15 mm (2.3288 inch)
Bore measuring point	40 mm (1.57 inch) from top of cylinder
Taper and out-of-round limit	Not specified

Pistons

Piston diameter	
Standard	58.940 to 58.955 mm (2.320 to 2.321 inch)
First oversize	59.5 mm (2.343 inch)
Second oversize	60.0 mm (2.362 inch)
Diameter measuring point	5.0 mm (0.197 inch) from bottom of skirt
Piston-to-cylinder clearance	
Standard	0.03 to 0.05 mm (0.0012 to 0.0020 inch)
Maximum	0.10 mm (0.0039 inch)
Ring side clearance	
Top ring	
Standard	0.03 to 0.07 mm (0.0012 to 0.0028 inch)
Maximum	0.10 mm (0.0039 inch)
Second ring	
Standard	0.02 to 0.06 mm (0.0008 to 0.0024 inch)
Maximum	0.10 mm (0.0039 inch)
Oil ring	Not specified
Ring thickness	
Top and second rings	0.8 mm (0.0315 inch)
Oil ring (spacer and rails)	1.5 mm (0.0591 inch)
Ring end gap	
Top and second rings	0.15 to 0.30 mm (0.0059 to 0.0118 inch)
Oil ring	0.2 to 0.6 mm (0.0079 to 0.0236 inch)
Ring width	
Top and second rings	2.1 mm (0.0827 inch)
Oil ring	2.2 mm (0.0866 inch)

Crankshaft, connecting rods and bearings
Main bearing oil clearance
    Standard .... 0.025 to 0.043 mm (0.0010 to 0.0017 inch)
    Maximum .... 0.08 mm (0.003 inch)
Connecting rod side clearance
    Standard .... 0.160 to 0.262 mm (0.0063 to 0.0103 inch)
    Maximum .... 0.5 mm (0.02 inch)
Connecting rod bearing oil clearance .... 0.043 to 0.066 mm (0.0017 to 0.0026 inch)
Crankshaft runout limit .... 0.03 mm (0.0012 inch)

Oil pump and relief valve
Inner to outer rotor clearance .... 0.03 to 0.09 mm (0.0012 to 0.0035 inch)
Outer rotor to housing clearance .... 0.03 to 0.08 mm (0.0012 to 0.0031 inch)
Bypass valve setting pressure .... 0.76 to 1.17 Bars (11 to 17 psi)
Relief valve opening pressure .... 4.47 to 5.44 Bars (64 to 78 psi)

Clutch and transmission
Friction plate thickness
    Standard .... 2.9 to 3.1 mm (0.1142 to 0.1220 inch)
    Minimum .... 2.8 mm (0.11 inch)
Steel plate thickness .... 1.8 to 2.2 mm (0.072 to 0.085 inch)
Steel plate warpage limit .... 0.1 mm (0.004 inch)
Pushrod bend limit .... 0.5 mm (0.02 inch)
Spring length
    Standard .... 33.5 mm (1.32 inch)
    Minimum .... 32.6 mm (1.28 inch)
Driveshaft and mainshaft runout limit .... 0.08 mm (0.0031 inch)

Torque specifications
Cam chain guide (intake side) Allen bolts .... 10 Nm (7.2 ft-lbs) (1)
Cam chain sprocket bolts .... 24 Nm (17 ft-lbs)
Cam chain tensioner mounting bolts .... 10 Nm (7.2 ft-lbs)
Cam chain tensioner cap bolt .... 10 Nm (7.2 ft-lbs)
Camshaft bearing cap bolts .... 10 Nm (7.2 ft-lbs)
Cylinder block coolant passage plug screws .... 7 Nm (5.1 ft-lbs)
Cylinder head nuts .... 25 Nm (18 ft-lbs)
Clutch boss nut .... 70 ft-lbs (50 Nm) (2)
Clutch cover bolts .... 10 Nm (7.2 ft-lbs)
Clutch push lever screw .... 5 Nm (3.6 ft-lbs) (1)
Clutch pushrod adjuster locknut .... 16 Nm (11 ft-lbs)
Clutch pressure plate bolts .... 6 Nm (4.3 ft-lbs)
Connecting rod cap nuts .... 23 Nm (17 ft-lbs) (3)
Crankcase bolts
    M8 x 1.25 .... 24 Nm (17 ft-lbs) (4)
    M6 x 1.0 .... 12 Nm (8.7 ft-lbs) (4)
Crankcase studs to crankcase .... 13 Nm (9.4 ft-lbs) (4)
Engine mounting bolts
    Upper rear and lower front .... 55 Nm (40 ft-lbs)
    Lower rear .... 45 Nm (32 ft-lbs)
Frame downtube bolts
    Upper .... 60 Nm (43 ft-lbs) (1)
    Lower .... 33 Nm (24 ft-lbs) (1)
Oil baffle plate screws .... 7 Nm (5.1 ft-lbs)
Oil cooler banjo bolts .... 25 Nm (18 ft-lbs)
Oil cooler hose bolts .... 32 Nm (23 ft-lbs)
Oil cooler mounting bolts .... 10 Nm (7.2 ft-lbs)
Oil pan mounting bolts .... 10 Nm (7.2 ft-lbs)
Oil passage plugs .... 37 Nm (27 ft-lbs)
Oil pickup bolts .... 10 Nm (7.2 ft-lbs)
Oil pump housing screw .... 7 Nm (5.1 ft-lbs)
Oil pump mounting bolts .... 10 Nm (7.2 ft-lbs) (1)
Shift cam retaining plate bolt .... 10 Nm (7.2 ft-lbs) (1)
Shift cam stopper lever bolt .... 10 Nm (7.2 ft-lbs) (1)
Starter clutch cover bolts .... 10 Nm (7.2 ft-lbs)
Starter clutch securing bolt .... 80 Nm (58 ft-lbs)
Valve cover bolts .... 10 Nm (7.2 ft-lbs)

1 Apply non-permanent thread locking agent to the threads.
2 Use a new lockwasher.
3 Apply molybdenum disulphide grease to the threads.
4 Apply engine oil to the threads.

2•4 FZR600 engine, clutch and transmission

1 General information

The engine/transmission unit is a liquid-cooled, in-line four. The valves are operated by double overhead camshafts which are chain driven off the crankshaft. The engine/transmission assembly is constructed from aluminium alloy. The crankcase is divided horizontally.

The crankcase incorporates a wet sump, pressure-fed lubrication system which uses a gear-driven oil pump, an oil filter, relief valve and an oil level switch. The starter clutch is mounted on the right side of the crankcase.

Power from the crankshaft is routed to the transmission via the clutch, which is of the coil spring, wet multi-plate type and is gear-driven off the crankshaft. The transmission is a six-speed, constant-mesh unit.

2 Operations possible with the engine in the frame

The components and assemblies listed below can be removed without having to remove the engine from the frame. If, however, a number of areas require attention at the same time, removal of the engine is recommended.

Gear selector mechanism external components
Starter motor
Alternator
Clutch assembly
Oil pump
Oil pan and relief valve
Valve cover, camshafts and lifters
Cam chain tensioner
Cylinder head
Cylinder block and pistons
Starter clutch
Camshaft chain (if soft link is fitted)

3 Operations requiring engine removal

It is necessary to remove the engine/transmission assembly from the frame and separate the crankcase halves to gain access to the following components:

Crankshaft, connecting rods and bearings
Transmission shafts
Shift cam and forks
Camshaft chain (see Section 2)

4 Major engine repair - general note

1 It is not always easy to determine when or if an engine should be completely overhauled, as a number of factors must be considered.

2 High mileage is not necessarily an indication that an overhaul is needed, while low mileage, on the other hand, does not preclude the need for an overhaul. Frequency of servicing is probably the single most important consideration. An engine that has regular and frequent oil and filter changes, as well as other required maintenance, will most likely give many miles of reliable service. Conversely, a neglected engine, or one which has not been broken in properly, may require an overhaul very early in its life.

3 Exhaust smoke and excessive oil consumption are both indications that piston rings and/or valve guides are in need of attention. Make sure oil leaks are not responsible before deciding that the rings and guides are bad. Refer to Chapter 1 and perform a cylinder compression check to determine for certain the nature and extent of the work required.

4 If the engine is making obvious knocking or rumbling noises, the connecting rod and/or main bearings are probably at fault.

5 Loss of power, rough running, excessive valve train noise and high fuel consumption rates may also point to the need for an overhaul, especially if they are all present at the same time. If a complete tune-up does not remedy the situation, major mechanical work is the only solution.

6 An engine overhaul generally involves restoring the internal parts to the specifications of a new engine. During an overhaul the piston rings are replaced and the cylinder walls are bored and/or honed. If a rebore is done, then new pistons are also required. The main and connecting rod bearings are generally replaced with new ones and, if necessary, the crankshaft is also replaced. Generally the valves are serviced as well, since they are usually in less than perfect condition at this point. While the engine is being overhauled, other components such as the carburetors and the starter motor can be rebuilt also. The end result should be a like-new engine that will give as many trouble free miles as the original.

HAYNES HINT *As a general rule, time is the primary cost of an overhaul so it doesn't pay to install worn or substandard parts.*

7 Before beginning the engine overhaul, read through all of the related procedures to familiarize yourself with the scope and requirements of the job. Overhauling an engine is not all that difficult, but it is time consuming. Plan on the motorcycle being tied up for a minimum of two weeks. Check on the availability of parts and make sure that any necessary special tools, equipment and supplies are obtained in advance.

8 Most work can be done with typical shop hand tools, although a number of precision measuring tools are required for inspecting parts to determine if they must be replaced. Often a dealer service department or motorcycle repair shop will handle the inspection of parts and offer advice concerning reconditioning and replacement.

9 As a final note, to ensure maximum life and minimum trouble from a rebuilt engine, everything must be assembled with care in a spotlessly clean environment.

5 Engine - removal and installation

Note: *Engine removal and installation should be done with the aid of an assistant to avoid damage or injury that could occur if the engine is dropped. A hydraulic floor jack should be used to support and lower the engine if possible (they can be rented at low cost).*

Removal

1 Support the bike securely so it can't be knocked over during this procedure.
2 Remove the fuel tank (see Chapter 5).
3 Remove the left, right and upper fairings and the seat (see Chapter 9).
4 Remove the air filter housing (see Chapter 5).
5 Drain the engine oil and coolant (see Chapter 1).
6 Remove the carburetors (see Chapter 5) and plug the intake openings with rags.
7 Remove the radiator and the coolant tubes on the intake side of the engine. Remove the radiator outlet tubes (see Chapter 4).
8 If you're working on a California model, disconnect the EXUP cables at the upper end (see Chapter 5). If you're working on an early UK model, remove the oil cooler (see Section 31).
9 Remove the exhaust system (see Chapter 5).
10 Disconnect the clutch cable (see Section 20).
11 Remove the engine sprocket cover and engine sprocket (see Chapter 7). It isn't necessary to remove the drive chain completely, but if the engine sprocket is difficult to remove, loosen the rear axle nut and chain adjusters, then push the rear wheel forward to create slack in the chain (see Chapter 1 for details).
12 Disconnect both battery cables from the battery.

Warning: Always disconnect the negative cable first and reconnect it last to prevent a battery explosion.

13 Refer to Chapter 10 and disconnect the following electrical connectors:
a) alternator
b) neutral, oil level and sidestand switches
c) spark plug wires
d) starter motor
e) engine ground cable

14 Remove the cover and detach the choke lever assembly from the left side of the motorcycle (see Chapter 4).
15 Detach the shift lever adjusting rod from the engine (see Section 21).

FZR600 engine, clutch and transmission 2•5

5.17a Remove the hex bolts from the upper end of each downtube . . .

5.17b . . . and the Allen bolts from the lower end . . .

5.17c . . . and unbolt the down tubes from the engine

5.18a The nut for the upper engine mounting bolt is beneath a plastic cap

5.18b The nut for the lower mounting bolt is inboard of the brake pedal

5.18c Slip the spacers back onto the mounting bolt so they won't be lost

16 Support the engine securely with a floor jack and a wood block.
17 Remove the bolts holding the downtubes to the frame **(see illustrations)**.
18 Remove the upper and lower engine mounting bolts and spacers **(see illustrations)**.
19 Make sure no wires or hoses are still attached to the engine assembly.

> **Warning:** *The engine is heavy and may cause injury if it falls. Be sure it's securely supported. Have an assistant help you steady the engine on the jack as you remove it.*

20 Slowly and carefully lower the engine assembly to the floor, then guide it out from under the bike **(see illustration)**.

Installation

21 Installation is the reverse of removal. Note the following points:
a) Don't tighten any of the engine mounting bolts until they all have been installed.
b) Use new gaskets at all exhaust pipe connections.
c) Tighten the engine mounting bolts and frame downtube bolts to the torques listed in this Chapter's Specifications.
d) Adjust the drive chain, clutch cable and throttle cables following the procedures in Chapter 1 and Chapter 5.
e) Be sure to refill the cooling system and engine oil before starting the engine.

6 Engine disassembly and reassembly - general information

> **HAYNES HINT** *Before disassembling the engine, clean the exterior with a degreaser and rinse it with water. A clean engine will make the job easier and prevent the possibility of getting dirt into the internal areas of the engine.*

1 In addition to the precision measuring tools mentioned earlier, you will need a torque wrench, a valve spring compressor, oil gallery brushes, a piston ring removal and installation tool, piston ring compressors and a clutch holder tool (which is described in Section 19). Some new, clean engine oil of the correct grade and type, some engine assembly lube (or moly-based grease), a tube of Yamaha Quick Gasket (part no. 11001-05-01) or equivalent, and a tube of RTV (silicone) sealant will also be required.
2 Although it may not be considered a tool, some Plastigauge should also be obtained to use for checking bearing oil clearances **(see illustrations)**.
3 An engine support stand made from short lengths of 2 x 4's bolted together will facilitate

5.20 Use a jack to lower the engine and have an assistant help guide it out of the frame

6.2a A selection of brushes is required for cleaning holes and passages in the engine components

2•6 FZR600 engine, clutch and transmission

6.2b Plastigauge is needed to check the crankshaft, connecting rod and camshaft oil clearances

6.3 An engine stand can be made from short lengths of 2 x 4 lumber and lag bolts or nails

7.7 Remove the valve cover mounting bolts

the disassembly and reassembly procedures **(see illustration)**. The perimeter of the mount should be just big enough to accommodate the engine oil pan. If you have an automotive-type engine stand, an adapter plate can be made from a piece of plate, some angle iron and some nuts and bolts.

4 When disassembling the engine, keep "mated" parts together (including gears, cylinders, pistons, etc. that have been in contact with each other during engine operation). These "mated" parts must be reused or replaced as an assembly.

5 Engine/transmission disassembly should be done in the following general order with reference to the appropriate Sections.
　Remove the camshafts
　Remove the cylinder head
　Remove the cylinder block
　Remove the pistons
　Remove the starter clutch and idle gears
　Remove the clutch
　Remove the oil pan
　Remove the external shift mechanism
　Remove the alternator and starter (see Chapter 10)
　Separate the crankcase halves
　Remove the crankshaft and connecting rods
　Remove the transmission shafts/gears
　Remove the shift cam/forks

6 Reassembly is accomplished by reversing the general disassembly sequence.

7 Valve cover - removal and installation

Note: *The valve cover can be removed with the engine in the frame. If the engine has been removed, ignore the steps which don't apply.*

Removal

1 Support the bike securely so it can't be knocked over during this procedure.
2 Remove the left and right fairings, fuel tank cover and seat (see Chapter 9).
3 Remove the radiator (see Chapter 4).

4 Remove the air cleaner housing, carburetors and exhaust system (see Chapter 5).
5 Remove the right frame downtube (see Section 5).
6 Remove the spark plugs (see Chapter 1).
7 Remove the valve cover bolts **(see illustration)**.
8 Lift the cover off the cylinder head **(see illustration)**. If it's stuck, don't attempt to pry

1 Washer
2 Rubber seals
3 Valve cover gasket
4 Spark plug
5 Cylinder head nut
6 Washer
7 Valve guide
8 Snap-ring
9 Head gasket
10 Valve cover
11 Cylinder head

7.8 Valve cover and cylinder head - exploded view

FZR600 engine, clutch and transmission 2•7

7.11 Make sure the cover fits into the groove on the head; apply silicone sealant to the corners of the gasket (arrowed)

7.12 The gasket tab (arrowed) should protrude when the valve cover is installed

7.13 Replace the rubber seals on the valve cover bolts if they're compressed or brittle

it off - tap around the sides with a plastic hammer to dislodge it.

Installation

9 Peel the rubber gasket from the cover. If it's cracked, hardened, has soft spots or shows signs of general deterioration, replace it with a new one.

10 Clean the mating surfaces of the cylinder head and the valve cover with lacquer thinner, acetone or brake system cleaner. Apply a thin film of RTV sealant to the half-circle cutouts on each side of the head.

11 Install the gasket to the cover. Make sure it fits completely into the cover groove **(see illustration)**. Apply a small amount of silicone sealer to the corners of the half-circle portions of the gasket.

12 Position the cover on the cylinder head, making sure the gasket doesn't slip out of place. The tab on the gasket should protrude from the front (exhaust) side of the engine **(see illustration)**.

13 Check the rubber seals on the valve cover bolts, replacing them if necessary **(see illustration)**. Install the bolts with their seals and washers, tightening them evenly to the torque listed in this Chapter's Specifications.

14 The remainder of installation is the reverse of removal.

8 Camshaft chain tensioner - removal and installation

Removal

Caution: Once you start to remove the tensioner bolts, you must remove the tensioner all the way and reset it before tightening the bolts. The tensioner extends and locks in place, so if you loosen the bolts partway and then retighten them, the tensioner or cam chain will be damaged.

1 Loosen the tensioner cap bolt while the tensioner is still installed **(see illustration)**.

8.1 Loosen the tensioner cap bolt before unbolting the tensioner from the engine

8.3 Tensioner components
1 Tensioner body
2 Outer spring
3 Inner spring
4 Copper washer
5 Cap bolt

8.5 Release the latch (arrowed) and compress the tensioner before installing it

2 Remove the tensioner mounting bolts and take it off the engine **(see illustration)**.
3 Remove the tensioner cap bolt and sealing washer **(see illustration)**.

Installation

4 Check the sealing washer on the cap bolt for cracks or hardening. It's a good idea to replace this washer whenever the tensioner cap is removed.
5 Release the one-way cam on the chain tensioner and compress the rod **(see illustration)**.
6 Turn the tensioner so the one-way cam is downward and install the tensioner on the cylinder block, using a new gasket **(see illustration)**. The word UP cast in the tensioner housing should be upward.

8.2 Remove the tensioner bolts and take the tensioner off

8.6 Use a new tensioner gasket

8.8 Install the springs, washer and cap bolt after the tensioner is installed on the engine

9.2 The small punch mark on each camshaft should be aligned with the mark on the bearing cap (arrowed)

9.4 Remove the bolts (arrowed) and lift off the upper chain guide

7 Tighten the mounting bolts to the torque listed in this Chapter's Specifications.

8 Install the tensioner springs, cap and sealing washer **(see illustration)**. Tighten the cap to the torque listed in this Chapter's Specifications.

9 Camshafts and lifters - removal, inspection and installation

Note: *This procedure can be performed with the engine in the frame.*

9.5a Remove the bearing caps evenly

Camshafts

Removal

1 Remove the valve cover (see Section 7).
2 Turn the engine to position no. 1 cylinder at TDC compression (see Chapter 1 - Valve clearances - check and adjustment). When the engine is positioned correctly, the punch marks on the camshafts will align with the marks on the bearing caps **(see illustration)**.
3 Remove the camshaft chain tensioner (see Section 8).
4 Remove the upper cam chain guide **(see illustration)**.
5 Unscrew the bearing cap bolts for the camshafts bearing caps, a little at a time, working from the outer to the inner bolts **(see illustration)**.
Caution: *If the bearing cap bolts aren't loosened evenly, the bearing caps may break. Because they're line-bored with the cylinder head, this may necessitate replacing the entire cylinder head. Remove the bolts and lift off the caps. Note that each bearing cap is labeled for position and direction. The small triangular mark on each cap points toward the clutch side of the engine (see illustration). The letters E and I indicate exhaust and intake sides of the engine. The caps labeled E1 and I1 go on the alternator side of the engine; the* caps labeled E2 and I2 go on the clutch side. *If you can't see the marks, make your own.*
6 Remove the bolts and lift off the bearing caps and their dowel pins **(see illustration)**.
7 Remove the camshafts. Keep the chain taut by wiring it to the engine so it can't fall down off the crankshaft. While the camshafts are out, don't allow the chain to go slack - the chain may fall off and bind between the crankshaft and case, which could damage these components. Also, cover the top of the cylinder head with a rag to prevent foreign objects from falling into the engine.
8 Lift the exhaust side (front) cam chain guide out of the engine **(see illustration)**.

Inspection

Note: *Before replacing camshafts or the cylinder head and bearing caps because of damage, check with local machine shops specializing in motorcycle engine work. In the case of the camshafts, it may be possible for cam lobes to be welded, reground and hardened, at a cost far lower than that of a new camshaft. If the bearing surfaces in the cylinder head are damaged, it may be possible for them to be bored out to accept bearing inserts. Due to the cost of a new cylinder head it is recommended that all options be explored before condemning it as trash!*

9.5b Note the location and position of the bearing cap identification marks

9.6 Remove the bearing cap dowels

9.8 Lift the exhaust side chain guide out of the engine

9.9 Inspect the bearing surfaces in the cylinder head and bearing caps

9.10a Check the camshaft lobes for wear - here's damage which will require replacement (or repair) of the camshaft

9.10b Measure the height of the camshaft lobes with a micrometer

9 Inspect the cam bearing surfaces of the head and the bearing caps (see illustration). Look for score marks, deep scratches and evidence of spalling (a pitted appearance).
10 Check the camshaft lobes for heat discoloration (blue appearance), score marks, chipped areas, flat spots and spalling (see illustration). Measure the height of each lobe with a micrometer (see illustration) and compare the results to the minimum lobe height listed in this Chapter's Specifications. If damage is noted or wear is excessive, the camshaft must be replaced.
11 Next, check the camshaft bearing oil clearances. Clean the camshafts, the bearing surfaces in the cylinder head and the bearing caps with a clean, lint-free cloth, then lay the cams in place in the cylinder head. Be sure the punch marks on the camshafts are upward (see illustration 9.2). Be sure to place the camshafts in the correct bearings; the exhaust and intake camshafts are identified by EX and IN marks (see illustration).
12 Cut twelve strips of Plastigauge and lay one piece on each bearing journal, parallel with the camshaft centerline.
13 Make sure the bearing cap dowels are installed (see illustration 9.6). Install the bearing caps in their proper positions (see Step 5). Tighten the bolts in two steps to the torque listed in this Chapter's Specifications.

Caution: Tighten the bearing caps evenly to specifications, starting with the inner bolts and working outward. While tightening, DO NOT let the camshafts rotate!

14 Now unscrew the bolts, a little at a time, and carefully lift off the bearing caps. Be sure to start with the outer bolts and work inward.
15 To determine the oil clearance, compare the crushed Plastigauge (at its widest point) on each journal to the scale printed on the Plastigauge container (see illustration). Compare the results to this Chapter's Specifications. If the oil clearance is greater than specified, measure the diameter of the cam bearing journal with a micrometer (see illustration). If the journal diameter is less than the specified limit, replace the camshaft with a new one and recheck the clearance. If the clearance is still too great, replace the cylinder head and bearing caps with new parts (see the Note that precedes Step 9).
16 Except in cases of oil starvation, the camshaft chain wears very little. If the chain has stretched excessively, which makes it difficult to maintain proper tension, replace it with a new one (see Section 27).
17 Check the sprockets for wear, cracks and other damage, replacing them if necessary. If the sprockets are worn, the chain is also worn, and also the sprocket on the crankshaft (which can only be remedied by replacing the crankshaft). If wear this severe is apparent, the entire engine should be disassembled for inspection.
18 Check the chain guides for wear or damage (see illustration). If it is worn or damaged, the chain may be worn out or improperly adjusted. Refer to Section 27 for camshaft chain replacement.

9.11 The exhaust and intake camshafts are identified by cast marks

Installation

19 Make sure the crankshaft is still at no. 1 TDC (refer to Chapter 1 - Valve clearances - check and adjustment).
20 Bolt the camshaft sprockets to the camshafts (if removed) and tighten the bolts to the torque listed in this Chapter's Specifications.

9.15a Lay a strip of Plastigauge (1) lengthwise along each journal

9.15b Measure the cam bearing journal diameter with a micrometer

9.18 Check the pad on the upper chain guide for score marks or damage

2•10 FZR600 engine, clutch and transmission

9.21 Lower the exhaust-side chain guide into the engine and make sure it rests securely on the bottom of the crankcase

9.23 Lay the exhaust camshaft in the engine; with the alignment mark slightly counterclockwise (anti-clockwise)

9.25 Lay the intake camshaft in the engine

21 Install the exhaust side chain guide (if removed) **(see illustration)**.
22 Make sure the bearing surfaces in the cylinder head and the bearing caps are clean, then apply a light coat of engine assembly lube or moly-based grease to each of them.
23 Apply a coat of moly-based grease to the lobes of the exhaust camshaft. Make sure the camshaft bearing journals are clean, then slip the exhaust camshaft through the chain and lay it in the cylinder head (the camshaft won't fit all the way down into the bearing saddles and locating slot because some of the lobes will be pointed downward). Make sure the small punch mark on the camshaft is very slightly counterclockwise (anti-clockwise) from its installed position (straight up) **(see illustration)**. Engage the chain with the sprocket so there is no slack in the exhaust side of the chain.
24 Carefully set the bearing caps in place with the small arrowhead cast in the top of each cap pointing toward the right (clutch) end of the engine. Make sure the caps are in their proper positions (see Step 5) and install the bolts. Tighten them in two stages to the torque listed in this Chapter's Specifications, working from the inner bolts outward. As the bearing caps are tightened, the camshaft should settle down into its bearing saddles, the locating flange on the left end of the camshaft should settle into its groove and the exhaust camshaft alignment mark should move into the straight-up position. If the alignment mark isn't positioned correctly, disengage the chain from the camshaft and turn the camshaft to align the mark.
25 Place the intake camshaft in its bearing saddles with its alignment mark just counterclockwise (anti-clockwise) from the straight-up position **(see illustration)**. Drape the chain over the intake camshaft sprocket so there is no slack in the upper run of the chain (between the two sprockets).
26 Insert a finger or wooden dowel in the cam chain tensioner hole and push against the chain to remove the slack in the upper run of the chain. Make sure the crankshaft mark is still in the no. 1 TDC position and both camshaft marks are in the straight-up positions.
27 If the crankshaft and camshaft alignment marks are not in the correct positions, lift the chain off the sprocket, turn the cam to obtain correct alignment and re-engage the chain with the sprocket.
28 Once all timing marks - those on the camshafts and alternator rotor - are aligned correctly, install the cam chain tensioner as described in Section 8.
Caution: If the marks are not aligned exactly as described, the valve timing will be incorrect and the valves may contact the pistons, causing extensive damage to the engine. Be sure to recheck all timing marks to make sure they haven't shifted.
29 Pour clean engine oil over the cam chain and along the camshafts. Use enough that it flows down onto the sprockets and the valve area.
30 Install the upper cam chain guide **(see illustration 9.4)**.
31 Turn the engine with a wrench on the crankshaft turning bolt. If you feel a sudden increase in resistance, stop turning. The valves may be hitting the pistons due to incorrect assembly. Find the problem and fix it before turning the engine any further, or serious damage may occur. Once again, check the alignment of the camshaft punch marks with the marks on the bearing caps and the mark on the alternator rotor with the crankcase seam.
32 The remainder of installation is the reverse of removal.

Valve lifters
Removal
33 Remove the camshafts following the procedure given above. Be sure to keep tension on the camshaft chain.
34 Make a holder with a separate section for each lifter and its valve adjusting shim (a pair of egg cartons will work). Label the sections according to cylinder number (1, 2, 3 or 4), valve number (starting from the left end of the engine) and whether the lifter belongs with an intake or exhaust valve. The lifters form a wear pattern with their bores and must be returned to their original locations if reused.
35 Pull the lifter out of the bore with a magnet together with its valve adjusting shim (see Chapter 1). If the lifters are stuck, spray the area around them with carburetor cleaner and let it soak in. Place the lifters in order in their holder.

Inspection
36 Check the lifters and their bores for wear, scuff marks, scratches or other damage. Yamaha doesn't provide specifications or wear tolerances for the lifters or their bores. If wear or damage is found, replace the lifters and cylinder head as a set.

Installation
37 Coat the lifters and their bores with clean engine oil.
38 Installation is the reverse of the removal steps. Be sure to reinstall a valve adjusting shim between the each valve and its lifter.

10 Cylinder head - removal and installation

Caution: The engine must be completely cool before beginning this procedure, or the cylinder head may become warped.
Note: *This procedure can be performed with the engine in the frame.*
Note: *In the following procedure, the camshafts are removed to access the cylinder head nuts. However, the camshaft bearing caps and camshafts are drilled to permit access to the cylinder head nuts without removing the camshafts; rubber caps plug the three access holes in each camshaft cap. If the latter method is adopted, the camchain must be split (see Section 27).*

Removal
1 Support the bike securely so it can't be knocked over during this procedure.
2 Remove the carburetors and exhaust system (see Chapter 5).
3 Remove the valve cover (see Section 7).
4 Remove the cam chain tensioner (see Section 8).
5 Remove the camshafts (see Section 9).

FZR600 engine, clutch and transmission 2•11

10.6a Remove the oil line banjo bolt from the cylinder head . . .

10.6b . . . unbolt the bracket from the cylinder block . . .

10.6c . . . and remove the banjo bolt from the crankcase

6 Unbolt the oil line from the cylinder head, cylinder block and crankcase **(see illustrations)**.

7 Loosen the cylinder head nuts, 1/2 turn at a time, in the reverse of the tightening sequence **(see illustration 7.8 and the accompanying illustration)**. Once all of the nuts are loose, remove the nuts and washers **(see illustrations)**.

8 Pull the cylinder head off the cylinder block studs, together with the lifters **(see illustration)**. Don't attempt to pry the head off by inserting a screwdriver between the head and the cylinder block - you'll damage the sealing surfaces.

9 Lift the head gasket off the cylinder block.

> **HAYNES HiNT** *If the head is stuck, tap upward with a rubber mallet to jar it loose, or use two wooden dowels inserted into the intake or exhaust ports to rock the head back and forth slightly (its movement will be limited by the studs).*

Stuff a clean rag into the cam chain tunnel to prevent the entry of debris.

10 Remove the dowel pins **(see illustration)**.

11 Check the cylinder head gasket and the mating surfaces on the cylinder head and block for leakage, which could indicate warpage. Refer to Section 12 and check the flatness of the cylinder head.

12 Clean all traces of old gasket material from the cylinder head and block. Be careful not to let any of the gasket material fall into the crankcase, the cylinder bores or the coolant passages.

Installation

13 Install the dowels on the cylinder head studs **(see illustration 10.10)**.

14 Lay the new gasket in place on the cylinder block. Make sure the UP cutout on the gasket is upright and toward the rear of the engine (if the word UP reads backwards, the gasket is upside down) **(see illustration)**. Never reuse the old gasket and don't use any type of gasket sealant.

10.7a Cylinder head TIGHTENING sequence

10.7b Remove the cylinder head nuts with an Allen bolt bit . . .

10.7c . . . and lift out the washers (you may need a magnet)

10.8 Lift the cylinder head off the studs

10.10 Find the dowels (arrowed) if they aren't in position

10.14 The UP cutout in the head gasket should be upright

2•12 FZR600 engine, clutch and transmission

10.16a Seat the cylinder head washers in their bores with a small screwdriver

10.16b Tighten the cylinder head nuts in sequence, in two stages

15 Carefully lower the cylinder head over the studs. It's helpful to have an assistant support the camshaft chain with a piece of wire so it doesn't fall and become kinked or detached from the crankshaft. When the head is resting against the cylinder block, wire the cam chain to another component to keep tension on it.

16 Install the head washers and nuts. Push the washers down with a small screwdriver to make sure they've seated completely **(see illustration)**. Starting with the inner nuts and working outward **(see illustration 10.7a)**, tighten the nuts to approximately half of the torque listed in this Chapter's Specifications **(see illustration)**.

17 Using the same sequence, tighten the nuts to the full torque listed in this Chapter's Specifications.

18 Install the camshafts, timing chain tensioner and valve cover (see Sections 9, 8 and 7).

19 Change the engine oil (see Chapter 1).

20 The remainder of installation is the reverse of the removal steps.

11 Valves/valve seats/valve guides - servicing

1 Because of the complex nature of this job and the special tools and equipment required, servicing of the valves, the valve seats and the valve guides (commonly known as a valve job) is best left to a professional.

2 The home mechanic can, however, remove and disassemble the head, do the initial cleaning and inspection, then reassemble and deliver the head to a dealer service department or properly equipped motorcycle repair shop for the actual valve servicing. Refer to Section 12 for those procedures.

3 The dealer service department will remove the valves and springs, recondition or replace the valves and valve seats, replace the valve guides, check and replace the valve springs, spring retainers and keepers/collets (as necessary), replace the valve seals with new ones and reassemble the valve components.

4 After the valve job has been performed, the head will be in like-new condition. When the head is returned, be sure to clean it again very thoroughly before installation on the engine to remove any metal particles or abrasive grit that may still be present from the valve service operations. Use compressed air, if available, to blow out all the holes and passages.

12 Cylinder head and valves - disassembly, inspection and reassembly

1 As mentioned in the previous Section, valve servicing and valve guide replacement should be left to a dealer service department or motorcycle repair shop. However, disassembly, cleaning and inspection of the valves and related components can be done (if the necessary special tools are available) by the home mechanic. This way no expense is incurred if the inspection reveals that service work is not required at this time.

2 To properly disassemble the valve components without the risk of damaging them, a valve spring compressor is absolutely necessary. This special tool can usually be rented, but if it's not available, have a dealer service department or motorcycle repair shop handle the entire process of disassembly, inspection, service or repair (if required) and reassembly of the valves.

Disassembly

3 Remove the lifters and their shims if you haven't already done so (see Section 9). Store the components in such a way that they can be returned to their original locations without getting mixed up.

4 Before the valves are removed, scrape away any traces of gasket material from the head gasket sealing surface. Work slowly and do not nick or gouge the soft aluminium of the head. Gasket removing solvents, which work very well, are available at most motorcycle shops and auto parts stores.

5 Carefully scrape all carbon deposits out of the combustion chamber area. A hand held wire brush or a piece of fine emery cloth can be used once the majority of deposits have

1 Intake camshaft
2 Sprocket
3 Valve lifter
4 Adjusting shim
5 Valve keepers (collets)
6 Valve spring retainer
7 Valve spring
8 Spring seat
9 Valve stem oil seal
10 Intake valve
11 Exhaust valve
12 Cam chain tensioner
13 Tensioner gasket
14 Intake side chain guide
15 Exhaust camshaft
16 Upper chain guide
17 Cam chain
18 Exhaust side chain guide

12.7a Valves and camshafts - exploded view

12.7b Take the valve out of the combustion chamber, but don't force it if it's stuck . . .

12.7c . . . check the area around the keeper groove (1) for burrs and remove any that you find

12.14 Measure the head along these lines with a feeler gauge and straightedge

been scraped away. Do not use a wire brush mounted in a drill motor, or one with extremely stiff bristles, as the head material is soft and may be eroded away or scratched by the wire brush.

6 Before proceeding, arrange to label and store the valves along with their related components so they can be kept separate and reinstalled in the same valve guides they are removed from (labeled plastic bags work well for this).

7 Compress the valve spring on the first valve with a spring compressor, then remove the keepers and the spring retainer from the valve assembly **(see illustration)**. Do not compress the springs any more than is absolutely necessary. Carefully release the valve spring compressor and remove the spring and the valve from the head **(see illustration)**. If the valve binds in the guide (won't pull through), push it back into the head and deburr the area around the keeper groove with a very fine file or whetstone **(see illustration)**.

8 Repeat the procedure for the remaining valves. Remember to keep the parts for each valve together so they can be reinstalled in the same location.

9 Once the valves have been removed and labeled, pull off the valve stem seals with pliers and discard them (the old seals should never be reused), then remove the spring seats.

10 Next, clean the cylinder head with solvent and dry it thoroughly. Compressed air will speed the drying process and ensure that all holes and recessed areas are clean.

11 Clean all of the valve springs, keepers, retainers and spring seats with solvent and dry them thoroughly. Do the parts from one valve at a time so that no mixing of parts between valves occurs.

12 Scrape off any deposits that may have formed on the valve, then use a motorized wire brush to remove deposits from the valve heads and stems. Again, make sure the valves do not get mixed up.

Inspection

13 Inspect the head very carefully for cracks and other damage. If cracks are found, a new head will be required. Check the cam bearing surfaces for wear and evidence of seizure. Check the camshafts and lifters for wear as well (see Section 9).

14 Using a precision straightedge and a feeler gauge, check the head gasket mating surface for warpage. Lay the straightedge lengthwise, across the head and diagonally (corner-to-corner), intersecting the head bolt holes, and try to slip a feeler gauge under it, on either side of each combustion chamber **(see illustration)**. The gauge should be the same thickness as the cylinder head warp limit listed in this Chapter's Specifications. If the feeler gauge can be inserted between the head and the straightedge, the head is warped and must either be machined or, if warpage is excessive, replaced with a new one. Minor surface imperfections can be cleaned up by sanding on a surface plate in a figure-eight pattern with 400 or 600 grit wet or dry sandpaper. Be sure to rotate the head every few strokes to avoid removing material unevenly.

15 Examine the valve seats in each of the combustion chambers. If they are pitted, cracked or burned, the head will require valve service that's beyond the scope of the home mechanic. Measure the valve seat width **(see illustration)** and compare it to this Chapter's Specifications. If it is not within the specified range, or if it varies around its circumference, valve service work is required.

16 Clean the valve guides to remove any carbon build-up, then measure the inside diameters of the guides (at both ends and the center of the guide) with a small hole gauge and a 0-to-1-inch micrometer **(see illustrations)**. Record the measurements for future reference. These measurements, along with the valve stem diameter measurements, will enable you to compute the valve stem-to-guide clearance. This clearance, when compared to the Specifications, will be one factor that will determine the extent of the valve service work required. The guides are measured at the ends and at the center to determine if they are worn in a bell-mouth pattern (more wear at the ends). If they are, guide replacement is an absolute must.

17 Carefully inspect each valve face for cracks, pits and burned spots. Check the valve stem

12.15 Measuring the valve seat width

12.16a Insert a small hole gauge into the valve guide and expand it so there's a slight drag when it's pulled out

12.16b Measure the small hole gauge with a micrometer

2•14 FZR600 engine, clutch and transmission

12.17 Check the valve face (A), stem (B) and keeper groove (C) for signs of wear and damage

12.18a Measure the valve stem diameter with a micrometer

12.18b Check the valve stem for bends with V-blocks and a dial indicator

and the keeper groove area for cracks **(see illustration)**. Rotate the valve and check for any obvious indication that it is bent. Check the end of the stem for pitting and excessive wear and make sure the margin is the specified width. The presence of any of the above conditions indicates the need for valve servicing.

18 Measure the valve stem diameter **(see illustration)**. By subtracting the stem diameter from the valve guide diameter, the valve stem-to-guide clearance is obtained. If the stem-to-guide clearance is greater than listed in this Chapter's Specifications, the guides and valves will have to be replaced with new ones. Also check the valve stem for bending. Set the valve in a V-block with a dial indicator touching the middle of the stem **(see illustration)**. Rotate the valve and note the reading on the gauge. If the stem runout exceeds the value listed in this Chapter's Specifications, replace the valve.

19 Check the end of each valve spring for wear and pitting. Measure the free length **(see illustration)** and compare it to this Chapter's Specifications. Any springs that are shorter than specified have sagged and should not be reused. Stand the spring on a flat surface and check it for squareness **(see illustration)**.

20 Check the spring retainers and keepers for obvious wear and cracks. Any questionable parts should not be reused, as extensive damage will occur in the event of failure during engine operation.

21 If the inspection indicates that no service work is required, the valve components can be reinstalled in the head.

Reassembly

22 Before installing the valves in the head, they should be lapped to ensure a positive seal between the valves and seats. This procedure requires coarse and fine valve lapping compound (available at auto parts stores) and a valve lapping tool.

> **TOOL TIP** *If a lapping tool is not available, a piece of rubber or plastic hose can be slipped over the valve stem (after the valve has been installed in the guide) and used to turn the valve.*

23 Apply a small amount of coarse lapping compound to the valve face **(see illustration)**, then slip the valve into the guide. **Note:** *Make sure the valve is installed in the correct guide and be careful not to get any lapping compound on the valve stem.*

24 Attach the lapping tool (or hose) to the valve and rotate the tool between the palms of your hands. Use a back-and-forth motion rather than a circular motion. Lift the valve off the seat and turn it at regular intervals to distribute the lapping compound properly. Continue the lapping procedure until the valve face and seat contact area is of uniform width and unbroken around the entire circumference of the valve face and seat **(see illustrations)**.

25 Carefully remove the valve from the guide and wipe off all traces of lapping compound.

12.19a Measure the free length of the valve springs

12.19b Check the valve springs for squareness

12.23 Apply the lapping compound very sparingly, in small dabs, to the valve face only

12.24a After lapping, the valve face should have a uniform, unbroken contact pattern (arrowed) . . .

12.24b . . . and the seat should be the specified width (arrowed) with a smooth unbroken appearance

FZR600 engine, clutch and transmission 2•15

12.28 A small dab of grease will help hold the keepers (collets) in place on the valve spring while the spring is released

13.3a Lift the cylinder block straight off the studs . . .

13.3b . . . and note the location of the dowels and oil jets (arrowed)

Use solvent to clean the valve and wipe the seat area thoroughly with a solvent soaked cloth.

26 Repeat the procedure with fine valve lapping compound, then repeat the entire procedure for the remaining valves.

27 Lay the spring seats in place in the cylinder head, then install new valve stem seals on each of the guides **(see illustration 12.7a)**. Use an appropriate size deep socket to push the seals into place until they are properly seated. Don't twist or cock them, or they will not seal properly against the valve stems. Also, don't remove them again or they will be damaged.

28 Coat the valve stems with assembly lube or moly-based grease, then install one of them into its guide. Next, install the springs and retainers, compress the springs and install the keepers. **Note:** *Install the springs with the tightly wound coils at the bottom (next to the spring seat). When compressing the springs with the valve spring compressor, depress them only as far as is absolutely necessary to slip the keepers into place. Apply a small amount of grease to the keepers* **(see illustration)** *to help hold them in place as the pressure is released from the springs. Make certain that the keepers are securely locked in their retaining grooves.*

29 Support the cylinder head on blocks so the valves can't contact the workbench top, then very gently tap each of the valve stems with a soft-faced hammer. This will help seat the keepers in their grooves.

30 Once all of the valves have been installed in the head, check for proper valve sealing by pouring a small amount of solvent into each of the valve ports. If the solvent leaks past the valve(s) into the combustion chamber area, disassemble the valve(s) and repeat the lapping procedure, then reinstall the valve(s) and repeat the check. Repeat the procedure until a satisfactory seal is obtained.

13 Cylinder block - removal, inspection and installation

Removal

1 Following the procedure given in Section 10, remove the cylinder head. Make sure the crankshaft is positioned at Top Dead Center (TDC) for cylinder no. 1.

2 Remove the coolant tube from the right side of the cylinder block (see Chapter 4).

3 Lift the cylinder block straight up to remove it **(see illustration)**. If it's stuck, tap around its perimeter with a soft-faced hammer. Don't attempt to pry between the block and the crankcase, as you will ruin the sealing surfaces. As you lift, note the location of the dowel pins and oil jet nozzles **(see illustration)**. Be careful not to let these drop into the engine. Remove the O-ring from the base of each cylinder.

4 Stuff clean shop towels around the pistons and remove the gasket and all traces of old gasket material from the surfaces of the cylinder block, cylinder head and crankcase.

Inspection

5 Don't attempt to separate the liners from the cylinder block.

6 Check the cylinder walls carefully for scratches and score marks.

7 Using the appropriate precision measuring tools, check each cylinder's diameter. Measure parallel to the crankshaft axis and across the crankshaft axis, at the depth from the top of the cylinder listed in this Chapter's Specifications **(see illustration)**. Average the two measurements and compare the results to this Chapter's Specifications. If the cylinder walls are tapered, out-of-round, worn beyond the specified limits, or badly scuffed or scored, have them rebored and honed by a dealer service department or a motorcycle repair shop. If a rebore is done, oversize pistons and rings will be required as well.

8 As an alternative, if the precision measuring tools are not available, a dealer service department or motorcycle repair shop will make the measurements and offer advice concerning servicing of the cylinders.

9 If they are in reasonably good condition and not worn to the outside of the limits, and if the piston-to-cylinder clearances can be maintained properly (see Section 14), then the cylinders do not have to be rebored; honing is all that is necessary.

10 To perform the honing operation you will need the proper size flexible hone with fine stones, or a "bottle brush" type hone, plenty of light oil or honing oil, some shop towels and an electric drill motor. Hold the cylinder block in a vice (cushioned with soft jaws or wood blocks) when performing the honing operation. Mount the hone in the drill motor, compress the stones and slip the hone into the cylinder. Lubricate the cylinder thoroughly, turn on the drill and move the hone up and down in the cylinder at a pace which will produce a fine crosshatch pattern on the cylinder wall with the crosshatch lines intersecting at approximately a 60-degree angle **(see illustration)**. Be sure to use plenty

13.7 Measure across the bore in two directions (X and Y), at the specified distance from the top of the bore

13.10 A bore in good condition will have an even crosshatched appearance, without vertical score marks

2•16 FZR600 engine, clutch and transmission

13.12 Lift out the oil jets and install new O-rings, then insert the oil jets firmly into their passages

13.13 Lubricate the cylinder bores with clean engine oil

13.14a Be sure the spray nozzles on the oil jets point in the proper direction (arrowed)

of lubricant and do not take off any more material than is absolutely necessary to produce the desired effect. Do not withdraw the hone from the cylinder while it is running. Instead, shut off the drill and continue moving the hone up and down in the cylinder until it comes to a complete stop, then compress the stones and withdraw the hone. Wipe the oil out of the cylinder and repeat the procedure on the remaining cylinders. Remember, do not remove too much material from the cylinder wall. If you do not have the tools, or do not desire to perform the honing operation, a dealer service department or motorcycle repair shop will generally do it for a reasonable fee.

11 Next, the cylinders must be thoroughly washed with warm soapy water to remove all traces of the abrasive grit produced during the honing operation. Be sure to run a brush through the bolt holes and coolant passages and flush them with running water. After rinsing, dry the cylinders thoroughly and apply a coat of light, rust-preventative oil to all machined surfaces.

12 Lift the oil jets out of their passages, replace the O-rings and reinstall the jets **(see illustration)**.

Installation

13 Lubricate the cylinder bores and pistons with plenty of clean engine oil **(see illustration)**.

14 Install the dowel pins and oil jet nozzles **(see illustration)**, then place a new cylinder base gasket on the crankcase **(see illustration)**. Make sure the UP mark on the gasket is upright and toward the front of the engine (if the UP cutout reads backwards, the gasket is upside down). Install new O-rings on the base of each cylinder **(see illustration)**.

15 Slowly rotate the crankshaft until two of the pistons are at the top of their travel and two are at the bottom.

16 Attach four piston ring compressors to the pistons and compress the piston rings. Large hose clamps can be used instead - just make sure they don't scratch the pistons, and don't tighten them too much.

17 Install the cylinder block over the pistons and carefully lower it down until the piston crowns fit into the cylinder liners **(see illustration)**. While doing this, pull the camshaft chain up, using a hooked tool or a piece of coat hanger. Also keep an eye on the cam chain guide to make sure it doesn't wedge against the block. Push down on the cylinder block, making sure the pistons don't get cocked sideways, until the bottoms of the cylinder liners slide down past the piston rings. A wood or plastic hammer handle can be used to gently tap the block down, but don't use too much force or the pistons will be damaged.

18 Slide the cylinder block down over the remaining two pistons and guide the rings into the bores.

19 Remove the piston ring compressors or hose clamps, being careful not to scratch the pistons.

20 The remainder of installation is the reverse of removal.

14 Pistons - removal, inspection and installation

1 The pistons are attached to the connecting rods with piston pins that are a slip fit in the pistons and rods.

2 Before removing the pistons from the rods, stuff a clean shop towel into each crankcase hole, around the connecting rods. This will prevent the circlips from falling into the crankcase if they are inadvertently dropped.

Removal

3 Using a sharp scribe, scratch the number of each piston into its crown (or use a felt pen if the piston is clean enough). Each piston should also have a triangular mark pointing to

13.14b Make sure the UP mark on the cylinder base gasket is positioned correctly

13.14c Install an O-ring on the bottom of each cylinder (arrowed)

13.17 You can install the cylinders over the rings using only a screwdriver, but it's a good idea to use a ring compressor

FZR600 engine, clutch and transmission 2•17

14.3a Mark the piston with its cylinder number (right arrow); the triangle points to the front (exhaust) side of the engine

14.3b Wear eye protection and pry out the clip with a pointed tool

14.4a Pull out the piston pin and lift the piston off the connecting rod

TOOL TIP

The piston pins should come out with hand pressure - if they don't, this removal tool can be fabricated with readily available parts
1 Bolt
2 Washer
3 Pipe*
4 Padding*
5 Piston
6 Washer**
7 Nut**

*Large enough for piston pin to fit inside
**Small enough to fit through piston pin bore

1 Dowel
2 Sealing washer (replace if removed)
3 Cylinder block
4 O-ring
5 Base gasket
6 Coolant drain plugs
7 Piston pin clip (replace if removed)
8 Piston
9 Piston pin
10 Piston pin clip (replace if removed)
11 Piston rings

14.4b Cylinder block and piston - exploded view

the front of the engine (see illustration). If not, scribe an arrow into the piston crown before removal. Support the first piston, grasp the circlip with a pointed tool or needle-nose pliers and remove it from the groove (see illustration).

4 Push the piston pin out from the opposite end to free the piston from the rod (see illustration). You may have to deburr the area around the groove to enable the pin to slide out (use a triangular file for this procedure). If the pin won't come out, remove the remaining circlip. Fabricate a piston pin removal tool from threaded stock, nuts, washers and a piece of pipe (see Tool Tip). Repeat the procedure for the other pistons (see illustration).

Inspection

5 Before the inspection process can be carried out, the pistons must be cleaned and the old piston rings removed.

6 Using a piston ring installation tool, carefully remove the rings from the pistons (see illustration). Do not nick or gouge the pistons in the process.

7 Scrape all traces of carbon from the tops of the pistons. A hand-held wire brush or a piece of fine emery cloth can be used once most of the deposits have been scraped away. Do not, under any circumstances, use a wire brush mounted in a drill motor to remove deposits from the pistons; the piston material is soft and will be eroded away by the wire brush.

14.6 Remove the piston rings with a ring removal and installation tool

14.11 Check the piston pin bore and the piston skirt for wear, and make sure the internal holes are clear (arrowed)

14.13 Measure the piston ring-to-groove clearance with a feeler gauge

14.14 Measure the piston diameter with a micrometer

A Specified distance from bottom of piston
B Piston diameter

8 Use a piston ring groove cleaning tool to remove any carbon deposits from the ring grooves. If a tool is not available, a piece broken off the old ring will do the job. Be very careful to remove only the carbon deposits. Do not remove any metal and do not nick or gouge the sides of the ring grooves.

9 Once the deposits have been removed, clean the pistons with solvent and dry them thoroughly. Make sure the oil return holes below the oil ring grooves are clear.

10 If the pistons are not damaged or worn excessively and if the cylinders are not rebored, new pistons will not be necessary. Normal piston wear appears as even, vertical wear on the thrust surfaces of the piston and slight looseness of the top ring in its groove. New piston rings, on the other hand, should always be used when an engine is rebuilt.

11 Carefully inspect each piston for cracks around the skirt, at the pin bosses and at the ring lands **(see illustration)**.

12 Look for scoring and scuffing on the thrust faces of the skirt, holes in the piston crown and burned areas at the edge of the crown. If the skirt is scored or scuffed, the engine may have been suffering from overheating and/or abnormal combustion, which caused excessively high operating temperatures. The oil pump and cooling system should be checked thoroughly. A hole in the piston crown, an extreme to be sure, is an indication that abnormal combustion (pre-ignition) was occurring. Burned areas at the edge of the piston crown are usually evidence of spark knock (detonation). If any of the above problems exist, the causes must be corrected or the damage will occur again.

13 Measure the piston ring-to-groove clearance by laying a new piston ring in the ring groove and slipping a feeler gauge in beside it **(see illustration)**. Check the clearance at three or four locations around the groove. Be sure to use the correct ring for each groove; they are different. If the clearance is greater than specified, new pistons will have to be used when the engine is reassembled.

14 Check the piston-to-bore clearance by measuring the bore (see Section 13) and the piston diameter. Make sure that the pistons and cylinders are correctly matched. Measure the piston across the skirt on the thrust faces at a 90-degree angle to the piston pin, at the distance from the bottom of the skirt listed in this Chapter's Specifications **(see illustration)**. Subtract the piston diameter from the bore diameter to obtain the clearance. If it is greater than specified, the cylinders will have to be rebored and new oversized pistons and rings installed. If the appropriate precision measuring tools are not available, the piston-to-cylinder clearances can be obtained, though not quite as accurately, using feeler gauge stock. Feeler gauge stock comes in 12-inch lengths and various thicknesses and is generally available at auto parts stores. To check the clearance, select a feeler gauge of the same thickness as the piston clearance listed in this Chapter's Specifications and slip it into the cylinder along with the appropriate piston. The cylinder should be upside down and the piston must be positioned exactly as it normally would be. Place the feeler gauge between the piston and cylinder on one of the thrust faces (90-degrees to the piston pin bore). The piston should slip through the cylinder (with the feeler gauge in place) with moderate pressure. If it falls through, or slides through easily, the clearance is excessive and a new piston will be required. If the piston binds at the lower end of the cylinder and is loose toward the top, the cylinder is tapered, and if tight spots are encountered as the feeler gauge is placed at different points around the cylinder, the cylinder is out-of-round. Repeat the procedure for the remaining pistons and cylinders. Be sure to have the cylinders and pistons checked by a dealer service department or a motorcycle repair shop to confirm your findings before purchasing new parts.

15 Apply clean engine oil to the pin, insert it into the piston and check for freeplay by rocking the pin back-and-forth **(see illustration)**. If the pin is loose, new pistons and pins must be installed.

16 Refer to Section 15 and install the rings on the pistons.

Installation

17 Install the pistons in their original locations with the arrows pointing to the front of the engine. Lubricate the pins and the rod bores with clean engine oil. Install new circlips in the grooves in the inner sides of the pistons (don't reuse the old circlips). Push the pins into position from the opposite side and install new circlips. Compress the circlips only enough for them to fit in the piston. Make sure the clips are properly seated in the grooves **(see illustration)**.

14.15 Slip the pin into the piston and try to wiggle it back-and-forth; if it's loose, replace the piston and pin

14.17 Make sure the piston pin clips are securely seated in the grooves (arrowed)

FZR600 engine, clutch and transmission 2•19

15.3a Square the ring in the bore by turning the piston upside down and tapping on the ring . . .

15.3b . . . then lift the piston out and check the ring end gap with a feeler gauge

15.5 If the end gap is too small, clamp a file in a vise and file the ring ends (from the outside in only) to enlarge the gap

15 Piston rings - installation

1 Before installing the new piston rings, the ring end gaps must be checked.
2 Lay out the pistons and the new ring sets so the rings will be matched with the same piston and cylinder during the end gap measurement procedure and engine assembly.
3 Insert the top (No. 1) ring into the bottom of the first cylinder and square it up with the cylinder walls by pushing it in with the top of the piston **(see illustration)**. The ring should be about one inch above the bottom edge of the cylinder. To measure the end gap, slip a feeler gauge between the ends of the ring **(see illustration)** and compare the measurement to the Specifications.
4 If the gap is larger or smaller than specified, double check to make sure that you have the correct rings before proceeding.
5 If the gap is too small, it must be enlarged or the ring ends may come in contact with each other during engine operation, which can cause serious damage. The end gap can be increased by filing the ring ends very carefully with a fine file **(see illustration)**. When performing this operation, file only from the outside in.
6 Excess end gap is not critical unless it is greater than 1 mm (0.04 inch). Again, double check to make sure you have the correct rings for your engine.
7 Repeat the procedure for each ring that will be installed in the first cylinder and for each ring in the remaining cylinder. Remember to keep the rings, pistons and cylinders matched up.
8 Once the ring end gaps have been checked/corrected, the rings can be installed on the pistons.
9 The oil control ring (lowest on the piston) is installed first. It is composed of three separate components. Slip the expander into the groove, then install the upper side rail **(see illustrations)**. Do not use a piston ring installation tool on the oil ring side rails as they may be damaged. Instead, place one end of the side rail into the groove between the spacer expander and the ring land. Hold it firmly in place and slide a finger around the piston while pushing the rail into the groove. Next, install the lower side rail in the same manner.
10 After the three oil ring components have been installed, check to make sure that both the upper and lower side rails can be turned smoothly in the ring groove.
11 Install the second (middle) ring next. It can be distinguished from the top ring by its RN mark (the top ring is marked R or not marked) **(see illustration)**. Do not mix the top and middle rings.
12 To avoid breaking the ring, use a piston ring installation tool and make sure that the identification mark is facing up **(see illustration 15.11)**. Fit the ring into the middle groove on the piston. Do not expand the ring any more than is necessary to slide it into place.
13 Finally, install the top ring in the same manner. Make sure the identifying mark is facing up.
14 Repeat the procedure for the remaining pistons and rings. Be very careful not to confuse the top and second rings.
15 Once the rings have been properly installed, stagger the end gaps, including those of the oil ring side rails **(see illustration)**.

15.9a Installing the oil ring expander - make sure the ends don't overlap

15.9b Installing an oil ring side rail - don't use a ring installation tool to do this

15.11 The second ring has an RN mark; the top ring has an R mark or no mark; make sure the marks on the rings face up

15.15 Arrange the ring gaps like this

1 Top compression ring
2 Oil ring lower rail
3 Oil ring upper rail
4 Second compression ring

2•20 FZR600 engine, clutch and transmission

16.6a Remove the oil pan bolts (arrowed) . . .

16.6b . . . this bolt secures the harness clip for the oil level sender . . .

16.6c . . . and take the oil pan off

16 Oil pan and relief valve - removal, relief valve inspection and installation

Note: *The oil pan can be removed with the engine in the frame.*

Removal

1 Support the bike securely so it can't be knocked over during this procedure.
2 Remove the left and right fairings and the fairing stay (see Chapter 9).
3 Disconnect the wires for the oil level switch and neutral switch (see Chapter 10).
4 Remove the exhaust system (see Chapter 5).
5 Drain the engine oil and remove the oil filter (see Chapter 1). If you're working on a model equipped with a spin-on oil filter, remove the filter mounting base **(see illustrations 22.8a, 22.8b and 22.8c)**.
6 Remove the oil pan bolts and detach the pan from the crankcase **(see illustrations)**.
7 Remove all traces of old gasket material from the mating surfaces of the oil pan and crankcase.
8 Remove the strainer from the oil pickup **(see illustration)**.
9 Unbolt the pickup from the crankcase and lift it off **(see illustrations)**.
10 Remove all traces of old gasket from the pickup and crankcase.
11 Remove the relief valve from the crankcase **(see illustration)**. It should pull out with light hand pressure. If it's stuck, rock it back and forth slightly.

Relief valve inspection

12 Push the plunger into the relief valve and check for free movement **(see illustration)**. If the valve sticks, perform Steps 13 through 15 to disassemble and inspect it.
13 Straighten the cotter pin and pull it out **(see illustration)**.

16.8 The arrow on the strainer cover points in the opposite direction from the front arrow cast in the oil pickup

16.9a Remove the pickup mounting bolts (arrowed) . . .

16.9b . . . and take the pickup off the engine

16.11 Pull the relief valve out of the case; it's a good idea to replace the O-ring whenever the relief valve is removed

16.12 Push in on the relief valve plunger to make sure it moves freely

16.13 Straighten the ends of the cotter pin and pull it out

FZR600 engine, clutch and transmission 2•21

16.14a Remove the spring retainer . . .

16.14b . . . the spring . . .

16.14c . . . and the plunger

16.16 Make sure the oil pan dowels are in position (arrowed)

14 Remove the spring retainer, spring and plunger **(see illustrations)**.
15 Check all parts for wear and damage. Clean the parts thoroughly, reassemble the valve and recheck its movement. If the valve still sticks, replace it.
Caution: If you re-use the relief valve, install a new cotter pin before reinstalling the relief valve in the engine.

Installation

16 Install the oil pan dowels **(see illustration)**. Install the relief valve in the crankcase, using a new O-ring.
17 Install the oil pickup and tighten the bolts to the torque listed in this Chapter's Specifications. Install the strainer on the pickup with its arrow pointing away from the relief valve.
18 Position a new gasket on the oil pan. A thin film of RTV sealant can be used to hold the gasket in place. Install the oil pan and bolts, tightening the bolts to the torque listed in this Chapter's Specifications, using a criss-cross pattern.
19 The remainder of installation is the reverse of removal. Install a new filter and fill the crankcase with oil (see Chapter 1), then run the engine and check for leaks.

17 Oil pump - oil pressure check, removal, inspection and installation

Note: The oil pump can be removed with the engine in the frame.

Oil pressure check

> **Warning:** *If the oil passage plug is removed when the engine is hot, hot oil will drain out - wait until the engine is cold before beginning this check.*

1 Remove the left and right fairings (see Chapter 9).
2 Remove the plug at the bottom of the crankcase on the right-hand side and install an oil pressure gauge **(see illustration)**.
3 Start the engine and watch the gauge while varying the engine rpm. The pressure should stay within the relief valve opening pressure listed in this Chapter's Specifications. If the pressure is too high, the relief valve is stuck closed. To check it, see Section 16.
4 If the pressure is lower than the standard, either the relief valve is stuck open, the oil pump is faulty, or there is other engine damage. Begin diagnosis by checking the relief valve (see Section 16), then the oil pump. If those items check out okay, chances are the bearing oil clearances are excessive and the engine needs to be overhauled.
5 If the pressure reading is in the desired range, allow the engine to warm up to normal operating temperature and check the pressure again, at the specified engine rpm. Compare your findings with this Chapter's Specifications.
6 If the pressure is significantly lower than specified, check the relief valve and the oil pump.

Removal

7 Remove the clutch (see Section 19).
8 Remove the oil pump mounting bolts and remove the pump **(see illustrations)**.

17.2 To check the oil pressure, remove the plug (arrowed) and connect an oil pressure gauge using the proper adapter

17.8a Insert an Allen bolt bit through the holes in the oil pump gear to remove the mounting bolts . . .

17.8b . . . then take off the pump

2•22 FZR600 engine, clutch and transmission

17.9a Remove the gasket...

17.9b ...and the dowel

17.11 Remove the Phillips screw (you may need an impact driver)...

9 Remove the oil pump gasket and dowel **(see illustrations)**.

Inspection

10 Wash the oil pump in solvent, then dry it off.
11 Remove the pump housing screws (use an impact driver if they're tight) **(see illustration)**. Lift off the housing.
12 Lift off the rotors **(see illustration)**.
13 Check the pump body and rotors for scoring and wear. If any damage or uneven or excessive wear is evident, replace the pump (individual parts aren't available).

> **HAYNES HiNT** *If you are rebuilding the engine, it's a good idea to install a new oil pump.*

14 Measure the clearance between the inner and outer rotor tips and between the outer rotor and housing **(see illustrations)**. Replace the pump if the clearance is excessive.
15 If the pump is good, reverse the disassembly steps to reassemble it. Make sure the pin is centered in the rotor shaft so it will align with the slot in the inner rotor **(see illustration)**.

Installation

16 Before installing the pump, prime it by pouring oil into it while turning the shaft by hand - this will ensure that it begins to pump oil quickly.
17 Installation is the reverse of removal, with the following additions:

a) Align the arrow mark on the pump body with the cast mark on the crankcase **(see illustration)**.
b) Use non-permanent thread locking agent on the pump mounting bolts and tighten the bolts to the torque listed in this Chapter's Specifications **(see illustration)**.

18 Starter clutch - removal, inspection and installation

Removal

1 Remove the left and right fairings (see Chapter 9).

17.12 ...and lift the housing and rotors off the pump shaft

17.14a Measure clearance between the inner rotor tip and the outer rotor (arrowed) with a feeler gauge

17.14b Measure clearance between the outer rotor and pump body with a feeler gauge (A) and rotor tips (B)

17.15 Make sure the pin (arrowed) is centered in the pump shaft

17.17a Align the arrow cast in the crankcase with the arrow cast in the pump body

17.17b Tighten the pump mounting bolts with an Allen bolt bit

FZR600 engine, clutch and transmission 2•23

18.2a Loosen the cover bolts (arrowed) evenly in a criss-cross pattern...

18.2b ... then take the cover off

18.3 Remove the gasket and dowels (arrowed)

2 Loosen the starter clutch cover bolts in a criss-cross pattern, 1/4 turn at a time, until all are loose, then lift the cover off **(see illustrations)**.
3 Remove the cover gasket and dowels **(see illustration)**.
4 Remove the idle gears **(see illustrations)**.
5 Remove the starter clutch securing bolt and washer **(see illustration)**.
6 Attach a three-legged puller (Yamaha tool no. YU-33270, part no. 90890-01362 or equivalent) to the starter clutch, then tighten the puller bolt to pull the starter clutch off **(see illustration)**.
7 Remove the woodruff key and starter clutch gear **(see illustration)**.

Inspection

8 Check the rollers inside the starter clutch for wear and damage **(see illustration)**. If any undesirable conditions can be seen, replace the starter clutch. Check the friction surface on the starter clutch gear for scoring or other defects. Replace the gear if the friction surface isn't perfectly smooth.
9 Place the starter clutch gear in the starter clutch and try to rotate it separately from the starter clutch **(see illustration overleaf)**. It should turn easily counterclockwise (anti-clockwise), but lock up when you try to

18.4a Remove the upper idle gear and its shaft...

18.4b ... then the starter drive gear...

18.4c ... then the lower idle gear and its shaft

18.5 Remove the starter clutch securing bolt and washer

18.6 Remove the starter clutch with a three-legged puller

18.7 Remove the woodruff key and starter clutch gear

18.8 Check the starter clutch rollers (right arrow) and the friction surface of the gear (left arrow) for wear or damage

2•24 FZR600 engine, clutch and transmission

18.9 Place the gear in the starter clutch and try to rotate it; it should turn freely in only one direction

18.10 Check the idle gears and shafts for wear or damage

18.11a Have the ball bearing inside the cover replaced if it's worn or damaged

18.11b Also check the needle roller bearing inside the crankcase

18.12 Install the woodruff key in the shaft

18.14a Install the starter drive gear . . .

turn it clockwise. If not, replace the starter clutch.

10 Check the idle gears for chipped or worn teeth **(see illustration)**. Check the shafts for wear. Replace them if any of these conditions are found.

11 Check the bearing inside the starter clutch cover and the idler gear bearing in the crankcase for wear, damage or looseness **(see illustrations)**. Have the bearings replaced by a Yamaha dealer or machine shop if their condition is in doubt.

Installation

12 Install the woodruff key in its slot (see illustration). Install the starter clutch gear on the shaft with its friction surface facing outward **(see illustration 18.7)**.

13 Install the starter clutch, washer and securing bolt **(see illustration 18.5)**. Tighten the center bolt to the torque listed in this Chapter's Specifications.

14 Install the starter drive gear and idle gears **(see illustrations)**.

15 Install the cover dowels and a new gasket **(see illustration 18.3)**.

16 Install the cover. Tighten its bolts in several stages, in a criss-cross pattern, to the torque listed in this Chapter's Specifications.

19 Clutch - removal, inspection and installation

Note: *The clutch can be removed with the engine in the frame.*

Removal

1 Support the bike securely so it can't be knocked over during this procedure. Remove the right fairing (see Chapter 9).

2 Drain the engine oil (see Chapter 1).

3 Loosen the clutch cover bolts 1/4 turn at a time in a criss-cross pattern, then remove the clutch cover **(see illustrations)**.

4 Loosen the pressure plate bolts evenly in a

18.14b . . . the lower idle gear and shaft . . .

18.14c . . . and the upper idle gear and shaft

19.3a Loosen the clutch cover bolts (arrowed) 1/4 turn at a time in a criss-cross pattern . . .

FZR600 engine, clutch and transmission 2•25

19.3b ... then take the cover off the engine ...

19.3c ... and remove the gasket

criss-cross pattern, then remove the bolts, springs and pressure plate **(see illustrations)**.
5 Remove the friction plates and steel plates **(see illustrations)**.
6 Remove the short pushrod and the steel ball that fits behind it **(see illustration)**.

1 Clutch housing
2 Thrust washer
3 Clutch boss
4 Friction plate
5 Steel plate
6 Pressure plate
7 Pressure plate spring
8 Short pushrod
9 O-ring
10 Lockwasher
11 Steel ball
12 Oil seal
13 Long pushrod
14 Release mechanism
15 Release mechanism housing
16 Collar
17 Thrust washer
18 Spacer
19 Bearing

19.3d Clutch - exploded view

19.4a Loosen the pressure plate bolts evenly with a Phillips screwdriver or socket ...

19.4b ... then remove the bolts and springs ...

19.4c ... and take off the pressure plate

19.5a Take off a friction plate ...

19.5b ... then a steel plate

19.6a Remove the short pushrod and steel ball, then remove the long pushrod from behind them ...

2•26 FZR600 engine, clutch and transmission

19.6b ... it can also be removed from the other side of the engine if the engine sprocket cover is removed

19.7a Bend back the tab on the lockwasher ...

19.7b ... hold the clutch from turning with a tool like the one shown here and remove the nut ...

19.7c ... you can make your own holding tool out of steel strap

19.8 Remove the grooved washer

19.9 Thread a pair of bolts into the spacer and pull it out

19.10 Remove the bearing

19.11 Remove the large and small washers

19.12 Check the inner and outer splines of the clutch boss for wear

19.13 Measure the clutch spring free length

There's another, longer pushrod behind the steel ball which can be removed for inspection with a magnet. If it won't come out easily, it can be removed from the other side of the engine if the engine sprocket cover is removed **(see illustration)**.

7 Bend back the lockwasher on the clutch boss nut **(see illustration)**. Remove the nut, using a special holding tool (Yamaha tool no. YM-91402, part no. 90890-04086 or equivalent) to prevent the clutch housing from turning **(see illustration)**. An alternative to this tool can be fabricated from some steel strap, bent at the ends and bolted together in the middle **(see illustration)**. Remove the lockwasher and discard it. Use a new one during installation.

8 Remove the clutch boss and thrust washer **(see illustration)**.

9 Thread a pair of bolts into the spacer and pull it out **(see illustration)**.

10 Pull out the bearing and remove the clutch housing **(see illustration)**.

11 Remove the thrust washer and collar from behind the clutch housing **(see illustration)**.

Inspection

12 Examine the splines on both the inside and the outside of the clutch boss **(see illustration)**. If any wear is evident, replace the clutch boss with a new one.

13 Measure the free length of the clutch springs **(see illustration)**. Replace the springs as a set if any one of them is not within the values listed in this Chapter's Specifications.

FZR600 engine, clutch and transmission 2•27

19.14 Measure the thickness of the friction plates

19.15 Check the metal plates for warpage

19.17 Check the slots in the clutch housing (arrowed) for uneven wear

14 If the lining material of the friction plates smells burnt or if it's glazed, new parts are required. If the metal clutch plates are scored or discolored, they must be replaced with new ones. Measure the thickness of each friction plate **(see illustration)** and compare the results to this Chapter's Specifications. Replace the friction plates as a set if any are near the wear limit.

15 Lay the metal plates, one at a time, on a perfectly flat surface (such as a piece of plate glass) and check for warpage by trying to slip a feeler gauge between the flat surface and the plate **(see illustration)**. The feeler gauge should be the same thickness as the warpage limit listed in this Chapter's Specifications. Do this at several places around the plate's circumference. If the feeler gauge can be slipped under the plate, it is warped and should be replaced with a new one.

16 Check the tabs on the friction plates for excessive wear and mushroomed edges. They can be cleaned up with a file if the deformation is not severe.

17 Check the edges of the slots in the clutch housing for indentations made by the friction plate tabs **(see illustration)**. If the indentations are deep they can prevent clutch release, so the housing should be replaced with a new one. If the indentations can be removed easily with a file, the life of the housing can be prolonged to an extent.

18 Check the pressure plate, thrust washers, spacer and collar for wear and damage. Replace any worn or damaged parts.

19 If you removed the long pushrod, make sure it isn't bent (roll it on a perfectly flat surface or use V-blocks and a dial indicator). Check both pushrods and the steel ball for wear or damage and replace them if defects are visible. Install a new O-ring on the short pushrod **(see illustration)**.

20 Check the release bearing and clutch housing bearing for wear, damage or roughness. Replace the bearings if their condition is uncertain or obviously bad. Check the bearing surface in the clutch housing and replace the clutch housing if it's worn or damaged **(see illustration)**.

21 Clean all traces of old gasket material from the clutch cover and its mating surface on the crankcase.

Installation

22 Install the collar, thrust washer and clutch housing.

23 Coat the clutch housing bearing with engine oil, then install the bearing and spacer **(see illustration 19.3d)**.

24 Install the thrust washer, the clutch boss, a new lockwasher and the clutch boss nut **(see illustration)**.

25 Tighten the clutch boss nut to the torque listed in this Chapter's Specifications, using the technique described in Step 7 to prevent the housing from turning.

26 Bend the lockwasher against one of the flats on the nut with pliers **(see illustration)**.

27 Coat the pushrods and steel ball with multi-purpose grease, then install the long pushrod, ball and short pushrod **(see illustrations)**.

19.19 Check the pushrods and steel ball for wear or damage; install a new O-ring on the short pushrod

19.20 Check the springs in the clutch housing for breakage; check the gear teeth for wear or damage

19.24 Place a new lockwasher on the shaft and install the nut

19.26 Bend the lockwasher against the nut

19.27a Install the long pushrod (narrow end first) . . .

2•28 FZR600 engine, clutch and transmission

19.27b ... the steel ball ...

19.27c ... and the short pushrod

19.28 Install a friction plate ...

19.29a ... then a steel plate ...

19.29b ... the rounded edge of each steel plate faces in toward the engine; the sharp edge faces out

19.30a After installing the last friction plate, align the marks on pressure plate and clutch boss (arrowed) ...

28 Coat one of the friction plates with engine oil and install it in the clutch housing **(see illustration)**. Engage the tabs on the friction plate with the slots in the clutch housing.
29 Install a steel plate on top of the friction plate with its rounded side inward **(see illustrations)**. Continue to install alternate friction and steel plates (a friction plate is the last one installed).
30 The remainder of installation is the reverse of the removal steps, with the following additions:

a) Align the hole in the pressure plate with the triangular mark on the clutch boss

(see illustration). Tighten the pressure plate bolts in several stages in a criss-cross pattern to the torque listed in this Chapter's Specifications.
b) Make sure the clutch cover dowels are in position and install a new gasket **(see illustration)**.
c) Install the shouldered clutch cover bolts in the same holes as the dowels **(see illustration)**. Tighten the clutch cover bolts in several stages to the torque listed in this Chapter's Specifications.

31 Fill the crankcase with the recommended type and amount of engine oil (see Chapter 1).

20 Clutch cable - removal and installation

1 Loosen the clutch cable locknut and adjusting nut at the handlebar (see Chapter 1).
2 Loosen the pinch bolt on the shift arm, then slide the arm off the shaft (see Section 21).
3 Remove the bolts and remove the engine sprocket cover (see Chapter 7).
4 Disconnect the lower end of the cable from the release mechanism and take the cable out **(see illustration)**.
5 Installation is the reverse of the removal steps. Adjust the cable (see Chapter 1).

19.30b ... and install the pressure plate screws, dowels and gasket. . .

19.30c ... install the cover with the shouldered bolts in the dowel holes

20.4 Disconnect the lower end of the cable from the release mechanism inside the engine sprocket cover

FZR600 engine, clutch and transmission 2•29

21.2 The marks on the shift shaft and shift arm must be aligned, or shifting problems will occur

21.3 Remove the bolt and slide the shift arm off the shaft

21.4 Remove the bracket bolts (arrowed) and take the bracket off together with the footpeg, shift pedal and linkage

21 External shift mechanism - removal, inspection and installation

Shift linkage and pedal

1 Support the bike securely so it can't be knocked over during this procedure.
2 Look for a punch mark on the end of the shift shaft **(see illustration)**. This should align with the mark in the arm. If you can't find it, make your own punch mark so the arm can be realigned correctly during installation.
3 Remove the lever pinch bolt **(see illustration)**. Pull the lever off the shaft, together with the linkage rod.
4 Remove the shift pedal/footpeg bracket bolts and take the assembly off **(see illustration)**. If necessary, remove the Allen bolt and separate the footpeg and shift pedal from the bracket.
5 Installation is the reverse of removal. Adjust the linkage as needed with the nuts on the linkage shaft.

Shift mechanism removal

6 Remove the shift pedal and linkage (Steps 1 through 4), clutch (see Section 19) and engine sprocket cover (see Chapter 7).
7 Slide the shift shaft out of the crankcase **(see illustration)**.
8 Remove the oil pump (see Section 17).

21.7 Pull the shift shaft out of the engine

9 Remove the stopper lever, and return spring **(see illustration)**.

Shift mechanism inspection

10 Inspect the shift shaft guide bar **(see illustration 21.9)**. If it's worn or damaged, replace it. If it's loose, unscrew it, apply a non-permanent thread locking compound to the threads, reinstall the guide bar and tighten it securely.
11 Check the shift shaft for bends and damaged splines. If the shaft is bent, you can attempt to straighten it, but replace it if the splines are damaged. Inspect the pawls and springs on the shift shaft and replace the shaft if they're worn or damaged **(see illustration)**.
12 Check the condition of the stopper lever and spring. Replace the stopper lever if it's

21.9 Remove the stopper lever bolt, then remove the lever and spring

worn where it contacts the shift cam. Replace the spring if it's distorted.
13 Inspect the pins on the end of the shift cam. If they're worn or damaged, you'll have to disassemble the crankcase to replace the shift cam.
14 Check the condition of the seals in the crankcase and engine sprocket cover (see Chapter 7). If they've been leaking, replace them.

Shift mechanism installation

15 Apply non-permanent thread locking agent to the threads of the stopper lever bolt **(see illustration)**, then install the stopper lever and return spring. Make sure the stopper lever engages the neutral detent in the shift cam **(see illustration)**. Tighten the

21.11 If the shift shaft springs and worn, distorted or broken, replace the shaft

21.15a Use non-permanent thread locking agent on the threads of the stopper lever bolt . . .

21.15b . . . and install the lever, making sure its spring is correctly engaged

2•30 FZR600 engine, clutch and transmission

21.18 Slide the shaft into the engine and position the ends of the large spring on either side of the guide bar (arrowed)

22.5 Crankcase bolt TIGHTENING sequence

bolt to the torque listed in this Chapter's Specifications.

16 Install the oil pump (see Section 17).

17 Apply high-temperature grease to the lip of the seal. Wrap the splines of the shift shaft with electrical tape, so the splines won't damage the seal as the shaft is installed.

18 Slide the shaft into the crankcase. Engage the pawls evenly with the pins on the shift cam and position the return spring over the guide bar **(see illustration)**. Adjust the pawls if they're not even.

19 The remainder of installation is the reverse of the removal steps.

20 Check the engine oil level and add some, if necessary (see 'Daily (pre-ride) checks at the beginning of this Manual).

22 Crankcase - disassembly and reassembly

1 To examine and repair or replace the crankshaft, primary chains, connecting rods, bearings, or transmission components, the crankcase must be split into two parts.

Disassembly

2 Remove the clutch and starter clutch covers and the oil pan. Remove the cylinder head, cylinder block and pistons (see Sections 10, 13 and 14). Remove the clutch if you are separating the crankcase halves to disassemble the transmission main shaft or remove the internal shift linkage (see Section 19).

3 Remove the water pump (see Chapter 4).

4 Remove the engine sprocket and the oil seal retainer behind it (see Chapter 7). Remove the alternator cover.

5 Remove the upper crankcase bolts, then the lower crankcase bolts, starting with the highest-numbered bolt and working to the lowest (the reverse of the tightening sequence) **(see illustration)**.

6 Carefully separate the crankcase halves, guiding the breather tube out of its opening as you do so **(see illustration)**. If they won't come easily, make sure all fasteners have been removed. Don't pry against the crankcase mating surfaces or they will leak. Once the halves are separated, remove the breather assembly **(see illustration)**.

7 Look for the oil jet and the dowels **(see illustrations)**. If they're not in one of the crankcase halves, locate them.

22.6a Guide the breather tube (arrowed) out as you separate the crankcase halves

22.6b The breather assembly is secured by four screws (arrowed)

22.7a Remove the oil jet (arrowed) . . .

22.7b . . . its O-ring should be replaced whenever the crankcase is disassembled

22.7c Find the case dowels if they're not in their holes

22.8a Unscrew the filter mount . . .

FZR600 engine, clutch and transmission 2•31

22.8b . . . lift the mount and base off the engine . . .

22.8c . . . and remove the O-ring

22.11 Rest the ends of the cylinder studs on a board to angle the case correctly for reassembly

8 On models with a one-piece oil filter, remove the filter mount and O-ring **(see illustrations)**.

9 Refer to Sections 23 through 30 for information on the internal components of the crankcase.

Reassembly

10 Make sure the crankshaft and transmission shafts are correctly positioned in the upper crankcase half (see Sections 25 and 28).

11 Place the ends of the crankcase studs on a piece of 2-by-4 lumber or equivalent **(see illustration)**. This will prevent the connecting rods from pushing against the workbench and forcing the crankshaft out of its bearings.

12 Remove all traces of sealant from the crankcase mating surfaces. Be careful not to let any fall into the case as this is done. Check to make sure the oil jet (with a new O-ring) and the two dowel pins are in place **(see illustrations 22.7a and 22.7b)**.

13 Pour some engine oil over the transmission gears, the crankshaft main bearings and the shift cam. Don't get any oil on the crankcase mating surfaces.

14 Apply a thin, even bead of Yamaha Bond or Quick Gasket sealant (part no. ACC-11001-05-01) or equivalent to the crankcase mating surfaces **(see illustration)**.

Caution: Don't apply an excessive amount of sealant. Don't let it contact the oil jet.

Don't apply it within 2 to 3 mm (0.8 to 1.2 inch) of the bearing inserts, as it will ooze out when the case halves are assembled and may obstruct oil passages and prevent the bearings from seating.

15 Check the position of the shift cam, shift forks and transmission shafts - make sure they're in the neutral position (see Section 28). Make sure the locating pins in the transmission bearings are positioned correctly.

16 Carefully assemble the crankcase halves over the dowels. While doing this, make sure the shift forks fit into their gear grooves. Guide the breather tube into position in its hole **(see illustration)**. Make sure the crankshaft end seal, transmission seal and clutch pushrod

seal are positioned correctly in the case **(see illustrations)**. The seals should fit flush with the case surfaces when the case halves are assembled.

Caution: The crankcase halves should fit together completely without being forced. If they're slightly apart, DO NOT force them together by tightening the crankcase bolts. The most likely reason they're apart is that the transmission bearing pins aren't positioned correctly. If the pins are forced against the crankcase halves, the cases will crack and have to be replaced.

17 Oil the threads and install the crankcase bolts in the correct holes **(see illustration 22.5)**. Bolts 1 through 12 have steel washers **(see illustration)**. Bolts 23 and 26

22.14 Apply sealant to the mating surface

22.16a Guide the breather tube into its opening

22.16b The transmission and pushrod seals should be flush with the crankcase surface

22.16c The crankshaft seal should be seated securely in its groove

22.17a Crankcase bolts one through 12 have steel washers (arrowed) . . .

2•32 FZR600 engine, clutch and transmission

22.17b ... bolts 23 and 26 secure wiring harness clips

22.17c ... bolt 29 has a copper washer ...

22.17d ... and bolt 34 secures a ground wire

secure wiring harness clips **(see illustration)**. Bolt 29 has a copper washer **(see illustration)**. Bolt 34 secures a ground wire **(see illustration)**.

18 Tighten the bolts in numerical order, referring to the numbers cast in the crankcase. Tighten all bolts to the torque listed in this Chapter's Specifications. **Note: There are different torque settings for the 8 mm bolts and the 6 mm bolts.**

19 Turn the mainshaft and the transmission driveshaft to make sure they turn freely. Also make sure the crankshaft turns freely.

20 Install the oil pan (see Section 16).

21 The remainder of assembly is the reverse of disassembly, with the following additions:
a) Once the external shift linkage is installed, shift the transmission through all the gear positions and back to Neutral.
b) Be sure to refill the engine oil.

23 Crankcase components - inspection and servicing

1 After the crankcases have been separated and the crankshaft, shift cam and forks and transmission components removed, the crankcases should be cleaned thoroughly with new solvent and dried with compressed air.

2 Remove any oil passage plugs that haven't already been removed. All oil passages should be blown out with compressed air **(see illustrations)**.

3 All traces of old gasket sealant should be removed from the mating surfaces. Minor damage to the surfaces can be cleaned up with a fine sharpening stone or grindstone **(see illustration)**.

Caution: Be very careful not to nick or gouge the crankcase mating surfaces or leaks will result. Check both crankcase halves very carefully for cracks and other damage.

4 Check the cam chain guides for wear (see Section 27). If they appear to be worn excessively, replace them.

5 If any damage is found that can't be repaired, replace the crankcase halves as a set.

24 Main and connecting rod bearings - general note

1 Even though main and connecting rod bearings are generally replaced with new ones during the engine overhaul, the old bearings should be retained for close examination as they may reveal valuable information about the condition of the engine.

2 Bearing failure occurs mainly because of lack of lubrication, the presence of dirt or other foreign particles, overloading the engine and/or corrosion. Regardless of the cause of bearing failure, it must be corrected before the engine is reassembled to prevent it from happening again.

3 When examining the bearings, remove the main bearings from the case halves and the rod bearings from the connecting rods and caps and lay them out on a clean surface in the same general position as their location on the crankshaft journals. This will enable you to match any noted bearing problems with the corresponding side of the crankshaft journal.

4 Dirt and other foreign particles get into the engine in a variety of ways. It may be left in the engine during assembly or it may pass through filters or breathers. It may get into the oil and from there into the bearings. Metal chips from machining operations and normal engine wear are often present. Abrasives are sometimes left in engine components after reconditioning operations such as cylinder honing, especially when parts are not thoroughly cleaned using the proper cleaning methods. Whatever the source, these foreign objects often end up imbedded in the soft bearing material and are easily recognized. Large particles will not imbed in the bearing and will score or gouge the bearing and journal. The best prevention for this cause of bearing failure is to clean all parts thoroughly and keep everything spotlessly clean during engine reassembly. Frequent and regular oil and filter changes are also recommended.

5 Lack of lubrication or lubrication breakdown has a number of interrelated

23.2a Make sure oil passages are clear ...

23.2b ... including this small one in the transmission bearing saddle (arrowed)

23.3 Small burrs can be removed from the gasket surfaces with a fine stone

FZR600 engine, clutch and transmission 2•33

25.2 Lift the crankshaft out with the connecting rods and cam chain

25.3 Push the center of the bearing sideways to tilt it out of its saddle

causes. Excessive heat (which thins the oil), overloading (which squeezes the oil from the bearing face) and oil leakage or throw off (from excessive bearing clearances, worn oil pump or high engine speeds) all contribute to lubrication breakdown. Blocked oil passages will also starve a bearing and destroy it. When lack of lubrication is the cause of bearing failure, the bearing material is wiped or extruded from the steel backing of the bearing. Temperatures may increase to the point where the steel backing and the journal turn blue from overheating.

6 Riding habits can have a definite effect on bearing life. Full throttle low speed operation, or lugging the engine, puts very high loads on bearings, which tend to squeeze out the oil film. These loads cause the bearings to flex, which produces fine cracks in the bearing face (fatigue failure). Eventually the bearing material will loosen in pieces and tear away from the steel backing. Short trip driving leads to corrosion of bearings, as insufficient engine heat is produced to drive off the condensed water and corrosive gases produced. These products collect in the engine oil, forming acid and sludge. As the oil is carried to the engine bearings, the acid attacks and corrodes the bearing material.

7 Incorrect bearing installation during engine assembly will lead to bearing failure as well. Tight fitting bearings which leave insufficient bearing oil clearances result in oil starvation. Dirt or foreign particles trapped behind a bearing insert result in high spots on the bearing which lead to failure.

8 To avoid bearing problems, clean all parts thoroughly before reassembly, double check all bearing clearance measurements and lubricate the new bearings with engine assembly lube or moly-based grease during installation.

25 Crankshaft and main bearings - removal, inspection, main bearing selection and installation

Crankshaft removal

1 Before removing the crankshaft check the endplay, using a dial indicator mounted in-line with the crankshaft. Yamaha doesn't provide endplay specifications, but if the endplay is excessive (more than a few thousandths of an inch), consider replacing the case halves.

2 Lift the crankshaft out, together with the connecting rods and cam chain and set them on a clean surface **(see illustration)**. Remove the oil seal from one end of the crankshaft.

3 The main bearing inserts can be removed from their saddles by pushing their centers to the side, then lifting them out **(see illustration)**. Keep the bearing inserts in order. The main bearing oil clearance should be checked, however, before removing the inserts (see Step 8).

Inspection

4 If you haven't already done so, mark and remove the connecting rods from the crankshaft (see Section 26).

5 Clean the crankshaft with solvent, using a rifle-cleaning brush to scrub out the oil passages. If available, blow the crank dry with compressed air. Check the main and connecting rod journals for uneven wear, scoring and pits **(see illustration)**. Rub a copper coin across the journal several times - if a journal picks up copper from the coin, it's too rough. Replace the crankshaft.

6 Check the primary gear and camshaft chain sprocket on the crankshaft for chipped teeth and other wear. If any undesirable conditions are found, replace the crankshaft. Check the chain as described in Section 27. Check the rest of the crankshaft for cracks and other damage. It should be magnafluxed to reveal hidden cracks - a dealer service department or motorcycle machine shop will handle the procedure.

7 Set the crankshaft on V-blocks and check the runout with a dial indicator touching each of the main journals, comparing your findings with this Chapter's Specifications. If the runout exceeds the limit, replace the crank.

Main bearing selection

8 To check the main bearing oil clearance, clean off the bearing inserts (and reinstall them, if they've been removed from the case) and lower the crankshaft into the upper half of the case. Cut four pieces of Plastigauge and lay them on the crankshaft main journals, parallel with the journal axis **(see illustration)**.

9 Very carefully, guide the lower case half down onto the upper case half. Install the lower crankcase retaining bolts and tighten them, using the recommended sequence, to the torque listed in this Chapter's Specifications **(see illustration)**.

Caution: DO NOT tighten the bolts unless the case halves fit together completely. Don't rotate the crankshaft!

10 Now, loosen the bolts in reverse sequence, remove them and carefully lift the lower case half off. Compare the width of the

25.5 Inspect the journals, gear and chain sprocket (arrowed) for wear, damage, pitted surfaces or chipped teeth

25.8 Lay a strip of Plastigauge lengthwise on the journal

25.9 Tighten the lower crankcase bolts in this sequence to check bearing clearance

2•34 FZR600 engine, clutch and transmission

25.10 Measuring the width of the crushed Plastigauge (be sure to use the correct scale - inch and metric are included)

A Plastigauge

crushed Plastigauge on each journal to the scale printed on the Plastigauge envelope to obtain the main bearing oil clearance **(see illustration)**. Write down your findings, then remove all traces of Plastigauge from the journals, using your fingernail or the edge of a credit card.

11 If the oil clearance falls into the specified range, no bearing replacement is required (provided they are in good shape). If the clearance is more than the standard range,

25.15b The numbers on the crankcase correspond with the crankshaft main journals no. 1 through no. 6

1	No. 1 journal	4	No. 4 journal
2	No. 2 journal	5	No. 5 journal
3	No. 3 journal	6	No. 6 journal

25.13 Measure the diameter of each crankshaft journal at several points to detect taper and out-of-round conditions

replace the bearing inserts with new ones of the same thickness and check the oil clearance once again. Always replace all of the inserts at the same time.

12 The clearance should be within the range listed in this Chapter's Specifications.

13 If the clearance is greater than the service limit listed in this Chapter's Specifications, measure the diameter of the crankshaft journals with a micrometer or vernier caliper **(see illustration)**. Yamaha doesn't provide journal diameter or wear specifications, but by measuring the diameter at a number of points around each journal's circumference, you'll be able to determine whether or not the journal is

BEARING COLOR CODE	
No. 1	Blue
No. 2	Black
No. 3	Brown
No. 4	Green
* No. 5	Yellow

* No. 5 applies only to the main journal bearing selection.

25.15c Subtract the crankshaft number from the crankcase number, then use that bearing number to select a color code

25.15a These numbers on the crankshaft indicate journal thickness - the first six relate to main journals and the last four to connecting rod journals

out-of-round. Take the measurement at each end of the journal, near the crank throws, to determine if the journal is tapered.

14 If any crank journal is out-of-round or tapered or the bearing clearance is beyond the limit listed in this Chapter's Specifications with new bearings, replace the crankshaft.

15 Use the number marks on the crankshaft and on the case to determine the bearing sizes required. The first six numbers on the crankshaft are the main journal numbers, starting with the left journal **(see illustrations)**. These correspond with the numbers on the upper crankcase half **(see illustration)**. To determine the bearing number for each bearing, subtract the crankshaft number from the case number. For example, the crankshaft number for journal no. 1 is 1 and the case number for journal no. 1 is 6. Subtracting 1 from 6 produces 5, which is the bearing number for journal no. 1. According to the accompanying chart, bearing no. 5 is color-coded yellow **(see illustration)**. The color codes are painted on the edges of the bearings **(see illustration)**.

Installation

16 Clean the bearing saddles in the case halves, then install the bearing inserts in their webs in the case **(see illustrations)**. When installing the bearings, use your hands only - don't tap them into place with a hammer.

25.15d The color codes, painted on the sides of the bearings, identify bearing thickness

25.16a Make sure the oil holes are clear (arrowed), then install the bearings in their saddles . . .

25.16b . . . engage the locating tab securely in its slot (arrowed)

FZR600 engine, clutch and transmission 2•35

25.17 Apply assembly lube to the bearing surfaces

25.21 Make sure the crankshaft seal is seated securely in its groove

25.22 Lay the crankshaft in the bearing saddles

17 Lubricate the bearing inserts with engine assembly lube or moly-based grease **(see illustration)**.
18 You can install the connecting rods on the crankshaft at this point (see Section 26).
19 Loop the camshaft chain over the crankshaft and engage it with its sprocket.
20 If the connecting rods are on the crankshaft, recheck side clearances (see Section 26).
21 Install the seal on the end of the crankshaft **(see illustration)**.
22 Carefully lower the crankshaft into place **(see illustration)**. If the connecting rods are on the crankshaft, guide them through their openings.
23 Assemble the case halves (see Section 22) and check to make sure the crankshaft and the transmission shafts turn freely.

26 Connecting rods and bearings - removal, inspection, bearing selection and installation

Removal

1 Before removing the connecting rods from the crankshaft, measure the side clearance of each rod with a feeler gauge **(see illustration)**. If the clearance on any rod is greater than that listed in this Chapter's Specifications, that rod will have to be replaced with a new one.
2 Using a center punch, mark the position of each rod and cap, relative to its position on the crankshaft (one through four, counting from the left side of the engine).
3 Unscrew the bearing cap nuts, separate the cap from the rod, then detach the rod from the crankshaft **(see illustrations)**. If the cap is stuck, tap on the ends of the rod bolts with a soft face hammer to free them.
4 Roll the bearing inserts sideways to separate them form the rods and caps **(see illustration)**. Keep them in order so they can be reinstalled in their original locations. Wash the parts in solvent and dry them with compressed air, if available.

Inspection

5 Check the connecting rods for cracks and other obvious damage. Lubricate the piston pin for each rod, install it in the proper rod and check for play **(see illustration)**. If it wobbles, replace the connecting rod and/or the pin.
6 Refer to Section 25 and examine the connecting rod bearing inserts. If they are scored, badly scuffed or appear to have been seized, new bearings must be installed. Always replace the bearings in the connecting rods as a set. If they are badly damaged, check the corresponding crankshaft journal.

26.1 Measure the clearance between the crankshaft and the big end of the connecting rod with a feeler gauge

26.3a Remove the connecting rod nuts (arrowed) ...

26.3b ... and separate the rod from the cap

26.4 Push the center of the bearing insert sideways to tilt it out of its saddle

26.5 Slip the piston pin into the rod and rock it back-and-forth to check for looseness

2•36 FZR600 engine, clutch and transmission

> **HAYNES HINT**: *Evidence of extreme heat, such as discoloration, indicates that lubrication failure has occurred. Be sure to thoroughly check the oil pump and pressure relief valves as well as all oil holes and passages before reassembling the engine.*

7 Have the rods checked for twist and bending at a dealer service department or other motorcycle repair shop.

Connecting rod bearing selection

8 If the bearings and journals appear to be in good condition, check the oil clearances as follows:
9 Start with the rod for the number one cylinder. Wipe the bearing inserts and the connecting rod and cap clean, using a lint-free cloth.
10 Install the bearing inserts in the connecting rod and cap. Make sure the tab on the bearing engages with the notch in the rod or cap.
11 Wipe off the connecting rod journal with a lint-free cloth. Lay a strip of Plastigauge across the top of the journal, parallel with the journal axis.
12 Position the connecting rod on the bottom of the journal, then install the rod cap and nuts. Tighten the nuts to the torque listed in this Chapter's Specifications, but don't allow the connecting rod to rotate at all.
13 Unscrew the nuts and remove the connecting rod and cap from the journal, being very careful not to disturb the Plastigauge. Compare the width of the crushed Plastigauge to the scale printed in the Plastigauge envelope to determine the bearing oil clearance.
14 If the clearance is within the range listed in this Chapter's Specifications and the bearings are in perfect condition, they can be reused. If the clearance is beyond the standard range, replace the bearing inserts with new inserts that have the same color code, then check the oil clearance once

26.18a The halves of the letter stamped on the rod should match perfectly when the rod is assembled

again. Always replace all of the inserts at the same time.
15 The clearance should be within the range listed in this Chapter's Specifications.
16 If the clearance is greater than the maximum clearance listed in this Chapter's Specifications, measure the diameter of the connecting rod journal with a micrometer. As with the main bearing journals, Yamaha doesn't provide diameter or wear limit specifications, but by measuring the diameter at a number of points around the journal's circumference, you'll be able to determine whether or not the journal is out-of-round. Take the measurement at each end of the journal to determine if the journal is tapered.
17 If any journal is tapered or out-of-round or bearing clearance is beyond the maximum listed in this Chapter's Specifications, replace the crankshaft.
18 Each connecting rod has a 3 or 4 stamped on it in ink **(see illustration)**; subtract the connecting rod journal number on the crankshaft from this to get a bearing number **(see illustration 25.15a)**. For example, the number on the connecting rod shown in illustration 26.18a is 4. The corresponding number for that connecting rod's journal, stamped into the crankshaft, is 2. Subtracting 2 from 4 produces 2, which is the bearing number for that journal. According to the chart **(see illustration 25.15c)**, bearing no. 2 is color-coded black. The color codes are painted

26.18b The color code is painted on the side of the bearing

on the edges of the bearings **(see illustration)**.
19 Repeat the bearing selection procedure for the remaining connecting rods.

Installation

20 Wipe off the bearing inserts, connecting rods and caps. Install the inserts into the rods and caps, using your hands only, making sure the tabs on the inserts engage with the notches in the rods and caps **(see illustrations)**. When all the inserts are installed, lubricate them with engine assembly lube or moly-based grease **(see illustration)**. Don't get any lubricant on the mating surfaces of the rod or cap.
21 Assemble each connecting rod to its proper journal, referring to the previously applied cylinder numbers. Make sure the Y mark on the rod is toward the left side of the engine **(see illustration)**. Also, the letter present at the rod/cap seam on one side of the connecting rod should fit together perfectly when the rod and cap are assembled **(see illustration 26.18a)**. If it doesn't, the wrong cap is on the rod. Fix this problem before assembling the engine any further.
22 When you're sure the rods are positioned correctly, lubricate the threads of the rod bolts with molybdenum disulphide grease and tighten the nuts to the torque listed

26.20a Be sure the tab fits in the notch

26.20b Apply assembly lube to the bearing

26.21 The Y mark on the rod faces the left side of the engine

FZR600 engine, clutch and transmission 2•37

26.22 Snug both nuts evenly, then tighten them to the correct torque in one continuous motion

27.6 The chain guide is secured to the crankcase by two Allen bolts (arrowed)

in this Chapter's Specifications **(see illustration)**. **Note:** *Snug both nuts evenly, then tighten them to the specified torque in a continuous motion. If you must stop before the nuts are fully tightened, loosen them completely, then retighten them to the specified torque.*

23 Turn the rods on the crankshaft. If any of them feel tight, tap on the bottom of the connecting rod caps with a hammer - this should relieve stress and free them up. If it doesn't, recheck the bearing clearance.

24 As a final step, recheck the connecting rod side clearances (see Step 1). If the clearances aren't correct, find out why before proceeding with engine assembly.

27 Camshaft chain and guides - removal, inspection and installation

Warning: *Although the cam chain can be cut and reconnected, this should be done by a qualified Yamaha technician with the proper special tool. Chain separation while the engine is running may cause engine seizure, leading to loss of control of the motorcycle. Yamaha replacement cam chains may be equipped with a master (soft) link; if you're not experienced with this type of chain, have the soft link connected by a qualified Yamaha technician.*

Removal

1 Remove the engine (see Section 5).
2 Separate the crankcase halves (see Section 22).
3 Remove the crankshaft (see Section 25).
4 Remove the chain from the crankshaft.
5 The cam chain front guide can be lifted from the cylinder head once the camshafts have been removed **(see illustration 9.8)**.
6 The cam chain rear guide is held in position by two Allen bolts **(see illustration)**. Separate the crankcase halves (see Section 22), then remove the Allen bolts and lift out the guide.

Inspection

7 Check the chain for binding and obvious damage. If these conditions are visible, or if the chain appears to be stretched, replace it.
8 Check the guides for deep grooves, cracking and other obvious damage, replacing them if necessary.

Installation

9 Installation of these components is the reverse of the removal procedure, with the following additions:
a) When installing the rear cam chain guide, apply a non-hardening thread locking compound to the threads of the bolts. Tighten the bolts to the torque listed in this Chapter's Specifications.
b) Apply engine oil to the faces of the guides and to the chain.

28 Transmission shafts - removal and installation

Removal

1 Remove the engine and clutch, then separate the case halves (see Sections 5, 19 and 22).
2 If you haven't already done so, remove the long clutch pushrod from the mainshaft (see Section 19).
3 Lift out the mainshaft, then the driveshaft **(see illustrations)**. If they are stuck, use a soft-face hammer and gently tap on the bearings on the ends of the shafts to free them. Lift out the half-circle retainer rings.
4 Refer to Section 29 for information pertaining to transmission shaft service and Section 30 for information pertaining to the shift cam and forks.

Installation

5 Install new half-circle retaining rings in their grooves in the crankcase **(see illustration)**.

28.3a Note the positions of the bearing pins and retainer rings (arrowed), then lift out the mainshaft . . .

28.3b . . . and the driveshaft

28.5 Place new retainer rings in their grooves and push them down flush with the crankcase surface

2•38 FZR600 engine, clutch and transmission

28.7 Make sure the transmission and clutch pushrod seals are in position

6 Carefully lower each shaft into place. The pins in the bearing outer races must engage with the locating holes in the crankcase, and the grooves in the crankcase and the ball bearing outer races must engage with the retaining rings (see illustration 28.3a).
Caution: If the pins are out of position and you try to force the crankcase halves together by tightening the bolts, the crankcase halves will crack and will have to be replaced.

7 The remainder of installation is the reverse of removal. Make sure the clutch pushrod seal and driveshaft end seal are in position **(see illustration)**.

8 Make sure the gears are in the neutral position. When they are, it will be possible to rotate the transmission shafts independently of each other. Align the shaft forks with the gear grooves.

29 Transmission shafts - disassembly, inspection and reassembly

Note: *When disassembling the transmission shafts, place the parts on a long rod or thread a wire through them to keep them in order and facing the proper direction.*

1 Remove the shafts from the case (see Section 28).

29.2a Transmission gears and shafts - exploded view

1 Mainshaft
2 Fifth pinion gear
3 Snap-ring
4 Third/fourth pinion gear
5 Sixth pinion gear
6 Second pinion gear
7 Bearing
8 Retainer ring
9 Driveshaft
10 Second wheel gear
11 Sixth wheel gear
12 Third wheel gear
13 Fourth wheel gear
14 Fifth wheel gear
15 First wheel gear
16 Flat washer
17 Dished washer

Mainshaft

Disassembly

2 Slide the bearing off the mainshaft **(see illustrations)**.

3 Press second and sixth pinion gears loose from the shaft together, then remove them from the shaft **(see illustrations)**.

4 Slide third-fourth pinion gear off the shaft **(see illustration)**.

29.2b Slide the bearing off the shaft

29.3a Press the shaft out of the second and sixth pinion gears . . .

29.3b . . . slide second pinion gear off . . .

FZR600 engine, clutch and transmission 2•39

29.4 Slide off the third-fourth pinion gear

29.5a Remove the snap-ring and thrust washer (arrowed) . . .

29.5b . . . and slide fifth pinion gear off

29.6 Press the bearing off the shaft if it's worn or damaged

29.12a Press sixth and second pinion gears onto the shaft

29.12b The assembled mainshaft should look like this

5 Remove the snap-ring and thrust washer, then slide fifth pinion gear off the shaft **(see illustrations)**.

Inspection

6 Wash all of the components in clean solvent and dry them off. Rotate the ball bearing on the shaft, feeling for tightness, rough spots and excessive looseness and listening for noises **(see illustration)**. If any of these conditions are found, replace the bearing with a press.

7 Check the ball bearing that was removed from the other end of the shaft and replace it if it has any of the conditions described in Step 6. The bearing should also be replaced if oil has been leaking from its seal.

8 Check the gear teeth for cracking and other obvious damage. Check the gear bushings and the surface in the inner diameter of each gear for scoring or heat discoloration. If the gear or bushing is damaged, replace it.

9 Inspect the dogs and the dog holes in the gears for excessive wear. Replace the paired gears as a set if necessary.

10 Place the shaft in V-blocks and check runout with a dial indicator. Replace the shaft if runout exceeds the value listed in this Chapter's Specifications.

Reassembly

11 During reassembly, always use new snap-rings. Lubricate the components with engine oil before assembling them.

12 Assembly is the reverse of the disassembly procedure with the following additions:
a) *The sharp side of the snap-ring faces away from the thrust washer; the rounded side faces toward the thrust washer.*
b) *Press sixth and second gears onto the mainshaft together **(see illustration)**.*
c) *Check the positions of the gears on the assembled shaft to make sure they are correct **(see illustration)**.*

Driveshaft

Disassembly

13 To disassemble the driveshaft, refer to the accompanying illustrations.

29.13a Take the dished washer off the driveshaft . . .

29.13b . . . slide off the needle roller bearing . . .

29.13c . . . remove the flat washer . . .

2•40 FZR600 engine, clutch and transmission

29.13d . . . slide off first wheel gear . . .

29.13e . . . slide off fifth wheel gear . . .

29.13f . . . remove the snap-ring . . .

29.13g . . . and the thrust washer . . .

29.13h . . . slide off fourth wheel gear . . .

29.13i . . . and third wheel gear . . .

29.13j . . . and sixth wheel gear . . .

29.13k . . . remove another snap ring . . .

29.13l . . . and thrust washer . . .

29.13m . . . and slide off second wheel gear . . .

29.13n . . . take the oil seal off the shaft . . .

29.13o . . . press off the collar and ball bearing if they're worn or damaged

FZR600 engine, clutch and transmission 2•41

29.15 The assembled driveshaft should look like this

30.3 Remove the stopper lever (if not already done), shift cam retainer bolts and the guide bar (arrowed)...

30.4a ...pull the fork shafts out of the case...

Inspection

14 Refer to Steps 6 through 10 above to inspect the driveshaft components. If the ball bearing and seal collar need to be replaced, remove them with a press; otherwise, they can be left on the shaft.

Reassembly

15 Assembly is the reverse of the disassembly procedure. Use new snap-rings and lubricate the components with engine oil before assembling them. Check the assembled shaft to make sure the gears are in the correct positions **(see illustration)**.

30 Shift cam and forks - removal, inspection and installation

Removal

1 Remove the engine, separate the crankcase halves and remove the transmission shafts (see Sections 5, 22 and 28).
2 Remove the external shift mechanism (see Section 21).
3 Remove the shift cam retainers **(see illustration)**.

4 Support the shift forks and pull the guide bars out **(see illustrations)**.
5 Pull the shift cam out of the case **(see illustration)**.

Inspection

6 Check the edges of the grooves in the shift cam for signs of excessive wear **(see illustration)**. Check the pins on each end of the shift cam for wear and damage **(see illustrations)**. If undesirable conditions are found, replace the shift cam.
7 Check the shift forks for distortion and wear,

30.4b ...and lift out the forks

30.5 Slide the shift cam out of the crankcase

30.6a Check the shift cam grooves for wear, especially at the tips (arrowed)

30.6b Check the pins at the end of the shift cam for wear...

30.6c ...if the neutral indicator pin is worn, remove the retainer screw...

30.6d ...and take out the pin and spring

2

2•42 FZR600 engine, clutch and transmission

30.7 Check the shift forks for wear at the tips (arrowed); check the guide bars for wear

30.9a The forks are numbered from left to right ...

30.9b ... when installed, the L, C and R marks should be positioned as shown (arrowed)

especially at the fork tips **(see illustration)**. If they are discolored or severely worn they are probably bent. If damage or wear is evident, check the shift fork groove in the corresponding gear as well. Inspect the guide pins and the shaft bore for excessive wear and distortion and replace any defective parts with new ones.

8 Check the shift fork guide bars for evidence of wear, galling and other damage **(see illustration 30.7)**. Make sure the shift forks move smoothly on the bar. If the bar is worn or bent, replace it with a new one.

Installation

9 Installation is the reverse of removal, noting the following points:
a) Lubricate all parts with engine oil before installing them.
b) Use the numbers on the forks to position them correctly. The forks are numbered from one to three, starting from the left side of the engine **(see illustration)**. The numbers face the left side of the engine when the forks are installed. The letters L, C and R (left, center and right) also indicate fork position **(see illustration)**.
c) Engage the follower pin on each shift fork with the shift cam as you pass the guide bar through the fork. Position the shift cam and forks in the neutral position **(see illustrations)**.
d) Apply a non-permanent locking agent to the threads of the shift cam retainer bolts **(see illustration)** and tighten them to the torque listed in this Chapter's Specifications.

30.9c Engage the pins with the grooves in the shift cam and place the cam and forks in the neutral position ...

30.9d ... in neutral, the notch in the end of the shift cam (arrowed) ...

30.9e ... will engage with the stopper lever (arrowed)

30.9f Apply a non-permanent thread locking agent to the shift cam retainer bolts and to the threads of the guide bar

FZR600 engine, clutch and transmission 2•43

1 Oil filter
2 Oil strainer
3 Oil pump
4 Oil cooler

31.2 Oil cooler details (UK models)

31 Oil cooler (early UK models) - removal and installation

1 Early UK models are equipped with an external oil cooler. The oil cooler on later models is mounted between the oil filter and crankcase (see Chapter 4).
2 To replace the oil lines, drain the engine oil and remove fairing panels as needed for access. Remove the oil line retaining bolts at the engine and banjo bolts at the cooler **(see illustration)**.
3 To replace the cooler, remove the oil line banjo bolts and cooler mounting bolts **(see illustration 31.2)**. Lift the cooler out.
4 Installation is the reverse of the removal steps. Use new sealing washers at the banjo fittings and new O-rings at the oil line fittings on the engine.

32 Initial start-up after overhaul

1 Make sure the engine oil level is correct and the cooling system is full, then remove the spark plugs from the engine. Place the engine kill switch in the Off position and unplug the primary (low tension) wires from the coils.
2 Turn on the key switch and crank the engine over with the starter several times to build up oil pressure. Reinstall the spark plugs, connect the wires and turn the switch to On.
3 Make sure there is fuel in the tank, then turn the fuel tap to the On position and operate the choke.
4 Start the engine and allow it to run at a moderately fast idle until it reaches operating temperature.
5 Check carefully for oil leaks and make sure the transmission and controls, especially the brakes, function properly before road testing the machine. Refer to Section 33 for the recommended break-in procedure.
6 Upon completion of the road test, and after the engine has cooled down completely, recheck the valve clearances (see Chapter 1).

33 Recommended break-in procedure

1 Any rebuilt engine needs time to break-in, even if parts have been installed in their original locations. For this reason, treat the machine gently for the first few miles to make sure oil has circulated throughout the engine and any new parts installed have started to seat.
2 Even greater care is necessary if the engine has been rebored or a new crankshaft has been installed. In the case of a rebore, the engine will have to be broken in as if the machine were new. This means greater use of the transmission and a restraining hand on the throttle until at least 500 miles (800 km) have been covered. There's no point in keeping to any set speed limit - the main idea is to keep from lugging (labouring) the engine and to gradually increase performance until the 500 mile (800 km) mark is reached. These recommendations can be lessened to an extent when only a new crankshaft is installed. Experience is the best guide, since it's easy to tell when an engine is running freely. The following recommendations, which Yamaha provides for new motorcycles, can be used as a guide:
a) *0 to 90 miles (0 to 150 km): Keep engine speed below 5,000 rpm. Turn off the engine after each hour of operation and let it cool for 5 to 10 minutes. Vary the engine speed and don't use full throttle.*
b) *90 to 300 miles (150 to 500 km): Don't run the engine for long periods above 6,500 rpm. Rev the engine freely through the gears, but don't use full throttle.*
c) *300 to 600 miles (500 to 1000 km): Don't use full throttle for prolonged periods and don't cruise at speeds above 8,000 rpm.*
d) *After 600 miles (1,000 km): Full throttle can be used. Don't exceed maximum recommended engine speed (redline).*
3 If a lubrication failure is suspected, stop the engine immediately and try to find the cause. If an engine is run without oil, even for a short period of time, severe damage will occur.

Notes

Chapter 3
FZR750/1000 engine, clutch and transmission

Contents

Camshaft and starter chains and guides - removal, inspection and installation	27	Hydraulic clutch component service and system bleeding	20
		Initial start-up after overhaul	33
Camshaft chain tensioner - removal and installation	8	Main and connecting rod bearings - general note	24
Camshafts and lifters - removal, inspection and installation	9	Major engine repair - general note	4
Clutch release mechanism	20	Oil and filter change	See Chapter 1
Clutch - removal, inspection and installation	19	Oil cooler and lines - removal and installation	32
Compression test	See Chapter 1	Oil pan and relief valve - removal, relief valve inspection and installation	16
Connecting rods and bearings - removal, inspection, bearing selection and installation	26	Oil pump - oil pressure check, removal, inspection and installation	17
Crankcase components - inspection and servicing	23	Operations possible with the engine in the frame	2
Crankcase - disassembly and reassembly	22	Operations requiring engine removal	3
Crankshaft and main bearings - removal, inspection, main bearing selection and installation	25	Pistons - removal, inspection and installation	14
		Piston rings - installation	See Chapter 2
Cylinder block - removal, inspection and installation	13	Recommended break-in procedure	34
Cylinder head and valves - disassembly, inspection and reassembly	12	Shift cam and forks - removal and installation	30
		Spark plug replacement	See Chapter 1
Cylinder head - removal and installation	10	Starter clutch and idle gears - removal, inspection and installation	31
Engine disassembly and reassembly - general information	6		
Engine - removal and installation	5	Transmission shafts - disassembly, inspection and reassembly	29
External oil lines - removal and installation	18	Transmission shafts - removal and installation	28
External shift mechanism - removal, inspection and installation	21	Valve cover - removal and installation	7
General information	1	Valves/valve seats/valve guides - servicing	11

Degrees of difficulty

Easy, suitable for novice with little experience	Fairly easy, suitable for beginner with some experience	Fairly difficult, suitable for competent DIY mechanic	Difficult, suitable for experienced DIY mechanic	Very difficult, suitable for expert DIY or professional

Specifications

FZR750R

General
Bore x stroke
   1987 and 1988 (US) .... 68.0 mm x 51.6 mm (2.6772 inches x 2.0315 inches)
   1989-on (UK) .... 72.0 x 46.0 mm (2.835 x 1.811 inches)
Displacement
   1987 and 1988 (US) .... 750 cc (45.8 cubic inches)
   1989-on (UK) .... 749 cc (45.7 cubic inches)
Compression ratio .... 11.2 to 1

Camshafts
Intake camshaft lobe height (1987 and 1988 - US)
   Standard .... 32.55 to 32.65 mm (1.2815 to 1.2854 inch)
   Minimum .... 32.45 mm (1.278 inch)
Intake camshaft lobe height (1989-on - UK)
   Standard .... 32.60 to 32.70 mm (1.2835 to 1.2874 inch)
   Minimum .... 32.50 mm (1.280 inch)

3•2 FZR750/1000 engine, clutch and transmission

Camshafts (continued)   FZR750R

Intake camshaft base circle
  Standard .... 24.95 to 25.05 mm (0.9823 to 0.9862 inch)
  Minimum .... 24.85 mm (0.978 inch)
Exhaust camshaft lobe height (1987 and 1988 - US)
  Standard .... 32.4 to 32.5 mm (1.2756 to 1.2795 inch)
  Minimum .... 32.3 mm (1.2717 inch)
Exhaust camshaft lobe height (1989-on - UK)
  Standard .... 33.0 to 33.1 mm (1.2992 to 1.3031 inch)
  Minimum .... 32.9 mm (1.30 inch)
Exhaust camshaft base circle
  Standard .... 24.95 to 25.05 mm (0.9823 to 0.9862 inch)
  Minimum .... 24.85 mm (0.978 inch)
Bearing oil clearance (cylinders 1 and 4) .... 0.020 to 0.054 mm (0.0008 to 0.0021 inch)
Bearing oil clearance (cylinders 2 and 3) .... 0.050 to 0.084 mm (0.0020 to 0.0033 inch)
Journal diameter .... 24.437 to 24.450 mm (0.9621 to 0.9626 inch)
Bearing bore (cylinders 1 and 4) .... 24.470 to 24.491 mm (0.9634 to 0.9642 inch)
Bearing bore (cylinders 2 and 3) .... 24.500 to 24.521 mm (0.9646 to 0.9654 inch)
Camshaft runout limit .... 0.03 mm (0.0012 inch)

Cylinder head, valves and valve springs

Cylinder head warpage limit .... 0.03 mm (0.0012 inch)
Valve stem bend limit .... 0.01 mm (0.0006 inch)
Valve head diameter (1987 and 1988 - US)
  Intake .... 20.9 to 21.1 mm (0.8228 to 0.8307 inch)
  Exhaust .... 22.9 to 23.1 mm (0.9016 to 0.9094 inch)
Valve head diameter (1989-on - UK)
  Intake .... 22.9 to 23.1 mm (0.9016 to 0.9094 inch)
  Exhaust .... 24.4 to 24.5 mm (0.9606 to 0.9685 inch)
Valve stem diameter (1987 and 1988 - US)
  Intake (standard) .... 4.975 to 4.990 mm (0.1959 to 0.1965 inch)
  Intake (minimum) .... 4.945 mm (0.1947 inch)
  Exhaust (standard) .... 4.960 to 4.975 mm (0.1953 to 0.1959 inch)
  Exhaust (minimum) .... 4.930 mm (0.1941 inch)
Valve stem diameter (1989-on - UK)
  Intake (standard) .... 4.475 to 4.490 mm (0.1762 to 0.1766 inch)
  Intake (minimum) .... 4.445 mm (0.175 inch)
  Exhaust (standard) .... 4.460 to 4.475 mm (0.1756 to 0.1762 inch)
  Exhaust (minimum) .... 4.430 mm (0.174 inch)
Valve head thickness limit (intake and exhaust) .... 0.6 to 0.8 mm (0.236 to 0.0315 inch)
Valve guide inside diameter (1987 and 1988 - US)
  Standard .... 5.000 to 5.012 mm (0.1969 to 0.1973 inch)
  Maximum .... 5.05 mm (0.1988 inch)
Valve guide inside diameter (1989-on - UK)
  Standard .... 4.500 to 4.512 mm (0.1772 to 0.1776 inch)
  Maximum .... 4.55 mm (0.179 inch)
Valve seat width (intake and exhaust) .... 0.9 to 1.1 mm (0.0354 to 0.0433 inch)
Valve face width
  1987 and 1988 (US) - intake and exhaust .... 1.98 to 2.55 mm (0.0780 to 0.1004 inch)
  1989-on (UK) - intake .... 1.49 to 2.48 mm (0.0587 to 0.0976 inch)
  1989-on (UK) - exhaust .... 1.76 to 2.76 mm (0.0693 to 0.1087 inch)
Valve spring free length (1987 and 1988 - US)
  Standard (intake and exhaust) .... 40.46 mm (1.593 inch)
  Minimum (intake and exhaust) .... 39.96 mm (1.573 inch)
Valve spring free length (1989-on - UK)
  Intake .... 40.38 mm (1.59 inch)
  Exhaust .... 44.40 mm (1.75 inch)
Valve spring installed length
  1987 and 1988 (US) .... 35.0 mm (1.378 inch)
  1989-on (UK) - intake .... 38.5 mm (1.44 inch)
  1989-on (UK) - exhaust .... 40.5 mm (1.59 inch)
Compressed pressure at installed length
  1987 and 1988 (US) .... 7.3 to 8.7 kg (16.1 to 19.2 lbs)
  1989-on (UK) - intake .... 12.2 to 13.2 kg (26.9 to 29.1 lbs)
  1989-on (UK) - exhaust .... 21 to 23 kg (46.3 to 50.7 lbs)
Valve spring bend limit (1987 and 1988) .... 1.7 mm (0.067 inch)
Valve spring bend limit (1989-on intake) .... 1.7 mm (0.067 inch)
Valve spring bend limit (1989-on exhaust) .... 1.9 mm (0.075 inch)

FZR750/1000 engine, clutch and transmission

Cylinder block
FZR750R
Bore diameter (1987 and 1988 - US) .... 68.000 to 68.005 mm (2.6772 to 2.6774 inches)
Bore diameter (1989-on - UK) .... 71.98 to 72.02 mm (2.834 to 2.835 inches)
Bore measuring point .... 40 mm (1.57 inch) from top of cylinder
Taper and out-of-round limit .... 0.05 mm (0.002 inch)

Pistons
Piston diameter (1987 and 1988 - US)
  Standard .... 69.93 to 69.94 mm (2.674 to 2.675 inch)
  First oversize .... 68.5 mm (2.697 inches)
  Second oversize .... 69.0 mm (2.717 inches)
  Diameter measuring point .... 3.0 mm (0.12 inch) from bottom of skirt
Piston diameter (1989-on - UK) .... 71.90 to 71.94 mm (2.831 to 2.832 inches)
Diameter measuring point .... 3.5 mm (0.14 inch) from bottom of skirt
Piston-to-cylinder clearance (1987 and 1988 - US) .... 0.06 to 0.08 mm (0.0024 to 0.0031 inch)
Piston-to-cylinder clearance (1989-on - UK) .... 0.07 to 0.09 mm (0.0028 to 0.0035 inch)
Ring side clearance (1987 and 1988 - US)
  Top and second .... 0.03 to 0.07 mm (0.0012 to 0.0028 inch)
  Oil ring .... Not specified
Ring side clearance (1989-on - UK)
  Top .... 0.03 to 0.07 mm (0.0012 to 0.0028 inch)
  Second and oil .... Not specified
Ring thickness (1987 and 1988 - US)
  Top ring .... 0.8 mm (0.0315 inch)
  Second ring .... 1.0 mm (0.0394 inch)
  Oil ring spacer .... 2.0 mm (0.0787 inch)
Ring thickness (1989-on - UK)
  Top ring .... 1.0 mm (0.0394 inch)
  Second ring .... Not specified
  Oil ring spacer .... 2.0 mm (0.0787 inch)
Ring end gap (1987 and 1988 - US)
  Top ring .... 0.15 to 0.30 mm (0.0059 to 0.0118 inch)
  Second ring .... 0.20 to 0.35 mm (0.0079 to 0.0138 inch)
  Oil ring .... 0.20 to 0.70 mm (0.0078 to 0.0276 inch)
Ring end gap (1989-on - UK)
  Top ring .... 0.15 to 0.30 mm (0.0059 to 0.0118 inch)
  Second ring .... Not specified
  Oil ring .... 0.10 to 0.60 mm (0.0039 to 0.0236 inch)
Ring width (1987 and 1988 - US)
  Top ring .... 2.6 mm (0.1024 inch)
  Second ring .... 2.8 mm (0.1102 inch)
  Oil ring .... 2.2 mm (0.0866 inch)
Ring width (1989-on - UK)
  Top and oil rings .... 2.8 mm (0.1102 inch)
  Second ring .... Not specified

Crankshaft, connecting rods and bearings
Main bearing oil clearance .... 0.040 to 0.064 mm (0.0016 to 0.0025 inch)
Connecting rod side clearance .... 0.160 to 0.262 mm (0.0063 to 0.0103 inch)
Connecting rod bearing oil clearance .... 0.032 to 0.056 mm (0.0013 to 0.0022 inch)
Crankshaft runout limit .... 0.03 mm (0.0012 inch)
Connecting rod bolt stretch - see text (UK FZR750) .... 0.15 to 0.19 mm (0.0059 to 0.0075 inch)

Oil pump and relief valve
Inner to outer rotor clearance limit .... 0.02 mm (0.008 inch)
Outer rotor to housing clearance limit .... 0.15 mm (0.006 inch)
Relief valve opening pressure .... 3.82 to 4.60 Bars (55.5 to 66.8 psi)

Clutch and transmission
Friction plate thickness .... 2.9 to 3.1 mm (0.1142 to 0.1220 inch)
Steel plate thickness .... 1.9 to 2.2 mm (0.075 to 0.085 inch)
Steel plate warpage limit .... 0.1 mm (0.004 inch)
Spring length (minimum) .... 54.0 mm (2.126 inches)
Driveshaft and mainshaft runout limit .... 0.08 mm (0.0031 inch)
Mainshaft gearset assembled length (1989-on - UK) .... 116.6 mm (4.59 inches)

3•4 FZR750/1000 engine, clutch and transmission

Torque specifications — FZR750R

Item	Torque
Alternator driveshaft bearing retainer	10 Nm (7.2 ft-lbs)
Cam chain guide (intake side) Allen bolts	10 Nm (7.2 ft-lbs)
Cam chain sprocket bolts	24 Nm (17 ft-lbs)
Cam chain tensioner mounting bolts	10 Nm (7.2 ft-lbs)
Cam chain tensioner cap bolt	20 Nm (14 ft-lbs)
Camshaft bearing cap bolts	10 Nm (7.2 ft-lbs)
Clutch bleed valve	6 Nm (4.3 ft-lbs)
Clutch boss nut	70 ft-lbs (50 Nm) (1)
Clutch cover bolts	10 Nm (7.2 ft-lbs)
Clutch hydraulic line union bolts	25 Nm (18 ft-lbs)
Clutch master cylinder bolts	9 Nm (6.5 ft-lbs)
Clutch master cylinder cap screws (1987 and 1988)	1 Nm (0.7 ft-lbs)
Clutch pressure plate bolts	8 Nm (5.8 ft-lbs)
Clutch release cylinder bolts	10 Nm (7.2 ft-lbs)
Connecting rod cap nuts (2)	
All except 1989-on	36 Nm (25 ft-lbs)
1989-on	
Initial torque	8 Nm (5.8 ft-lbs)
Final torque	42 Nm (30 ft-lbs) (6)
Crankcase bolts	
9 mm	32 Nm (23 ft-lbs) (3)
8 mm	24 Nm (17 ft-lbs) (3)
6 mm	12 Nm (8.7 ft-lbs) (3)
Crankcase studs to crankcase	10 Nm (7.2 ft-lbs) (3)
Crankshaft end cover screws	7 Nm (5.1 ft-lbs)
Cylinder head nuts	
1987 and 1988	25 Nm (18 ft-lbs) (3)
1989-on	41 Nm (30 ft-lbs) (3)
Engine mounting bolts	
1987 and 1988 (tighten in order listed)	
Lower rear bolt	42 Nm (30 ft-lbs)
Upper rear bolt	55 Nm (40 ft-lbs)
Upper front downtube bolts	63 Nm (46 ft-lbs)
Lower front downtube bolts	63 Nm (46 ft-lbs)
Forward lower downtube bolts	28 Nm (20 ft-lbs)
Rearward lower downtube bolts	28 Nm (20 ft-lbs)
Lower front engine bolt	55 Nm (40 ft-lbs)
Frame slit pinch bolt	15 Nm (11 ft-lbs)
Fairing stay bolts	15 Nm (11 ft-lbs)
1989-on (UK)	
Front of engine stay to frame	55 Nm (40 ft-lbs)
Rear of engine stay to frame	23 Nm (17 ft-lbs)
Lower rear mounting bolt	47 Nm (34 ft-lbs)
Pinch bolts	15 Nm (11 ft-lbs)
Neutral switch screws	4 Nm (2.9 ft-lbs) (4)
Oil baffle plate bolts	10 Nm (7.2 ft-lbs)
Oil cooler banjo bolts	25 Nm (18 ft-lbs)
Oil line (external) banjo bolts	21 Nm (15 ft-lbs)
Oil pan mounting bolts	10 Nm (7.2 ft-lbs)
Oil passage plugs	Not specified
Oil pick-up bolts	10 Nm (7.2 ft-lbs)
Oil pump body screws	10 Nm (7.2 ft-lbs)
Oil pump mounting bolts	10 Nm (7.2 ft-lbs)
Shift cam retainer bolt	10 Nm (7.2 ft-lbs) (4)
Shift mechanism stopper lever bolts	
All except 1989-on (UK)	10 Nm (7.2 ft-lbs) (4)
1989-on (UK)	22 Nm (16 ft-lbs)
Starter chain guide bolts	10 Nm (7.2 ft-lbs)
Starter clutch bolts	25 Nm (18 ft-lbs) (5)
Transmission bearing retainer screws	10 Nm (7.2 ft-lbs) (4)
Valve cover bolts	10 Nm (7.2 ft-lbs)

1 Use a new lockwasher.
2 Apply molybdenum disulphide grease to the threads.
3 Apply engine oil to the threads.
4 Apply non-permanent thread locking agent to the threads.
5 Apply non-permanent thread locking agent to the threads and stake the bolts after installation.
6 Final tightness is determined by bolt stretch; see text.

FZR1000

General
Bore x stroke	
1987 and 1988	75.0 mm x 56.0 mm (2.9528 x 2.2047 inches)
1989-on	75.5 mm x 56.0 mm (2.972 x 2.2047 inches)
Displacement (1987 and 1988)	989 cc (60.3 cubic inches)
Displacement (1989-on)	1002 cc (61.15 cubic inches)
Compression ratio (1987 and 1988)	11.2 to 1
Compression ratio (1989-on)	12.0 to 1

Camshafts
Intake camshaft lobe height (standard)	32.55 to 32.65 mm (1.2815 to 1.2854 inch)
Intake camshaft lobe height (minimum)	32.45 mm (1.278 inch)
Base circle (standard)	24.95 to 25.05 mm (0.9823 to 0.9862 inch)
Base circle (minimum)	24.85 mm (0.978 inch)
Exhaust camshaft lobe height	
1987 and 1988 (standard)	32.4 to 32.5 mm (1.2756 to 1.2795 inch)
1987 and 1988 (minimum)	32.3 mm (1.2717 inch)
1989-on (standard)	32.95 to 33.05 mm (1.2972 to 1.3012 inches)
1989-on (minimum)	32.85 mm (1.293 inch)
Base circle (standard)	24.95 to 25.05 mm (0.9823 to 0.9862 inch)
Base circle (minimum)	24.85 mm (0.978 inch)
Bearing oil clearance (cylinders 1 and 4)	0.020 to 0.054 mm (0.0008 to 0.0021 inch)
Bearing oil clearance (cylinders 2 and 3)	0.050 to 0.084 mm (0.0020 to 0.0033 inch)
Journal diameter	24.437 to 24.450 mm (0.9621 to 0.9626 inch)
Bearing bore (cylinders 1 and 4)	24.470 to 24.491 mm (0.9634 to 0.9642 inch)
Bearing bore (cylinders 2 and 3)	24.500 to 24.521 mm (0.9646 to 0.9654 inch)
Camshaft runout limit	0.03 mm (0.0012 inch)

Cylinder head, valves and valve springs
Cylinder head warpage limit	0.03 mm (0.0012 inch)
Valve stem bend limit	0.01 mm (0.0006 inch)
Valve head diameter (intake)	23.4 to 23.6 mm (0.9213 to 0.9291 inch)
Valve head diameter (exhaust)	24.9 to 25.1 mm (0.9803 to 0.9882 inch)
Valve stem diameter (1987 and 1988)	
Intake (standard)	4.975 to 4.990 mm (0.1959 to 0.1965 inch)
Intake (minimum)	4.945 mm (0.1947 inch)
Exhaust (standard)	4.960 to 4.975 mm (0.1953 to 0.1959 inch)
Exhaust (minimum)	4.930 mm (0.1941 inch)
Valve stem diameter (1989-on)	
Intake (standard)	4.475 to 4.490 mm (0.1762 to 0.1768 inch)
Intake (minimum)	4.445 mm (0.175 inch)
Exhaust (standard)	4.460 to 4.475 mm (0.1756 to 0.1762 inch)
Exhaust (minimum)	4.43 mm (0.174 inch)
Valve head thickness limit (intake)	0.45 to 0.95 mm (0.0177 to 0.0374 inch)
Valve head thickness limit (exhaust)	0.75 to 1.25 mm (0.0295 to 0.0492 inch)
Valve guide inside diameter (intake and exhaust)	
1987 and 1988 (standard)	5.000 to 5.012 mm (0.1969 to 0.1973 inch)
1987 and 1988 (maximum)	5.05 mm (0.1988 inch)
1989-on (standard)	4.500 to 4.512 mm (0.1772 to 0.1776 inch)
1989-on (maximum)	4.55 mm (0.179 inch)
Valve seat width (intake and exhaust)	
Standard	0.9 to 1.1 mm (0.0354 to 0.0433 inch)
Limit	1.8 mm (0.071 inch)
Valve face width (intake and exhaust)	1.63 to 2.90 mm (0.0642 to 0.1142 inch)
Valve spring free length (1987 and 1988)	
Intake	39.76 mm (1.565 inch)
Exhaust	39.96 mm (1.573 inch)
Valve spring free length (1989-on)	
Intake	40.73 mm (1.604 inch)
Exhaust	44.01 mm (1.733 inch)
Valve spring installed length (all)	35.0 mm (1.378 inch)
Compressed pressure at installed length	
1987 and 1988	7.3 to 8.7 kg (16.1 to 19.2 lbs)
1989-on	12.2 to 13.2 kg (26.9 to 29.1 lb)
Valve spring bend limit	1.7 mm (0.067 inch)

3•6 FZR750/1000 engine, clutch and transmission

Cylinder block
FZR1000

Bore diameter (1987 and 1988)	75.000 to 75.005 mm (2.9528 to 2.9529 inches)
Bore diameter (1989-on)	75.500 to 75.505 mm (2.9724 to 2.9726 inches)
Bore measuring point	40 mm (1.57 inch) from top of cylinder
Taper and out-of-round limit	0.05 mm (0.002 inch)

Pistons

Piston diameter (1987 and 1988)	
Standard	74.93 to 74.94 mm (2.949 to 2.950 inches)
Oversize	75.5 mm (2.97 inches)
Piston diameter (1989-on)	
Standard	75.425 to 75.440 mm (2.700 to 2.970 inches)
Oversize	76.0 mm (3.00 inches)
Diameter measuring point	3.0 mm (0.12 inch) from bottom of skirt
Piston-to-cylinder clearance	0.06 to 0.08 mm (0.0024 to 0.0031 inch)
Ring side clearance	
Top ring (standard)	0.03 to 0.07 mm (0.0012 to 0.0028 inch)
Top ring (maximum)	0.15 mm (0.0059 inch)
Second ring (standard)	0.02 to 0.06 mm (0.0008 to 0.0024 inch)
Second ring (maximum)	0.15 mm (0.0059 inch)
Oil ring	Not specified
Ring thickness	
Top ring	0.8 mm (0.0315 inch)
Second ring (1987 and 1988)	1.0 mm (0.0394 inch)
Second ring (1989-on)	0.8 mm (0.0315 inch)
Oil ring spacer (1987 and 1988)	2.0 mm (0.0787 inch)
Oil ring spacer (1989-on)	1.5 mm (0.0591 inch)
Ring end gap	
Top and second rings (standard)	0.3 to 0.5 mm (0.0118 to 0.0197 inch)
Top and second rings (maximum)	0.7 mm (0.0276 inch)
Oil ring	0.20 to 0.80 mm (0.0078 to 0.0315 inch)
Ring width	
Top and second rings (1987 and 1988)	3.1 mm (0.1220 inch)
Top and second rings (1989-on)	2.8 mm (0.1102 inch)
Oil ring	2.5 mm (0.0984 inch)

Crankshaft, connecting rods and bearings

Main bearing oil clearance	0.020 to 0.044 mm (0.0008 to 0.0017 inch)
Connecting rod side clearance	0.160 to 0.262 mm (0.0063 to 0.0103 inch)
Connecting rod bearing oil clearance	0.032 to 0.056 mm (0.0013 to 0.0022 inch)
Crankshaft runout limit	0.03 mm (0.0012 inch)

Oil pump and relief valve

Inner to outer rotor clearance limit	0.2 mm (0.008 inch)
Outer rotor to housing clearance	0.15 mm (0.006 inch)
Relief valve opening pressure	3.82 to 4.60 Bars (55.5 to 66.8 psi)

Clutch and transmission

Friction plate thickness	2.9 to 3.1 mm (0.1142 to 0.1220 inch)
Friction plate service limit	2.8 mm (0.11 inch)
Steel plate thickness	1.9 to 2.1 mm (0.075 to 0.083 inch)
Steel plate warpage limit	0.1 mm (0.004 inch)
Spring length (minimum)	54.0 mm (2.126 inches)
Driveshaft and mainshaft runout limit	0.08 mm (0.0031 inch)

Torque specifications

Alternator driveshaft bearing retainer	10 Nm (7.2 ft-lbs)
Cam chain guide (intake side) Allen bolts	10 Nm (7.2 ft-lbs)
Cam chain sprocket bolts	24 Nm (17 ft-lbs)
Cam chain tensioner mounting bolts	10 Nm (7.2 ft-lbs)
Cam chain tensioner cap bolt	20 Nm (14 ft-lbs)
Camshaft bearing cap bolts	10 Nm (7.2 ft-lbs)
Clutch bleed valve	6 Nm (4.3 ft-lbs)
Clutch boss nut	70 ft-lbs (50 Nm) (1)
Clutch cover bolts	10 Nm (7.2 ft-lbs)
Clutch hydraulic line union bolts	25 Nm (18 ft-lbs)
Clutch master cylinder bolts	9 Nm (6.5 ft-lbs)

Torque specifications (continued)

FZR1000

Clutch master cylinder cap screws	2 Nm (1.4 ft-lbs)
Clutch pressure plate bolts	8 Nm (5.8 ft-lbs)
Clutch release cylinder bolts	10 Nm (7.2 ft-lbs)
Connecting rod cap nuts (2)	36 Nm (25 ft-lbs)
Crankcase bolts	
9 mm	32 Nm (23 ft-lbs) (3)
8 mm	24 Nm (17 ft-lbs) (3)
6 mm	12 Nm (8.7 ft-lbs) (3)
Crankcase studs to crankcase	10 Nm (7.2 ft-lbs) (3)
Crankshaft end cover screws	7 Nm (5.1 ft-lbs)
Cylinder head nuts	
1987 and 1988	37 Nm (27 ft-lbs) (3)
1989-on	41 Nm (30 ft-lbs) (3)
Engine mounting bolts	
1987 and 1988 (tighten in order listed)	
Lower rear bolt	42 Nm (30 ft-lbs)
Upper rear bolt	55 Nm (40 ft-lbs)
Upper front downtube bolts	63 Nm (46 ft-lbs)
Lower front downtube bolts	63 Nm (46 ft-lbs)
Forward lower downtube bolts	28 Nm (20 ft-lbs)
Rearward lower downtube bolts	28 Nm (20 ft-lbs)
Lower front engine bolt	55 Nm (40 ft-lbs)
Frame slit pinch bolt	15 Nm (11 ft-lbs)
Fairing stay bolts	15 Nm (11 ft-lbs)
1989-on	
Lower rear mounting bolt	55 Nm (40 ft-lbs)
Upper rear mounting bolt	60 Nm (43 ft-lbs)
Frame to cylinder head bolts	60 Nm (43 ft-lbs)
Frame to cylinder block bolts	33 Nm (24 ft-lbs)
Rear pinch bolts	15 Nm (11 ft-lbs)
Center and front pinch bolts	22 Nm (16 ft-lbs)
Neutral switch screws	4 Nm (2.9 ft-lbs) (4)
Oil baffle plate bolts	10 Nm (7.2 ft-lbs)
Oil cooler banjo bolts	25 Nm (18 ft-lbs)
Oil line (external) banjo bolts	21 Nm (15 ft-lbs)
Oil pan mounting bolts	10 Nm (7.2 ft-lbs)
Oil passage plugs	Not specified
Oil pick-up bolts	10 Nm (7.2 ft-lbs)
Oil pump body screws	10 Nm (7.2 ft-lbs)
Oil pump mounting bolts	10 Nm (7.2 ft-lbs)
Shift cam retainer bolt	10 Nm (7.2 ft-lbs) (4)
Shift mechanism stopper lever bolts	10 Nm (7.2 ft-lbs) (4)
Starter chain guide bolts	10 Nm (7.2 ft-lbs)
Starter clutch bolts	25 Nm (18 ft-lbs) (5)
Transmission bearing retainer screws	10 Nm (7.2 ft-lbs) (4)
Valve cover bolts	10 Nm (7.2 ft-lbs)

1 Use a new lockwasher.
2 Apply molybdenum disulphide grease to the threads.
3 Apply engine oil to the threads.
4 Apply non-permanent thread locking agent to the threads.
5 Apply non-permanent thread locking agent to the threads and stake the bolts after installation.
6 Final tightness is determined by bolt stretch; see text.

1 General information

The engine/transmission unit is a liquid-cooled, in-line four. The valves are operated by double overhead camshafts which are chain driven off the crankshaft. The engine/transmission assembly is constructed from aluminum alloy. The crankcase is divided horizontally.

The crankcase incorporates a wet sump, pressure-fed lubrication system which uses a gear-driven oil pump, an oil filter, relief valve and an oil level switch. Also contained in the crankcase is the starter motor clutch.

Power from the crankshaft is routed to the transmission via the clutch, which is of the coil spring, wet multi-plate type and is gear-driven off the crankshaft. The transmission is a five-speed (FZR1000) or six-speed (FZR750), constant-mesh unit.

2 Operations possible with the engine in the frame

The components and assemblies listed below can be removed without having to remove the engine from the frame. If, however, a number of areas require attention at the same time, removal of the engine is recommended.

Gear selector mechanism external components
Water pump
Starter motor
Alternator
Clutch assembly
Valve cover, camshafts and lifters
Cam chain tensioner
Cylinder head
Cylinder block and pistons
Oil pan and pump
Camshaft chain (if soft link is fitted)

3 Operations requiring engine removal

It is necessary to remove the engine/transmission assembly from the frame and separate the crankcase halves to gain access to the following components:

Crankshaft, connecting rods and bearings
Transmission shafts
Shift cam and forks
Camshaft chain (see Section 2) and starter chain
Starter clutch

4 Major engine repair - general note

1 It is not always easy to determine when or if an engine should be completely overhauled, as a number of factors must be considered.
2 High mileage is not necessarily an indication that an overhaul is needed, while low mileage, on the other hand, does not preclude the need for an overhaul. Frequency of servicing is probably the single most important consideration. An engine that has regular and frequent oil and filter changes, as well as other required maintenance, will most likely give many miles of reliable service. Conversely, a neglected engine, or one which has not been broken in properly, may require an overhaul very early in its life.
3 Exhaust smoke and excessive oil consumption are both indications that piston rings and/or valve guides are in need of attention. Make sure oil leaks are not responsible before deciding that the rings and guides are bad. Refer to Chapter 1 and perform a cylinder compression check to determine for certain the nature and extent of the work required.
4 If the engine is making obvious knocking or rumbling noises, the connecting rod and/or main bearings are probably at fault.
5 Loss of power, rough running, excessive valve train noise and high fuel consumption rates may also point to the need for an overhaul, especially if they are all present at the same time. If a complete tune-up does not remedy the situation, major mechanical work is the only solution.
6 An engine overhaul generally involves restoring the internal parts to the specifications of a new engine. During an overhaul the piston rings are replaced and the cylinder walls are bored and/or honed. If a rebore is done, then new pistons are also required. The main and connecting rod bearings are generally replaced with new ones and, if necessary, the crankshaft is also replaced. Generally the valves are serviced as well, since they are usually in less than perfect condition at this point. While the engine is being overhauled, other components such as the carburetors and the starter motor can be rebuilt also. The end result should be a like-new engine that will give as many trouble free miles as the original.
7 Before beginning the engine overhaul, read through all of the related procedures to familiarize yourself with the scope and requirements of the job. Overhauling an engine is not all that difficult, but it is time consuming. Plan on the motorcycle being tied up for a minimum of two weeks. Check on the availability of parts and make sure that any necessary special tools, equipment and supplies are obtained in advance.
8 Most work can be done with typical shop hand tools, although a number of precision measuring tools are required for inspecting parts to determine if they must be replaced. Often a dealer service department or motorcycle repair shop will handle the inspection of parts and offer advice concerning reconditioning and replacement. As a general rule, time is the primary cost of an overhaul so it doesn't pay to install worn or substandard parts.
9 As a final note, to ensure maximum life and minimum trouble from a rebuilt engine, everything must be assembled with care in a spotlessly clean environment.

5 Engine - removal and installation

Note: *Engine removal and installation should be done with the aid of an assistant to avoid damage or injury that could occur if the engine is dropped. A hydraulic floor jack should be used to support and lower the engine if possible (they can be rented at low cost).*

Removal

1 Support the bike securely so it can't be knocked over during this procedure.
2 Remove the fuel tank (see Chapter 5).
3 Remove the left and right fairings, the front fairing (1989 and later FZR1000), the left and right side covers and seat (see Chapter 9).
4 Disconnect the negative cable from the battery, then disconnect the positive cable (see Chapter 1).

Warning: *Always disconnect the negative cable first and reconnect it last to prevent a battery explosion.*

5 Remove the air filter housing (see Chapter 5).
6 Disconnect the spark plug wires (see Chapter 1).
7 If you're working on a 1989 or later model, remove the air baffle plate together with the ignition coils (see Chapter 6).
8 Drain the engine oil and coolant (see Chapter 1).
9 Remove the carburetors (see Chapter 5) and plug the intake openings with rags.
10 Remove the radiator and the coolant tubes on the intake side of the engine. Remove the radiator outlet tubes (see Chapter 4).
11 Remove the oil cooler (see Section 32).
12 If you're working on an EXUP model, disconnect the EXUP cables at the upper end (see Chapter 5). On UK FZR750 models, remove the EXUP servo motor.
13 Remove the exhaust system (see Chapter 5).
14 Remove the external shift linkage from the shift shaft (see Section 21).
15 Disconnect the clutch cable or remove the release cylinder (see Section 20).
16 Remove the engine sprocket cover and engine sprocket (see Chapter 7). It isn't necessary to remove the drive chain completely, but if the engine sprocket is difficult to remove, loosen the rear axle nut and chain adjusters, then push the rear wheel forward to create slack in the chain (see Chapter 1 for details).
17 Refer to Chapter 10 and disconnect the following electrical connectors:
   a) *alternator*
   b) *neutral switch*
   c) *oil level switch*
   d) *starter motor*
   e) *sidestand switch*
   f) *pickup coil*
18 Disconnect the engine ground lead from the crankcase (refer to crankcase reassembly procedures in Section 22).
19 Support the engine securely with a floor jack and a wood block **(see illustration)**.

5.19 Place a jack under the oil pan (use a wooden block between the jack and oil pan to protect the pan)

FZR750/1000 engine, clutch and transmission 3•9

5.22a Loosen the collar pinch bolts but don't loosen the engine mounting bolt (arrowed) yet . . .

5.22b . . . also loosen the pinch bolts at the rear mount but not the engine mounting bolt (arrowed) yet

5.22c Loosen the pinch bolt on the upper rear mounting bolt collar at the left . . .

1987 and 1988 models

20 Remove the bolts holding the downtubes to the frame (see Chapter 7).
21 Remove the upper and lower engine mounting bolts and spacers.

1989 and later FZR1000 models

22 Loosen the spacer pinch bolts at the front and rear of the engine on each side, and at the back of the engine on top **(see illustrations)**.
23 Remove the nuts from the engine mounting bolts and remove the bolts **(see illustrations)**.

1989 and later FZR750 models

24 Loosen the pinch bolts at the lower rear of the engine and the rear of the engine stay.
25 Loosen the bolts at the front of the engine stay.
26 Remove the lower rear mounting bolt, then the lower rear engine stay bolts.
27 Unbolt the front of the engine stay from the frame.

All models

28 Make sure no wires or hoses are still attached to the engine assembly.

⚠ *Warning: The engine is heavy and may cause injury if it falls. Be sure it's securely supported. Have an assistant help you steady the engine on the jack as you remove it.*

29 Slowly and carefully lower the engine assembly to the floor, then guide it out from under the bike to the right **(see illustration)**.

Installation

30 Installation is the reverse of removal. Note the following points:
   a) *Don't tighten any of the engine mounting bolts until they all have been installed.*

5.22d . . . and at the right (arrowed)

5.23a Remove the outer nut and exhaust hanger bracket from the lower rear mounting bolt . . .

5.23b . . . remove the inner nut . . .

5.23c . . . pull out the lower rear mounting bolt . . .

5.23d . . . and remove the upper rear mounting bolt

5.29 Have an assistant steady the engine while you lower the jack

3

3•10 FZR750/1000 engine, clutch and transmission

b) If you're working on a 1987 or 1988 model, tighten the mounting bolts in the order and to the torque listed in this Chapter's Specifications. Tighten the downtube bolts with the full weight of the engine resting on them.
c) If you're working on a 1989 or later model, be sure the mounting bolt collars are in place (see illustrations).
d) Use new gaskets at all exhaust pipe connections.
e) Tighten the engine mounting bolts and frame downtube bolts (if equipped) to the torques listed in this Chapter's Specifications.
f) Adjust the drive chain and throttle cable(s)s following the procedures in Chapter 1.
g) Be sure to refill the cooling system and engine oil before starting the engine.

6 Engine disassembly and reassembly - general information

HAYNES HiNT *Before disassembling the engine, clean the exterior with a degreaser and rinse it with water. A clean engine will make the job easier and prevent the possibility of getting dirt into the internal areas of the engine.*

1 In addition to the precision measuring tools mentioned earlier, you will need a torque wrench, a valve spring compressor, oil gallery brushes, a piston ring removal and installation tool, piston ring compressors and a clutch holder tool (which is described in Section 19). Some new, clean engine oil of the correct grade and type, some engine assembly lube (or moly-based grease), a tube of Yamaha Quick Gasket (part no. ACC11001-05-01) or equivalent, and a tube of RTV (silicone) sealant will also be required.
2 Although it may not be considered a tool, some Plastigauge should also be obtained to use for checking bearing oil clearances (see illustrations).
3 An engine support stand made from short lengths of 2 x 4's bolted together will facilitate the disassembly and reassembly procedures (see illustration). The perimeter of the mount should be just big enough to accommodate the engine oil pan. If you have an automotive-type engine stand, an adapter plate can be made from a piece of plate, some angle iron and some nuts and bolts.
4 When disassembling the engine, keep "mated" parts together (including gears, cylinders, pistons, etc. that have been in contact with each other during engine operation). These "mated" parts must be reused or replaced as an assembly.
5 Engine/transmission disassembly should be done in the following general order with reference to the appropriate Sections.
   Remove the camshafts
   Remove the cylinder head
   Remove the cylinder block
   Remove the pistons
   Remove the clutch
   Remove the oil pan
   Remove the external shift mechanism
   Remove the alternator and starter (see Chapter 10)
   Separate the crankcase halves
   Remove the crankshaft and connecting rods

5.30a Be sure the mounting bolt collars are in place at the sides of the frame (arrowed) . . .

5.30b . . . and where the upper rear mounting bolt passes through (arrowed)

   Remove the transmission shafts/gears
   Remove the shift cam/forks
   Remove the starter clutch and idle gears
6 Reassembly is accomplished by reversing the general disassembly sequence.

7 Valve cover - removal and installation

Note: *The valve cover can be removed with the engine in the frame. If the engine has been removed, ignore the steps which don't apply.*

Removal

1 Support the bike securely so it can't be knocked over during this procedure.
2 Remove the left and right fairings, front fairing (1989 and later models) and seat (see Chapter 9).
3 Remove the fuel tank (see Chapter 5).
4 Remove the radiator (see Chapter 4) and oil cooler (see Section 32).
5 Remove the air cleaner housing. If you're working on a 1989 or later model, remove the air baffle plate (see Chapter 5).
6 If you're working on a 1987 or 1988 model, remove the right frame downtube (see Section 5).
7 Remove the spark plugs (see Chapter 1).

6.2a A selection of brushes is required for cleaning holes and passages in the engine components

6.2b Plastigauge is needed to check the crankshaft, connecting rod and camshaft oil clearances

6.3 An engine stand can be made from short lengths of 2 x 4 lumber and lag bolts or nails

FZR750/1000 engine, clutch and transmission 3•11

7.8 Remove the valve cover bolts . . .

7.9a . . . and lift the cover off the engine; note the dab of sealer (arrowed)

8 Remove the valve cover bolts **(see illustration)**.
9 Lift the cover off the cylinder head **(see illustrations)**. If it's stuck, don't attempt to pry it off - tap around the sides with a plastic hammer to dislodge it.

Installation

10 Peel the rubber gasket from the cover. If it's cracked, hardened, has soft spots or shows signs of general deterioration, replace it with a new one.
11 Clean the mating surfaces of the cylinder head and the valve cover with lacquer thinner, acetone or brake system cleaner. Apply a thin film of RTV sealant to the half-circle cutouts on each side of the head **(see illustration)**.
12 Install the gasket to the cover. Make sure it fits completely into the cover groove. Apply a small amount of silicone sealer to the corners of the half-circle portions of the gasket **(see illustration 7.9a)**.
13 Position the cover on the cylinder head, making sure the gasket doesn't slip out of place. The tab on the gasket should protrude from the front (exhaust) side of the engine **(see illustration)**.

7.9b Valve cover and cylinder head - exploded view

1 Washer
2 Rubber seals
3 Valve cover gasket
4 Spark plug
5 Valve guide
6 Snap-ring
7 Cylinder head end nuts and washers
8 Cylinder head upper section (camshaft case)
9 Gasket
10 Cylinder head main section

14 Check the rubber seals on the valve cover bolts, replacing them if necessary **(see illustration)**. Install the bolts with their seals and washers, tightening them evenly to the torque listed in this Chapter's Specifications.
15 The remainder of installation is the reverse of removal.

7.11 Apply a thin film of sealer to the half-circle cutouts in the cylinder head

7.13 The tab at the front of the gasket (arrowed) should protrude when the gasket is installed

7.14 Replace the rubber grommets on the valve cover bolts (arrowed) if they're cracked or deteriorated

3•12 FZR750/1000 engine, clutch and transmission

8.1 Loosen the tensioner cap bolt before unbolting the tensioner from the engine

8.2 Remove the tensioner bolts and take the tensioner off

1 Intake camshaft
2 Sprocket
3 Exhaust camshaft
4 Upper cam chain guide
5 Cam chain tensioner
6 Tensioner gasket
7 Intake side (rear) cam chain guide
8 Exhaust side (front) cam chain guide
9 Cam chain

8.3 Camshafts, tensioner and cam chain components - exploded view

8 Camshaft chain tensioner - removal and installation

Removal

Caution: *Once you start to remove the tensioner bolts, you must remove the tensioner all the way and reset it before tightening the bolts. The tensioner extends and locks in place, so if you loosen the bolts partway and then retighten them, the tensioner or cam chain will be damaged.*

1 Loosen the tensioner cap bolt while the tensioner is still installed **(see illustration)**.
2 Remove the tensioner mounting bolts and take it off the engine **(see illustration)**.

3 Remove the tensioner cap bolt and sealing washer **(see illustration)**.

Installation

4 Check the sealing washer on the cap bolt for cracks or hardening. It's a good idea to replace this washer whenever the tensioner cap is removed.
5 Release the one-way cam on the chain tensioner and compress the rod **(see illustration)**.
6 Turn the tensioner so the one-way cam is downward and install the tensioner on the cylinder block, using a new gasket **(see illustration)**. The word Up cast in the tensioner housing should be upward.
7 Tighten the mounting bolts to the torque listed in this Chapter's Specifications.

8 Install the tensioner springs, cap and sealing washer **(see illustration)**. Tighten the cap to the torque listed in this Chapter's Specifications.

9 Camshafts and lifters - removal, inspection and installation

Note: *This procedure can be performed with the engine in the frame.*

Camshafts

Removal

1 Remove the valve cover (see Section 7).
2 Turn the engine to position no. 1 cylinder at TDC compression (see Chapter 1 - Valve

8.5 Release the one-way cam (arrowed) and compress the tensioner before installing it

8.6 Install the tensioner body with a new gasket

8.8 Install the plunger, springs, washer and cap bolt after the tensioner is installed on the engine

FZR750/1000 engine, clutch and transmission 3•13

9.2 Align the small punch mark on each camshaft with the mark on the bearing cap (arrowed)

9.4 Remove the bolts (arrowed) and lift off the upper chain guide

9.5a Remove the bearing caps evenly

clearances - check and adjustment). When the engine is positioned correctly, the dots on the camshafts will align with the marks on the bearing caps **(see illustration)**.

3 Remove the camshaft chain tensioner (see Section 8).

4 Remove the upper cam chain guide **(see illustration)**.

5 Unscrew the cam bearing cap bolts, a little at a time, working from the outer to the inner bolts **(see illustration)**.

Caution: If the bearing cap bolts aren't loosened evenly, the bearing caps may break. Because they're line-bored with the cylinder head, this may necessitate replacing the entire cylinder head. Remove the bolts and lift off the caps.

Note that each bearing cap is labeled EX for exhaust (front side of the engine) or IN for intake (rear side of the engine) **(see illustration)**. They're also numbered from 1 through 4, starting at the left side of the engine.

6 Remove the bolts and lift off the bearing caps and their dowel pins **(see illustration)**.

7 Remove the camshafts. Keep the chain taut by wiring it to the engine so it can't fall down off the crankshaft. While the camshafts are out, don't allow the chain to go slack - the chain may fall off and bind between the crankshaft and case, which could damage these components. Also, cover the top of the cylinder head with a rag to prevent foreign objects from falling into the engine.

8 Lift the exhaust side (front) cam chain guide out of the engine **(see illustration)**.

Inspection

Note: *Before replacing camshafts or the cylinder head and bearing caps because of damage, check with local machine shops specializing in motorcycle engine work. In the case of the camshafts, it may be possible for cam lobes to be welded, reground and hardened, at a cost far lower than that of a new camshaft. If the bearing surfaces in the cylinder head are damaged, it may be possible for them to be bored out to accept bearing inserts. Due to the cost of a new cylinder head it is recommended that all options be explored before condemning it as trash!*

9 Inspect the cam bearing surfaces of the head and the bearing caps **(see illustration)**. Look for score marks, deep scratches and evidence of spalling (a pitted appearance).

10 Check the camshaft lobes for heat discoloration (blue appearance), score marks, chipped areas, flat spots and spalling **(see illustration)**. Measure the height of each lobe

9.5b Note the location and position of the bearing cap identification marks

9.6 Remove the bearing cap dowels (arrowed)

9.8 Lift the exhaust side chain guide out of the engine

9.9 Inspect the bearing surfaces in the cylinder head and bearing caps

9.10a Check the camshaft lobes - here's damage which will require ccamshaft replacement (or repair)

3•14 FZR750/1000 engine, clutch and transmission

9.10b Measure the height of the camshaft lobes with a micrometer

9.11 Camshafts are identified by lobes per cylinder; the intake has three, the exhaust two

9.15a Compare the crushed Plastigauge (1) to the scale

with a micrometer **(see illustration)** and compare the results to the minimum lobe height listed in this Chapter's Specifications. If damage is noted or wear is excessive, the camshaft must be replaced.

11 Next, check the camshaft bearing oil clearances. Clean the camshafts, the bearing surfaces in the cylinder head and the bearing caps with a clean, lint-free cloth, then lay the cams in place in the cylinder head. Be sure the punch marks on the camshafts are upward **(see illustration 9.2)**. Be sure to place the camshafts in the correct bearings; the exhaust camshaft has a total of eight lobes and the intake camshafts has twelve lobes **(see illustration)**.

12 Cut one strip of Plastigauge for each bearing journal and lay it the pieces on the journals, parallel with the camshaft centerline.

13 Make sure the bearing cap dowels are installed (see illustration 9.6). Install the bearing caps in their proper positions (see Step 5). Tighten the bolts in two steps to the torque listed in this Chapter's Specifications.

Caution: Tighten the bearing caps evenly to specifications, starting with the inner bolts and working outward. While tightening, DO NOT let the camshafts rotate!

14 Now unscrew the bolts, a little at a time, and carefully lift off the bearing caps. Be sure to start with the outer bolts and work inward.

15 To determine the oil clearance, compare the crushed Plastigauge (at its widest point) on each journal to the scale printed on the Plastigauge container **(see illustration)**. Compare the results to this Chapter's Specifications. If the oil clearance is greater than specified, measure the diameter of the cam bearing journal with a micrometer **(see illustration)**. If the journal diameter is less than the specified limit, replace the camshaft with a new one and recheck the clearance. If the clearance is still too great, replace the cylinder head and bearing caps with new parts (see the Note that precedes Step 9).

16 Except in cases of oil starvation, the camshaft chain wears very little. If the chain has stretched excessively, which makes it difficult to maintain proper tension, replace it with a new one (see Section 27).

17 Check the sprockets for wear, cracks and other damage, replacing them if necessary. If the sprockets are worn, the chain is also worn, and also the sprocket on the crankshaft (which can only be remedied by replacing the crankshaft). If wear this severe is apparent, the entire engine should be disassembled for inspection.

18 Check the front guide and upper chain guide's rubber pad for wear or damage. If it is worn or damaged, the chain may be worn out or improperly adjusted. Refer to Section 27 for chain replacement.

Installation

19 Make sure the crankshaft is still at no. 1 TDC (refer to Chapter 1 - Valve clearances - check and adjustment).

20 Bolt the camshaft sprockets to the camshafts (if removed) and tighten the bolts to the torque listed in this Chapter's Specifications.

21 Install the exhaust side chain guide (if removed) **(see illustration)**.

22 Make sure the bearing surfaces in the cylinder head and the bearing caps are clean, then apply a light coat of engine assembly lube or moly-based grease to each of them.

23 Apply a coat of moly-based grease to the lobes of each camshaft. Make sure the camshaft bearing journals are clean, then slip the exhaust camshaft through the chain and lay it in the cylinder head (the camshaft won't fit all the way down into the bearing saddles and locating slot because some of the lobes will be pointed downward). Make sure the small punch mark on the camshaft is very slightly forward from its installed position (straight up) **(see illustration)**. Engage the chain with the sprocket so there is no slack in the exhaust side of the chain.

24 Place the intake camshaft in its bearing saddles with its alignment mark just forward

9.15b Measure the cam bearing journal diameter with a micrometer

9.21 Lower the front (exhaust side) chain guide into the engine and make sure it rests securely on the bottom of the crankcase

9.23 Lay the camshaft in the engine; with the alignment mark slightly counterclockwise (anti-clockwise)

FZR750/1000 engine, clutch and transmission 3•15

9.24 Lay the intake camshaft in the engine

9.25a Install the exhaust bearing caps; the alignment mark (arrowed) should be next to the camshaft punch mark

9.25b Install the intake bearing caps - the alignment marks will be out of position until the caps are bolted down

of the straight-up position **(see illustration)**. Drape the chain over the intake camshaft sprocket so there is no slack in the upper run of the chain (between the two sprockets).

25 Make sure the dowels are in position **(see illustration 9.6)**. Carefully set the bearing caps in place **(see illustrations)**. Make sure the caps are in their proper positions (see Step 5) and install all of the bolts except the four that secure the upper chain guide. Tighten them in two stages to the torque listed in this Chapter's Specifications, working from the inner bolts outward. As the bearing caps are tightened, the camshaft should settle down into its bearing saddles, the locating flange on the camshaft should settle into its groove and the exhaust camshaft alignment mark should move into the straight-up position. If the alignment mark isn't positioned correctly, disengage the chain from the camshaft and turn the camshaft to align the mark.

26 Insert a finger or wooden dowel in the cam chain tensioner hole and push against the chain to remove the slack in the upper run of the chain. Make sure the crankshaft mark is still in the no. 1 TDC position and both camshaft marks are in the straight-up positions.

27 If the crankshaft and camshaft alignment marks are not in the correct positions, lift the chain off the sprocket, turn the cam to obtain correct alignment and re-engage the chain with the sprocket.

28 Once all timing marks - those on the camshafts and crankshaft - are aligned

correctly, install the cam chain tensioner (see Section 8).

Caution: If the marks are not aligned exactly as described, the valve timing will be incorrect and the valves may contact the pistons, causing extensive damage to the engine. Be sure to recheck all timing marks to make sure they haven't shifted.

29 Pour clean engine oil over the cam chain and along the camshafts. Use enough so it flows down onto the sprockets and the valve area.

30 Install the upper cam chain guide **(see illustration)**.

31 Turn the engine with a wrench on the crankshaft turning bolt. If you feel a sudden increase in resistance, stop turning. The valves may be hitting the pistons due to incorrect assembly. Find the problem and fix it before turning the engine any further, or serious damage may occur. After two full turns, recheck the alignment of the camshaft punch marks with the marks on the bearing caps and the timing mark pointer with the line next to the T mark. If all marks are not in correct alignment, remove the cam bearing caps and reposition the camshaft(s) in the cam chain so the marks are correctly aligned.

32 The remainder of installation is the reverse of removal.

Valve lifters
Removal

33 Remove the camshafts following the procedure given above. Be sure to keep tension on the camshaft chain.

34 Make a holder with a separate section for each lifter and its valve adjusting shim (several egg cartons will work). Label the sections according to cylinder number (1, 2, 3 or 4), valve number (starting from the left end of the engine) and whether the lifter belongs with an intake or exhaust valve. The lifters form a wear pattern with their bores and must be returned to their original locations if reused.

35 Pull the lifter out of the bore with a magnet together with its valve adjusting shim (see Chapter 1). If the lifters are stuck, spray the area around them with carburetor cleaner and let it soak in. Place the lifters and shims in order in their holder.

Inspection

36 Check the lifters and their bores for wear, scuff marks, scratches or other damage. Yamaha doesn't provide specifications or wear tolerances for the lifters or their bores. If lifter wear or damage is found, replace the lifters as a set. Lifters are available in several oversizes for later FZR750 models. If the bores are worn or damaged, replace the camshaft case.

Installation

37 Coat the lifters and their bores with clean engine oil.

38 Installation is the reverse of the removal steps. Be sure to reinstall a valve adjusting shim between the each valve and its lifter.

10 Cylinder head - removal and installation

Caution: The engine must be completely cool before beginning this procedure, or the cylinder head may become warped.

Note: This procedure can be performed with the engine in the frame.

Note: In the following procedure, the camshafts are removed to access the cylinder head nuts. However, the camshaft bearing caps and camshafts are drilled to permit access to the cylinder head nuts without removing the camshafts; rubber caps plug the access hole(s) in each camshaft cap. If the latter method is adopted, the camchain must be split (see Section 27).

9.25c Install the cap bolts and tighten them evenly, working from the inner bolts outward

9.30 After the other cap bolts are tightened and the tensioner installed, install the upper chain guide

10.8a Remove the cylinder head end nuts with a socket . . .

10.8b . . . and remove the center nuts with an Allen bolt bit

10.8c It isn't necessary to remove the case bolts (arrowed) in order to remove the cylinder head

Removal

1 Support the bike securely so it can't be knocked over during this procedure.
2 Remove the carburetors and exhaust system (see Chapter 5).
3 Remove the valve cover (see Section 7).
4 Remove the cam chain tensioner (see Section 8).
5 Remove the camshafts (see Section 9).
6 Remove the coolant tube and thermostat housing from the rear of the engine (see Chapter 4).
7 Remove the external oil line from the rear of the engine (see Section 18).
8 Loosen the cylinder head nuts, 1/2 turn at a time, in the reverse of the tightening sequence (see illustration 10.15b and the accompanying illustrations). Once all of the nuts are loose, remove the nuts and washers.

Caution: Don't remove the bolts that hold the camshaft case to the cylinder head (see illustration), or you'll break the seal and the cylinder head halves will have to be completely separated to reseal it.

9 Pull the cylinder head off the cylinder block studs, together with the lifters **(see illustration)**. Don't attempt to pry the head off by inserting a screwdriver between the head and the cylinder block - you'll damage the sealing surfaces.

> **HAYNES HiNT** *If the head is stuck, tap upward with a rubber mallet to jar it loose, or use two wooden dowels inserted into the intake or exhaust ports to rock the head back and forth slightly (its movement will be limited by the studs).*

10 Lift the head gasket off the cylinder block and remove the dowel pins **(see illustration)**. Stuff a clean rag into the cam chain tunnel to prevent the entry of debris.
11 Check the cylinder head gasket and the mating surfaces on the cylinder head and block for leakage, which could indicate warpage. Refer to Section 12 and check the flatness of the cylinder head.
12 Clean all traces of old gasket material from the cylinder head and block. Be careful not to let any of the gasket material fall into the crankcase, the cylinder bores or the oil or coolant passages.

Installation

13 Install the dowels on the cylinder head studs and lay the new gasket in place on the cylinder block **(see illustration)**. Make sure the UP cutout on the gasket is upright and toward the rear of the engine (if the word UP reads backwards, the gasket is upside down) **(see illustration)**. Never reuse the old gasket and don't use any type of gasket sealant.
14 Carefully lower the cylinder head over the studs. It's helpful to have an assistant support the camshaft chain with a piece of wire so it doesn't fall and become kinked or detached from the crankshaft. When the head is resting against the cylinder block, wire the cam chain to another component to keep tension on it. When the head is installed, the UP mark on the gasket should protrude and be upright **(see illustration)**.

10.9 Lift the cylinder head off the studs

10.10 Lift the gasket off

10.13a Make sure the dowels (arrowed) are in position and place the new gasket over the studs

10.13b The UP cutout in the head gasket should be upright

10.14 The UP cutout in the gasket should be visible when the head is installed

FZR750/1000 engine, clutch and transmission 3•17

15 Install the head washers and nuts. Push the washers down with a small screwdriver to make sure they've seated completely **(see illustration)**. Starting with the inner nuts and working outward, tighten the nuts to approximately half of the torque listed in this Chapter's Specifications **(see illustration)**.

16 Using the same sequence, tighten the nuts to the torque listed in this Chapter's Specifications.

17 Install the camshafts, timing chain tensioner and valve cover (see Sections 9, 8 and 7).

18 Change the engine oil (see Chapter 1).

19 The remainder of installation is the reverse of the removal steps.

11 Valves/valve seats/valve guides - servicing

1 Because of the complex nature of this job and the special tools and equipment required, servicing of the valves, the valve seats and the valve guides (commonly known as a valve job) is best left to a professional.

2 The home mechanic can, however, remove and disassemble the head, do the initial cleaning and inspection, then reassemble and deliver the head to a dealer service department or properly equipped motorcycle repair shop for the actual valve servicing. Refer to Section 12 for those procedures.

3 The dealer service department will remove the valves and springs, recondition or replace the valves and valve seats, replace the valve guides, check and replace the valve springs, spring retainers and keepers/collets (as necessary), replace the valve seals with new ones and reassemble the valve components.

4 After the valve job has been performed, the head will be in like-new condition. When the head is returned, be sure to clean it again very thoroughly before installation on the engine to remove any metal particles or abrasive grit that may still be present from the valve service operations. Use compressed air, if available, to blow out all the holes and passages.

12 Cylinder head and valves - disassembly, inspection and reassembly

1 As mentioned in the previous Section, valve servicing and valve guide replacement should be left to a dealer service department or motorcycle repair shop. However, disassembly, cleaning and inspection of the valves and related components can be done (if the necessary special tools are available) by the home mechanic. This way no expense is incurred if the inspection reveals that service work is not required at this time.

2 To properly disassemble the valve components without the risk of damaging them, a valve spring compressor is absolutely

10.15a Seat the cylinder head washers in their bores with a small screwdriver

necessary. This special tool can usually be rented, but if it's not available, have a dealer service department or motorcycle repair shop handle the entire process of disassembly, inspection, service or repair (if required) and reassembly of the valves.

Disassembly

3 Remove the lifters and their shims if you haven't already done so (see Section 9). Store the components in such a way that they can be returned to their original locations without getting mixed up. Unbolt the camshaft case

12.7a Valve components - exploded view

1 Valve lifter
2 Adjusting shim
3 Valve keepers (collets)
4 Valve spring retainer
5 Valve spring
6 Spring seat
7 Valve stem oil seal
8 Valve

10.15b Cylinder head TIGHTENING sequence

from the cylinder head so the valves can be removed **(see illustration 7.9b)**.

4 Before the valves are removed, scrape away any traces of gasket material from the head gasket sealing surface. Work slowly and do not nick or gouge the soft aluminum of the head. Gasket removing solvents, which work very well, are available at most motorcycle shops and auto parts stores.

5 Carefully scrape all carbon deposits out of the combustion chamber area. A hand held wire brush or a piece of fine emery cloth can be used once the majority of deposits have been scraped away. Do not use a wire brush mounted in a drill motor, or one with extremely stiff bristles, as the head material is soft and may be eroded away or scratched by the wire brush.

6 Before proceeding, arrange to label and store the valves along with their related components so they can be kept separate and reinstalled in the same valve guides they are removed from (labeled plastic bags work well for this).

7 Compress the valve spring on the first valve with a spring compressor, then remove the keepers/collets and the spring retainer from the valve assembly **(see illustration)**. Do not compress the springs any more than is absolutely necessary. Carefully release the valve spring compressor and remove the spring and the valve from the head **(see illustration)**. If the valve binds in the guide (won't pull through), push it back into the head and deburr the area around the

12.7b Take the valve out of the combustion chamber, but don't force it if it's stuck . . .

3•18 FZR750/1000 engine, clutch and transmission

12.7c ... check the area around the keeper groove (1) for burrs and remove any that you find

keeper/collet groove with a very fine file or whetstone **(see illustration)**.
8 Repeat the procedure for the remaining valves. Remember to keep the parts for each valve together so they can be reinstalled in the same location.
9 Once the valves have been removed and labeled, pull off the valve stem seals with pliers and discard them (the old seals should never be reused), then remove the spring seats.
10 Next, clean the cylinder head with solvent and dry it thoroughly. Compressed air will speed the drying process and ensure that all holes and recessed areas are clean.
11 Clean all of the valve springs, keepers, retainers and spring seats with solvent and dry them thoroughly. Do the parts from one valve at a time so that no mixing of parts between valves occurs.
12 Scrape off any deposits that may have formed on the valve, then use a motorized wire brush to remove deposits from the valve heads and stems. Again, make sure the valves do not get mixed up.

Inspection

13 Inspection is the same as for FZR600 models. Refer to procedures in Chapter 2 and this Chapter's Specifications.

Reassembly

14 Reassembly is the reverse of the disassembly procedure. Before installing the valves in the head, they should be lapped to

13.4a Lift the cylinder block straight off the studs

12.15 Check all around the edge of each valve (arrowed) for solvent leakage

ensure a positive seal between the valves and seats. Refer to Chapter 2 for details of the lapping procedure.
15 Once all of the valves have been installed in the head, check for proper valve sealing by pouring a small amount of solvent into each of the valve ports. If the solvent leaks past the valve(s) into the combustion chamber area **(see illustration)**, disassemble the valve(s) and repeat the lapping procedure, then reinstall the valve(s) and repeat the check. Repeat the procedure until a satisfactory seal is obtained.

13 Cylinder block - removal, inspection and installation

Removal

1 Following the procedure given in Section 10, remove the cylinder head. Make sure the crankshaft is positioned at Top Dead Center (TDC) for cylinder no. 1.
2 Remove the external oil line from the rear of the engine (see Section 18).
3 Remove the coolant tube from the rear of the cylinder block (see Chapter 4).
4 Lift the cylinder block straight up to remove it **(see illustrations)**. If it's stuck, tap around its perimeter with a soft-faced hammer. Don't attempt to pry between the block and the crankcase, as you will ruin the sealing surfaces. As you lift, note the location of the dowel pins and oil jet nozzles. Be careful not to let these drop into the engine.
5 Stuff clean shop towels around the pistons and remove the gasket and all traces of old gasket material from the surfaces of the cylinder block, cylinder head and crankcase.

1 Circlip
2 Piston pin
3 Piston
4 Circlip
5 Dowels
6 Head gasket
7 Cylinder block
8 Cylinder base O-rings
9 Cylinder base gasket

13.4b Cylinder block and piston components

13.7 Measure across the bore in two directions (X and Y), at the specified distance from the top of the bore

13.10 Move the hone quickly up-and-down and be careful not to remove too much material

13.12 Insert the oil jets into their passages and be sure the spray nozzles point in the proper direction

Inspection

6 Check the cylinder walls carefully for scratches and score marks (don't attempt to separate the liners from the cylinder block).

7 Using the appropriate precision measuring tools, check each cylinder's diameter. Measure parallel to the crankshaft axis and across the crankshaft axis, at the depth from the top of the cylinder listed in this Chapter's Specifications (see illustration). Average the two measurements and compare the results to this Chapter's Specifications. If the cylinder walls are tapered, out-of-round, worn beyond the specified limits, or badly scuffed or scored, have them rebored and honed by a dealer service department or a motorcycle repair shop. If a rebore is done, oversize pistons and rings will be required as well.

8 As an alternative, if the precision measuring tools are not available, a dealer service department or motorcycle repair shop will make the measurements and offer advice concerning servicing of the cylinders.

9 If they are in reasonably good condition and not worn to the outside of the limits, and if the piston-to-cylinder clearances can be maintained properly (see Section 14), then the cylinders do not have to be rebored; honing is all that is necessary.

10 To perform the honing operation you will need the proper size flexible hone with fine stones, or a "bottle brush" type hone, plenty of light oil or honing oil, some shop towels and an electric drill motor. Hold the cylinder block in a vise (cushioned with soft jaws or wood blocks) when performing the honing operation. Mount the hone in the drill motor, compress the stones and slip the hone into the cylinder. Lubricate the cylinder thoroughly, turn on the drill and move the hone up and down in the cylinder at a pace which will produce a fine crosshatch pattern on the cylinder wall with the crosshatch lines intersecting at approximately a 60-degree angle (see illustration). Be sure to use plenty of lubricant and do not take off any more material than is absolutely necessary to produce the desired effect. Do not withdraw the hone from the cylinder while it is running. Instead, shut off the drill and continue moving the hone up and down in the cylinder until it comes to a complete stop, then compress the stones and withdraw the hone. Wipe the oil out of the cylinder and repeat the procedure on the remaining cylinder. Remember, do not remove too much material from the cylinder wall. If you do not have the tools, or do not desire to perform the honing operation, a dealer service department or motorcycle repair shop will generally do it for a reasonable fee.

11 Next, the cylinders must be thoroughly washed with warm soapy water to remove all traces of the abrasive grit produced during the honing operation. Be sure to run a brush through the bolt holes and flush them with running water. After rinsing, dry the cylinders thoroughly and apply a coat of light, rust-preventative oil to all machined surfaces.

12 Lift the oil jets out of their passages, replace the O-rings and reinstall the jets (see illustration).

Installation

13 Lubricate the cylinder bores and pistons with plenty of clean engine oil.

14 Make sure the oil jets are installed correctly (see illustration 13.12). Install the dowel pins and place a new cylinder base gasket on the crankcase (see illustration). Make sure the UP mark on the gasket is upright and toward the front of the engine (if the UP cutout reads backwards, the gasket is upside down) (see illustration). Install new O-rings on the base of each cylinder (see illustration 13.4b).

15 Slowly rotate the crankshaft until two of the pistons are at the top of their travel and two are at the bottom.

16 Attach four piston ring compressors to the pistons and compress the piston rings. Large hose clamps can be used instead - just make sure they don't scratch the pistons, and don't tighten them too much.

17 Install the cylinder block over the pistons and carefully lower it down until the piston crowns fit into the cylinder liners (see illustration). While doing this, pull the camshaft chain up, using a hooked tool or a piece of coat hanger. Also keep an eye on the

13.14a Make sure there's a dowel (arrowed) at each front corner, then install the base gasket . . .

13.14b . . . make sure the UP mark on the cylinder base gasket is positioned correctly

13.17 You can install the cylinders using a screwdriver, but it's a good idea to use ring compressors

14.3a Mark the piston with its cylinder number; the arrow points to the exhaust side of the engine

14.3b Wear eye protection and pry out the clip with a pointed tool

14.4 Pull out the piston pin and lift the piston off the connecting rod

cam chain guide to make sure it doesn't wedge against the block. Push down on the cylinder block, making sure the pistons don't get cocked sideways, until the bottoms of the cylinder liners slide down past the piston rings. A wood or plastic hammer handle can be used to gently tap the block down, but don't use too much force or the pistons will be damaged.

18 Slide the cylinder block down over the remaining two pistons and guide the rings into the bores.

19 Remove the piston ring compressors or hose clamps, being careful not to scratch the pistons.

20 The remainder of installation is the reverse of removal.

14 Pistons - removal, inspection and installation

1 The pistons are attached to the connecting rods with piston pins that are a slip fit in the pistons and rods.

2 Before removing the pistons from the rods, stuff a clean shop towel into each crankcase hole, around the connecting rods. This will prevent the circlips from falling into the crankcase if they are inadvertently dropped.

Removal

3 Using a sharp scribe, scratch the number of each piston into its crown (or use a felt pen if the piston is clean enough). Each piston should also have an arrow pointing toward the front of the engine **(see illustration)**. If not, scribe an arrow into the piston crown before removal. Support the first piston, grasp the circlip with a pointed tool or needle-nose pliers and remove it from the groove **(see illustration)**.

4 Push the piston pin out from the opposite end to free the piston from the rod **(see illustration)**. You may have to deburr the area around the groove to enable the pin to slide out (use a triangular file for this procedure). If the pin won't come out, remove the remaining circlip. Fabricate a piston pin removal tool from threaded stock, nuts, washers and a piece of pipe (see Chapter 2 for details).

5 Remove the remaining pistons in the same manner.

Inspection

6 Inspection is the same as for FZR600 models (see Chapter 2 and this Chapter's Specifications). The oil holes inside the pistons differ slightly **(see illustration)**.

Installation

7 Install the pistons in their original locations with the arrows pointing to the front of the engine. Lubricate the pins and the rod bores with clean engine oil. Install new circlips in the grooves in the inner sides of the pistons (don't reuse the old circlips). Push the pins into position from the opposite side and install new circlips. Compress the circlips only enough for them to fit in the piston. Make sure the clips are properly seated in the grooves **(see illustration)**.

15 Piston rings - installation

This procedure is the same as for FZR600 models (see Chapter 2 for details).

16 Oil pan and relief valve - removal, relief valve inspection and installation

Note: *The oil pan can be removed with the engine in the frame.*

Removal

1 Support the bike securely so it can't be knocked over during this procedure.

2 Remove fairing panels as necessary for access (see Chapter 9).

3 Disconnect the wires for the oil level switch and neutral switch (see Chapter 10).

4 Remove the exhaust system (see Chapter 5).

5 Drain the engine oil and remove the oil filter (see Chapter 1).

6 Detach the oil cooler lines from the engine (see Section 32).

7 Remove the oil pan bolts and detach the pan from the crankcase **(see illustrations)**.

14.6 Check the piston pin bore and skirt for wear, and make sure the holes are clear (arrowed)

14.7 Make sure the piston pin clips are securely seated in the grooves (arrowed)

16.7a Remove the oil pan bolts . . .

FZR750/1000 engine, clutch and transmission 3•21

16.7b . . . and take the oil pan off

16.8 Remove the dowels and the oil pickup mounting bolts (arrowed)

16.10 Pull the relief valve out of the case; it's a good idea to replace the O-ring

8 Unbolt the pickup from the crankcase and lift it off **(see illustration)**.
9 Remove all traces of old gasket from the oil pan and crankcase.
10 Remove the relief valve from the crankcase **(see illustration)**. It should pull out with light hand pressure. If it's stuck, rock it back and forth slightly.
11 Remove the oil pipes from the crankcase **(see illustrations)**.
12 Unbolt the baffle from the oil pan **(see illustration)**.
13 If necessary, remove the clutch oil return pipe. Remove the snap-ring that holds the pipe against the crankcase **(see illustration)**. Remove the clutch cover (see Section 19) and withdraw the pipe into the clutch housing **(see illustration)**.

Relief valve inspection

14 This is the same as for FZR600 models (see Chapter 2 for details).

Installation

15 Install the oil pan dowels **(see illustration)**. Install the relief valve in the crankcase, using a new O-ring.
16 Install new O-rings on the oil pipes and pickup **(see illustration)**.
17 Install the oil pipes and pickup and tighten the bolts securely.

16.11a Remove the oil pipes; one can be pulled out, the other is secured by bolts (arrowed) (FZR1000 shown)

16.11b Remove the remaining bolts (arrowed) and take the oil pipe out of the crankcase (FZR1000 shown)

16.12 Remove the baffle from the oil pan

16.13a Remove the snap-ring from the clutch oil return pipe . . .

16.13b . . . and withdraw the pipe (the clutch cover will have to be removed to do this)

16.15 Make sure the oil pan dowels are in position (arrowed)

16.16 Inspect the O-rings on the pipes and pickup; it's a good idea to replace these with new ones

3•22 FZR750/1000 engine, clutch and transmission

16.18 These two oil pan bolts secure a fairing bracket

18 Position a new gasket on the oil pan. A thin film of RTV sealant can be used to hold the gasket in place. Install the oil pan and bolts, tightening the bolts to the torque listed in this Chapter's Specifications, using a criss-cross pattern. Two of the bolts secure a fairing bracket on later FZR1000 models **(see illustration)**.

19 The remainder of installation is the reverse of removal. Install a new filter and fill the crankcase with oil (see Chapter 1), then run the engine and check for leaks.

17 Oil pump - oil pressure check, removal, inspection and installation

Note: *The oil pump can be removed with the engine in the frame.*

Oil pressure check

⚠ *Warning: If the oil passage plug is removed when the engine is hot, hot oil will drain out - wait until the engine is cold before beginning this check.*

1 Remove fairing panels as necessary for access (see Chapter 9).
2 Remove the plug at the bottom of the crankcase on the right-hand side and install an oil pressure gauge **(see illustration)**.
3 Start the engine and watch the gauge while varying the engine rpm. The pressure should stay within the relief valve opening pressure listed in this Chapter's Specifications. If the pressure is too high, the relief valve is stuck closed. To remove and inspect it, see Section 16 and Chapter 2.
4 If the pressure is lower than the standard, either the relief valve is stuck open, the oil pump is faulty, or there is other engine damage. Begin diagnosis by checking the relief valve, then the oil pump. If those items check out okay, chances are the bearing oil clearances are excessive and the engine needs to be overhauled.
5 If the pressure reading is in the desired range, allow the engine to warm up to normal operating temperature and check the pressure again, at the specified engine rpm. Compare your findings with this Chapter's Specifications.
6 If the pressure is significantly lower than specified, check the relief valve and the oil pump.

Removal

7 Remove the clutch (see Section 19).
8 Remove the oil pump mounting bolts and remove the pump **(see illustrations)**.
9 Remove the oil pump gasket and dowel **(see illustration)**.

Inspection

10 This is the same as for FZR600 models (see Chapter 2 and this Chapter's Specifications).

Installation

11 Before installing the pump, prime it by pouring oil into it while turning the shaft by hand - this will ensure that it begins to pump oil quickly. Align the drive tooth and drive slot with with the same mounting bolt hole so they will mesh when installed.

17.2 To check the oil pressure, remove the plug (arrowed) and connect an oil pressure gauge

17.8a Turn the pump gear to provide access to the mounting bolts

17.8b Insert an Allen key (arrowed) through the holes in the gear to remove the bolts (oil pan removed for clarity) . . .

17.8c . . . one of the bolts can be removed; the others can't, but they can be loosened enough for pump removal . . .

17.8d . . . with all three bolts loose, take the pump off

17.9 Remove the gasket and dowel (arrowed)

FZR750/1000 engine, clutch and transmission 3•23

17.12a The pump drive tooth (arrowed) must align with the water pump impeller slot

17.12b Align the arrowhead mark on the pump body with the arrow cast in the crankcase

18.4 Remove the banjo bolts; on FZR1000 models remove the bracket bolt (arrowed)

12 Installation is the reverse of removal, with the following additions:
a) Engage the drive tooth on the pump with its corresponding notch in the water pump impeller *(see illustration)*.
b) Align the arrowhead mark on the pump body with the cast arrow on the crankcase *(see illustration)*.

18 External oil lines - removal and installation

1 FZR1000 models use a single Y-shaped oil line with one fitting on the crankcase and two fittings on the cylinder head. FZR750 models use two oil lines that run from a single fitting on the crankcase to two fittings in the cylinder head.
2 Remove the left and right fairings (see Chapter 9).
3 Remove the fuel tank, air filter housing and carburetors (see Chapter 5).
4 At the top of the oil lines, remove two banjo bolts; if you're working on an FZR1000, remove the bracket bolt *(see illustration)*.
5 At the bottom of the oil line, remove the banjo bolt *(see illustration)*.
6 Take off the oil lines and their sealing washers.

18.5 Remove the banjo bolt at the crankcase (FZR1000 shown)

7 Installation is the reverse of the removal steps. Be sure to use a new sealing washer on each side of each banjo bolt and tighten them to the specified torque *(see illustration)*. On FZR750 models, position the oil lines so they don't touch any part of the engine except the cam chain tensioner.

19 Clutch - removal, inspection and installation

Note: The clutch can be removed with the engine in the frame.

18.7 Use a new sealing washer on both sides of each banjo fitting (FZR1000 shown)

Removal

1 Support the bike securely so it can't be knocked over during this procedure. Remove the right fairing (see Chapter 9).
2 Drain the engine oil (see Chapter 1).
3 Loosen the clutch cover bolts 1/4 turn at a time in a criss-cross pattern, then remove the cover, gasket and dowels *(see illustrations)*.
4 Loosen the pressure plate bolts evenly in a criss-cross pattern, then remove the bolts, springs and pressure plate *(see illustrations)*.

19.3a Loosen the clutch cover bolts evenly . . .

19.3b . . . then take off the cover

19.4a Loosen the pressure plate bolts evenly

3•24 FZR750/1000 engine, clutch and transmission

1 Pressure plate
2 Thrust washer
3 Bearing
4 Short pushrod and O-ring
5 Steel ball
6 Nut
7 Lockwasher
8 Friction plates (with red paint mark - outer plate has slot in tab)*
9 Cushion spring
10 Center friction plate (with blue paint mark)*
11 Steel plates
12 Clutch boss
13 Thrust washer (shown smooth; may have grooves)
14 Clutch housing
15 Bearing
16 Collar
17 Thrust washer (shown grooved; may be smooth)
18 Long pushrod
19 Oil seal
20 Release cylinder (except UK FZR750)
21 Release lever (UK FZR750)

*Friction plates interchangeable on UK FZR750

19.4b Clutch - exploded view

5 Remove the thrust washer and bearing from the short clutch pushrod **(see illustration)**.

6 On all except UK FZR750 models, remove the four outer friction plates, one center friction plate and the related steel plates **(see illustration)**. The outermost friction plate has a slot in one of its tabs which must be lined up with the marks on the clutch housing. The four outer and four inner friction plates have red paint marks and the center friction plate has a blue paint mark. Look for these marks as soon as you remove the plates and make your own marks if they aren't visible. On UKFZR750 models, the plates are interchangeable

7 Remove the short pushrod and the steel ball that fits behind it **(see illustration)**.

19.5 Remove the thrust washer and bearing

19.6 The clutch plate with the slot (arrowed) is installed next to the pressure plate (all except UK FZR750)

19.7a Remove the short pushrod and steel ball

FZR750/1000 engine, clutch and transmission 3•25

19.7b Remove the long pushrod; it can be removed from the other side of the engine, as shown here

19.8a Remove the cushion spring . . .

19.8b . . . then remove the remaining steel plates and friction plates

There's another, longer pushrod behind the steel ball which can be removed for inspection with a magnet. If it won't come out easily, it can be removed from the other side of the engine if the clutch release cylinder or lever is removed **(see illustration)**.

8 Remove the cushion spring and the remaining steel plates and friction plates **(see illustrations)**.

9 Bend back the lockwasher on the clutch boss nut **(see illustration)**. Loosen the nut, using a special holding tool (Yamaha tool no. YM-91402, part no. 90890-04086 or equivalent) to prevent the clutch housing from turning (see Chapter 2 for details). An alternative to this tool can be fabricated from some steel strap, bent at the ends and bolted together in the middle. Once the nut is loose, remove the nut and lockwasher and discard the lockwasher **(see illustrations)**. Use a new lockwasher during installation.

10 Remove the clutch boss and thrust washer **(see illustrations)**. **Note:** *The thrust washer may be grooved or smooth. Be sure to note which it is, because there's another washer behind the clutch housing which is not interchangeable.*

11 Thread a bolt into the collar and pull it out **(see illustration)**. Once the spacer is out, pull out the bearing.

12 Remove the clutch housing **(see illustration)**.

19.9a Bend back the lockwasher tab . . .

19.9b . . . remove the clutch nut . . .

19.9c . . . and remove the lockwasher

19.10a Slide the clutch boss (arrowed) off the transmission shaft . . .

19.10b . . . and remove the thrust washer

19.11 Thread a bolt (or two bolts if necessary) into the collar, then pull on the bolts to remove the collar

19.12 Remove the clutch housing

3•26 FZR750/1000 engine, clutch and transmission

19.13 Remove the remaining thrust washer

19.16a Position the clutch boss on the transmission shaft and install the collar . . .

19.16b . . . then slide the bearing in between the collar and clutch housing

13 Remove the thrust washer from behind the clutch housing (see illustration). Note whether it's grooved or smooth.

Inspection

14 This is the same as for FZR600 models (see Chapter 2 and this Chapter's Specifications).

Installation

15 Install the thrust washer (see illustration 19.10b) and clutch housing.
16 Coat the clutch housing bearing with engine oil, then install the bearing and collar (see illustrations). Be sure the gear on the back of the clutch housing engages the oil pump gear.
17 Install the thrust washer, the clutch boss, a new lockwasher and the clutch boss nut (see illustration).
18 Tighten the clutch boss nut to the torque listed in this Chapter's Specifications, using the technique described in Step 9 to prevent the hub from turning.
19 Bend the lockwasher against one of the flats on the nut with pliers (see illustration).
20 On all except UKFZR750 models coat one of the red-painted friction plates with engine oil and install it in the clutch housing. Engage the tabs on the friction plate with the slots in the clutch housing.
21 Install a steel plate on top of the friction plate with its rounded side inward. Continue to install alternate friction and steel plates until you've installed four friction plates with steel plates next to them. Always install friction plates and steel plates next to each other; never install a steel plate next to a steel plate or a friction plate next to a friction plate.

22 Install the blue-painted friction plate and cushion spring (see illustration 19.4b).
23 Install the remaining steel plates and red-painted friction plates.
24 Install the friction plate with the notch in one tab last. Align the notch with the marks on the clutch housing (see illustration).
25 On UKFZR750 models, install a friction plate first, then alternate steel and friction plates.
26 Coat the pushrods and steel ball with multipurpose grease, then install the long pushrod, the steel ball and the short pushrod (see illustrations).
27 The remainder of installation is the reverse of the removal steps, with the following additions:
  a) Align the hole in the pressure plate with the mark on the clutch boss (see illustration).

19.17 Install the lockwasher so its tabs fit into the clutch housing slots

19.19 Install the nut, tighten it to the specified torque and bend the lockwasher against the nut

19.24 Align the slot in the outer friction plate with the marks on the clutch housing (except UK FZR750)

1 Slotted tab on outer friction plate
2 Clutch housing

19.26a Install the long pushrod with its rounded end away from the steel ball, then install the steel ball . . .

19.26b . . . then install the short pushrod and its O-ring

19.27a Align the marks on the clutch boss and pressure plate (arrowed)

FZR750/1000 engine, clutch and transmission 3•27

19.27b Fit the oil tube into its hole in the clutch cover (arrowed)

20.2 Remove the union bolt from the clutch line (arrowed)

20.3a Remove the master cylinder clamp bolts (arrowed)

b) Tighten the pressure plate bolts in several stages in a criss-cross pattern to the torque listed in this Chapter's Specifications.

c) Make sure the clutch cover dowels are in position and install a new gasket.

d) Fit the oil tube into its hole in the cover as the cover is installed **(see illustration)**.

e) Tighten the clutch cover bolts in several stages to the torque listed in this Chapter's Specifications.

28 Fill the crankcase with the recommended type and amount of engine oil (see Chapter 1).

20 Clutch release mechanism

Master cylinder removal

1 Disconnect the electrical connector from the clutch interlock switch beneath the master cylinder.

2 Place a towel under the master cylinder to catch any spilled fluid, then remove the union bolt from the master cylinder fluid line **(see illustration)**.

Caution: Brake fluid will damage paint. Wipe up any spills immediately and wash the area with soap and water.

3 Remove the master cylinder clamp bolts and take the cylinder body off the handlebar **(see illustrations)**.

Master cylinder overhaul

4 Remove the lever pivot bolt and nut and take off the lever **(see illustration)**.

5 Remove the cap and rubber diaphragm from the reservoir **(see illustration 20.3b)**.

1 Reservoir cap
2 Diaphragm
3 Piston assembly
4 Sealing washers
5 Dowel
6 Release cylinder spring
7 Piston seal
8 Piston
9 Dust seal

20.3b Clutch hydraulic system - exploded view

20.4 Remove the pivot bolt and nut and separate the lever from the cylinder

3•28 FZR750/1000 engine, clutch and transmission

20.6 Remove the rubber boot, pushrod and spring

20.7a Remove the snap-ring from the bore . . .

20.7b . . . and take out the piston assembly, cup, spring seat and spring

6 Remove the rubber boot, pushrod and spring from the master cylinder **(see illustration)**.
7 Remove the snap ring and retaining ring, then dump out the piston and primary cup, secondary cup and spring **(see illustrations)**. If they won't come out, blow compressed air into the fluid line hole.

⚠️ **Warning: The piston may shoot out forcefully enough to cause injury. Point the piston at a block of wood or a pile of rags inside a box and apply air pressure gradually. Never point the end of the cylinder at yourself, including your fingers.**

8 Thoroughly clean all of the components in clean brake fluid (don't use any type of petroleum-based solvent).

9 Check the piston and cylinder bore for wear, scratches and rust. If the piston shows these conditions, replace it and both rubber cups as a set. If the cylinder bore has any defects, replace the entire master cylinder.
10 Install the spring in the cylinder bore, wide end first.
11 Coat a new cup with brake fluid and install it in the cylinder, wide side first.
12 Coat the piston with brake fluid and install it in the cylinder.
13 Install the retaining ring. Press the piston into the bore and install the snap ring to hold it in place **(see illustration)**.
14 Install the rubber boot, pushrod and spring.
15 When you install the lever, align the hole in the lever bushing with the pushrod **(see illustration)**.

Master cylinder installation

16 Installation is the reverse of the removal steps, with the following additions:
  a) *The arrow next to the UP mark on the clamp must point upward. Position the master cylinder at 10-degrees from horizontal (see illustration 20.3b).*
  b) *Tighten the clamp bolts to the torque listed in this Chapter's Specifications.*
  c) *Fill and bleed the clutch hydraulic system.*
  d) *Operate the clutch lever and check for fluid leaks.*

Release cylinder removal

17 Place rags and a container beneath the release cylinder to catch spilled fluid, then remove the union bolt and place the end of the hose in the container to let the fluid drain **(see illustration)**.
Caution: Brake fluid will damage paint. Wipe up any spills immediately and wash the area with soap and water.
18 Remove the cylinder mounting bolts and take it off.

Release cylinder overhaul

19 Pull the dust seal off the cylinder **(see illustration 20.3b)**.
20 Remove the piston and spring. If they won't come out, blow compressed air into the fluid line hole.

⚠️ **Warning: The piston may shoot out forcefully enough to cause injury. Point the piston at a block of wood or a pile of rags inside a box and apply air pressure gradually. Never point the end of the cylinder at yourself, including your fingers.**

21 Separate the spring from the piston **(see illustration)**.
22 Thoroughly clean all of the components in clean brake fluid (don't use any type of petroleum-based solvent).
23 Check the piston and cylinder bore for wear, scratches and rust. If the piston shows these conditions, replace it and the seal as a

20.13 Make sure the snap-ring seats in its groove

20.15 Align the lever bushing hole with the pushrod (arrowed)

20.17 Disconnect the fluid line and remove the mounting bolts (arrowed) and take the cylinder off

20.21 Take the spring off the piston

FZR750/1000 engine, clutch and transmission 3•29

20.23 If you plan to reuse the piston, remove the seals and install new ones

20.27 Remove the rubber cap from the bleed valve (arrowed)

set. If the cylinder bore has any defects, replace the entire release cylinder. If the piston and bore are good, carefully remove the seals from the piston and install new ones **(see illustration)**.

Release cylinder installation

24 Installation is the reverse of the removal procedure, with the following additions:
 a) Use new sealing washers on the fluid line.
 b) Tighten the cylinder mounting bolts and fluid line union bolt to the torques listed in this Chapter's Specifications.
 c) Bleed the clutch (see below).
 d) Operate the clutch and check for fluid leaks.

21.2 The punch marks on the shift lever and shaft (arrowed) should be aligned

21.4 Loosen the locknut and rotate the linkage rod to detach it from the rear adjuster

Clutch bleeding

25 Support the motorcycle upright and point the front wheel straight ahead.
26 Remove the master cylinder cap and diaphragm. Top up the master cylinder with fluid to the upper edge of the fluid level window, then set the diaphragm and cap on the reservoir (but don't install the screws yet).
27 Remove the cap from the bleed valve **(see illustration)**. Place a box wrench (ring spanner) over the bleed valve. Attach a rubber tube to the valve fitting and put the other end of the tube in a container. Pour enough clean brake fluid into the container to cover the end of the tube.
28 Rapidly squeeze the clutch lever several times, then hold it in. With the clutch lever held in, open the bleed valve 1/4-turn with the wrench, let air and fluid escape, then tighten the valve.
29 Release the clutch lever.
30 Repeat Steps 28 and 29 until there aren't any more bubbles in the fluid flowing into the container. Top off the master cylinder with fluid, then reinstall the diaphragm and cap and tighten the screws to the specified torque.

Cable replacement (UK FZR750 models)

31 Loosen the cable adjusters at the handlebar and at the lower end of the cable near the release lever. Unbolt the release lever cover, straighten the lock tab and disconnect the cable from the release lever. Note how the cable is routed through the holder near the steering head, then disconnect it from the clutch lever and remove it.
32 Installation is the reverse of removal. Adjust the cable as described in Chapter 1.

21 External shift mechanism - removal, inspection and installation

Shift lever and pedal removal and installation

1 Support the bike securely so it can't be knocked over during this procedure.
2 Look for punch marks on the end of the shift shaft and lever **(see illustration)**. If you can't find them, make your own punch marks so the lever can be realigned correctly during installation.
3 Remove the lever pinch bolt. Pull the lever off the shaft, together with the linkage rod.
4 Loosen the locknut and unscrew the linkage rod from the rear adjuster **(see illustration)**.
5 Remove the shift pedal/footpeg bracket bolts and take the assembly off. If necessary, remove the Allen bolt and separate the footpeg and shift pedal from the bracket.
6 Installation is the reverse of removal. Position the linkage so the bottom of the shift pedal is even with the threads on the forward end of the linkage rod **(see illustration)**. The shift arm should be at 90-degrees to the linkage rod. Adjust the linkage as needed with the nuts on the linkage rod (see Chapter 1).

Shift mechanism removal

7 Remove the shift lever and linkage (Steps 1 through 4) and the engine sprocket cover (see Chapter 7).

1 Adjusting nuts
2 Linkage rod
A 90-degrees
a Shift pedal
b Threads on linkage rod

21.6 Shift linkage details

3•30 FZR750/1000 engine, clutch and transmission

21.8a Slide the bushing off the shift shaft . . .

21.8b . . . pry the C-clip away from the shaft . . .

21.8c . . . and remove the washer

8 Remove the shift shaft bushing, C-clip and washer **(see illustrations)**.
9 Remove the clutch (see Section 19).
10 Slide the shift shaft out of the crankcase **(see illustration)**.
11 Remove the oil pump (see Section 17).
12 Unbolt the stopper lever and the stopper plate and the stopper plate that secures the shift fork guide bar, then remove the stopper lever return spring **(see illustrations)**.

Shift mechanism inspection

13 Inspect the return spring guide bar **(see illustration 21.12b)**. If it's worn or damaged, replace it. If it's loose, unscrew it, install a new lockwasher, reinstall the guide bar and tighten it securely. Bend the tab of the new lockwasher securely against one of the flats on the guide bar.
14 Check the shift shaft for bends and damage to the splines. If the shaft is bent, you can attempt to straighten it, but if the splines are damaged it will have to be replaced. Inspect the pawls and springs on the shift shaft and replace the shaft if they're worn or damaged.
15 Check the condition of the stopper lever and spring. Replace the stopper lever if it's worn where it contacts the shift cam. Replace the spring if it's distorted.
16 Inspect the pins on the end of the shift cam. If they're worn or damaged, you'll have to disassemble the crankcase to replace the shift cam.

Shift mechanism installation

17 Position the stopper lever return spring on the crankcase and engage its end with the stop **(see illustration)**.
18 Apply non-permanent thread locking agent to the threads of the shift fork guide bar retainer bolt, then install the retainer over the return spring. Apply the same thread locking agent to the stopper lever bolt, then install the stopper lever. Make sure the stopper lever engages the neutral detent in the shift cam and the spring is hooked over the lever **(see illustration)**. Tighten the bolts to the torque listed in this Chapter's Specifications.
19 Install the oil pump (see Section 17).
20 Apply high-temperature grease to the lip of the seal. Wrap the splines of the change lever shaft with electrical tape, so the splines won't damage the seal as the shaft is installed.
21 Slide the shaft into the crankcase. Engage the pawls evenly with the pins on the shift cam and position the return spring over the guide bar **(see illustration)**.
22 The remainder of installation is the reverse of the removal steps.
23 Check the engine oil level and add some, if necessary (see 'Daily (pre-ride) checks at the beginning of this Manual).

21.10 Pull the shift shaft out of the crankcase

21.12a Unbolt the stopper lever and the stopper plate (arrowed) . . .

21.12b . . . and remove the stopper plate and return spring; check the guide bar (arrowed) for looseness

21.17 Position the return spring like this

21.18 The stopper lever (left arrow) in the neutral detent on the shift cam; the return spring (right arrow) hooked over the stopper lever

FZR750/1000 engine, clutch and transmission 3•31

21.21 The shift shaft looks like this when it's installed correctly

22.6 Use a Torx bit to remove the bearing retainer screws (arrowed)

22 Crankcase - disassembly and reassembly

1 To examine and repair or replace the crankshaft, starter and camshaft chains, connecting rods, bearings, or transmission components, the crankcase must be split into two parts.

Disassembly

2 Remove the cylinder head, cylinder block and pistons (see Sections 10, 13 and 14). Remove the clutch (see Section 19).
3 Remove the water pump (see Chapter 4).
4 Remove the alternator and starter (see Chapter 10).
5 Remove the engine sprocket (see Chapter 7).
6 Remove the bearing retainers from behind the engine sprocket (see illustration) and from behind the clutch (see illustration 19.13).

Caution: Use the correct size Torx bit to remove the screws. Don't use an Allen bit or the screw heads will be rounded out.
7 Remove the cover from each end of the crankshaft (see illustrations).
8 Remove the pickup coil (see Chapter 6).

9 Remove the oil pan (see Section 16).
10 Remove the upper crankcase bolts, then the lower crankcase bolts, starting with the highest-numbered bolt and working to the lowest (reverse of the tightening sequence) **(see illustration)**.

22.7a Remove the crankshaft end covers . . .

22.7b . . . there's one at each end of the crankshaft

22.10 Crankcase bolt TIGHTENING sequence (typical; bolt numbers are cast in the crankcase)

A Upper crankcase   B Lower crankcase

3•32 FZR750/1000 engine, clutch and transmission

22.11 With the crankcase upside down, lift the bottom half off the top half

11 Carefully separate the crankcase halves **(see illustration)**. If they won't come easily, make sure all fasteners have been removed. Don't pry against the crankcase mating surfaces or they will leak.

12 Look for the oil jets, dowel(s) with O-rings and large dowel (where fitted) **(see illustrations)**. If they're not in one of the crankcase halves, locate them.

13 Refer to Sections 23 through 31 for information on the internal components of the crankcase.

Reassembly

14 Make sure the crankshaft, starter clutch and transmission shafts are correctly positioned in the upper crankcase half (see Sections 25, 28 and 31).

15 Place the ends of the crankcase studs on a piece of 2-by-4 lumber or equivalent **(see illustration on page 3•34)**. This will prevent the connecting rods from pushing against the workbench and forcing the crankshaft out of its bearings.

16 Remove all traces of sealant from the crankcase mating surfaces. Be careful not to let any fall into the case as this is done. Check to make sure the oil jet (with a new O-ring) and the dowel pins are in place. The 1987-88 FZR1000 and US FZR750 models have two small dowels with O-rings, all other models

1 Shift fork guide bar
2 Stopper lever
3 Guide bar stopper plate
4 Right shift fork (labeled R)
5 Center shift fork (labeled C)
6 Left shift fork (labeled L)
7 Shift cam
8 Bearing retainer
9 Main bearings
10 O-rings

22.12a Lower crankcase components

FZR750/1000 engine, clutch and transmission 3•33

1. Alternator drive shaft
2. Bearing retainer plate
3. Starter idle gear
4. Starter clutch gear
5. Starter clutch
6. Starter chain
7. Chain guide
8. Alternator damper
9. Oil jet
10. O-ring

22.12b Upper crankcase components

22.12c Look for the inner dowel(s) (arrowed) . . .

22.12d . . . and their corresponding O-ring(s) in the mating surface of the crankcase

22.12e Locate this dowel on the edge of the crankcase - 1991-on FZR1000

3•34 FZR750/1000 engine, clutch and transmission

22.12f There's an oil jet for each pair of cylinders

22.15 Rest the crankcase studs as shown

22.18 Apply sealant to the mating surfaces

have a single dowel with O-ring **(see illustration 22.12c)**. The 1991-on FZR1000 models havv a single large dowel in the crankcase rear edge **(see illustration 22.12e)**.

17 Pour some engine oil over the transmission gears, the crankshaft main bearings and the shift cam. Don't get any oil on the crankcase mating surfaces.

18 Apply a thin, even bead of Yamaha Bond or Quick Gasket sealant (part no. ACC-11001-05-01) or equivalent to the crankcase mating surfaces **(see illustration)**.

Caution: Don't apply an excessive amount of sealant. Don't let it contact the oil jet. Don't apply it within 2 to 3 mm (0.8 to 1.2 inch) of the bearing inserts, as it will ooze out when the case halves are assembled and may obstruct oil passages and prevent the bearings from seating.

19 Check the position of the shift cam, shift forks and transmission shafts - make sure they're in the neutral position (see Section 28). Make sure the locating pins in the transmission bearings are positioned correctly.

20 Carefully assemble the crankcase halves over the dowels. While doing this, make sure the shift forks fit into their gear grooves. Make sure the transmission seal and clutch pushrod seal are positioned correctly in the case **(see illustration)**. The seals should fit flush with the case surfaces when the case halves are assembled.

Caution: The crankcase halves should fit together completely without being forced.

If they're slightly apart, DO NOT force them together by tightening the crankcase bolts. The most likely reason they're apart is that the transmission bearing pins aren't positioned correctly. If the pins are forced against the crankcase halves, the cases will crack and have to be replaced.

21 Oil their threads and install the crankcase bolts in the correct holes **(see illustration 22.10)**. Bolts 7 through 10 have steel washers **(see illustration)**. Bolt 25 has a copper washer **(see illustration)**. Bolt 31 secures a ground wire **(see illustration)**.

22 Tighten the bolts in numerical order, referring to the numbers cast in the crankcase. Tighten all bolts to the torque listed in this Chapter's Specifications. **Note:** *There are different torque settings for the 9 mm bolts, 8 mm bolts and the 6 mm bolts.*

23 Turn the mainshaft and the transmission driveshaft to make sure they turn freely. Also make sure the crankshaft turns freely.

24 Install the oil pan (see Section 16).

25 The remainder of assembly is the reverse of disassembly, with the following additions:
 a) Once the external shift linkage is installed, shift the transmission through all the gear positions and back to Neutral.
 b) Use new O-rings in the crankshaft end covers. Apply a small amount of sealant to the covers where they cross the crankcase seam **(see illustration)**.
 c) Be sure to refill the engine oil.

22.20 The transmission and clutch pushrod seals should look this when the cases are assembled

22.21a The four end bolts have steel washers

22.21b Bolt 25 has a copper washer

22.21c Bolt 31 secures a ground wire

22.25 Install the O-rings and place sealant where the end covers meet the crankcase seam (arrowed)

FZR750/1000 engine, clutch and transmission 3•35

23.2a This oil line is secured by bolts (arrowed)

23.2b Remove the securing bolt (arrowed) . . .

23.2c . . . and slide the oil spray tube out of the crankcase

23 Crankcase components - inspection and servicing

1 After the crankcases have been separated and the crankshaft, starter clutch, shift cam and forks and transmission components removed, the crankcases should be cleaned thoroughly with new solvent and dried with compressed air.
2 All oil passages should be blown out with compressed air. Internal oil lines should be removed and flushed with solvent **(see illustrations)**. Remove any oil passage plugs that haven't already been removed **(see illustration)**.
3 Remove the oil baffles **(see illustration)**.
4 Check the starter clutch and idle gears (see Section 31).
5 All traces of old gasket sealant should be removed from the mating surfaces. Minor damage to the surfaces can be cleaned up with a fine sharpening stone or grindstone. *Caution: Be very careful not to nick or gouge the crankcase mating surfaces or leaks will result. Check both crankcase halves very carefully for cracks and other damage.*
6 Check the starter chain guide and cam chain rear guide for wear. If they appear to be worn excessively, replace them.
7 If any damage is found that can't be repaired, replace the crankcase halves as a set.

24 Main and connecting rod bearings - general note

1 Even though main and connecting rod bearings are generally replaced with new ones during the engine overhaul, the old bearings should be retained for close examination as they may reveal valuable information about the condition of the engine.
2 Bearing failure occurs mainly because of lack of lubrication, the presence of dirt or other foreign particles, overloading the engine and/or corrosion. Regardless of the cause of bearing failure, it must be corrected before the engine is reassembled to prevent it from happening again.
3 When examining the bearings, remove the main bearings from the case halves and the rod bearings from the connecting rods and caps and lay them out on a clean surface in the same general position as their location on the crankshaft journals. This will enable you to match any noted bearing problems with the corresponding side of the crankshaft journal.
4 Dirt and other foreign particles get into the engine in a variety of ways. It may be left in the engine during assembly or it may pass through filters or breathers. It may get into the oil and from there into the bearings. Metal chips from machining operations and normal engine wear are often present. Abrasives are sometimes left in engine components after reconditioning operations such as cylinder honing, especially when parts are not thoroughly cleaned using the proper cleaning methods. Whatever the source, these foreign objects often end up imbedded in the soft bearing material and are easily recognized. Large particles will not imbed in the bearing and will score or gouge the bearing and journal. The best prevention for this cause of bearing failure is to clean all parts thoroughly and keep everything spotlessly clean during engine reassembly. Frequent and regular oil and filter changes are also recommended.
5 Lack of lubrication or lubrication breakdown has a number of interrelated causes. Excessive heat (which thins the oil), overloading (which squeezes the oil from the bearing face) and oil leakage or throw off (from excessive bearing clearances, worn oil pump or high engine speeds) all contribute to lubrication breakdown. Blocked oil passages will also starve a bearing and destroy it. When lack of lubrication is the cause of bearing failure, the bearing material is wiped or extruded from the steel backing of the bearing. Temperatures may increase to the point where the steel backing and the journal turn blue from overheating.
6 Riding habits can have a definite effect on bearing life. Full throttle low speed operation, or lugging (labouring) the engine, puts very high loads on bearings, which tend to squeeze out the oil film. These loads cause the bearings to flex, which produces fine cracks in the bearing face (fatigue failure). Eventually the bearing material will loosen in pieces and tear away from the steel backing. Short trip riding leads to corrosion of bearings, as insufficient engine heat is produced to drive off the condensed water and corrosive gases produced. These products collect in the engine oil, forming acid and sludge. As the oil is carried to the engine bearings, the acid attacks and corrodes the bearing material.
7 Incorrect bearing installation during engine assembly will lead to bearing failure as well. Tight fitting bearings which leave insufficient bearing oil clearances result in oil starvation. Dirt or foreign particles trapped behind a bearing insert result in high spots on the bearing which lead to failure.

23.2d Remove any oil passage plugs not removed already

23.3 Unbolt the oil baffle plates

3•36 FZR750/1000 engine, clutch and transmission

25.2a Lift the crankshaft out of the case

25.2b Set the crankshaft, connecting rods and chains on a clean surface

25.5 Inspect the journals, gear and chain sprockets for wear, damage, pitted surfaces or chipped teeth

8 To avoid bearing problems, clean all parts thoroughly before reassembly, double check all bearing clearance measurements and lubricate the new bearings with engine assembly lube or moly-based grease during installation.

25 Crankshaft and main bearings - removal, inspection, main bearing selection and installation

Removal

1 Before removing the crankshaft check the endplay, using a dial indicator mounted in-line with the crankshaft. Yamaha doesn't provide endplay specifications, but if the endplay is excessive (more than a few thousandths of an inch), consider replacing the case halves.

2 Lift the crankshaft out, together with the connecting rods, starter chain and cam chain and set them on a clean surface (see illustrations). Remove the oil seal from one end of the crankshaft and the blind plug from the other end.

3 The main bearing inserts can be removed from their saddles by pushing their centers to the side, then lifting them out. Keep the bearing inserts in order. The main bearing oil clearance should be checked, however, before removing the inserts (see Step 8).

Inspection

4 If you haven't already done so, mark and remove the connecting rods from the crankshaft (see Section 26).

5 Clean the crankshaft with solvent, using a rifle-cleaning brush to scrub out the oil passages. If available, blow the crank dry with compressed air. Check the main and connecting rod journals for uneven wear, scoring and pits (see illustration). Rub a copper coin across the journal several times - if a journal picks up copper from the coin, it's too rough. Replace the crankshaft.

6 Check the primary gear and chain sprockets on the crankshaft for chipped teeth and other wear. If any undesirable conditions are found, replace the crankshaft. Check the chain as described in Section 27. Check the rest of the crankshaft for cracks and other damage. It should be magnafluxed to reveal hidden cracks - a dealer service department or motorcycle machine shop will handle the procedure.

7 Set the crankshaft on V-blocks and check the runout with a dial indicator touching each of the main journals, comparing your findings with this Chapter's Specifications. If the runout exceeds the limit, replace the crank.

Main bearing selection

8 Checking the main bearing clearance and selecting bearings is the same as for FZR600 models, except that the crankshaft has five main bearings instead of six, so the first five numbers on the crankshaft refer to the main journals (see illustration). The corresponding numbers for the main bearing bores are stamped in the crankcase (see illustration). Refer to this Chapter's Specifications.

Installation

9 Clean the bearing saddles in the case halves, then install the bearing inserts in their webs in the case (see illustration). When installing the bearings, use your hands only - don't tap them into place with a hammer.

10 Lubricate the bearing inserts with engine assembly lube or moly-based grease.

11 You can install the connecting rods on the crankshaft at this point if they were removed (see Section 26).

12 Loop the camshaft and starter chains over the crankshaft and engage them with their sprockets.

13 Carefully lower the crankshaft into place. If the connecting rods are on the crankshaft, guide them through their openings.

14 Assemble the case halves (see Section 22) and check to make sure the crankshaft and the transmission shafts turn freely.

25.8a These numbers on the crankshaft indicate journal diameter; the first five numbers relate to main bearing journals and the last four to connecting rod journals

25.8b The numbers on the crankcase correspond with the crankshaft main journals no. 1 through no. 5

A No. 5 journal
B No. 4 journal
C No. 3 journal
D No. 2 journal
E No. 1 journal

25.9 Make sure the tab on each bearing fits into the notch in the case

FZR750/1000 engine, clutch and transmission 3•37

26.1 Inspect each connecting rod; if the bore is scored, the rod and piston pin should be replaced

26.2 The number on the connecting rod is used for bearing selection

26 Connecting rods and bearings - removal, inspection, bearing selection and installation

Removal and inspection

1 These procedures are the same as for FZR600 models (see Chapter 2). Pay special attention to the piston pin bore at the top of each rod (see illustration). If it's scored or shows signs of seizure, the rod should be replaced.

Connecting rod bearing selection

2 Bearing selection is the same as for FZR600 models (see Chapter 2), except that the bearing selection number on the connecting rod may be 5 (see illustration). Use this number together with the last four numbers on the crankshaft to select connecting rod bearings (see illustration 25.8a). Refer to this Chapter's Specifications.

Installation

3 On all except 1989 and later (UK) FZR750 models, this is the same as for the FZR600 (see Chapter 2 and this Chapter's Specifications).

4 On UK FZR750 models, the connecting rod bolts must be discarded and replaced with new ones whenever they're removed. **Note: New connecting rod bolts may be tightened to measure bearing clearance with Plastigauge, then installed and run in the engine.** Connecting rod bolt stretch must be measured during the tightening process. Measure and record the length of the bolts before tightening (measure at several points on the end of the bolt and calculate the average of the measurements). Tighten the bolts to the initial torque, then to the final torque. Measure the length of each bolt after tightening to calculate bolt stretch; if it has stretched more than the maximum listed in this Chapter's Specifications, replace the bolt. If it hasn't yet stretched the minimum amount listed in the Specifications, keep tightening until bolt stretch is within the specified range (each 10-degrees of tightening increases bolt length by approximately 0.022 mm/0.00087 inch). Never loosen the bolts to bring bolt stretch within the specified range.

27 Camshaft and starter chains and guides - removal, inspection and installation

⚠ **Warning: Although the cam chain can be cut and reconnected, this should be done by a qualified Yamaha technician with the proper service tool. Chain separation while the engine is running may cause engine seizure, leading to loss of control of the motorcycle. Yamaha replacement cam chains may be equipped with a master (soft) link; if you're not experienced with this type of chain, have the soft link connected by a qualified Yamaha technician.**

Removal

1 Remove the engine (see Section 5).
2 Separate the crankcase halves (see Section 22).
3 Remove the crankshaft (see Section 25).
4 Remove the chains from the crankshaft.

5 The cam chain front guide can be lifted from the cylinder head (see illustration 9.8).
6 The cam chain rear guide is held in position by two Allen bolts (see illustration). Separate the crankcase halves (see Section 22), then remove the Allen bolts and lift out the guide.
7 The starter chain guide is held in place by two hex-head bolts (see illustration). Separate the crankcase halves (see Section 22), remove the starter clutch (see Section 31), then remove the Allen bolts and lift out the guide.

Inspection

8 Check the chains for binding and obvious damage. If these conditions are visible, or if the chains appear to be stretched, replace them.
9 Check the guides for deep grooves, cracking and other obvious damage, replacing them if necessary.

Installation

10 Installation of these components is the reverse of the removal procedure, with the following additions:
 a) When installing the rear cam chain guide or the starter chain guide, apply a non-hardening thread locking compound to the threads of the bolts. Tighten the bolts to the torque listed in this Chapter's Specifications.
 b) Apply engine oil to the faces of the guides and to the chain.

27.6 The cam chain rear guide is held in place by two Allen bolts (arrowed)

27.7 The starter chain guide is held in place by two hex bolts (arrowed)

3•38 FZR750/1000 engine, clutch and transmission

28.4 Lift out the mainshaft (upper arrow), then the driveshaft (lower arrow)

28.6 Install a new half-circle retaining ring; center the rings in the grooves and seat them securely

28 Transmission shafts - removal and installation

Removal

1 If you plan to remove the engine sprocket, it will be easier to remove the sprocket nut while the engine is still in the frame (see Chapter 7).

2 Remove the engine and clutch, then separate the case halves (see Sections 5, 19 and 22).

3 If you haven't already done so, remove the long clutch pushrod from the mainshaft (see Section 19).

4 Lift out the mainshaft, then the driveshaft (see illustration). If they are stuck, use a soft-face hammer and gently tap on the bearings on the ends of the shafts to free them. Lift out the half-circle retainer rings.

5 Refer to Section 29 for information pertaining to transmission shaft service and Section 30 for information pertaining to the shift cam and forks.

Installation

6 Install new half-circle retaining rings in their grooves in the crankcase (see illustration).

7 Carefully lower each shaft into place. The pins in the bearing outer races must engage with the locating holes in the crankcase, and the grooves in the crankcase and the ball bearing outer races must engage with the retaining rings (see illustrations).

Caution: If the pins are out of position and you try to force the crankcase halves together by tightening the bolts, the crankcase halves will crack and will have to be replaced.

8 The remainder of installation is the reverse of removal. Make sure the clutch pushrod seal and driveshaft end seal are in position (see illustration).

9 Make sure the gears are in the neutral position. When they are, it will be possible to rotate the transmission shafts independently of each other.

29 Transmission shafts - disassembly, inspection and reassembly

Note: *When disassembling the transmission shafts, place the parts on a long rod or thread a wire through them to keep them in order and facing the proper direction. Some of the steps require a press. If you don't have one, it may be more practical to have a Yamaha dealer disassemble and reassemble the shafts.*

1 FZR750 models have a six-speed transmission; FZR1000 models have a five-

28.7a At the engine sprocket end, the bearings have pins that lie flat against the case (arrowed)

28.7b At the clutch end of the driveshaft, the small bearing has a pin that lies flat against the case

28.8 Install the transmission seal and clutch pushrod seal

FZR750/1000 engine, clutch and transmission 3•39

29.2a Five-speed transmission gears and shafts - exploded view

1 Half-circle bearing retainer
2 Ball bearing
3 First wheel gear
4 Fourth wheel gear
5 Snap-ring
6 Thrust washer
7 Third wheel gear
8 Fifth wheel gear
9 Bushings
10 Driveshaft
11 Second wheel gear
12 Ball bearing
13 Collar
14 Snap-ring
15 Oil seal
16 Engine sprocket
17 Lockwasher
18 Nut
19 Ball bearing
20 Mainshaft
21 Fourth pinion gear
22 Third pinion gear
23 Plain washer
24 Fifth pinion gear
25 Second pinion gear
26 Ball bearing

29.2b Take the ball bearing off

29.3a Slide off the first wheel gear . . .

29.3b . . . the bushing will have to be pressed off if it's worn or damaged

29.3c . . . slide off the fourth wheel gear

29.4a Remove the snap-ring . . .

speed. The two designs are the same except that the six-speed has an additional gear on the driveshaft and a paired gear on the mainshaft where the five-speed has only a single gear. Remove the shafts from the case (see Section 28).

Five-speed transmission

Driveshaft disassembly

2 Slide the bearing off the driveshaft **(see illustrations)**.
3 Slide off the first wheel gear and fourth wheel gear **(see illustrations)**.
4 Remove the snap-ring and thrust washer **(see illustrations)**.

3•40 FZR750/1000 engine, clutch and transmission

29.4b . . . and thrust washer

29.5a Slide off the third wheel gear . . .

29.5b . . . and fifth wheel gear (this bushing is also a press fit)

5 Slide the third wheel gear and fifth wheel gear off the shaft **(see illustrations)**.

6 If you haven't already done so, remove the nut, lockwasher and engine sprocket from the other end of the shaft **(see illustrations)**.

7 Remove the oil seal and bearing snap-ring (if equipped) from the shaft **(see illustration 29.2a and the accompanying illustration)**.

8 Press the collar, bearing and second wheel gear off the shaft **(see illustration)**.

Driveshaft inspection

9 Wash all of the components in clean solvent and dry them off. Rotate the ball bearing on the shaft, feeling for tightness, rough spots and excessive looseness and listening for noises. If any of these conditions are found, replace the bearing with a press.

10 Check the ball bearing that was removed from the other end of the shaft and replace it if it has any of the conditions described in Step 6. The bearing seal should be replaced if oil has been leaking from it; it's a good idea to replace the seal whenever the engine is disassembled this far.

11 Check the gear teeth for cracking and other obvious damage. Check the gear bushings and the surface in the inner diameter of each gear for scoring or heat discoloration. If the gear or bushing is damaged, replace it.

12 Inspect the dogs and the dog holes in the gears for excessive wear **(see illustrations)**.

Replace the paired gears as a set if necessary.

13 Place the shaft in V-blocks and check runout with a dial indicator. Replace the shaft if runout exceeds the value listed in this Chapter's Specifications.

Driveshaft reassembly

14 During reassembly, always use new snap-rings. Lubricate the components with engine oil before assembling them.

15 Assembly is the reverse of the disassembly procedure with the following additions:

a) *The sharp side of the snap-ring faces away from the thrust washer; the rounded side faces toward the thrust washer.*

29.6a If you haven't already done so, flatten the lockwasher tab (arrowed) . . .

29.6b . . . and remove the nut

29.7 Remove the seal

29.8 Press off the collar, bearing and second wheel gear

29.12a Pay attention to the shift dog corners (arrowed); if worn, the transmission will jump out of gear . . .

29.12b . . . also check the edges of the gear slots (arrowed); if they're rounded off, replace the gear

FZR750/1000 engine, clutch and transmission 3•41

29.15a Place the second wheel gear on the driveshaft, then press on the bearing and collar . . .

29.15b . . . the installed parts should look like this; make sure the gears spin freely

29.15c The assembled driveshaft should look like this

b) Press the collar, bearing and second wheel gear onto the shaft together **(see illustrations)**.

c) Check the positions of the gears on the assembled shaft to make sure they are correct **(see illustration)**.

Mainshaft disassembly

16 To disassemble the mainshaft, refer to the accompanying **illustrations**.

Mainshaft inspection

17 Refer to Steps 9 through 13 above to inspect the mainshaft components. If the ball bearing and bushing need to be replaced, remove them with a press **(see illustration)**; otherwise, they can be left on the shaft.

29.16a Take the bearing off the mainshaft

29.16b Support the fifth pinion gear and press the shaft out of second pinion gear . . .

29.16c . . . then take off second pinion gear . . .

29.16d . . . and fifth pinion gear

29.16e Slide the bushing off . . .

29.16f . . . and remove the plain washer

29.16g Slide off third pinion gear

29.16h Remove the snap-ring . . .

3•42 FZR750/1000 engine, clutch and transmission

29.16i ... and thrust washer

29.16j Slide off fourth pinion gear

29.17 If the bushing or ball bearing is worn, press it off the shaft; if the gear is worn or damaged the entire shaft must be replaced

Mainshaft reassembly

18 Assembly is the reverse of the disassembly procedure, with the following additions:
a) Use new snap-rings and lubricate the components with engine oil before assembling them.
b) Press the second pinion gear and fifth pinion gear into the shaft together (see illustration). Be sure the gears turn freely after installation; if they don't, they may have been pressed on too far.
c) Check the assembled shaft to make sure the gears are in the correct positions (see illustration).

Six-speed transmission
Driveshaft disassembly

19 Slide the bearing off the driveshaft (see illustration).
20 Slide off the first wheel gear and fifth wheel gear.
21 Remove the snap ring and thrust washer.

22 Slide the fourth wheel gear, third wheel gear and sixth wheel gear off the shaft.
23 If you haven't already done so, remove the nut, lockwasher and engine sprocket from the other end of the shaft.
24 Remove the oil seal from the shaft.
25 Press the collar, bearing and second wheel gear off the shaft.

29.18a Press fifth pinion gear and second pinion gear onto the shaft and make sure they turn freely

29.18b The assembled mainshaft should look like this

1 Half-circle bearing retainer
2 Ball bearing
3 First wheel gear
4 Fifth wheel gear
5 Snap-ring
6 Thrust washer
7 Fourth wheel gear
8 Third wheel gear
9 Sixth wheel gear
10 Plain bearings
11 Driveshaft
12 Second wheel gear
13 Collar
14 Snap-ring
15 Oil seal
16 Engine sprocket
17 Lockwasher
18 Nut
19 Mainshaft
20 Fifth pinion gear
21 Third/fourth pinion gear
22 Plain washer
23 Plain bearing
24 Sixth pinion gear
25 Second pinion gear

29.19 Six-speed transmission - exploded view

FZR750/1000 engine, clutch and transmission 3•43

30.3 Remove the shift cam retaining bolt

30.4 Pull out the guide bar and remove the shift forks

Driveshaft inspection

26 Refer to Steps 9 through 13 above to inspect the driveshaft and its components.

Driveshaft reassembly

27 Assembly is the reverse of the disassembly procedure, with the following additions:
  a) Use new snap-rings and lubricate the components with engine oil before assembling them. The sharp side of the snap-ring faces away from the thrust washer; the rounded side is toward the thrust washer.
  b) Press the collar, bearing and second wheel gear onto the shaft together **(see illustrations 29.15a and 29.15b)**.

Mainshaft disassembly

28 This is essentially the same as for five-speed models, except that the gear next to second pinion gear is the sixth pinion gear, and a combined third-fourth pinion gear is installed in the same location as the third pinion gear on five-speed models.

Mainshaft inspection

29 Perform Steps 9 through 13 above to inspect the mainshaft components.

Mainshaft reassembly

30 Assembly is the reverse of the disassembly procedure, with the following additions:

  a) Use new snap-rings and lubricate the components with engine oil before assembling them.
  b) Press the second pinion gear and sixth pinion gear into the shaft together. Be sure the gears turn freely after installation; if they don't, they may have been pressed on too far.
  c) Check the assembled shaft to make sure the gears are in the correct positions.

30 Shift cam and forks - removal, inspection and installation

Removal

1 Remove the engine and separate the crankcase halves (see Sections 5 and 22).
2 Remove the external shift mechanism (see Section 21).
3 Remove the shift cam retaining bolt **(see illustration)**.
4 Support the shift forks and pull the guide bar out **(see illustration)**.
5 Pull the shift cam out of the case **(see illustration)**.

Inspection

6 This is the same as for FZR600 models (see Chapter 2 for details). Refer to **illustration 22.12a** in this Chapter.

Installation

7 Installation is the reverse of removal, noting the following points:
  a) Lubricate all parts with engine oil before installing them.
  b) Use the letters on the forks to position them correctly. The forks are lettered L, C and R, starting from the left side of the engine **(see illustration)**.
  c) Engage the follower pin on each shift fork with the shift cam as you pass the guide bar through the fork. Position the shift cam and forks in the neutral position **(see illustrations)**.
  d) Apply a non-permanent locking agent to the threads of the shift cam retaining bolt and tighten it to the torque listed in this Chapter's Specifications.

31 Starter clutch and idle gears - removal, inspection and installation

1 The starter clutch on FZR750 models is removed and installed in the same manner as for FZR1000 models. Disassembly and inspection are the same as for the FZR600 (see Chapter 2 for details).

30.5 Slide the shift cam out

30.7a The letters on the forks indicate left, center and right

30.7b Engage the pins on the shift forks with the grooves in the shift cam

3•44 FZR750/1000 engine, clutch and transmission

31.4a Unbolt the oil plug plate . . .

31.4b . . . take off the plate and gasket . . .

31.4c . . . and pull out the spray nozzle

31.5 Remove the shaft and lift out the starter idle gears

31.6a Remove the bearing retainer bolts . . .

Removal

2 Remove the engine, separate the crankcase halves and remove the transmission shafts (see Sections 5, 22 and 28).
3 Remove the oil line above the starter clutch and idle gears (see illustrations 23.2b and 23.2c).
4 Remove the plug plate and gasket, then pull the oil nozzle out of the case (see illustrations).
5 Pull out the shaft and remove the starter idle gears (see illustration).
6 Remove the bolts and take off the retainer that secures the alternator drive shaft bearing (see illustrations).
7 Take the bearing out of its bore (see illustration). Note: *If the bearing is tight in its bore, it will be necessary to remove the alternator driveshaft and bearing together with a slide hammer* (see illustration).
8 Support the starter clutch with one hand and pull out the alternator driveshaft with the other (see illustration).
9 Disengage the starter clutch from the chain and lift it out of the engine (see illustration).

Disassembly, inspection and reassembly (FZR1000 models)

10 Lift the starter sprocket and starter clutch gear out of the starter clutch (see illustrations).

31.6b . . . and lift off the retainer

31.7 Take out the bearing; if tight, remove the bearing and alternator drive shaft with a slide hammer

31.8 Pull out the alternator drive shaft

31.9 Disengage the starter clutch from the chain and lift it out

31.10a Lift the starter sprocket out of the starter clutch gear . . .

FZR750/1000 engine, clutch and transmission 3•45

31.10b ... and lift the starter clutch gear out of the starter clutch

31.12 Place the gear in the starter clutch and try to turn it in both directions; it should go one way only

31.14 If the bearing in the crankcase is worn or damaged, have it replaced by a Yamaha dealer

31.15a Align the pin on the nozzle with the slot in the case (arrowed), then push the nozzle in

31.15b Position the tab on the plug plate in the crankcase slot (arrowed)

31.15c The starter clutch and idle gears should look like this when they're installed

11 Check the sprocket and gears for chipped or worn teeth. Check the idle gear shaft and its bearing surface inside the gear for wear or damage. If any defects are found, replace the affected parts.

12 Place the gear in the starter clutch and try to turn it in both directions **(see illustration)**. The gear should turn in one direction only. If it goes both ways or neither way, replace the starter clutch.

13 Check the starter clutch rollers for wear or damage. Replace the starter clutch if defects are found.

14 Place the bearing on the alternator driveshaft. Rotate the bearing and check for roughness, looseness or noise. If it's defective, replace it. Also check the ball bearing in the case **(see illustration)**. Have the bearing replaced by a Yamaha dealer if it's worn or damaged.

Installation

15 Installation is the reverse of the removal steps, with the following additions:
 a) Be sure the pin on the oil spray nozzle fits into the groove in the case and the tab on the plug plate fits into the slot in the case **(see illustrations)**.
 b) Use non-permanent thread locking agent on the threads of the bearing retainer bolts for the alternator shaft.
 c) Check to be sure the idle gear and starter clutch gear are correctly engaged after installation **(see illustration)**.

32 Oil cooler and lines - removal and installation

1 To replace the oil lines, drain the engine oil and remove fairing panels as needed for access.

2 If you're working on an FZR1000, remove the oil line fitting bolts at the engine, the retaining bracket bolts at the engine and the banjo bolts at the cooler **(see illustrations)**.

3 If you're working on an FZR750, remove the oil line banjo bolts from the front of the engine just below the oil filter.

4 Detach the cooler from its mountings and lift it out.

32.2a Unbolt the oil line fittings from the sides of the engine (FZR1000) ...

32.2b ... unbolt the retainer brackets from the engine ...

32.2c ... and remove the banjo bolts at the oil cooler (arrowed)

33 Initial start-up after overhaul

1 Make sure the engine oil level is correct and the cooling system is full, then remove the spark plugs from the engine. Place the engine kill switch in the Off position and unplug the primary (low tension) wires from the coils.
2 Turn on the key switch and crank the engine over with the starter several times to build up oil pressure. Reinstall the spark plugs, connect the wires and turn the switch to On.
3 Make sure there is fuel in the tank, then turn the fuel tap to the On position and operate the choke.
4 Start the engine and allow it to run at a moderately fast idle until it reaches operating temperature.
5 Check carefully for oil leaks and make sure the transmission and controls, especially the brakes, function properly before road testing the machine. Refer to Section 34 for the recommended break-in procedure.
6 Upon completion of the road test, and after the engine has cooled down completely, recheck the valve clearances (see Chapter 1).

34 Recommended break-in procedure

1 Any rebuilt engine needs time to break-in, even if parts have been installed in their original locations. For this reason, treat the machine gently for the first few miles to make sure oil has circulated throughout the engine and any new parts installed have started to seat.
2 Even greater care is necessary if the engine has been rebored or a new crankshaft has been installed. In the case of a rebore, the engine will have to be broken in as if the machine were new. This means greater use of the transmission and a restraining hand on the throttle until at least 500 miles (800 Km) have been covered. There's no point in keeping to any set speed limit - the main idea is to keep from lugging (labouring) the engine and to gradually increase performance until the 500 mile (800 Km) mark is reached. These recommendations can be lessened to an extent when only a new crankshaft is installed. Experience is the best guide, since it's easy to tell when an engine is running freely. The following recommendations, which Yamaha provides for new motorcycles, can be used as a guide:
   a) *0 to 90 miles (0 to 150 km): Keep engine speed below 5,000 rpm. Turn off the engine after each hour of operation and let it cool for 5 to 10 minutes. Vary the engine speed and don't use full throttle.*
   b) *90 to 300 miles (150 to 500 km): Don't run the engine for long periods above 6,500 rpm. Rev the engine freely through the gears, but don't use full throttle.*
   c) *300 to 600 miles (500 to 1000 km): Don't use full throttle for prolonged periods and don't cruise at speeds above 8,000 rpm.*
   d) *After 600 miles (1000 km): Full throttle can be used. Don't exceed maximum recommended engine speed (redline).*
3 If a lubrication failure is suspected, stop the engine immediately and try to find the cause. If an engine is run without oil, even for a short period of time, severe damage will occur.

Chapter 4
Cooling system

Contents

Coolant level check .... See 'Daily (pre-ride) checks	Radiator cap - check 2
Coolant reservoir - removal and installation 3	Radiator - removal and installation 7
Coolant temperature gauge and sender unit - check and	Thermostat - removal, check and installation 6
replacement 5	Water jacket joint (FZR600 models) - removal and installation 9
Cooling fan and thermostatic switch - check and replacement 4	Water jacket joints (FZR750/1000 models) - removal and
Cooling system check .... See Chapter 1	installation 10
Cooling system draining, flushing and refilling .... See Chapter 1	Water pump - check, removal, disassembly, inspection and
General information 1	installation 8

Degrees of difficulty

Easy, suitable for novice with little experience	Fairly easy, suitable for beginner with some experience	Fairly difficult, suitable for competent DIY mechanic	Difficult, suitable for experienced DIY mechanic	Very difficult, suitable for expert DIY or professional

Specifications

General
Coolant type	See Chapter 1
Mixture ratio	See Chapter 1
Cooling system capacity	See Chapter 1
Radiator cap pressure rating	
FZR600	
1989 models	0.69 to 0.96 bar (10 to 14 psi)
1990-on models	0.93 to 1.24 bar (13.5 to 18 psi)
FZR750/1000	
1987 and 1988 models	0.76 to 1.03 bar (11 to 15 psi)
1989-on models	0.93 to 1.24 bar (13.5 to 18 psi)
Thermostat rating	
Opening temperature	80 to 84-degrees C (176 to 183-degrees F)
Fully open at	95-degrees C (203-degrees F)
Valve travel (when fully open)	Not less than 8 mm (5/16 inch)
Fan thermoswitch continuity	
Heating up	
Below 98-degrees C (208.4-degrees F)	No continuity
Above 105 ± 3-degrees C (221 ± 5.4-degrees F)	Continuity
Cooling down	
105 to 98-degrees C (221 to 208.4-degrees F)	Continuity
Below 98-degrees C (208.4-degrees F)	No continuity

Torque specifications
Coolant tube bolts	10 Nm (7.2 ft-lbs)
Thermostat housing cover bolts	10 Nm (7.2 ft-lbs)
Water jacket joint bolts	10 Nm (7.2 ft-lbs)
Water pump bolts	10 Nm (7.2 ft-lbs)
Water pump cover bolts	10 Nm (7.2 ft-lbs)
Cooling fan thermoswitch	8 Nm (5.9 ft-lbs)
Temperature gauge sender unit	
1987 and 1988 FZR1000, US FZR750	14 Nm (10.3 ft-lbs)
All FZR600 models, UK FZR750, 1989-on FZR1000	15 Nm (11 ft-lbs)

4•2 Cooling system

1 Radiator
2 Water pump
3 Thermostat housing
4 Thermostat valve
5 Pressure cap

1.1a Cooling system details (1989 and 1990 FZR600 models shown; later models similar)

1 Radiator
2 Water pump
3 Thermostat housing
4 Thermostat
5 Pressure cap

1.1b Cooling system details (US FZR750 and all 1987 and 1988 FZR1000 models)

1 General information

The models covered by this manual are equipped with a liquid cooling system which utilizes a water/antifreeze mixture to carry away excess heat produced during the combustion process **(see illustrations)**. The cylinders are surrounded by water jackets, through which the coolant is circulated by the water pump. The pump is mounted to the left side of the crankcase and driven by the oil pump shaft. The coolant passes through hoses and tubes, around the cylinders and to the thermostat. When the engine is warm, the thermostat opens and allows coolant to flow down into the radiator (which is mounted on the frame downtubes to take advantage of maximum air flow), where it is cooled by the passing air, routed through another hose and back to the water pump, where the cycle is repeated.

An electric fan, mounted behind the radiator and automatically controlled by a thermostatic switch, provides a flow of cooling air through the radiator when the motorcycle is not moving.

The coolant temperature sender unit, threaded into the radiator, senses the temperature of the coolant and controls the coolant temperature gauge on the instrument cluster.

On all UK FZR750 models and all 1991-on FZR 600 and 1000 models, coolant is routed around the oil filter adapter on the front of the crankcase and then back into the cooling system.

The entire system is sealed and pressurized. The pressure is controlled by a valve which is part of the radiator cap. By pressurizing the coolant, the boiling point is raised, which prevents premature boiling of the coolant. An overflow hose, connected between the radiator and reservoir tank, directs coolant to the tank when the radiator cap valve is opened by excessive pressure. The coolant is automatically siphoned back to the radiator as the engine cools.

Many cooling system inspection and service procedures are considered part of routine maintenance and are included in 'Daily (pre-ride) checks at the beginning of this Manual and Chapter 1.

⚠ *Warning: Do not allow antifreeze to come in contact with your skin or painted surfaces of the motorcycle. Rinse off spills immediately with plenty of water. Antifreeze is highly toxic if ingested. Never leave antifreeze lying around in an open container or in puddles on the floor; children and pets are attracted by its sweet smell and may drink it. Check with local authorities (councils) about disposing of used antifreeze. Many communities*

Cooling system 4•3

have collection centers which will see that antifreeze is disposed of safely.

⚠️ **Warning:** Do not remove the pressure cap from the thermostat housing when the engine and radiator are hot. Scalding hot coolant and steam may be blown out under pressure, which could cause serious injury. To open the pressure cap, remove the right side panel on the inside of the fairing. When the engine has cooled, lift up the panel and place a thick rag, like a towel, over the radiator cap; slowly rotate the cap counterclockwise (anti-clockwise) to the first stop. This procedure allows any residual pressure to escape. When the steam has stopped escaping, press down on the cap while turning counterclockwise (anti-clockwise) and remove it.

2 Radiator cap - check

If problems such as overheating and loss of coolant occur, check the entire system as described in Chapter 1. The radiator cap opening pressure should be checked by a dealer service department or service station equipped with the special tester required to do the job. If the cap is defective, replace it with a new one.

3 Coolant reservoir - removal and installation

1 Remove the seat and the right side cover (left for UK FZR750) (see Chapter 9).
2 Disconnect the coolant hoses from the reservoir and catch any escaped coolant.
3 Remove the reservoir mounting screws and take it out.
4 Installation is the reverse of the removal steps.

4 Cooling fan and thermostatic switch - check and replacement

Check

1 If the engine is overheating and the cooling fan isn't coming on, first remove the seat or rear side cover (as applicable) and check the fuses. If the fuse is blown, check the fan circuit for a short to ground/earth (see the *Wiring diagrams* at the end of this book). Check that the battery is fully charged.
2 If the fuses are all good, check for proper continuity at the red and brown wire terminals of the ignition main switch connector (see Chapter 10). Replace the switch if necessary and recheck the fan.

1 Pressure cap
2 Engine-mounted coolant tube
3 Thermostat housing
4 Thermostat
5 Water jacket joint
6 Reservoir tank
7 Water pump outlet tube
8 Water pump
9 Water pump inlet hose
10 Radiator
11 Temperature sender
12 Thermoswitch (for cooling fan)

1.1c Cooling system details (1989-on FZR1000 models; UK FZR750 models similar) - part one

1 Pressure cap
2 Thermoswitch (for cooling fan)
3 Temperature sender
4 Radiator
5 Fan
6 Water pump outlet tube
7 Water pump

1.1d Cooling system details (1989-on FZR1000 models; UK FZR750 models similar) - part two

4•4 Cooling system

4.3 Connect a battery directly to the fan terminals

1 Blue wire terminal
2 Black wire terminal

3 If the fuses and main switch are good, follow the wiring harness from the fan motor to the electrical connector and unplug the connector **(see illustration)**. Using two jumper wires, apply battery voltage to the terminals in the fan motor side of the electrical connector. If the fan doesn't work, replace the motor.

4 If the fan does come on, the problem lies in the fan thermoswitch or the wiring that connects the components. Remove the jumper wires and reconnect the electrical connector to the fan.

5 Unplug the electrical connector from the fan thermoswitch on the thermostat housing or radiator **(see illustrations)**. Connect the terminals in the wiring harness together with a jumper wire. If the fan comes on, the circuit to the motor is good and the switch is defective.

6 Before replacing the switch, test it. Unscrew the switch and immerse it in a pan of water (but keep the electrical terminals out of the water) **(see illustration)**. Connect an ohmmeter between the terminals, heat the water and compare the readings with those listed in this Chapter's Specifications. Let the

4.5a The thermoswitch and gauge sender on 1987/1988 FZR750/1000 and all FZR600 are mounted on the thermostat housing (FZR600 shown)

1 Fan thermoswitch
2 Temperature sender
3 Ground (earth) wire

water cool and note the ohmmeter readings as it cools If the readings aren't within the specified ranges, replace the switch.

Replacement

Fan motor

⚠️ *Warning: The engine must be completely cool before beginning this procedure.*

1 Radiator
2 Fan assembly
3 Filler neck
4 Pressure cap
5 Stone shield
6 Radiator outlet hose
7 Radiator outlet tube
8 O-ring (always replace)
9 Radiator inlet hose

4.5b The thermoswitch and gauge sender on 1989-on FZR750/1000 are mounted on the radiator

1 Fan thermoswitch
2 Ground (earth) wire
3 Temperature sender

7 Disconnect the cable from the negative terminal of the battery and remove the radiator (see Section 7).
8 Remove the three bolts or nuts securing the fan bracket to the radiator **(see illustrations)**. Separate the fan and bracket from the radiator.
9 If you're working on an FZR600, remove the bolt that retains the blades to the fan motor shaft **(see illustration 4.8a or 4.8b)** and

4.6 Place the thermoswitch in water, but don't get the terminals wet

1 Thermoswitch
2 Water
3 Thermometer

4.8a Radiator and fan details - 1989 and 1990 FZR600 models

Cooling system 4•5

4.8b Radiator and fan details - 1991-on FZR600 models

1. Radiator
2. Fan assembly
3. Filler neck
4. Pressure cap
5. Radiator outlet hose
6. Radiator inlet hose
7. Oil cooler (1991-on UK models)
8. Oil cooler outlet hose (1991-on UK models)
9. Oil cooler inlet hose (1991-on UK models)

4.8c Radiator and fan details - 1989-on FZR1000 models (FZR750 and earlier FZR1000 models similar)

1. Radiator inlet hoses and tube
2. Fan and motor assembly
3. Radiator
4. Radiator outlet hose
5. Stone shield
6. Pressure cap
7. O-ring (always replace)

4•6 Cooling system

4.8d The fan bracket is secured by three nuts or screws

On FZR600 models, one screw is located inside the fan shroud (lower arrow)

remove the fan blade assembly from the motor.
10 If you're working on an FZR600, remove the screws that attach the fan motor to the bracket **(see illustration 4.8a or 4.8b)** and detach the motor from the bracket.
11 Installation is the reverse of the removal steps.

Thermoswitch

⚠️ *Warning: The engine must be completely cool before beginning this procedure.*

12 Prepare the new switch by wrapping the new threads with Teflon tape or by coating the threads with RTV sealant.
13 Disconnect its electrical connector and unscrew the switch from the thermostat housing or radiator.
14 Quickly install the new switch, tightening it to the specified torque.
15 Connect the electrical connector to the switch. Check, and if necessary, add coolant to the system (see 'Daily (pre-ride) checks at the beginning of this Manual).

5 Coolant temperature gauge and sender unit - check and replacement

Check

1 If the engine has been overheating but the coolant temperature gauge hasn't been indicating a hotter than normal condition, begin with a check of the coolant level (see 'Daily (pre-ride) checks at the beginning of this Manual). If it's low, add the recommended type of coolant and be sure to locate the source of the leak.
2 Check the fuse and ignition switch (see Chapter 10) and replace them if necessary. Check that the battery is fully charged.

1987 and 1988 models

3 Remove the upper and right fairings (see Chapter 9).
4 Remove the headlight assembly (see Chapter 10).

5 Locate the coolant temperature sender unit, which is screwed into the thermostat housing **(see illustration 4.5a)**. Disconnect the electrical connector from the sender unit, turn the ignition key to the On position (don't crank the engine over) and note the temperature gauge - it should read Cold.
6 Turn the key off and connect one end of a jumper wire to the sender unit wire and ground/earth the other end. Turn the key back on and watch the needle on the temperature gauge; it should swing over to the Hot mark.
Caution: Turn the key off as soon as the needle moves to the Hot mark or the gauge may be damaged.
7 If the gauge passes both of these tests, but doesn't operate correctly under normal riding conditions, the temperature sender unit is probably defective and must be replaced. Before replacing, test the sender in the same way as the fan thermoswitch (see Section 4) and compare the ohmmeter readings to those listed in this Chapter's Specifications.
8 If the gauge didn't respond to the tests properly, either the wire to the gauge is bad or the gauge itself is defective.

1989 and later models

9 Test the temperature sender in the same way as the fan thermoswitch (see Section 4) and compare the ohmmeter readings to those listed in this Chapter's Specifications. Replace the sender if it's defective.
10 Refer to the Wiring diagrams at the end of Chapter 10 and locate the brown wire and black wire for the temperature gauge in the instrument cluster connector.
11 Connect a DC voltmeter with a 0 to 20-volt range between the wires. On the harness side of the connector (positive meter lead to brown wire terminal, and negative to black) and turn the ignition switch to On. The voltmeter should indicate approximately 12 volts. If it does, the wiring to the gauge is good and the connections at the gauge or the gauge itself are probably bad. If there's a low reading or no voltage at all, there's a break or poor connection in the wiring to the gauge.

6.5a It may be easier to remove the housing mounting bolt and pull it away from the harness for access

Replacement

Sender unit

⚠️ *Warning: The engine must be completely cool before beginning this procedure.*

12 Prepare the new sender unit by wrapping the threads with Teflon tape or coating them with silicone sealant.
13 Disconnect its electrical connector and unscrew the sender unit from the thermostat housing or radiator and quickly install the new unit, tightening it to the specified torque.
14 Connect the electrical connector to the sender unit. Check, and if necessary, add coolant to the system (see 'Daily (pre-ride) checks at the beginning of this Manual).

Temperature gauge

15 Refer to Chapter 10 for the coolant temperature gauge replacement procedure.

6 Thermostat - removal, check and installation

⚠️ *Warning: The engine must be completely cool before beginning this procedure.*

Removal

1 If the thermostat is functioning properly, the coolant temperature gauge should rise to the normal operating temperature quickly and then stay there, only rising above the normal position occasionally when the engine gets abnormally hot. If the engine does not reach normal operating temperature quickly, or if it overheats, the thermostat should be removed and checked, or replaced with a new one.
2 Refer to Chapter 1 and drain the cooling system.

FZR600 models

3 Remove the fuel tank cover and fairings (see Chapter 9).
4 Remove the fuel tank and air filter housing (see Chapter 5).
5 Remove the thermostat housing cover **(see illustrations)**. Note that the rearward bolt secures a ground/earth wire.

6.5b Remove the housing cover bolts; the rearward bolt secures a ground (earth) wire (arrowed)

Cooling system 4•7

1 Radiator hose
2 Thermostat housing cover
3 Thermostat
4 Thermostat housing
5 Coolant hose
6 Radiator hose
7 Coolant pipe
8 Coolant pipe
9 Water jacket joint
10 O-rings
11 O-ring
12 Upper coolant tube
13 O-ring
14 Water pump cover (1991-on models)
15 O-ring
16 Water pump housing
17 O-ring

1989 and 1990 models

6.5c Thermostat and water pump details (FZR600 models)

6 Note the position of the relief hole, then lift out the thermostat **(see illustration)**.

1987 and 1988 FZR750/1000 models

7 Remove the left and right fairings and the side covers (see Chapter 9).
8 Remove the fuel tank and air filter housing (see Chapter 5).
9 Remove the filler neck/thermostat cover from the thermostat housing **(see illustration 1.1b)**.
10 Note the position of the relief hole (it should be upward), then lift out the thermostat.
11 If you're working on a model with a separate cover O-ring, check it and replace it if its condition is in doubt. It's a good idea to replace the O-ring as a matter of course.

1989 and later FZR750/1000 models

12 Remove the left, right and front fairings (see Chapter 9).
13 Remove the seat (see Chapter 9).
14 Remove the fuel tank. Remove the air filter housing (FZR750 models) or carburetors (FZR1000 models) (see Chapter 5).
15 If necessary for access, remove the outlet water jacket joint (see Section 10), together with the thermostat housing. On FZR750 models, disconnect the electrical connectors

6.6 The relief hole (upper arrow) must align with the protrusion on the thermostat housing (lower arrow)

4•8 Cooling system

6.16a Remove the thermostat housing bolts (arrowed)

for the ignition coils, handlebar switches, clutch switch and ignition switch.
16 Unbolt the thermostat cover from the housing **(see illustrations)**.
17 Note the position of the relief hole, then lift out the thermostat **(see illustrations)**.

Check

18 Remove any coolant deposits, then visually check the thermostat for corrosion, cracks and other damage. If it was open when it was removed, the thermostat is defective.
19 To check the thermostat operation, submerge it in a container of water along with a thermometer. The thermostat should be suspended so it does not touch the sides of the container.

⚠ *Warning: Antifreeze is poisonous. Do not use a cooking pan to test the thermostat.*

20 Gradually heat the water in the container with a hot plate or stove and check the temperature when the thermostat first starts to open.
21 Compare the opening temperature to the values listed in this Chapter's Specifications.
22 Continue heating the water until the valve is fully open.
23 Measure how far the thermostat valve has opened and compare to the value listed in this Chapter's Specifications.
24 If these specifications are not met, or if the thermostat doesn't open while the water is heated, replace it with a new one.

Installation
25 Install the thermostat into the housing, making sure the relief hole is positioned correctly.
26 If you're working on a model with a separate O-ring, install a new one in the groove.
27 Place the cover on the housing and install the bolts, tightening them securely.
28 The remainder of installation is the reverse of the removal steps. Fill the cooling system with the recommended coolant (see Chapter 1).

1 Thermostat housing cover
2 Thermostat
3 Thermostat housing
4 Outlet water jacket joint
5 Inlet water jacket joint
6 Water pump outlet tube
7 Bearing
8 Oil seal
9 Dowel
10 Mechanical seal
11 Impeller shaft
12 Sealing washer

6.16b Thermostat and water pump details - 1989-on FZR1000 models (1989-on FZR750 models similar)

6.17a The relief hole in the thermostat (arrowed) is upward when the thermostat is installed...

6.17b ...its bridge (lower arrows) aligns with the slots in the thermostat housing (upper arrows)

Cooling system 4•9

7.6a Loosen the hose clamp and disconnect the upper (inlet) hose ...

7.6b ... and the lower (outlet) hose (arrowed)

7.7 Unbolt the radiator brace from the radiator and from the frame

7 Radiator - removal and installation

Warning: *The engine must be completely cool before beginning this procedure.*

1 Support the bike securely so it can't be knocked over during this procedure.
2 Drain the cooling system (see Chapter 1).

FZR600 models

3 Remove the fuel tank cover and fairings (see Chapter 9).
4 Remove the fuel tank and air filter housing (see Chapter 5).
5 Follow the wiring from the fan motor to the electrical connector and disconnect it.
6 Loosen the radiator hose clamps **(see illustrations)**. Work the hoses free from the fittings, taking care not to damage the fittings in the process. Disconnect the oil cooler hose on 1991-on models.
7 Remove the radiator mounting bolts **(see illustration)**. Take the radiator out.

US FZR750, all 1987 and 1988 FZR1000 models

8 Remove the fairings, engine grille and side covers (see Chapter 9).
9 Remove the fuel tank and air filter housing (see Chapter 5).
10 Loosen the radiator hose clamps. Work the hoses free from the fittings, taking care not to damage the fittings in the process **(see illustration 1.1b)**.
11 Remove the mounting nut from the upper right corner of the radiator. Remove the upper and lower radiator mounting bolts and take the radiator out.

UK FZR750 and all 1989-on FZR1000 models

12 Remove the left, right and front fairings (see Chapter 9).
13 Remove the seat (see Chapter 9).
14 Remove the fuel tank and air filter housing (see Chapter 5).
15 Disconnect the wiring connector for the fan thermoswitch and temperature sender, as well as the sender ground/earth wire **(see illustration 4.5b)**.
16 Disconnect the fan motor connector. Disconnect the ground/earth wire for the fan switch (if equipped).
17 Disconnect the radiator hoses **(see illustrations)**. Disconnect the oil cooler hose on all FZR750 models and 1991-on FZR1000 models.
18 Remove the radiator mounting bolts **(see illustrations)**. Take the radiator out.

HAYNES HiNT *If the radiator fins are bent or flattened, straighten them very carefully with a small screwdriver.*

All models

19 Inspect the radiator mounting bushings. Replace them if they're cracked or deteriorated.

20 Installation is the reverse of the removal steps, with the following additions:
 a) Don't forget to connect the fan switch ground/earth wire (if equipped).
 b) On all models, fill the cooling system with the recommended coolant (see Chapter 1).

7.17a Loosen the hose clamp (arrowed) and disconnect the lower radiator hose ...

7.17b ... and the upper radiator hose

7.18a Remove the radiator lower mounting bolts (arrowed) ...

7.18b ... and the upper mounting bolts (arrowed)

4•10 Cooling system

8.5 On later FZR600, loosen the clamp and disconnect the hose; on early models, unbolt the lower tube

8.6a On all FZR600 models, unbolt the upper coolant tube from the water pump . . .

8.6b . . . and from the water jacket joint

8 Water pump - check, removal, disassembly, inspection and installation

Warning: *The engine must be completely cool before beginning this procedure.*

Check and removal

1 Visually check the area around the water pump for coolant leaks. Try to determine if the leak is simply the result of a loose hose clamp or deteriorated hose.

2 Support the bike securely so it can't be knocked over during this procedure.
3 Remove the left fairing panel (see Chapter 9) and the drive chain cover (see Chapter 7).
4 Drain the engine coolant following the procedure in Chapter 1.

FZR600 models

5 Disconnect the lower hose or coolant tube from the water pump (see illustration 6.5a and the accompanying illustration).
6 Unbolt the upper coolant tube from the water pump and pull its upper end out of the water jacket joint (see illustration 6.5a and the accompanying illustrations).

7 Remove both mounting bolts and take the pump off (see illustrations).

FZR750/1000 models

8 Disconnect the lower hose from the water pump (see illustration).
9 Unbolt the coolant tube bracket from the engine (see illustration).
10 Remove the water pump mounting bolts and pull the water pump away from the engine, separating the coolant tube from the cylinder block as you do so (see illustration 6.16b and the accompanying illustrations).

8.7a Remove the lower mounting bolt . . .

8.7b . . . and the upper mounting bolt . . .

8.7c . . . and pull the water pump out of the engine

8.8 On FZR750/1000, disconnect the lower hose from the water pump (or unbolt the lower coolant tube) . . .

8.9 . . . unbolt the upper coolant tube bracket from the engine

Cooling system 4•11

8.10a Remove the pump mounting bolts (arrowed) and pull the pump off the engine . . .

8.10b . . . together with the coolant tube; replace the O-ring (arrowed) whenever the tube is removed . . .

8.10c . . . the water pump O-ring (arrowed) should also be replaced

8.12a Remove the water pump cover bolts . . .

Disassembly and inspection

11 Check the shaft seal for leaks.
 a) If you're working on an FZR600, replace the water pump if the seal has been leaking.
 b) If you're working on an FZR750/1000, the water pump can be disassembled for seal replacement. However, the job requires a press and special tools and should be done by a Yamaha dealer.

12 Remove the pump cover bolts and take the cover off (see illustrations).

13 Try to wiggle the pump impeller back-and-forth and in-and-out. Check the impeller blades for corrosion.
 a) If you're working on an FZR600 and you can feel movement or the impeller blades are heavily corroded, the water pump must be replaced.
 b) If you're working on an FZR750/1000 and you can feel movement or the impeller blades are heavily corroded, the water pump can be disassembled for bearing replacement. However, the job requires a press and special tools and should be done by a Yamaha dealer.

14 If the impeller blades are heavily corroded, flush the system thoroughly (it would also be a good idea to check the internal condition of the radiator).

15 Remove the O-ring from its groove with a pointed tool and install a new one (see illustration).

8.12b . . . and take the cover off

8.15 Remove the cover O-ring from the groove with a pointed tool and install a new one

4•12 Cooling system

8.17a Remove the water pump O-ring and install a new one (FZR600 shown; others similar)

8.17b There's an O-ring at each end of the tube; these should be replaced each time it is removed

8.17c Align the slot in the water pump (arrowed) . . .

8.17d . . . with the drive tooth on the oil pump shaft

16 Install the cover and tighten the bolts to the torque listed in this Chapter's Specifications.

Installation

17 Installation is the reverse of the removal steps with the following additions:

a) Install new O-rings on the water pump and the coolant tube **(see illustrations)**.

b) If you're working on an FZR750/1000, install the coolant tube on the water pump, then install the assembled water pump and coolant tube on the engine **(see illustration 8.10b)**.

c) Align the slot in the water pump shaft with the drive tooth in the oil pump shaft **(see illustrations)**.

d) Tighten the mounting bolts to the torque listed in this Chapter's Specifications.

9 Water jacket joint (FZR600 models) - removal and installation

Warning: The engine must be completely cool for this procedure.

1 Refer to Chapter 1 and drain the cooling system.
2 Remove the fuel tank cover and fairings (see Chapter 9).
3 Remove the fuel tank and air filter housing (see Chapter 5).
4 Remove the water pump upper tube **(see illustrations 8.6a and 8.6b)**.
5 Remove the water jacket mounting bolts and take the water jacket off the cylinder block **(see illustration 6.5a and the accompanying illustration)**.
6 Installation is the reverse of the removal steps, with the following additions:

a) Use new O-rings and lubricate them with multi-purpose grease.
b) Tighten the mounting bolts to the torque listed in this Chapter's Specifications.

9.5 Remove the mounting bolts (arrowed) and take the water jacket off; use new O-rings

Cooling system 4•13

10.6a Remove the mounting bolts (arrowed) . . .

10.6b . . . and pull the outlet water jacket joint out of the cylinder block

10.7 Remove the mounting bolts (arrowed) and take the inlet water jacket joint off

10 Water jacket joints (FZR750/1000 models) - removal and installation

1987 and 1988 models

1 Remove the left and right fairings and the side covers (see Chapter 9).
2 Refer to Chapter 1 and drain the cooling system. Remove the fuel tank and air filter housing (see Chapter 5).

1989 and later models

3 Remove the left, right and front fairings (see Chapter 9).
4 Remove the seat (see Chapter 9).
5 Remove the fuel tank and carburetors (see Chapter 5). Refer to Chapter 1 and drain the cooling system.
6 Remove the mounting bolts and pull the outlet water jacket joint out of the cylinder block **(see illustrations)**.

10.8a Use new O-rings . . .

All models

7 Remove the mounting bolts and take the inlet water jacket joint off the cylinder block **(see illustration)**.
8 Installation is the reverse of the removal steps, with the following additions:

10.8b . . . and lubricate them with multi-purpose grease

a) *Use new O-rings and lubricate them with multi-purpose grease* **(see illustrations)**.
b) *Tighten the mounting bolts to the torque listed in this Chapter's Specifications.*

4

Notes

Chapter 5
Fuel and exhaust systems

Contents

Air filter housing - removal and installation 4	Exhaust system - removal, EXUP inspection and installation 13
Air filter element - servicing . . . . See Chapter 1	Fuel pump and relay - replacement 15
Air induction system (California FZR600 models) - inspection and	Fuel pump - circuit check and fuel pump test 14
component replacement 16	Fuel reserve system . . . . See Chapter 10
Carburetor overhaul - general information 6	Fuel system - check and filter replacement . . . . See Chapter 1
Carburetors and intake manifolds - removal and installation 7	Fuel tank - cleaning and repair 3
Carburetors - disassembly, cleaning and inspection 8	Fuel tank - removal and installation 2
Carburetors - reassembly and fuel level adjustment 10	General information 1
Carburetors - separation and reassembly 9	Idle fuel/air mixture adjustment - general information 5
Carburetor synchronization . . . . See Chapter 1	Idle speed - check and adjustment . . . . See Chapter 1
Choke cable - removal and installation 12	Throttle cables - removal, installation and adjustment 11
Evaporation control system (California models) - inspection and	Throttle operation/grip freeplay - check and adjustment . . . See Chapter 1
canister replacement 17	

Degrees of difficulty

Easy, suitable for novice with little experience	**Fairly easy,** suitable for beginner with some experience	**Fairly difficult,** suitable for competent DIY mechanic	**Difficult,** suitable for experienced DIY mechanic	**Very difficult,** suitable for expert DIY or professional

Specifications

Fuel tank capacity
FZR600
  Main tank . . . . 18 liters (4.8 US gal, 4.0 Imperial gal)
  Reserve . . . . 3.4 liters (0.9 US gal, 0.75 Imperial gal)

FZR750
  1987 and 1988 - US
    Main tank . . . . 20 liters (5.3 US gal, 4.4 Imperial gal)
    Reserve . . . . 4.5 liters (1.19 US gal, 0.99 Imperial gal)
  1989-on - UK
    Main tank . . . . 19 liters (5.0 US gal, 4.2 Imperial gal)
    Reserve . . . . 4.0 liters (1.06 US gal, 0.88 Imperial gal)

FZR1000
  1987 and 1988
    Main tank . . . . 20 liters (5.3 US gal, 4.4 Imperial gal)
    Reserve . . . . 4.5 liters (1.19 US gal, 0.99 Imperial gal)
  1989-on
    Main tank . . . . 19 liters (5.0 US gal, 4.2 Imperial gal)
    Reserve . . . . 3.5 liters, 0.92 US gal, 0.77 Imperial gal)

Fuel grade
All 1987 and 1988, 1989-on UK . . . . Regular
1989-on US . . . . Unleaded

5•2 Fuel and exhaust systems

Idle speed
FZR600 .... 1150 to 1250 rpm
FZR750
    1987 and 1988 (US) .... 1000 to 1100 rpm
    1989-on (UK) .... 1150 to 1250 rpm
FZR1000 .... 950 to 1050 rpm

FZR600 carburettor
Type .... Mikuni BDST32 (four)
Jet sizes - US models
    Main jet 107.5
    Main air jet 65
    Jet needle/clip position
        1989 non-California 5CFZ4/2
        California 5CFZ7/1
    Needle jet .... Y-O
    Pilot air jet 132.5
    Pilot jet 32.5
    Pilot screw .... 3.0 (preset)
    Valve seat size 1.2
    Starter jet
        Except California 52.5
        California 50
Jet sizes - UK models
    Main jet 107.5
    Main air jet 65
    Jet needle/clip position 5CFZ4/2
    Needle jet .... Y-O
    Pilot air jet 112.5
    Pilot jet 30
    Pilot screw .... 3 turns out
    Valve seat size 1.2
    Starter jet 52.5
Fuel level .... 3.8 to 4.8 mm (0.15 to 0.19 inch)

FZR750 (US) carburettor
Type .... Mikuni BD34 (four)
Main jet
    Cylinders 1 and 4 .... 107.5
    Cylinders 2 and 3 105
Main air jet 65
Jet needle/clip position
    Cylinders 1 and 4 .... 5CDZ/6
    Cylinders 2 and 3 .... 5CEZ/6
Needle jet .... Y-O
Pilot air jet 125
Pilot jet 15
Pilot screw 2.0
Valve seat size 1.2
Starter jet 30
Fuel level .... 7.3 to 9.3 mm (0.287 to 0.366 inch)

FZR750 (UK) carburettor
Type .... Mikuni BDST38 (four)
Main jet
    Cylinders 1 and 4 .... 122.5
    Cylinders 2 and 3 .... 117.5
Main air jet 50
Jet needle 5CEW-11
Needle jet .... Y-O
Pilot air jet 125
Pilot jet 42.5
Pilot screw .... 2-1/2 turns out
Valve seat size 1.6
Starter jet 57.5
Fuel level .... 7.8 to 8.8 mm (0.31 to 0.35 inch)

Fuel and exhaust systems

FZR1000 (1987 and 1988) carburettor

Type	Mikuni BDS37 (four)
Jet sizes - US models	
Main jet (except California)	
Cylinders 1 and 4	110
Cylinders 2 and 3	107.5
Main jet (California)	
Cylinders 1 and 4	107.5
Cylinders 2 and 3	105
Main air jet	65
Jet needle/clip position	
Except California	5CT/2
California	5CZ/3
Needle jet	Y-O
Pilot air jet	117.5
Pilot jet	
Except California	17.5
California	20
Pilot screw	
Except California	3.0 (preset)
California	2.0 (preset)
Valve seat size	1.5
Starter jet	30
Jet sizes - UK models	
Main jet	
Cylinders 1 and 4	110
Cylinders 2 and 3	107.5
Main jet (model 2LF00)	
Cylinders 1 and 4	92.5
Cylinders 2 and 3	90
Main air jet	65
Jet needle/clip position	5CFZ2/4
Needle jet	Y-O
Pilot air jet	115
Pilot jet	20
Pilot screw	2-1/2 turns out
Valve seat size	1.5
Starter jet	30
Fuel level	7.3 to 9.3 mm (0.287 to 0.366 inch)

FZR1000 (1989-on) carburettor

Type	Mikuni BDST38 (four)
Jet sizes - US models	
Main jet	
Cylinders 1 and 4	125
Cylinders 2 and 3	122.5
Main air jet	85
Jet needle	5CEW9
Needle jet	Y-O
Pilot air jet	125
Pilot jet	37.5
Pilot screw	Preset
Valve seat size	1.7
Starter jet	60
Jet sizes - UK models	
Main jet	
Cylinders 1 and 4	125
Cylinders 2 and 3	122.5
Main air jet	85
Jet needle/clip position	5CEW8/3
Needle jet	Y-O
Pilot air jet	115
Pilot jet	40
Pilot screw	
1989	2-1/2 turns out
1990-on	3 turns out
Valve seat size	1.7
Starter jet	60

5•4 Fuel and exhaust systems

FZR1000 (1989-on) carburettor (continued)
Fuel level
1989 .... 10.5 to 11.5 mm (0.41 to 0.45 inch)
1990-on .... 10.6 to 11.6 mm (0.42 to 0.46 inch)

Tightening torques

FZR600
Carburetor connecting bolts/nuts
    Upper .... 3 Nm (26 in-lbs)
    Lower .... 5 Nm (43 in-lbs)
Exhaust pipe-to-cylinder head nuts .... 10 Nm (7.2 ft-lbs)
Muffler/silencer clamp bolt .... 20 Nm (14 ft-lbs)
Exhaust pipe support bolt .... 20 Nm (14 ft-lbs)
Muffler/silencer bracket bolt .... 20 Nm (14 ft-lbs)
EXUP pulley and cover bolts .... 10 Nm (7.2 ft-lbs)
Exhaust pipe blind plug (CO test) .... 10 Nm (7.2 ft-lbs)

FZR750/1000 models
Carburetor connecting screws (early models) or bolts/nuts (late models)
    Upper .... 3 Nm (26 in-lbs)
    Lower .... 5 Nm (43 in-lbs)
Exhaust pipe-to-cylinder head nuts (all except 1989-on FZR750R) ... 10 Nm (7.2 ft-lbs)
Exhaust flange-to-cylinder head bolts (1989-on FZR750R) .... 20 Nm (14 ft-lbs)
Exhaust pipe support bolt
    All except 1989-on FZR750R .... 25 Nm (18 ft-lbs)
    1989-on FZR750R .... 20 Nm (14 ft-lbs)
Muffler bracket bolt .... 20 Nm (14 ft-lbs)
EXUP pulley and cover bolts .... 10 Nm (7.2 ft-lbs)
Exhaust pipe and muffler stay (1989-on FZR750R) .... 10 Nm (7.2 ft-lbs)
Rear exhaust pipe to EXUP valve (1989-on FZR750R) .... 10 Nm (7.2 ft-lbs)

1 General information

The fuel system consists of the fuel tank, the fuel tap and filter, the carburetors and the connecting lines, hoses and control cables and an electric fuel pump.

The carburetors used on these motorcycles are four Mikunis with butterfly-type throttle valves. For cold starting, an enrichment circuit is actuated by a cable and the choke lever mounted on the left side of the frame.

The exhaust system is a four-into-one design. California and some UK models are equipped with Yamaha's Exhaust Ultimate Powervalve (EXUP). This valve, mounted in the exhaust system, regulates exhaust backpressure to increase performance and reduce exhaust emissions.

Many of the fuel system service procedures are considered routine maintenance items and for that reason are included in Chapter 1.

2 Fuel tank - removal and installation

Warning: Gasoline (petrol) is extremely flammable, so take extra precautions when you work on any part of the fuel system. Don't smoke or allow open flames or bare light bulbs near the work area, and don't work in a garage where a natural gas-type appliance (such as a water heater or clothes dryer) is present. If you spill any fuel on your skin, rinse it off immediately with soap and water. When you perform any kind of work on the fuel system, wear safety glasses and have a fire extinguisher suitable for class B fires on hand.

FZR600 models

1 The fuel tank is mounted beneath a plastic cover and is held in place at the forward end by a through-bolt which secures a mount on the tank to two brackets on the frame. The rear of the tank is fastened to a bracket, which also secures the tank cover.

2 Remove the seat and disconnect the cable from the negative terminal of the battery.

3 Remove the cap from the fuel tank **(see illustration)**.

4 Remove the two Allen bolts that secure the cap flange to the tank cover **(see illustration)**.

5 Remove the screws at the front and rear of the tank cover **(see illustrations)**. Lift the cover off the mount **(see illustration)**.

6 Turn the fuel tap off and remove the knob **(see illustration)**.

7 Disconnect the electrical connector for the fuel tank sender pump **(see illustration)**.

2.3 Use the key to unlock and remove the fuel tank cap

2.4 Remove the bolts (arrowed) securing the cover to the tank (they're identified by triangular marks)

Fuel and exhaust systems 5•5

2.5a Remove the cover screws at the rear . . .

2.5b . . . and at the front . . .

2.5c . . . and lift the cover off the mounts

8 On California models, disconnect the vapor hose from the valve at the right side of the tank (see illustration).
9 Disconnect the fuel line at the carburetors (see illustration).
10 Remove the mounting bolts at the rear and front of the tank and lift the tank off (see illustrations).
11 Before installing the tank, check the condition of the vapor hose (California models). and rubber mounting dampers (see illustrations) - if they're hardened, cracked, or show any other signs of deterioration, replace them.
12 If necessary, pour the fuel from the tank, disconnect the hose and remove the

2.6 Remove the fuel tap knob

2.7 Locate and disconnect the electrical connectors for the fuel sender and fuel pump

2.8 Disconnect the vapor hose (California models)

2.9 Disconnect the fuel line at the carburetors; clean up any spilled fuel so it won't be a fire hazard

2.10a Unbolt the tank bracket at the rear . . .

2.10b . . . and remove the mounting bolt at the front

2.11a Inspect the vapor hose on the tank (California models) . . .

2.11b . . . the mount on top of the tank (be sure to reinstall the reinforcing washers) . . .

5•6 Fuel and exhaust systems

2.11c ... and the mount at the front of the tank

2.12 Disconnect the fuel line and remove the mounting screws (arrowed) to remove the fuel tap

2.15 Turn the fuel tap to Off and disconnect the electrical connector for the fuel level sender (arrowed)

mounting screws, then separate the fuel tap from the tank **(see illustration)**.

13 When replacing the tank, reverse the above procedure. Make sure the tank seats properly and does not pinch any control cables or wires. If difficulty is encountered when trying to slide the tank cover onto the dampers, a small amount of light oil should be used to lubricate them.

1987 and 1988 FZR750 and all FZR1000 models

14 Remove the seat. If you're working on a 1987 or 1988 model, remove the side covers (see Chapter 9).

15 Turn the fuel tap knob to Off **(see illustration)**. If you're working on a 1987 or 1988 model, remove the fuel tap screws.

16 Follow the wiring harness from the fuel level sender to the connector and disconnect the connector **(see illustration 2.15)**.

17 Disconnect the hose from the breather fitting at the rear of the tank and remove the rear mounting bolt **(see illustration)**.

18 Remove the mounting bolt from the front of the tank **(see illustration)**.

19 Lift the tank off the mounts and disconnect the fuel line **(see illustrations)**. On California models, disconnect the canister hose from the valve **(see illustration)**.

20 If necessary for access to other components, remove the tank mounting bracket **(see illustration)**.

21 Perform Steps 11 through 13 above to inspect and reinstall the tank.

1989-on FZR750 models

22 Disconnect the breather hose from the rollover valve. Undo the two quick-release fasteners on either side of the tank front cover and release the air intake spring bands on the inside of the fairing. Remove the front cover, pulling the breather hose through the grommet. Unbolt and lift off the seat.

23 Remove the tank mounting bolts **(see illustration)**.

2.17 Disconnect the hose from the fitting (left arrow) and remove the rear mounting bolt (right arrow)

2.18 Hold the nut with a wrench and remove the front mounting bolt

2.19a Lift the tank and disengage the mounting dampers . . .

2.19b . . . and disconnect the fuel line; wipe up any spilled fuel so it doesn't become a fire hazard

2.19c On California models, disconnect the canister hose from the valve

2.20 Unbolt the tank mounting bracket and lift it off if necessary for access to other components

Fuel and exhaust systems 5•7

24 Carefully note how the drain hose is routed, then disconnect it from the rear of the tank.
25 Remove the locating dampers from the rear mountings.
26 Disconnect the fuel line and vacuum line from the fuel tap.
27 Disconnect the fuel pump electrical connector and lift the tank off.
28 Drain the tank if fuel tap or pump removal is required. Remove the tap mounting screws to free it. Always use a new tap seal on installation. Refer to Section 15 for pump removal.
29 Before installing the tank, check the condition of the locating dampers and hoses - if they're hardened, cracked or show other signs of deterioration, replace them.
30 Reverse the removal steps to install. Make sure the hoses are routed correctly, the tank is seated properly and no hoses or cables are pinched.

3 Fuel tank - cleaning and repair

1 All repairs to the fuel tank should be carried out by a professional who has experience in this critical and potentially dangerous work. Even after cleaning and flushing of the fuel system, explosive fumes can remain and ignite during repair of the tank.
2 If the fuel tank is removed from the vehicle, it should not be placed in an area where sparks or open flames could ignite the fumes coming out of the tank. Be especially careful inside garages where a natural gas-type appliance is located, because the pilot light could cause an explosion.

4 Air filter housing - removal and installation

1 Remove the seat (see Chapter 9) and the fuel tank (see Section 2).
2 If you're working on an FZR750/1000, remove the mounting screw at the front of the air cleaner housing (see illustration). Loosen

2.23 Fuel tank details (1989-on FZR750 models)

1 Fuel tank assembly
2 Yamaha emblems
3 Front mounting bolt
4 Special washer
5 Fuel tank bracket
6 Flange bolt
7 Tank front cover
8 Trim
9 Grommet
10 Quick-release fastener
11 Special washer
12 Spring plate
13 Damper
14 Cap
15 Filler cover
16 Allen bolt
17 Rollover valve
18 Allen bolt
19 O-ring
20 Plate washer
21 Breather hose
22 Clip
23 Drain hose
24 Clip
25 Fuel tap
26 Tap seal
27 Screw
28 Locating damper
29 Plate washer
30 Locating damper
31 Rear mounting bolt
32 Fuel pump
33 Seal
34 Pan head screw
35 Spring washer
36 Plate washer
37 Fuel line
38 Clip
39 Locating damper
40 Locating damper
41 Locating damper
42 Plate washer
43 Bolt

4.2a On FZR750/1000 models, remove the screw at the front of the air filter housing

5•8 Fuel and exhaust systems

4.2b Loosen the clamping band screw on each carburetor joint; this is an FZR600 . . .

4.2c . . . and this is an FZR1000

the clamps that secure the air box to the carburetors (see illustrations). Pull the air box upward, away from the carburetors.
3 Lift the air box, disconnect the hoses and take the air box out (see illustrations).
4 Installation is the reverse of the removal steps.

5 Idle fuel/air mixture adjustment - general information

1 Due to the increased emphasis on controlling motorcycle exhaust emissions, certain governmental regulations have been formulated which directly affect the carburetion of this machine. In order to comply with the regulations, the carburetors on some models have a metal sealing plug pressed into the hole over the pilot screw (which controls the idle fuel/air mixture) on each carburetor, so they can't be tampered with. These should only be removed in the event of a complete carburetor overhaul, and even then the screws should be returned to their original settings. The pilot screws on other models are accessible, but the use of an exhaust gas analyzer is the only accurate way to adjust the idle fuel/air mixture and be sure the machine doesn't exceed the emissions regulations.
2 If the engine runs extremely rough at idle or continually stalls, and if a carburetor overhaul does not cure the problem, take the motorcycle to a Yamaha dealer service department or other repair shop equipped with an exhaust gas analyzer. They will be able to properly adjust the idle fuel/air mixture to achieve a smooth idle and restore low speed performance.

6 Carburetor overhaul - general information

1 Poor engine performance, hesitation, hard starting, stalling, flooding and backfiring are all signs that major carburetor maintenance may be required.
2 Keep in mind that many so-called carburetor problems are really not carburetor problems at all, but mechanical problems within the engine or ignition system malfunctions. Try to establish for certain that the carburetors are in need of maintenance before beginning a major overhaul.
3 Check the fuel filter, the fuel lines, the fuel tank cap vent (if equipped), the intake manifold hose clamps, the vacuum hoses, the air filter element, the cylinder compression, the spark plugs, the carburetor synchronization and the fuel pump before assuming that a carburetor overhaul is required.
4 Most carburetor problems are caused by dirt particles, varnish and other deposits which build up in and block the fuel and air passages. Also, in time, gaskets and O-rings shrink or deteriorate and cause fuel and air leaks which lead to poor performance.
5 When the carburetor is overhauled, it is generally disassembled completely and the parts are cleaned thoroughly with a carburetor cleaning solvent and dried with filtered, unlubricated compressed air. The fuel and air passages are also blown through with compressed air to force out any dirt that may have been loosened but not removed by the solvent. Once the cleaning process is complete, the carburetor is reassembled using new gaskets, O-rings and, generally, a new inlet needle valve and seat.
6 Before disassembling the carburetors, make sure you have a carburetor rebuild kit (which will include all necessary O-rings and other parts), some carburetor cleaner, a supply of rags, some means of blowing out the carburetor passages and a clean place to work.

4.3a Disconnect the vapor hose . . .

4.3b . . . and the breather hose and air induction hose (if equipped) (this is an FZR600) . . .

4.3c . . . and this is an FZR1000

Fuel and exhaust systems 5•9

7.4 Loosen the clamping screw on the intake manifold (arrowed) (carburetors removed for clarity)

7.6 Lift the carburetor assembly clear of the intake manifolds

7.8a Disconnect the vacuum line (if equipped) from the intake manifold . . .

> **HAYNES HINT**: *It is recommended that only one carburetor be overhauled at a time to avoid mixing up parts.*

7 Don't separate the carburetors from each other unless one of the joints between them is leaking. The carburetors can be overhauled completely without being separated, and reconnecting them properly can be difficult without special factory equipment.

7 Carburetors and intake manifolds - removal and installation

⚠ *Warning: Gasoline (petrol) is extremely flammable, so take extra precautions when you work on any part of the fuel system. Don't smoke or allow open flames or bare light bulbs near the work area, and don't work in a garage where a natural gas-type appliance (such as a water heater or clothes dryer) is present. If you spill any fuel on your skin, rinse it off immediately with soap and water. When you perform any kind of work on the fuel system, wear safety glasses and have a class B type fire extinguisher (flammable liquids) on hand.*

Removal

FZR600 models

1 Remove the seat and fairings (see Chapter 9).

2 Remove the fuel tank (see Section 2).
3 Remove the air filter housing (see Section 4).
4 Loosen the clamp screws on the intake manifolds (the rubber tubes that connect the carburetors to the engine) **(see illustration)**.
5 Disconnect the fuel line from the carburetor assembly and remove the inline strainer.
6 Lift the carburetor assembly clear of the intake manifold tubes **(see illustration)**. Raise the assembly up far enough to disconnect the throttle and choke cables (see Sections 11 and 12).
7 After the carburetors have been removed, stuff clean rags into the intake manifold tubes to prevent the entry of dirt or other objects.
8 Inspect the intake manifold tubes **(see illustrations)**. If they're cracked or brittle, replace them.

7.8b . . . remove the mounting bolts (arrowed) and take the manifold off the engine

FZR750/1000 models

9 If you're working on a 1987 or 1988 model, remove the seat and side covers (see Chapter 9).
10 If you're working on a 1989 or later model, remove the left fairing (see Chapter 9).
11 Remove the fuel tank (see Section 2).
12 Remove the air filter housing (see Section 4).
13 Loosen the clamp screws on the intake manifolds (the rubber tubes that connect the carburetors to the engine) **(see illustration)**.
14 Disconnect the fuel line from the carburetor assembly and remove the inline strainer (if equipped) **(see illustrations)**.
15 Disconnect the breather hose from the carburetor assembly **(see illustration)**.
16 Lift the carburetor assembly clear of the intake manifold tubes. Raise the assembly up

7.13 Loosen the screw on each clamping band (arrowed)

7.14a Disconnect the fuel line . . .

7.14b . . . and remove the inline strainer (if equipped) from the fitting

7.15 Disconnect the breather hose

5•10 Fuel and exhaust systems

7.18a Pull the rubber manifold off the aluminum manifold

7.18b Remove the mounting bolts (arrowed) and detach the aluminum manifold from the engine

far enough to disconnect the throttle and choke cables (see Sections 11 and 12).
17 After the carburetors have been removed, stuff clean rags into the intake manifold tubes to prevent the entry of dirt or other objects.
18 Inspect the intake manifold tubes **(see illustrations)**. If they're cracked or brittle, replace them.

Installation

19 Position the assembly over the intake manifold tubes. Lightly lubricate the ends of the throttle cables with multi-purpose grease and attach them to the throttle pulley. Make sure the accelerator and decelerator cables are in their proper positions.
20 Tilt the front of the assembly down and insert the fronts of the carburetors into the intake manifold tubes. Push the assembly forward and tighten the clamps.
21 Install the air filter housing (see Section 4).
22 Make sure the ducts from the air filter housing are seated properly, then slide the spring bands into position.
23 Connect the choke cable to the assembly (see Section 12).
24 Adjust the throttle grip freeplay (see Chapter 1).
25 The remainder of installation is the reverse of the removal steps.
26 Check and, if necessary, adjust the idle speed and carburetor synchronization (see Chapter 1).

8 Carburetors - disassembly, cleaning and inspection

> **Warning:** *Gasoline (petrol) is extremely flammable, so take extra precautions when you work on any part of the fuel system. Don't smoke or allow open flames or bare light bulbs near the work area, and don't work in a garage where a natural gas-type appliance (such as a water heater or clothes dryer) is present. If you spill any fuel on your skin, rinse it off immediately with soap and water. When you perform any kind of work on the fuel system, wear safety glasses and have a fire extinguisher suitable for class B type fires (flammable liquids) on hand.*

FZR600 models

Disassembly

1 Remove the carburetors from the machine as described in Section 7. Set the assembly on a clean working surface. **Note:** *Unless the O-rings on the fuel and vent fittings between the carburetors are leaking, don't detach the carburetors from their mounting brackets. Also, work on one carburetor at a time to avoid getting parts mixed up. It's possible to overhaul the carburetors without removing them from the brackets* **(see illustration)**.
2 Remove the vent hoses **(see illustrations)**.

8.1 Carburetors (FZR600 models) - exploded view

1 Upper bracket bolt
2 Throttle stop screw and spring
3 Float chamber vent hose
4 Lower bracket bolt
5 Synchronizing screw
6 Float
7 Float pivot pin
8 Float chamber cover
9 Needle jet
10 Float chamber drain screw
11 Needle valve and seat
12 Pilot jet
13 Main jet
14 Choke plunger
15 Pilot screw
16 Throttle piston
17 Jet needle
18 Choke shaft
19 O-ring
20 Inline strainer

Fuel and exhaust systems 5•11

8.2a Squeeze the spring clamps and slide them down the vent hoses . . .

8.2b . . . and detach the hoses from the float chamber covers

8.3 Remove the bracket mounting screws and take off the throttle stop screw and bracket

3 Remove the throttle stop screw and bracket **(see illustration)**.
4 Remove the float chamber cover screws and lift off the covers **(see illustrations)**.
5 Remove the starter jet, main jet and pilot jet **(see illustrations)**.
6 The pilot (idle mixture) screw is located in the front of the carburetor body. On US models, this screw is hidden behind a plug which will have to be removed if the screw is to be taken out. To do this, drill a hole in the plug, being careful not to drill into the screw, then pry the plug out or remove it with a small slide hammer. On all models, turn the pilot screw in, counting the number of turns until it bottoms lightly **(see illustration)**. Record that

8.4a Remove the float chamber cover screws (arrowed) . . .

8.4b . . . and lift the float chamber covers off in pairs

8.5a The float chamber contains the main jet (1), starter jet (2) and pilot jet (3)

8.5b Unscrew the starter jet . . .

8.5c . . . the pilot jet . . .

8.5d . . . and the main jet

8.6a Remove the plug and turn the pilot screw (arrowed) in until it bottoms lightly . . .

8.6b . . . then remove the screw, spring, washer and O-ring

5•12 Fuel and exhaust systems

8.7 Work the O-ring free of its bore and lift the needle valve assembly out together with the floats

8.8a Unscrew the jet holder bolt with a box wrench (ring spanner) . . .

8.8b . . . lift out the bolt; the projection on the jet holder (arrowed) aligns with a slot in the jet . . .

8.8c . . . and lift out the jet holder; use a new O-ring and be sure the pin aligns with the slot (arrowed)

8.9a Unscrew the pilot air jet (arrowed) . . .

number for use when installing the screw. Now remove the pilot screw along with its spring, washer and O-ring **(see illustration)**.

7 Work the needle valve O-ring free of its bore and lift out the float and needle valve assembly **(see illustration)**.

8 Remove the jet holder bolt, washer and jet holder **(see illustrations)**.

9 Remove the pilot air jet **(see illustrations)**.

10 Remove the vacuum chamber cover screws **(see illustration)**.

11 Lift off the cover, spring and throttle piston, then separate the piston spring from the throttle piston **(see illustrations)**.

12 Take the jet needle and washer out of the throttle piston **(see illustration)**.

8.9b . . . and lift it out of its bore

8.10 Remove the vacuum chamber cover screws

8.11a Lift off the cover and spring and note the location of the small O-ring (arrowed) . . .

8.11b . . . lift out the throttle piston, diaphragm and jet needle, and remove the piston support (arrowed)

8.11c Separate the spring from the throttle piston

8.12 Lift the jet needle and washer out of the throttle piston

Fuel and exhaust systems 5•13

8.13 Compress the choke shaft clips and slide them out of their bores, then take off the choke shaft

8.14a Squeeze the tab on one side, then on the other, while applying light steady pressure . . .

8.14b . . . until the choke plunger can be lifted out of its bore

13 Compress the choke shaft clips and take them out of their bores **(see illustration)**. Remove the choke shaft from the carburetor assembly.

14 Squeeze the retaining tangs on the choke plunger while applying gentle pressure on the retainer, then pull the choke plunger out of its bore **(see illustrations)**.

Inspection

15 Remove the O-rings from the float chamber covers **(see illustration)**.

16 If fuel has been leaking from the fittings between the float chamber covers, pull them apart, install new O-rings and reassemble the covers **(see illustration)**.

17 Check the filter screen on the needle valve seat **(see illustration)** and replace it if it's torn or can't be cleaned.

18 Pull out the float pivot pin and separate the floats and needle valve from the needle valve seat **(see illustrations)**. Check the tip of the needle valve. If it has grooves or scratches in it, it must be replaced. Push in on the rod in the other end of the needle valve, then release it - if it doesn't spring back, replace the valve needle.

19 Check the operation of the choke plunger. If it doesn't move smoothly, replace it, along with the return spring. Inspect the needle on the end of the choke plunger and replace it if it's worn.

20 Check the tapered portion of the pilot screw for wear or damage. Replace the pilot screw if necessary.

8.15 The float chamber cover O-rings should be replaced whenever the carburetors are overhauled

8.16 If the fittings between pairs of float chamber covers leak, remove them and install new O-rings

8.17 Make sure the fuel strainer (arrowed) is clean; if it's torn or can't be cleaned, replace it

8.18a Pull the float pivot pin out . . .

8.18b . . . separate the needle valve seat from the floats . . .

8.18c . . . replace the needle valve if it's worn at the tip (arrowed) (use a new one if it's in the rebuild kit) . . .

8.18d . . . check the tang (arrowed) that contacts the needle valve; replace the floats if the tang is worn

5•14 Fuel and exhaust systems

8.29 Carburetors (1987 and 1988 FZR750/1000 models) exploded view

1. Upper bracket
2. Throttle stop screw
3. Fuel overflow hose
4. Lower bracket
5. Synchronizing screw
6. Float
7. Float pivot pin
8. Pilot air jet
9. Needle jet
10. Fuel drain screw
11. Needle valve and seat
12. Pilot jet
13. Main jet
14. Choke plunger assembly
15. Pilot screw
16. Throttle piston
17. Fuel line
18. Choke shaft
19. O-ring

21 Check the carburetor body, float chamber cover and vacuum chamber cover for cracks, distorted sealing surfaces and other damage. If any defects are found, replace the faulty component, although replacement of the entire carburetor will probably be necessary (check with your parts supplier for the availability of separate components).
22 Check the diaphragm for splits, holes and general deterioration. Holding it up to a light will help to reveal problems of this nature.
23 Insert the throttle piston in the carburetor body and see that it moves up-and-down smoothly. Check the surface of the piston for wear. If it's worn excessively or doesn't move smoothly in the bore, replace the carburetor.
24 Check the jet needle for straightness by rolling it on a flat surface (such as a piece of glass). Replace it if it's bent or if the tip is worn.
25 Operate the throttle shaft to make sure the throttle butterfly valve opens and closes smoothly. If it doesn't, replace the carburetor.
26 Check the floats for damage. This will usually be apparent by the presence of fuel inside one of the floats. If the floats are damaged, they must be replaced.

Cleaning

Caution: Use only a petroleum based solvent for carburetor cleaning. Don't use caustic cleaners.

27 Submerge the metal components in the solvent for approximately thirty minutes (or longer, if the directions recommend it).
28 After the carburetor has soaked long enough for the cleaner to loosen and dissolve most of the varnish and other deposits, use a brush to remove the stubborn deposits. Rinse it again, then dry it with compressed air. Blow out all of the fuel and air passages in the main body.

Caution: Never clean the jets or passages with a piece of wire or a drill bit, as they will be enlarged, causing the fuel and air metering rates to be upset.

1987 and 1988 FZR750/1000 models

Disassembly

29 Remove the choke shaft screws and take off the choke shaft **(see illustration)**. These screws have been secured with non-permanent thread locking agent, so you may need an impact driver.
30 Remove the choke plunger nut, spring and plunger.
31 Remove four screws and take off the vacuum chamber cover. Remove the spring and throttle piston.
32 Unscrew the jet needle plug, then remove the spring, washer and jet needle.
33 Remove the float chamber cover screws, then lift off the cover and remove the gasket.
34 Pull out the float pivot pin and remove the float and needle valve.
35 Remove the needle valve seat screw and needle valve seat.
36 Remove the main jet, washer, main jet holder and its washer.
37 Remove the needle jet from its passage inside the float chamber.
38 Unscrew the pilot air jet from its bore in the intake passage of the carburetor.
39 The pilot (idle mixture) screw is located in the front of the carburetor body. On US models, this screw is hidden behind a plug which will have to be removed if the screw is to be taken out. To do this, drill a hole in the plug, being careful not to drill into the screw, then pry the plug out or remove it with a small slide hammer. On all models, turn the pilot screw in, counting the number of turns until it bottoms lightly. Record that number for use when installing the screw. Now remove the pilot screw along with its spring, washer and O-ring.

Inspection and cleaning

40 Perform Steps 15 through 28 above to inspect and clean the carburetors.

Fuel and exhaust systems 5•15

1 Carburetor set
2 Carburetor body
3 Carburetor components
4 Vacuum chamber cover
5 Vacuum chamber cover screw
6 Float chamber drain plug
7 Washer
8 Panhead screw
9 Screw
10 Bolt
11 O-ring
12 Float pivot pin
13 Floats
14 Choke plunger
15 Pilot screw set
16 O-ring
17 Vacuum chamber cover
18 Throttle piston
19 Piston valve support
20 Diaphragm spring
21 Jet needle
22 Needle jet holder
23 Main jet washer
24 Needle jet bolt
25 O-ring
26 O-ring
27 O-ring
28 Needle valve and seat
29 Washer
30 Lockwasher
31 Main jet
32 Needle jet
33 Pilot air jet
34 Pilot jet
35 Starter jet
36 Main air jet
37 Pipe clip
38 Plate washer
39 Nut
40 Throttle synchronizing screw
41 Rod
42 Choke shaft clip
43 Ring
44 Nipple
45 Pipe
46 Choke connecting tube
47 Seal
48 Strainer
49 O-ring
50 Pipe
51 Throttle stop screw
52 Plate washer
53 Nut
54 Choke connecting tube
55 Screw
56 Nipple
57 O-ring
58 Hose
59 Clamp

8.41 Carburetors (1989-on FZR750 models) exploded view

1989-on FZR750 models

Disassembly

41 Remove the choke shaft clips and take off the choke shaft **(see illustration)**.
42 Squeeze the retaining tangs on the choke plunger while applying gentle pressure on the retainer, then lift the choke plunger out of its bore.
43 Remove two screws that secure the vacuum chamber cover. Hold the cover down and turn it about 45-degrees counterclockwise (anti-clockwise), then lift it off. Remove the spring, throttle piston, jet needle and O-ring.
44 Unscrew the jet needle plug, then remove the spring, washer and jet needle.
45 Remove the float chamber cover screws, then lift off the cover and remove the O-ring.
46 Pull out the float pivot pin and remove the float and needle valve.
47 Remove the needle valve seat.
48 Remove the main jet and its washer.
49 Remove the pilot jet and starter jet.
50 Unscrew the needle jet bolt and remove the needle jet holder and its O-ring from the carburetor body.
51 Remove the throttle piston support and the needle jet.
52 Turn the pilot air screw in until it bottoms lightly, then count the number of turns required to remove it and write this down. Remove the pilot air screw and its spring, washer and O-ring.
53 Remove the pilot air jet and main air jet from their bores in the intake passage.

5•16 Fuel and exhaust systems

1 Fuel strainer
2 Fuel feed joint
3 Needle valve seat
4 Needle valve
5 O-ring
6 Floats
7 Jet holder
8 Starter jet
9 Main jet
10 Pilot jet
11 Pilot air jet
12 Pilot air screw
13 Overflow hose joint
14 Ventilation hose joint
15 Choke shaft joint
16 Choke plunger
17 Choke shaft
18 Choke shaft clip
19 Jet needle
20 Piston valve
21 Needle jet
22 Throttle piston support

8.55 Carburetors (1989-on FZR1000 models) - exploded view

8.56 Remove the float chamber cover screws

59 Remove the needle jet bolt, needle jet holder, and O-ring.
60 Remove the pilot air jet (see illustration 8.9a).
61 Turn the carburetor over and remove the vacuum chamber cover screws.
62 Lift off the cover, spring and throttle piston, then separate the spring from the throttle piston. Remove the needle jet and throttle valve support.
63 Take the jet needle and washer out of the throttle piston.
64 Compress the choke shaft clips and take them out of their bores (see illustration 8.13). Remove the choke shaft from the carburetor assembly.
65 Squeeze the retaining tangs on the choke plunger while applying gentle pressure on the retainer, then lift the choke plunger out of its bore (see illustrations 8.14a and 8.14b).

Inspection and cleaning

66 Perform Steps 15 through 28 above to clean and inspect the carburetor.

Inspection and cleaning

54 Perform Steps 15 through 28 above to inspect and clean the carburetors.

1989-on FZR1000 models

Disassembly

55 Remove the choke shaft, throttle stop screw and bracket (see illustration).
56 Remove the float chamber cover screws and lift off the float chamber cover (see illustration).
57 Work the needle valve O-ring free of its bore and lift out the float and needle valve assembly (see illustration). Pull out the float pivot pin and unhook the needle valve from the float (see illustrations).
58 Remove the starter jet, main jet and pilot jet.

9 Carburetors - separation and reassembly

1 The carburetors needn't be separated for normal overhaul. If you need to separate them (to replace a carburetor body, for example), remove them (see Section 7) and refer to the following procedure.

8.57a Work the O-ring free of its bore and remove the needle valve and seat assembly

8.57b Pull out the float pivot pin

8.57c Unhook the needle valve from the float

Fuel and exhaust systems 5•17

FZR600 and all 1989-on FZR750/1000 models

2 Remove the choke shaft (see Section 8).
3 Remove the nuts from the two long bolts that hold the carburetors together (the upper bracket bolt and the lower bracket bolt) **(see illustration 8.1, 8.41 or 8.55)**.
4 Note how the synchronizing screws and springs are assembled (see Chapter 1). As you pull the carburetors apart, keep track of the synchronizer screw springs. They should stay with the adjusting screws, but if they don't, find them and install them as shown in Chapter 1 so they aren't lost.
5 Pull out the upper and lower bracket bolts and remove the spacers and fittings from between the carburetors.
6 Assembly is the reverse of the disassembly procedure. Before tightening the connecting bolts, place the carburetor assembly on a surface plate with the manifold side down. Use new O-rings on the fuel and vent line fittings. Tighten the connecting bolts and nuts to the torque listed in this Chapter's Specifications.

1987 and 1988 FZR750/1000 models

7 If you're going to separate the carburetors, remove eight screws each from the upper bracket and the lower bracket. These screws are secured with thread locking agent, so you'll probably need an impact driver.
8 Note how the synchronizing screws and springs are assembled (see Chapter 1). As you pull the carburetors apart, keep track of the synchronizer screw springs. They should stay with the adjusting screws, but if they don't, find them and install them as shown in Chapter 1 so they aren't lost.
9 Assembly is the reverse of the disassembly procedure. Before tightening the connecting screws, make sure all four throttle valves are fully closed. Use new O-rings on the fuel and vent line fittings. Use non-permanent thread locking agent on the screw threads. Tighten the connecting bolts and nuts to the torque listed in this Chapter's Specifications.

10 Carburetors - reassembly and fuel level adjustment

Caution: *When installing the jets, be careful not to over-tighten them - they're made of soft material and can strip or shear easily.*
Note: *When reassembling the carburetors, be sure to use the new O-rings, gaskets and other parts supplied in the rebuild kit.*

Reassembly

1 Assembly is the reverse of the disassembly steps, with the following additions.

FZR600 models

2 Install the pilot screw (if removed) along with its spring, washer and O-ring, turning it in until it seats lightly. Now, turn the screw out

10.3 Be sure to install this small O-ring in its groove (arrowed)

the number of turns that was previously recorded. On US models, install a new metal plug in the hole over the screw. Apply a little bonding agent around the circumference of the plug after it has been seated.
3 Be sure to install the small O-ring in its groove when installing the vacuum chamber cover **(see illustration)**.
4 Engage the choke shaft with the choke plunger **(see illustration)**.

1987 and 1988 FZR750/1000 models

5 When installing the diaphragm, be sure the tab on the edge of the diaphragm engages the notch in the carburetor body.

1989-on FZR750/1000 models

6 If you removed the throttle piston support, align the tabs on its ends with the slots in the carburetor body.
7 Align the groove on the needle jet with the projection on the jet housing. Align the pin on the jet housing with the slot in the carburetor body.
8 Be sure to install the main jet and starter jet in the correct positions (the main jet has a larger orifice).
9 Align the projection on the needle valve seat with the slot in the carburetor body.
10 If you've separated the cap from the vacuum chamber cover, apply a thin coating of grease to its O-ring. Align the three projections on the cap with the slots in the cover, insert the cap, push it down and turn it clockwise until it stops.

Fuel level adjustment

Warning: *Gasoline (petrol) is extremely flammable, so take extra precautions when you work on any part of the fuel system. Don't smoke or allow open flames or bare light bulbs near the work area, and don't work in a garage where a natural gas-type appliance (such as a water heater or clothes dryer) is present. If you spill any fuel on your skin, rinse it off immediately with soap and water. When you perform any kind of work on the fuel system, wear safety glasses and have a fire extinguisher suitable for class B type fires (flammable liquids) on hand.*

11 Support the bike securely so it can't be knocked over during this procedure.

10.4 The choke shaft should engage the choke plungers like this

12 Support the bike so the carburetors are upright.
13 Attach Yamaha service tool no. YM-01312 (part no. 90890-01312) to the drain fitting on the bottom of one of the carburetor float chamber covers (all four will be checked). This is a clear plastic tube graduated in millimeters **(see illustration)**. On 1987 and 1988 models, you'll also need an adapter (tool no. YM-01329/part no. 90890-01329). An alternative is to use a length of clear plastic tubing and an accurate ruler. Hold the graduated tube (or the free end of the clear plastic tube) vertically against the carburetor body.
14 Unscrew the drain screw at the bottom of the float chamber cover a couple of turns, then start the engine and let it idle - fuel will flow into the tube. Wait for the fuel level to stabilize, then note how far the fuel level is above the float chamber line **(see illustration 10.13)**.
15 Measure the distance between the line on the float chamber/carburetor body and the top of the fuel level in the tube or gauge. This distance is the fuel level - write it down on a piece of paper, screw in the drain screw, then move on to the next carburetor and check it the same way.
16 Compare your fuel level readings to the value listed in this Chapter's Specifications. If the fuel level in any carburetor is incorrect, remove the carburetors (see Section 7), then remove the float chamber cover from the carburetor(s) with the incorrect fuel level. Make sure the needle valve and seat are in good condition, then bend the tang slightly up or down as necessary. Reinstall the float chamber cover(s) and carburetors, then recheck fuel level.

10.13 Fuel level adjustment details

5•18 Fuel and exhaust systems

11.4a Loosen the cable locknut and adjusting nut (if equipped) and lift the cable out of the bracket . . .

11.4b . . . if the decelerator cable doesn't have an adjusting nut, lift it and guide it through the slot (arrowed)

11.4c Lift the cable out of its groove in the throttle pulley and slide it sideways to disengage it

11 Throttle cables - removal, installation and adjustment

1 Remove the fuel tank (see Section 2).
2 Loosen the accelerator cables with the adjusters (see Throttle operation/grip freeplay - check and adjustment in Chapter 1).
3 Remove the handlebar switch mounting screws and separate the halves of the handlebar switch (see Chapter 10).
4 Detach the accelerator and decelerator cables from the throttle grip pulley and from the throttle pulley at the carburetors **(see illustrations)**. Remove the cables, noting how they are routed.
5 Unscrew the throttle grip weight and take the throttle grip off the handlebar **(see illustrations)**.

11.5a Throttle and choke cable details (FZR600 models)

1	Throttle grip	6	Left handlebar grip	10	Clutch cable
2	Right handlebar	7	Grip end weights	11	Accelerator cable
3	Right handlebar boss	8	Clutch cable adjuster locknut	12	Decelerator cable
4	Left handlebar boss	9	Clutch cable adjuster	13	Choke cable
5	Left handlebar			14	Choke lever assembly

11.5b Throttle and choke cable details (1989-on FZR1000 models shown; others similar)

1	Throttle grip	6	Left handlebar grip	10	Rubber damper
2	Right handlebar	7	Grip end weights	11	Accelerator cable
3	Right handlebar boss	8	Accelerator cable adjuster locknut	12	Decelerator cable
4	Left handlebar boss	9	Accelerator cable adjuster	13	Choke cable
5	Left handlebar			14	Choke lever assembly

Fuel and exhaust systems 5•19

12.3a Unbolt the choke lever from the frame (this is an FZR600)...

12.3b ... and this is an FZR1000

12.4 Turn the lever around and disengage the cable from the pulley

6 Clean the handlebar and apply a light coat of multi-purpose grease.
7 Route the cables into place. Make sure they don't interfere with any other components and aren't kinked or bent sharply.
8 Lubricate the ends of the accelerator and decelerator cables with multi-purpose grease and connect them to the throttle pulleys at the carburetors and at the throttle grip.
9 Follow the procedure outlined in Chapter 1, Throttle operation/grip freeplay - check and adjustment, to adjust the cables.
10 Turn the handlebars back and forth to make sure the cables don't cause the steering to bind. With the engine idling, turn the handlebars back and forth and make sure idle speed doesn't change. If it does, find and fix the cause before riding the motorcycle.
11 Install the fuel tank.

12 Choke cable - removal and installation

1 Remove the fuel tank (see Section 2).
2 Remove the left fairing panel (see Chapter 9).
3 Unbolt the choke lever from the frame (see illustrations).

12.5 Loosen the bracket screw and disengage the cable from the choke shaft

4 Turn the choke lever around, align the cable with the slot in the pulley and disengage the cable (see illustration).
5 At the carburetor end of the cable, loosen the screw that secures the outer housing in the bracket enough that you can separate the cable from the bracket. Align the inner cable with the slot in the choke shaft bracket, then separate the cable end from the bracket (see illustration).
6 Installation is the reverse of the removal steps. Lubricate the pulley end of the choke cable with a film of multi-purpose grease.

13 Exhaust system - removal, EXUP inspection and installation

Removal

All except 1989-on FZR750 models

1 Remove the left and right fairings (see Chapter 9).
2 Remove the exhaust pipe holder nuts at the cylinder head and slide the holders off the mounting studs (see illustrations).

1 Exhaust pipes
2 Gaskets
3 EXUP shaft bushings*
4 Grease seal*
5 Gasket*
6 EXUP valve*
7 Valve housing*
8 Cable bracket*
9 EXUP cables*
10 Washer*
11 Pulley*
12 EXUP valve cover*
13 Muffler gasket
14 Muffler
*Not used on US 49-state models or UK FZR600 models

13.2a Exhaust system details (except 1989-on FZR750 models)

5•20 Fuel and exhaust systems

13.2b Remove the nuts . . .

13.2c . . . and slide the retainers off the studs

13.3 The EXUP cables can be disconnected from the servo motor without changing the adjustment

13.4a Remove the mounting bolt (this is an FZR600) . . .

13.4b . . . and this is an FZR1000

13.4c Unbolt the muffler bracket

1 Muffler/silencer
2 EXUP cable
3 EXUP cable
4 Muffler/silencer clamp
5 Gasket
6 EXUP valves
7 Exhaust flanges
8 Pulley cover
9 Pulley
10 Timing gear cover
11 Timing gears
12 Valve shafts
13 Bushings
14 Valve case
15 Spring
16 Exhaust pipe

13.7 Exhaust system (1989-on FZR750 models)

3 On EXUP-equipped models, disconnect the cables from the EXUP servo motor **(see illustration)**. This will eliminate the need to adjust the cables.

4 Remove the mounting bolt beneath the engine and detach the muffler/silencer from the bracket near the right rear footpeg **(see illustrations)**. Lower the pipes and muffler/silencer away from the bike and take them out.

5 If necessary, loosen the clamp bolts and separate the muffler/silencer from the pipes.

1989-on FZR750 models

6 Remove the left and right fairings (see Chapter 9).

7 Loosen the locknuts on the EXUP cables all the way and turn the adjusters in as far as they will go. Remove the EXUP pulley cover and disconnect the cables, then remove the washer and the EXUP cable holder **(see illustration)**.

8 Unhook the springs that secure the exhaust pipes to the exhaust flanges at the cylinder head.

9 Remove the exhaust pipe gaskets, exhaust flanges and flange gaskets.

10 Unhook the springs that secure the exhaust pipes to the valve case. Label the pipes for reinstallation, then disconnect the pipes.

11 Remove the mounting bolts for the rear exhaust pipe and muffler/silencer. Take the exhaust system out.

Fuel and exhaust systems 5•21

13.21 Remove the bolts (arrowed) and take off the cover

13.23 The notch should be aligned with the hole (1)

13.24 Loosen the locknuts (arrowed) and turn the adjusters

12 If necessary, loosen the clamp and disconnect the muffler from the rear pipe. Detach the rear pipe and gasket from the EXUP valve case.

EXUP inspection

All except 1989-on FZR750 models

13 Twist the shaft and check its movement **(see illustration 13.2a)**. If it sticks, remove the cover and lubricate the ends of the shaft and the bushings with molybdenum disulfide grease. If that doesn't help, replace the valve.

1989-on FZR750 models

14 Remove the timing gear cover from the valve. Note the position of the match marks on the timing gears; they should be aligned when both valves are closed.
15 Note which side of the shafts the valves are attached to, then remove the valves **(see illustration 13.7)**.
16 Remove the spring, then remove the circlip, washer, lower valve shaft and the remaining washer.
17 Remove the circlip from the upper valve shaft, then remove the washer, shaft and remaining washer.
18 If the shafts or timing gears are worn or damaged, remove the gears from the shafts.
19 Check the bushings in the valve and all removed parts for wear or damage and replace any parts with visible defects.
20 Assembly is the reverse of the disassembly steps, with the following additions:

13.26 Turn the servo motor pulley clockwise until it stops

a) *Lubricate the bushings, shafts and washers with molybdenum disulfide grease.*
b) *If the timing gears were removed, install them with their toothed sides facing in the same direction as the valve attachment surfaces on the shafts.*
c) *Be sure the match marks on the timing gears are aligned when the valves are closed.*

EXUP cable adjustment

21 Remove the cover from the EXUP valve **(see illustration)**.
22 Turn the ignition switch to On. If the EXUP servo motor doesn't operate, refer further diagnosis to a Yamaha dealer.
23 Check the alignment marks **(see illustration)**. If they're aligned, no further adjustment is necessary. If they aren't aligned, adjust the cables (see below).
24 Loosen the cable adjuster locknuts and turn the adjuster in **(see illustration)**. Insert a 4 mm (0.16 inch) alignment pin through the pulley and into the hole.
25 Turn the adjusters counterclockwise (anti-clockwise) just enough to eliminate free-play in the cables, then turn them clockwise one half turn and tighten the locknuts.
26 Remove the alignment pin and turn off the ignition switch. Turn the pulley on the EXUP servo motor **(see illustration)** clockwise by hand until it stops, then turn on the ignition switch again. The EXUP pulley should move back to the aligned position. If it doesn't, try

13.27 Use new gaskets at the cylinder head

readjusting it. If that doesn't work, refer further service to a Yamaha dealer.

Installation

27 Installation is the reverse of removal, with the following additions:
a) *Use new gaskets at the cylinder head **(see illustration)**.*
b) *Tighten all fasteners to the torque settings listed in this Chapter's Specifications.*

14 Fuel pump - circuit check and fuel pump test

1 With the engine kill switch in the On position, the fuel pump should start and run for approximately five seconds after the ignition is switched on. It should shut off once the carburetor float bowls are full, then run again once the engine is started.
2 The fuel pump circuit consists of the pump, the pump relay, the digital igniter unit (which controls the fuel pump as well as ignition timing), the engine kill switch, the ignition switch, the main and ignition fuses, the battery and related wiring.
3 If you're working on an FZR600, remove the seat, fuel tank cover and fuel tank (see Chapter 9 and Section 2).
4 If you're working on a 1987 or 1988 model, remove the seat, left side cover, fuel tank and air filter housing (see Chapter 9, Section 2 and Section 4).
5 If you're working on a 1989 or later FZR750R model, remove the upper and lower fairing panels, fresh air duct, inner panels, seat, fuel tank and air filter housing (see Chapter 9, Section 2 and Section 4).
6 If you're working on a 1989 or later FZR1000, remove the seat, fuel tank, left side cover and air filter housing (see Chapter 9, Section 2 and Section 4).

All models

7 Check the battery condition and charge (see Chapter 1).
8 Check the main and ignition fuses, the ignition switch and the engine kill switch (see

5•22 Fuel and exhaust systems

14.9 Connect a voltmeter to the relay connector

1 Relay connector
2 Voltmeter positive lead
3 Red/white wire terminal
4 Voltmeter negative lead (to ground/earth)

14.11 Connect a jumper wire between the blue/black and red/white wire terminals

1 Connector
2 Blue/black wire terminal
3 Red/white wire terminal
4 Jumper wire

14.12 Connect a voltmeter to the relay connector

1 Relay connector
2 Voltmeter positive lead
3 Blue/black wire terminal
4 Voltmeter negative lead (to ground/earth)

Chapter 10). Replace them if they're defective, then try the fuel pump again.

1987 and 1988 models

Pump won't run

9 If the pump won't run while the engine is running, or if it won't run for five seconds with the ignition switch On and the kill switch in Run, check battery voltage to the pump. Disconnect the electrical connector at the relay and connect a 20-volt DC voltmeter between the red/white wire terminal in the harness and a good grounding/earthing point (bare metal on the motorcycle frame) **(see illustration)**.

10 Turn the ignition switch to On and the engine kill switch to Run. The voltmeter should indicate at least 12 volts.

a) If the reading is less than 12 volts, check the wiring in the fuel pump circuit for breaks or bad connections. Be sure to check the battery terminal connections and the battery ground/earth cable connection to the motorcycle.

b) If the reading is at least 12 volts, the wiring is good. If the pump won't run with the engine running, go to Step 11. If the pump won't run for five seconds with the ignition switch On and the kill switch in Run, go to Step 12.

11 Connect a short length of wire between the blue/black wire terminal and the red/white wire terminal in the harness side of the relay connector **(see illustration)**. With the ignition switch On and the kill switch in Run, the fuel pump should run.

a) If the fuel pump won't run, test it (see below).

b) If the fuel pump now runs, check the wiring and connections in the fuel pump circuit. If they're good, the fuel pump relay is probably defective. Replace it.

12 Reconnect the connector to the fuel pump relay. Insert the voltmeter positive probe into the back of the blue/black wire connector and connect the voltmeter negative lead to ground/earth (bare metal on the motorcycle) **(see illustration)**. With the ignition switch On and the kill switch in Run, the voltmeter should indicate at least 11 volts.

a) If voltage is less than 11 volts, the fuel pump relay is probably defective. Replace it.

b) If voltage is 11 volts or more, check the wiring and connections in the fuel pump circuit. If they're good, the fuel pump is probably defective. Test it (see below).

Pump won't shut off after 30 seconds

13 Perform Steps 7 and 8 and Step 12 above.

a) If voltage is less than 11 volts in Step 12, the digital igniter is probably defective. Since it's an expensive part that can't be returned once purchased, consider having a Yamaha dealer verify your test results before replacing the igniter.

b) If voltage is 11 volts or more in Step 10, check the wiring and connections in the fuel pump circuit. If they're good, the fuel pump relay is probably defective. Replace it.

1989-on models

14 Perform Steps 9 and 10 above.

15 Disconnect the wiring connector from the fuel pump relay **(see illustrations)**. Connect a 12-volt battery and an ohmmeter to the relay terminals shown. If the ohmmeter shows continuity, the relay is good. If not, replace the relay.

16 If the relay is good, test the fuel pump (see Step 17).

Fuel pump test (all models)

17 Disconnect the wiring connector from the fuel pump. Connect the pump directly to the battery with two lengths of wire (positive to blue/black; negative to black). If the pump doesn't run, replace it.

14.15a Connect a battery and ohmmeter to the relay connector

1 Blue/black terminal (ohmmeter positive lead)
2 Red/white terminal (ohmmeter negative lead and wire from battery positive terminal)
3 Blue/red terminal (wire from battery negative terminal)

14.15b Connect a battery and ohmmeter to the relay connector

1 Ohmmeter positive lead (to red/white)
2 Ohmmeter negative lead (to blue/black)
3 Wire from battery positive terminal (to blue/white)
4 Wire from battery negative terminal (to blue/red)

Fuel and exhaust systems 5•23

15 Fuel pump and relay - replacement

Fuel pump relay replacement

1 Disconnect the wiring connector from the relay.
2 Remove the relay from its mounting bracket, install a new one and reconnect the wiring connector.

Fuel pump replacement

All except 1989-on FZR750R models

3 Squeeze the fuel line clamps and push the ends of the fuel lines off the pump fittings **(see illustrations)**.
4 Disconnect the pump wiring connector. Remove the mounting nuts or bolts and take the pump out.
5 Installation is the reverse of the removal steps. Connect the fuel lines and wiring connector.

1989-on FZR750R models

6 Remove and drain the fuel tank (see Section 2).
7 Remove the pump mounting screws, then lower the pump and gasket out of the tank **(see illustration 2.23)**.
8 Installation is the reverse of the removal steps.

16 Air induction system (California FZR600 models) - inspection and component replacement

1 The air induction system uses exhaust gas pulses to suck fresh air into the exhaust ports, where it mixes with hot combustion gases. The additional oxygen provided by the fresh air allows combustion to continue for a longer time, reducing unburned hydrocarbons in the exhaust **(see illustration)**. Reed valves allow the flow of air into the ports and prevent exhaust gas from flowing into the system. The air cut valve shuts off the flow of air into the system during deceleration to prevent backfiring.
2 Check the hoses for loose connections, damage and deterioration. Tighten or replace loose or damaged hoses.
3 To replace system components, unbolt the system mounting plate from the frame **(see illustration)**. Disconnect the air hose and the metal tubes **(see illustrations)**, then take the

15.3a The FZR600 pump is on the tank; slide the clamps (lower arrows) and disconnect the hoses, Remove the mounting nuts from the studs (upper arrows)

15.3b The FZR1000 pump is on the frame; slide the clamps (lower arrow), then disconnect the lower hose and the upper hose (upper arrow)

16.1 Air induction system details

1 Reed valve assembly
2 Air filter housing
3 Air cut valve
A To cylinders
B To no. 3 cylinder
C To no. 4 cylinder

16.3a Unbolt the reed valve assembly . . .

16.3b . . . disconnect the air intake hose . . .

16.3c . . . and the air induction tubes . . .

5•24 Fuel and exhaust systems

16.3d ... and take the reed valve assembly off

16.5 To remove a reed valve from the assembly, disconnect the hoses and remove the bolts (arrowed)

assembly off the motorcycle **(see illustration)**.

4 To replace the air cut valve, remove the retaining clip screw and disconnect the hoses.

5 To replace reed valves, remove the mounting bolts and disconnect the hoses **(see illustration)**.

6 Installation is the reverse of the removal steps.

17 Evaporation control system (California models) - inspection and canister replacement

1 The evaporation control system used on California models prevents fuel vapor from escaping into the atmosphere. When the engine isn't running, the vapor is stored in a canister, then routed into the combustion chambers for burning when the engine starts **(see illustrations)**.

2 The hoses should be checked periodically for loose connections, damage and deterioration. Tighten or replace the hoses as needed.

3 To remove the canister, remove the seat and fuel tank (see Chapter 9 and Section 2).

Disconnect the hoses and remove the mounting bolts **(see illustrations)**.

4 Inspect the rubber mounting bushings and replace them if they're cracked or deteriorated. Bolt the canister to its bracket and reconnect the hoses.

1 Carburetor
2 Canister
3 To atmosphere
4 To carburetor
A Side view
B Bottom view

17.1a Evaporation control system details (FZR600 models)

17.1b Evaporation control system details (FZR1000 models)

Fuel and exhaust systems 5•25

17.3a Disconnect the hoses and remove the mounting bolts (this is an FZR600) . . .

17.3b . . . and this is an FZR1000

Notes

Chapter 6
Ignition system

Contents

General information	1	Ignition system - check	2
Igniter - check, removal and installation	5	Pickup coils - check, removal and installation	4
Ignition coils - check, removal and installation	3	Spark plugs - replacement	See Chapter 1

Degrees of difficulty

| **Easy,** suitable for novice with little experience | **Fairly easy,** suitable for beginner with some experience | **Fairly difficult,** suitable for competent DIY mechanic | **Difficult,** suitable for experienced DIY mechanic | **Very difficult,** suitable for expert DIY or professional |

Specifications

Ignition system

Ignition coil primary resistance	1.8 to 2.2 ohms at 20-degrees C (68-degrees F)
Ignition coil secondary resistance	
All except 1987 and 1988 UK FZR1000	9,600 to 14,400 ohms at 20-degrees C (68-degrees F)
1987 and 1988 UK FZR1000	10,800 to 13,200 ohms at 20-degrees C (68-degrees F)
Spark plug cap resistance	9,000 to 11,000 ohms at 20-degrees C (68-degrees F)
Arcing distance	6 mm (1/4 inch)
Pickup coil resistance	135 to 165 ohms at 20-degrees C (68-degrees F)
Ignition timing	Not adjustable
Spark plugs	See Chapter 1

1 General information

This motorcycle is equipped with a battery operated, fully transistorized, breakerless ignition system. The system consists of the following components:

Pickup coil
Igniter unit
Battery and fuse
Ignition coils
Spark plugs
Ignition (main) and engine kill (stop) switches
Primary and secondary circuit wiring

The transistorized ignition system functions on the same principle as a breaker point DC ignition system with the pickup unit and igniter performing the tasks previously associated with the breaker points and mechanical advance system. As a result, adjustment and maintenance of ignition components is eliminated (with the exception of spark plug replacement).

All models use a digital microprocessor and a single pickup coil. The digital microprocessor system also increases ignition coil primary current during starting, prevents excessive engine speed and controls the electric fuel pump.

Because of their nature, the individual ignition system components can be checked but not repaired. If ignition system troubles occur, and the faulty component can be isolated, the only cure for the problem is to replace the part with a new one. Keep in mind that most electrical parts, once purchased, can't be returned. To avoid unnecessary expense, make very sure the faulty component has been positively identified before buying a replacement part.

2 Ignition system - check

Warning: Because of the very high voltage generated by the ignition system, extreme care should be taken when these checks are performed.

1 If the ignition system is the suspected cause of poor engine performance or failure to start, a number of checks can be made to isolate the problem.
2 Make sure the engine kill switch is in the Run position.

Engine will not start

3 Disconnect one of the spark plug wires, connect the wire to a spare spark plug and lay the plug on the engine with the threads contacting the engine. If necessary, hold the spark plug with an insulated tool. Crank the engine over and make sure a well-defined, blue spark occurs between the spark plug electrodes.

Warning: Don't remove one of the spark plugs from the engine to perform this check - atomized fuel being pumped out of the open spark plug hole could ignite, causing severe injury!

4 If no spark occurs, the following checks should be made:
5 Unscrew a spark plug cap from a plug wire and check the cap resistance with an ohmmeter. If the resistance exceeds Specifications, replace it with a new one. Repeat this check on the remaining plug caps.

6•2 Ignition system

6 Make sure all electrical connectors are clean and tight. Check all wires for shorts, opens and correct installation.

7 Check the battery voltage with a voltmeter and - on models equipped with batteries having removable filler caps - check the specific gravity with a hydrometer (see Chapter 1). If the voltage is less than 12-volts or if the specific gravity is low, recharge the battery.

8 Check the ignition fuse and the fuse connections. If the fuse is blown, replace it with a new one; if the connections are loose or corroded, clean or repair them.

9 Refer to Chapter 10 and check the ignition switch, engine kill switch, neutral switch and sidestand switch.

10 Refer to Section 3 and check the ignition coil primary and secondary resistance.

11 Refer to Section 4 and check the pickup coil resistance.

12 On 1989 and later models, disconnect the electrical connector from the relay assembly behind the left side cover (FZR600 and 1000) or under the seat (FZR750). Connect an ohmmeter as follows:
  a) Positive lead to relay assembly terminal pin that connects to blue-yellow wire;
  b) Negative lead to relay assembly terminal pin that connects to sky blue wire.

The ohmmeter should indicate continuity (little or no resistance). Switch the ohmmeter leads; it should now indicate very high or infinite resistance. If the readings aren't as described, the diode is bad and the relay assembly will have to be replaced. Before you buy this non-returnable part, have the ignition system tested by a Yamaha dealer or other qualified technician. **Note:** *If the preceding checks produce positive results but there is still no spark at the plug, the igniter may be at fault. Have the ignition system tested by a Yamaha dealer or other qualified technician.*

Engine starts but misfires

13 If the engine starts but misfires, make the following checks before deciding that the ignition system is at fault.

14 The ignition system must be able to produce a spark across a six millimeter (1/4-inch) gap (minimum). A simple test fixture **(see illustration)** can be constructed to make sure the minimum spark gap can be jumped. Make sure the fixture electrodes are positioned six millimeters apart.

15 Connect one of the spark plug wires to the protruding test fixture electrode, then attach the fixture's alligator clip to a good engine ground/earth.

16 Crank the engine over (it will probably start and run on the remaining cylinders) and see if well-defined, blue sparks occur between the test fixture electrodes. If the minimum spark gap test is positive, the ignition coil for that cylinder (and its companion cylinder) is functioning properly. Repeat the check on one of the spark plug wires that is connected to the other coil. If the spark will not jump the gap during either test, or if it is weak (orange colored), refer to steps 5 through 11 of this Section and perform the component checks described.

3 Ignition coils - check, removal and installation

Check

1 In order to determine conclusively that the ignition coils are defective, they should be tested by an authorized Yamaha dealer service department which is equipped with the special electrical tester required for this check.

2 However, the coils can be checked visually (for cracks and other damage) and the primary and secondary coil resistances can be measured with an ohmmeter. If the coils are undamaged, and if the resistances are as specified, they are probably capable of proper operation.

2.14 A spark gap tester can be made from a block of wood, a large clip, two nails, a screw and wire

3 To check the coils for physical damage, they must be removed (see Step 9). To check the resistances, simply remove the fuel tank (see Chapter 5), unplug the primary circuit electrical connectors from the coil(s) and remove the spark plug wires from the plugs that are connected to the coil being checked. Mark the locations of all wires before disconnecting them.

4 To check the coil primary resistance, attach one ohmmeter lead to one of the primary terminals and the other ohmmeter lead to the other primary terminal in the connector **(see illustration)**.

5 Place the ohmmeter selector switch in the Rx1 position and compare the measured resistance to the value listed in this Chapter's Specifications.

6 If the coil primary resistance is as specified, check the coil secondary resistance. Remove the spark plug caps, disconnect the meter leads from the primary terminals and attach them to the spark plug wire terminals **(see illustration)**.

7 Place the ohmmeter selector switch in the Rx100 position and compare the measured

3.4 To test the primary resistance, connect the ohmmeter between the primary terminals in the connector

1 Coils
2 Gray wire terminal (cylinders 2 and 3)
3 Red/white wire terminal (cylinders 2 and 3)
4 Orange wire terminal (cylinders 1 and 4)
5 Red/white wire terminal (cylinders 1 and 4)

3.6 To test the coil secondary resistance, connect the ohmmeter between the spark plug wires

1 Coil   2 Spark plug wires

Ignition system 6•3

3.9 Disconnect the coil primary connectors (this is an FZR1000)

3.11 On FZR600 with bracket-mounted coils, remove the bolt (upper arrow); unscrew the mounting bolt (lower arrow) to remove the coils

3.12a On later FZR1000 models, unbolt the coil bracket . . .

resistance to the values listed in this Chapter's Specifications.
8 If the resistances are not as specified, the coil is probably defective and should be replaced with a new one.

Removal and installation

9 To remove the coils, refer to Chapter 5 and remove the fuel tank, then disconnect the spark plug wires from the plugs. Remove the coil cover (if equipped). After labeling them with tape to aid in reinstallation, unplug the coil primary circuit electrical connectors (see illustration).
10 If you're working on a model with separately mounted coils, remove the coil mounting bolt and take the coil out.
11 If you're working on an FZR600 with bracket-mounted coils, unbolt the bracket and remove it from the frame (see illustration). Remove the coil mounting bolt and take the coil(s) off the bracket.
12 If the coils are bracket-mounted, support the coils with one hand and remove the coil bracket mounting bolt, then withdraw the coil bracket (see illustrations). Unbolt the individual coil(s) from the bracket (see illustration).
13 Installation is the reverse of removal. Make sure the primary circuit electrical connectors are attached to the proper terminals and the plug wires to the correct plugs.

3.12b . . . lift the bracket out of the frame together with the coils . . .

3.12c . . . and detach the coil(s) from the bracket

4 Pickup coil - check, removal and installation

Check

1 Follow the wiring harness from the pickup coil to the connector, then unplug the connector (see illustrations).
2 Probe the terminals in the pickup coil connector with an ohmmeter and compare the resistance reading with the value listed in this Chapter's Specifications.
3 Set the ohmmeter on the highest resistance range. Measure the resistance between a good ground and each terminal in the electrical connector. The meter should read infinity.
4 If the pickup coil fails either of the above tests, it must be replaced.

Removal

FZR600 models

5 Remove the alternator cover from the left side of the engine (see Chapter 10).
6 Unscrew the pickup coil mounting screws and remove the pickup coil (see illustration).

FZR750/1000 models

7 Remove the pickup coil mounting bolts and

4.1a Follow the wiring (arrowed) from the alternator cover to the connector, and disconnect it

4.1b The wiring harness on FZR750/1000 models is protected by a metal cover
1 Harness cover
2 Pickup coil mounting bolts

4.6 On FZR600, remove the mounting screws (arrowed) and take the pickup coil out of the cover

6

6•4 Ignition system

remove the pickup coil from the right side of the engine **(see illustration 4.1b)**.

Installation

8 Installation is the reverse of the removal steps.

5 Igniter - check, removal and installation

Check

1 The igniter is checked by process of elimination (when all other possible causes have been checked and eliminated, the igniter is at fault). Because the igniter is expensive and can't be returned once purchased, consider having a Yamaha dealer test the ignition system before you buy a new igniter.

5.3a The digital igniter is mounted under the seat (this is an FZR600) . . .

5.3b . . . and this is an FZR1000 (FZR750 models similar)

Removal and installation

2 Remove the seat (see Chapter 9).
3 Unplug the electrical connectors. Remove the mounting screws and take the igniter out **(see illustrations)**.
4 Installation is the reverse of the removal steps.

Chapter 7
Frame, suspension and final drive

Contents

Cartridge forks - disassembly, inspection and reassembly 9
Conventional forks - disassembly, inspection and reassembly 8
Drive chain - removal, cleaning and installation 16
Drive chain and sprockets - check, adjustment
    and lubrication .... See Chapter 1
Footpegs and pads - removal and installation 3
Fork oil change 6
Forks - removal and installation 7
Frame - inspection and repair 2
General information 1
Handlebars - removal and installation 5
Rear shock absorber - removal, inspection and installation 11
Rear suspension linkage - removal, check and installation 12
Rear wheel coupling/rubber damper - check and replacement 18
Sidestand - maintenance 4
Sprockets - check and replacement 17
Steering head bearings - replacement 10
Suspension adjustments 19
Swingarm bearings - check 13
Swingarm bearings - inspection and replacement 15
Swingarm - removal and installation 14

Degrees of difficulty

Easy, suitable for novice with little experience	Fairly easy, suitable for beginner with some experience	Fairly difficult, suitable for competent DIY mechanic	Difficult, suitable for experienced DIY mechanic	Very difficult, suitable for expert DIY or professional

Specifications

FZR600

Fork spring length
    Standard .... 415 mm (16.3 inches)
    Minimum .... 410 mm (16.1 inches)
Fork oil capacity .... 435 cc (14.9 US fl oz, 15.3 Imp fl oz)
Fork oil level (fully compressed) .... 101 mm (3.98 inches) below top of inner fork tube
Rear spring free length
    Standard .... 180.5 mm (7.11 inches)
    Minimum .... 170.5 mm (6.71 inches)
Rear spring installed length .... 170.0 mm (6.69 inches)
Swingarm end play and side play limits .... 1 mm (0.04 inch)
Suspension settings (rear spring preload)
    Hard 7
    Standard 3
    Soft 1

Torque specifications

Footpegs to bracket .... 55 Nm (40 ft-lbs)
Footpeg bracket to frame .... 22 Nm (16 ft-lbs)
Frame downtubes to frame
    Front .... 60 Nm (43 ft-lbs)
    Rear .... 33 Nm (24 ft-lbs)
Rear frame section to frame
    Upper bolts (M10) .... 64 Nm (46 ft-lbs)
    Lower bolts (M12) .... 88 Nm (64 ft-lbs)
Front forks
    Cap bolt to fork .... Not specified
    Damper rod bolt .... 40 Nm (29 ft-lbs)*
Handlebars and steering stem
    Handlebar to boss Allen bolts .... 23 Nm (17 ft-lbs)
    Handlebar boss to fork tube pinch bolts .... 13 Nm 9.5 ft-lbs)
    Lower triple clamp bolts .... 22 Nm (16 ft-lbs)
    Upper triple clamp bolts .... 26 Nm (19 ft-lbs)
    Steering stem nut .... 110 Nm (80 ft-lbs)
    Grip weight to handlebar .... 25 Nm (18 ft-lbs)

Torque specifications (FZR600 continued)

Rear shock absorber pivot bolts/nuts	40 Nm (29 ft-lbs)
Rear suspension linkage	
Relay arm to frame	40 Nm (29 ft-lbs)
Tie rods to relay arm	40 Nm (29 ft-lbs)
Tie rods to frame	40 Nm (29 ft-lbs)
Swingarm pivot shaft nut	90 Nm (65 ft-lbs)
Drive chain front sprocket	60 Nm (43 ft-lbs)
Drive chain rear sprocket	32 Nm (23 ft-lbs)
Engine sprocket cover bolts	10 Nm (7.2 ft-lbs)

*Apply non-permanent thread locking agent to the damper rod bolt threads.

FZR750 (1987 and 1988)

Fork spring length	
Standard	529 mm (20.84 inches)
Minimum	524 mm (20.63 inches)
Fork oil capacity	434 cc (14.7 US fl oz, 15.31 Imp fl oz)
Fork oil level (fully compressed)	138 mm (5.43 inches) below top of inner fork tube
Swingarm end play and side play limits	1 mm (0.04 inch)
Front fork spring preload adjustment	
Minimum	Full counterclockwise (anti-clockwise)
Standard	Position 6
Maximum	Full clockwise
Front fork damping adjustment	
Minimum	Setting 1
Standard	Setting 2
Maximum	Setting 4
Rear spring preload adjustment	
Minimum	157 mm (6.2 inches)
Standard	175 mm (6.9 inches)
Maximum	180 mm (7.1 inches)
Rear shock damping adjustment	
Maximum (slower)	Zero
Standard	5 clicks out
Minimum (faster)	10 clicks out

Torque specifications

Footpegs to bracket	55 Nm (40 ft-lbs)
Front footpeg bracket to frame	28 Nm (20 ft-lbs)
Frame downtubes to frame	
Front	63 Nm (46 ft-lbs)
Rear	28 Nm (20 ft-lbs)
Rear frame section to frame (M10)	55 Nm (40 ft-lbs)
Front forks	
Cap bolt to fork	23 Nm (17 ft-lbs)
Damper rod bolt	62 Nm (45 ft-lbs)*
Handlebars and steering stem	
Handlebar to upper triple clamp Allen bolts	9 Nm (6.5 ft-lbs)
Handlebar to fork tube pinch bolts	20 Nm (14 ft-lbs)
Lower triple clamp bolts	20 Nm (14 ft-lbs)
Upper triple clamp bolts	20 Nm (14 ft-lbs)
Steering stem nut	110 Nm (80 ft-lbs)
Grip weight to handlebar	26 Nm (19 ft-lbs)
Rear shock absorber pivot bolts/nuts	
Upper	42 Nm (30 ft-lbs)
Lower	40 Nm (28 ft-lbs)
Rear suspension linkage	
Relay arm to frame	48 Nm (35 ft-lbs)
Tie rods to relay arm	74 Nm (54 ft-lbs)
Tie rods to frame	74 Nm (54 ft-lbs)
Swingarm pivot shaft nut	90 Nm (65 ft-lbs)
Drive chain front sprocket nut	60 Nm (43 ft-lbs)
Drive chain rear sprocket nuts	55 Nm (40 ft-lbs)
Engine sprocket cover bolts	Not specified

*Apply non-permanent thread locking agent to the damper rod bolt threads.

FZR750 (1989-on)

Fork spring length
  Standard .... 367 mm (5.12 inches)
  Minimum .... 363 mm (14.3 inches)
Fork oil capacity .... 437 cc (14.8 US fl oz, 15.4 Imp fl oz)
Fork oil level (fully compressed) .... 131 mm (5.16 inches) below top of inner fork tube
Swingarm end play and side play limits .... 1 mm (0.04 inch)
Front fork preload adjustment
  Maximum .... Groove 1
  Standard .... Groove 6
  Minimum .... Groove 9
Front fork rebound damping adjustment
  Maximum .... Fully turned in
  Standard .... 8 clicks out from full-in
  Minimum .... 10 clicks out from full-in
Front fork compression damping adjustment
  Maximum .... Fully turned in
  Standard .... 8 clicks out from full-in
  Minimum .... 10 clicks out from full-in
Front fork height adjustment
  Highest .... Groove 1
  Lowest .... Groove 5
Rear spring preload adjustment
  Maximum .... 15 mm (0.6 inch) on scale
  Standard (and minimum) .... Zero mm (zero inch) on scale
Rear shock rebound damping adjustment
  Maximum .... Fully turned in
  Standard .... 12 clicks out
  Minimum (faster) .... 23 clicks out
Rear shock compression damping adjustment
  Maximum .... Fully turned in
  Standard .... 15 clicks out
  Minimum (faster) .... 23 clicks out

Torque specifications

Front footpegs to bracket .... 55 Nm (40 ft-lbs)
Front footpeg bracket to frame .... 28 Nm (20 ft-lbs)
Rear frame section to frame (M8) .... 30 Nm (22 ft-lbs)
Front forks
  Cap bolt to fork .... 23 Nm (17 ft-lbs)
  Preload adjuster locknut .... 15 Nm (11 ft-lbs)
  Damper rod bolt .... 40 Nm (29 ft-lbs)*
Handlebars and steering stem
  Handlebar to spacer through-bolt .... 8 Nm (5.8 ft-lbs)
  Handlebar to fork tube clamp bolts .... 8 Nm (5.8 ft-lbs)
  Lower triple clamp bolts .... 23 Nm (17 ft-lbs)
  Upper triple clamp bolts .... 20 Nm (14 ft-lbs)
  Steering stem bolt .... 55 Nm (40 ft-lbs)
  Grip weight to handlebar .... 26 Nm (19 ft-lbs)
Rear shock absorber pivot bolts/nuts
  Upper .... 42 Nm (30 ft-lbs)
  Lower .... 40 Nm (28 ft-lbs)
Rear suspension linkage
  Relay arm to frame .... 45 Nm (32 ft-lbs)
  Tie rods to relay arm .... 70 Nm (50 ft-lbs)
  Tie rods to frame .... 70 Nm (50 ft-lbs)
Swingarm pivot shaft nut .... 130 Nm (94 ft-lbs)
Drive chain front sprocket nut .... 70 Nm (50 ft-lbs)
Drive chain rear sprocket nuts .... 55 Nm (40 ft-lbs)
Engine sprocket cover bolts .... 10 Nm (7.2 ft-lbs)

Apply non-permanent thread locking agent to the damper rod bolt threads.

FZR1000 (1987 and 1988)

Fork spring length
    Standard .... 533 mm (20.98 inches)
    Minimum .... 528 mm (20.79 inches)
Fork oil capacity .... 425 cc (14.4 US fl oz, 15.0 Imp fl oz)
Fork oil level (fully compressed) .... 143 mm (5.63 inches) below top of inner fork tube
Swingarm end play and side play limits .... 1 mm (0.04 inch)
Front fork preload adjustment
    Maximum .... Groove 1
    Standard .... Groove 5
    Minimum .... Groove 7
Rear spring preload adjustment length
    Maximum .... 20.5 mm (0.81 inch)
    Standard .... 14.5 mm (0.57 inch)
    Minimum .... 12.5 mm (0.49 inch)
Recommended suspension settings
    With rider only
        Front .... Groove 4 to 7
        Rear .... 12.5 to 16.5 mm (0.49 to 0.65 inch)
    With passenger OR accessories and equipment
        Front .... Groove 2 to 5
        Rear .... 14.5 to 18.5 mm (0.57 to 0.73 inch)
    With passenger AND accessories and equipment
        Front .... Groove 1 to 4
        Rear .... 16.5 to 20.5 mm (0.65 to 0.81 inch)

Torque specifications

Footpegs to bracket .... 55 Nm (40 ft-lbs)
Front footpeg bracket to frame .... 28 Nm (20 ft-lbs)
Frame downtubes to frame
    Front .... 63 Nm (46 ft-lbs)
    Rear .... 28 Nm (20 ft-lbs)
Rear frame section to frame (M10) .... 55 Nm (40 ft-lbs)
Front forks
    Cap bolt to fork .... 23 Nm (17 ft-lbs)
    Damper rod bolt .... 62 Nm (45 ft-lbs)*
Handlebars and steering stem
    Handlebar to upper triple clamp Allen bolts .... 9 Nm (6.5 ft-lbs)
    Handlebar to fork tube pinch bolts .... 20 Nm (14 ft-lbs)
    Lower triple clamp bolts .... 20 Nm (14 ft-lbs)
    Upper triple clamp bolts .... 20 Nm (14 ft-lbs)
    Steering stem nut .... 110 Nm (80 ft-lbs)
    Grip weight to handlebar .... 26 Nm (19 ft-lbs)
Rear shock absorber pivot bolts/nuts
    Upper .... 42 Nm (30 ft-lbs)
    Lower .... 40 Nm (28 ft-lbs)
Rear suspension linkage
    Relay arm to frame .... 48 Nm (35 ft-lbs)
    Tie rods to relay arm .... 74 Nm (54 ft-lbs)
    Tie rods to frame .... 74 Nm (54 ft-lbs)
Swingarm pivot shaft nut .... 90 Nm (65 ft-lbs)
Drive chain front sprocket nut .... 70 Nm (50 ft-lbs)
Drive chain rear sprocket nuts .... 55 Nm (40 ft-lbs)
Engine sprocket cover bolts .... 10 Nm (7.2 ft-lbs)

*Apply non-permanent thread locking agent to the damper rod bolt threads.

FZR1000 (1989)

Fork spring length
    Standard .... 321.3 mm (12.6 inches)
    Minimum .... 318 mm (12.5 inches)
Fork oil capacity (fully compressed) .... 535 cc (18.1 US fl oz, 18.9 Imp fl oz)
Fork oil level (fully compressed) .... 116 mm (4.57 inches) below top of inner fork tube
Swingarm end play and side play limits .... 1 mm (0.04 inch)
Front fork preload adjustment
    Maximum .... 4 (fully turned in)
    Standard 2
    Minimum 1

FZR1000 (1989) (continued)

Rear spring preload adjustment length
   Maximum .... 47.5 mm (1.87 inch)
   Standard .... 40.5 mm (1.59 inch)
   Minimum .... 37.5 mm (1.87 inch)
Rear shock damping adjustment
   Maximum .... Zero (fully turned in)
   Standard .... 7 clicks out
   Minimum .... 9 clicks out
Recommended suspension settings
  With rider only
   Front .... 1 or 2
   Rear preload .... 37.5 to 42.5 mm (1.48 to 1.67 inch)
   Rear damping .... 5 to 9 clicks out
  With passenger OR accessories and equipment
   Front .... 2 or 3
   Rear preload .... 40 to 45 mm (1.57 to 1.77 inch)
   Rear damping .... 4 to 7 clicks out
  With passenger AND accessories and equipment
   Front .... 3 or 4
   Rear preload .... 42.5 to 47.5 mm (1.57 to 1.77 inch)
   Rear damping .... 3 to 6 clicks out

Torque specifications

Footpegs to bracket .... 55 Nm (40 ft-lbs)
Footpeg brackets to frame .... 28 Nm (20 ft-lbs)
Rear frame section to frame (M10) .... 55 Nm (40 ft-lbs)
Front forks
  Cap bolt to fork .... Not specified
  Damper rod bolt* .... 62 Nm (45 ft-lbs)
Handlebars and steering stem
  Handlebar boss to upper triple clamp Allen bolts .... 20 Nm (14 ft-lbs)
Handlebars and steering stem
  Handlebar to boss Allen bolts .... 28 Nm (20 ft-lbs)
  Lower triple clamp bolts .... 23 Nm (17 ft-lbs)
  Upper triple clamp bolts .... 23 Nm (17 ft-lbs)
  Steering stem nut .... 110 Nm (80 ft-lbs)
Handlebars and steering stem
  Grip weight to handlebar .... 25 Nm (18 ft-lbs)
Rear shock absorber pivot bolts/nuts
  Upper .... 42 Nm (30 ft-lbs)
  Lower .... 40 Nm (28 ft-lbs)
Rear suspension linkage
  Relay arm to frame .... 48 Nm (35 ft-lbs)
  Tie rods to relay arm and swingarm .... 74 Nm (54 ft-lbs)
Swingarm pivot shaft nut .... 130 Nm (94 ft-lbs)
Drive chain front sprocket nut .... 70 Nm (50 ft-lbs)
Drive chain rear sprocket nuts .... 60 Nm (43 ft-lbs)
Engine sprocket cover bolts .... 10 Nm (7.2 ft-lbs)

FZR1000 (1990-on)

Fork spring length
  1990
   Standard .... 321.3 mm (12.6 inches)
   Minimum .... 318 mm (12.5 inches)
  1991 through 1993
   Standard .... 331.5 mm (13.1 inches)
   Minimum .... 328 mm (12.9 inches)
  1994-on
   Standard .... 340 mm (13.4 inches)
   Minimum .... 335 mm (13.2 inches)

FZR1000 (1990-on) (continued)

Fork oil capacity
   1990 .... 535 cc (18.1 US fl oz, 18.9 Imp fl oz)
   1991-on .... See Chapter 1
Fork oil level (fully compressed)
   1990 .... 116 mm (4.57 inches) below top of inner fork tube
   1991-on .... See Chapter 1
Swingarm end play and side play limits .... 1 mm (0.04 inch)
Front fork preload adjustment (1990 through 1993)
   Maximum (hardest) .... Groove 1
   Standard .... Groove 5
   Minimum (softest) .... Groove 7
Front fork preload adjustment (1994-on)
   Maximum (hardest) .... Groove 1
   Standard .... Groove 4
   Minimum (softest) .... Groove 5
Rear spring preload adjustment length
   Maximum .... 47.5 mm (1.87 inch)
   Standard .... 40.5 mm (1.59 inch)
   Minimum .... 37.5 mm (1.87 inch)
Rear shock damping adjustment
   Maximum .... Zero (full in)
   Standard .... 7 clicks out
   Minimum .... 9 clicks out
Recommended suspension settings
   With rider only
     Front .... Groove 4 to 7
     Rear preload .... 37.5 to 42.5 mm (1.48 to 1.67 inch)
     Rear damping .... 5 to 9 clicks out
   With passenger OR accessories and equipment
     Front .... Groove 2 to 5
     Rear preload .... 40 to 45 mm (1.57 to 1.77 inch)
     Rear damping .... 4 to 7 clicks out
   With passenger AND accessories and equipment
     Front .... Groove 1 to 4
     Rear preload .... 42.5 to 47.5 mm (1.57 to 1.77 inch)
     Rear damping .... 3 to 6 clicks out

Torque specifications

Footpegs to bracket .... 55 Nm (40 ft-lbs)
Footpeg brackets to frame .... 28 Nm (20 ft-lbs)
Rear frame section to frame (M10) .... 55 Nm (40 ft-lbs)
Front forks
   Cap bolt to fork
     1990 .... Not specified
     1991 through 1993 .... 23 Nm (17 ft-lbs)
     1994-on .... 25 Nm (18 ft-lbs)
   Adjuster bolt locknut
     1991 through 1993 .... 15 Nm (11 ft-lbs)
     1994-on .... 25 Nm (18 ft-lbs)
   Damper rod bolt*
     1990 .... 62 Nm (45 ft-lbs)
     1991 through 1993 .... 40 Nm (29 ft-lbs)
     1994-on .... 23 Nm (17 ft-lbs)
Handlebars and steering stem
   Handlebar boss to upper triple clamp Allen bolts
     1990 .... 20 Nm (14 ft-lbs)
     1991 through 1993 .... 19 Nm (13 ft-lbs)
     1994-on .... 28 Nm (20 ft-lbs)
Handlebars and steering stem
   Handlebar to boss Allen bolts .... 28 Nm (20 ft-lbs)
   Lower triple clamp bolts .... 23 Nm (17 ft-lbs)
   Upper triple clamp bolts .... 23 Nm (17 ft-lbs)
   Steering stem nut .... 110 Nm (80 ft-lbs)
Handlebars and steering stem
   Grip weight to handlebar
     1990 through 1993 .... 25 Nm (18 ft-lbs)
     1994-on .... 30 Nm (22 ft-lbs)

Frame, suspension and final drive 7•7

Torque specifications (FZR1000 1990-on continued)

Rear shock absorber pivot bolts/nuts
- Upper .... 42 Nm (30 ft-lbs)
- Lower .... 40 Nm (28 ft-lbs)

Rear suspension linkage
- Relay arm to frame .... 48 Nm (35 ft-lbs)
- Tie rods to relay arm and swingarm .... 74 Nm (54 ft-lbs)

Swingarm pivot shaft nut .... 130 Nm (94 ft-lbs)
Drive chain front sprocket nut .... 70 Nm (50 ft-lbs)
Drive chain rear sprocket nuts .... 60 Nm (43 ft-lbs)
Engine sprocket cover bolts .... 10 Nm (7.2 ft-lbs)

1 General information

FZR600 models and 1987 and 1988 FZR750/1000 models use a frame with detachable downtubes. The rear section of the frame on all models is detachable.

The front forks on FZR600 models, 1987 and 1988 FZR750R models and 1987 through 1990 FZR1000 models are of the conventional coil spring, hydraulically-damped telescopic type. The 1989 and later FZR750R and the 1991 and later FZR1000 use cartridge forks. The front forks on FZR750/1000 models include adjustments for fork spring preload; 750 models also include damping adjustments.

The rear suspension is Yamaha's Monocross design, which consists of a single shock absorber, a linkage which provides progressive damping and spring rate, and a swingarm. The shock absorber preload is adjustable on all models. The damping settings are adjustable on 750 and later 1000 models.

The final drive uses an endless chain (which means it doesn't have a master link). A rubber damper (often called a "cush drive") is installed between the rear wheel coupling and the wheel.

2 Frame - inspection and repair

1 The frame should not require attention unless accident damage has occurred. In most cases, frame replacement is the only satisfactory remedy for such damage. A few frame specialists have the jigs and other equipment necessary for straightening the frame to the required standard of accuracy, but even then there is no simple way of assessing to what extent the frame may have been overstressed.

2 After the machine has accumulated a lot of miles, the frame should be examined closely for signs of cracking or splitting at the welded joints. Corrosion can also cause weakness at these joints. Loose engine mount bolts can cause ovaling or fracturing of the mounting tabs. Minor damage can often be repaired by welding, depending on the extent and nature of the damage.

3 Remember that a frame which is out of alignment will cause handling problems. If misalignment is suspected as the result of an accident, it will be necessary to strip the machine completely so the frame can be thoroughly checked.

3 Footpegs and pads - removal and installation

All except 1989-on FZR750 models

1 To replace a rubber pad, remove the screws and lift it off (see illustration). Position the new pad and install the screws.

2 To remove a front footpeg, detach the brake master cylinder pushrod, brake pedal spring and stoplight switch spring (right side) or gearshift linkage (left side). Unbolt the footpeg bracket from the frame (see illustration).

3 Remove the Allen bolt that secures the footpeg to the bracket and remove the footpeg and brake pedal.

4 To remove a rear footpeg from its bracket, remove the cotter pin and pivot pin (or pivot bolt and nut) and take the footpeg off (see

3.1 The footpeg pads are secured by screws (arrowed)

3.2 Remove the master cylinder clevis pin (left arrow) and remove the bracket bolts (right arrows) (FZR600 shown)

7•8 Frame, suspension and final drive

illustrations). To remove the bracket, unbolt the muffler/silencer bracket from it (right side only). Unbolt the footpeg bracket from the frame.

1989-on FZR750 models

5 Remove the bolt from underneath the footpeg and withdraw the footpeg from its bracket.

All models

6 Installation is the reverse of removal. Lubricate the footpeg pivot as well as the bearing surfaces of the brake pedal and gearshift linkage arm (if removed). Tighten the bracket-to-frame and footpeg-to-bracket bolts to the torque listed in this Chapter's Specifications. Use new cotter pins. Adjust the gearshift linkage (see Chapter 1).

4 Sidestand - maintenance

1 The sidestand is attached to a bracket on the frame. An extension spring(s) anchored to the bracket ensures that the stand is held in the retracted position (see illustrations).
2 Make sure the pivot bolt is tight and the extension spring is in good condition and not overstretched. An accident is almost certain to occur if the stand extends while the machine is in motion.

5 Handlebars - removal and installation

1 The handlebars on all except 1989 and later FZR750 models are individual assemblies that slip over the tops of the fork tubes, each being retained by pinch bolts. The handlebars on 1989 and later FZR750 models are individual assemblies which are secured to the fork tubes by integral clamps.

FZR600 models

2 If you're going to remove the handlebar from the handlebar boss, remove the rubber

3.4a Rear footpeg details (FZR600 models)
1 Footpeg pivot pin
2 Muffler/silencer mounting bolt (right side only)
3 Footpeg bracket bolts

3.4b Rear footpeg details (FZR1000 models)
1 Footpeg pivot bolt
2 Muffler/silencer mounting bracket (right side only)
3 Footpeg bracket bolts

4.1a Sidestand mounting details (FZR600)
1 Retracting springs
2 Pivot nut
3 Switch mounting screws

4.1b Sidestand mounting details (1989-on FZR1000)
1 Switch bracket bolts
2 Sidestand bracket bolts
3 Sidestand pivot bolt

plug and remove the Allen bolt that secures the bar (see illustration).
3 If the handlebars must be removed for access to other components, such as the forks or the steering head, simply remove the bolts and slip the handlebar(s) off the fork tubes (see illustrations). It's not necessary to disconnect the cables, wires or hoses, but it is a good idea to support the assembly with a piece of wire or rope, to avoid unnecessary

strain on the cables, wires and the brake or clutch hose.
4 If the handlebars are to be removed completely, refer to Chapter 2 for clutch cable removal procedures, Chapter 8 for the brake master cylinder removal procedures, Chapter 5 for the throttle cable removal procedure and Chapter 10 for the switch removal procedure.
5 Check the handlebars for cracks and distortion and replace them if any undesirable

5.2 The handlebar is secured to the boss by an Allen bolt behind this plastic plug (arrowed)

5.3a The handlebar boss is secured by pinch bolts (arrowed) . . .

5.3b . . . loosen them with an Allen wrench

Frame, suspension and final drive 7•9

5.5 Align the pin with the hole (arrowed)

5.6a Pry out the plastic plugs with a pointed tool . . .

5.6b . . . remove the bolts that locate the handlebar bosses, and the steering stem nut (arrowed)

conditions are found. When installing the handlebars, align the pin in the upper triple clamp with the hole in the handlebar boss **(see illustration)**. Tighten the bolts to the torque listed in this Chapter's Specifications.

FZR750/1000 models (except 1989-on FZR750R)

6 Pry the plastic plugs out of the upper triple clamp, then remove the Allen bolts that secure the triple clamp to the handlebars **(see illustrations)**.
7 Remove the steering stem nut. Loosen the pinch bolts that secure the upper triple clamp to the forks and lift the triple clamp off **(see illustration)**.
8 To remove the handlebar from the handlebar boss on 1989 and later FZR1000 models, remove the Allen bolt that secures the handlebar **(see illustration)**.
9 If the handlebars must be removed for access to other components, such as the forks or the steering head, simply slip the handlebar(s) off the fork tubes **(see illustrations)**. It's not necessary to disconnect the cables, wires or hoses, but it is a good idea to support the assembly with a piece of

5.7 Loosen the pinch bolts with an Allen wrench

wire or rope, to avoid unnecessary strain on the cables, wires and the brake or clutch hose.
10 If the handlebars are to be removed completely, refer to Chapter 3 for clutch master cylinder removal procedures, Chapter 8 for the brake master cylinder removal procedures, Chapter 5 for the throttle cable removal procedure and Chapter 10 for the switch removal procedure.
11 Check the handlebars for cracks and distortion and replace them if any undesirable conditions are found. Be sure to reinstall the

5.8 Remove the Allen bolt (arrowed) to separate the handlebar from the boss

handlebar dampers (1989 and later FZR1000 models). Tighten the bolts to the torque listed in this Chapter's Specifications.

1989-on FZR750

12 Remove the clutch lever bracket from the left handlebar.
13 Remove the master cylinder and its reservoir from the right handlebar.
14 Disconnect the brake light switch electrical connectors and remove the handlebar switches (see Chapter 10).

5.9a Note the rubber dampers (1989-on FZR1000; the upper one fits on top of the handlebar boss (arrowed) . . .

5.9b . . . while the lower damper fits over the fork tube

7•10 Frame, suspension and final drive

15 Unscrew the grip ends and take off the left handlebar grip **(see illustration)**.
16 Pull back the rubber cover and separate the halves of the throttle cable housing.
17 Disconnect the throttle cables and remove the throttle grip.
18 Remove the handlebar clamp bolts, followed by the long through-bolt and remove the handlebar.
19 Installation is the reverse of the removal steps. Slide the spacer up against its triple clamp and install the handlebar and its clamp. Insert the long through-bolt through the hole in the spacer and thread it into the triple clamp. Tighten the clamp bolts to the torque listed in this Chapter's specification (tighten the inner bolts fully before tightening the outer bolts).

6 Fork oil change

1 Grip ends
2 Throttle grip
3 Throttle cablehousing
4 Right handlebar
5 Handlebar clamp
6 Handlebar spacer
7 Handlebar spacer
8 Handlebar clamp
9 Left handlebar
10 Left handlebar grip
11 Through-bolts

5.15 Handlebar details (1989-on FZR750 models)

Conventional forks

1 Support the bike securely so it can't be knocked over during this procedure. Remove the fairing and position a jack with a block of wood on the jack head under the engine to support the motorcycle when the fork cap bolts are removed.
2 Loosen the handlebar pinch bolts (FZR600) or the upper triple clamp pinch bolts (FZR750/1000).

3 Unscrew the fork cap and lift it out **(see illustrations)**. If you're working on an FZR750/1000, lift out the spring washer **(see illustration)**. On all models, remove the spacer, spring seat and spring **(see illustration)**.
4 Place a drain pan under the fork leg and remove the drain screw **(see illustration)**.

Warning: Do not allow fork oil to contact the brake discs, pads or tire. If it does, clean the discs with brake system cleaner, replace the pads with new ones or wash the tire clean before riding the motorcycle.

5 After most of the oil has drained, slowly compress and release the forks to pump out the remaining oil. An assistant will most likely be required to do this.
6 Check the drain screw gasket and fork cap O-ring for damage and replace them if necessary **(see illustration)**. Clean the

6.3a Unscrew the fork cap (this is an FZR600) . . .

6.3b . . . and this is an FZR1000 equipped with spring preload adjusters

6.3c On FZR750/1000 models, lift out the spring washer (arrowed) . .

6.3d . . . and on all models remove the spacer, spring seat and spring

1 Spring
2 Spring seat
3 Spacer
4 Fork cap and O-ring

6.4 Remove the fork drain screw (arrowed) and its gasket

6.6 Replace the O-ring on the fork cap if it's damaged or deteriorated

Frame, suspension and final drive 7•11

threads of the drain screw with solvent and let it dry, then install the screw and gasket, tightening it securely.
7 Pour the type and amount of fork oil, listed in this Chapter's Specifications, into the fork tube through the opening at the top **(see illustration)**.
8 Remove the jack from under the engine and slowly pump the forks a few times to purge the air. Measure the level of the oil in the fork with the fork fully compressed and without the spring in position. Compare it to the value listed in this Chapter's Specifications. Add or remove oil as necessary.
9 Install the spring, spring seat and spacer **(see illustration)**. If you're working on an FZR750/1000, install the spring washer.
10 Coat the O-ring on the cap bolt with a thin layer of multi-purpose grease.
11 Install the O-ring and the cap bolt. Tighten the cap bolt securely.
12 The remainder of installation is the reverse of the removal steps. Tighten all fasteners to the torque listed in this Chapter's Specifications.

Cartridge forks

13 Changing the oil in cartridge forks requires removal and partial disassembly of the forks (see Section 9).

7 Forks - removal and installation

Removal

1 Support the bike securely so it can't be knocked over during this procedure.
2 Place a jack under the engine and raise it slightly to lift the front tire off the ground.
3 Remove the brake calipers and front wheel (see Chapter 8).
4 Remove the front fender (see Chapter 9).

FZR600 models

5 Loosen the clamp bolts in the handlebar bosses, then lift the handlebars off the forks and support them from above (see Section 5).

6.7 Pour the specified amount of fork oil into the top of the fork

6 Remove any wiring harness clamps or straps from the fork tubes.
7 If the fork will be disassembled after removal, read through the disassembly procedure (see Section 8), paying special attention to the damper rod bolt removal steps. If you don't have the necessary special tool or a substitute for it, you can remove the damper rod bolt before the fork is disassembled, while the spring tension will keep the damper rod from spinning inside the fork tube.
8 If the forks will be disassembled after removal, refer to Section 6 and loosen the fork caps.
9 Loosen the fork upper and lower triple clamp bolts **(see illustrations)**, then slide the fork tubes down and remove the forks from the motorcycle.

HAYNES HiNT *If the fork legs are seized, spray the area with penetrating oil and allow time for it to soak in before trying again.*

1987 and 1988 FZR750; all FZR1000 models

10 Remove the left, right and front fairing panels and the front fender (see Chapter 9).
11 If you're working on a 1987 through 1993 model, remove the seat, the fuel tank and the air cleaner housing (see Chapters 5 and 9).

6.9 The spring seat fits on the spring like this

Disconnect the electrical connector for the ignition switch.
12 If you're working on a 1991 through 1993 model, remove the tie wrap that secures the horn electrical connector.
13 Remove the upper triple clamp and the handlebars (see Section 5).
14 Loosen the lower triple clamp bolts **(see illustration)**, then slide the fork tubes down and remove the forks from the motorcycle.

1989-on FZR750 models

15 Remove the lower fairing (see Chapter 9).
16 Remove the handlebars (see Section 5).
17 Loosen the upper and lower triple clamp bolts, then slide the fork tubes down and remove the forks and handlebar spacers from the motorcycle.

Installation

18 Slide each fork leg into the lower triple clamp.
19 Slide the fork legs up, installing the tops of the tubes into the upper triple clamp. Position the top of the fork tube the distance above the upper triple clamp listed in this Chapter's Specifications.
20 The remainder of installation is the reverse of the removal procedure. Tighten all fasteners to the torques listed in this Chapter's Specifications and the Chapter 8 Specifications.
21 Pump the front brake lever several times to bring the pads into contact with the discs.

7.9a Loosen the upper triple clamp bolt . . .

7.9b . . . and the lower triple clamp bolt

7.14 The forks are held in the lower triple clamps by a pair of clamp bolts

7•12 Frame, suspension and final drive

1 Fork cap
2 O-ring
3 Spacer
4 Spring seat
5 Spring
6 Rebound spring
7 Damper rod
8 Oil lock piece
9 Inner fork tube
10 Dust seal
11 Retainer
12 Oil seal
13 Seal spacer
14 Guide bushing
15 Outer fork tube
16 Gasket
17 Drain screw
18 Copper washer
19 Damper rod bolt

8.2a Front fork (FZR600 models) - exploded view

8.3 Pour the oil into a pan

8.4 Pry the dust seal out of the outer fork tube

8.5 Pry the retainer out of its groove

8.6a The tool to hold the damper rod from turning while the damper rod bolt is loosened or tightened

1 Handle   2 Adapter

8.2b Remove the fork cap with a socket or box wrench (ring spanner)

8 Conventional forks - disassembly, inspection and reassembly

FZR600 models

Disassembly

1 Remove the forks following the procedure in Section 6. Work on one fork leg at a time to avoid mixing up the parts.

2 Remove the fork cap and O-ring (it should have been loosened before the forks were removed) **(see illustrations)**. Remove the spacer, spring seat and spring.

3 Invert the fork assembly over a container and allow the oil to drain out **(see illustration)**.

4 Pry the dust seal from the outer tube **(see illustration)**.

5 Pry the retaining ring from its groove in the outer tube **(see illustration)**. Remove the ring and the washer that's present underneath it.

6 Prevent the damper rod from turning using a holding handle (Yamaha tool no. YM-01326, part no. 90890-01326) and adapter (Yamaha tool no. YM-01300-01, part no. 90890-01294) **(see illustration)**. Unscrew the Allen bolt at the bottom of the outer tube and remove the copper washer **(see illustration)**.

7 Pull the damper rod and the rebound spring from the top of the fork tube. Don't remove

8.6b Remove the damper rod bolt and copper washer

Frame, suspension and final drive 7•13

8.8 Use a slide-hammer motion to separate the outer tube guide bushing from the outer tube

8.9 The oil lock piece (arrowed) fits on the narrow end of the damper rod

8.10 Once the fork tubes are separated, slide the oil seal, spacer and guide bushing off the inner tube

1 Slide bushing
2 Guide bushing
3 Seal spacer
4 Oil seal

the Teflon ring from the damper rod unless a new one will be installed.

8 Hold the outer tube and yank the inner tube away from it, repeatedly (like a slide hammer), until the seal and outer tube guide bushing pop loose **(see illustration)**.
9 Remove the oil lock piece **(see illustration)**.
10 Slide the oil seal, spacer and guide bushing from the inner tube **(see illustration)**.

Inspection

11 Clean all parts in solvent and blow them dry with compressed air, if available. Check the inner and outer fork tubes, the guide bushings and the damper rod for score marks, scratches, flaking of the chrome and excessive or abnormal wear. Look for dents in the tubes and replace them if any are found. Check the fork seal seat for nicks, gouges and scratches. If damage is evident, leaks will occur around the seal-to-outer tube junction. Replace worn or defective parts with new ones.
12 Have the inner fork tube checked for runout at a dealer service department or other repair shop.

⚠ *Warning: If the fork tube is bent, it should not be straightened; replace it with a new one.*

13 Measure the overall length of the long spring and check it for cracks and other damage. Compare the length to the minimum length listed in this Chapter's Specifications. If it's defective or sagged, replace both fork springs with new ones. Never replace only one spring.

Reassembly

14 Always replace the slide bushing (the one that won't come off that's on the bottom of the inner tube) (see illustration 8.10). Pry it apart at the slit and slide it off. Make sure the new one seats properly.
15 Install the rebound spring on the damper rod. Install the damper rod in the inner fork tube, then let it slide slowly down until it protrudes from the bottom of the inner fork tube.
16 Install the oil lock piece over the end of the damper rod that protrudes from the fork tube **(see illustrations)**.
17 Install the inner fork tube in the outer fork tube.
18 Apply non-permanent thread locking agent to the damper rod bolt, then install the bolt and tighten it to the torque listed in this Chapter's Specifications **(see illustration)**. Hold the damper rod from turning with the

8.16a Let the damper rod protrude from the inner fork tube and install the oil lock piece . . .

tool used in Step 6. **Note:** *If you didn't use the tool, tighten the damper rod bolt after the fork spring and cap bolt are installed.*

19 Slide the outer guide bushing down the inner tube. Using a special bushing driver (Yamaha tool no. YM-33963 and 01372, part nos. 90890-01367 and 90890-01372 or equivalent) and a used guide bushing placed

8.16b . . . the damper rod and oil lock piece should look like this when they're assembled

8.18 Use a new washer, and install the damper rod bolt with thread locking agent on the threads

7

7•14 Frame, suspension and final drive

8.19 Drive the guide bushing into position with a special tool like this one

on top of the guide bushing being installed, drive the bushing into place until it is fully seated. If you don't have access to one of these tools, it is highly recommended that you take the assembly to a Yamaha dealer service department or other motorcycle repair shop to have this done.

20 Slide the oil seal spacer down the inner tube, into position over the guide bushing.

21 Lubricate the lips and the outer diameter of the oil seal with the recommended fork oil (see Chapter 1) and slide it down the inner tube, with the seal lip facing up. Drive the seal into place with the same tools used to drive in the guide bushing **(see illustration)**. If you

TOOL TIP

It is possible to drive the bushing into place using a section of pipe and an old guide bushing. Wrap tape around the ends of the pipe to prevent it from scratching the fork tube.

don't have access to these, it is recommended that you take the assembly to a Yamaha dealer service department or other motorcycle repair shop to have the seal driven in. If you are very careful, the seal can be driven in with a hammer and a drift punch. Work around the circumference of the seal, tapping gently on the outer edge of the seal until it's seated. Be careful - if you distort the seal, you'll have to disassemble the fork again and end up taking it to a dealer anyway!

22 Install the retainer, making sure the ring is completely seated in its groove **(see illustration)**.
23 Install the dust seal, making sure it seats completely **(see illustration)**. The same tool used to drive in the oil seal can be used for the dust seal.
24 Install the drain screw and a new gasket, if it was removed.
25 Add the recommended type and amount of fork oil (see Section 6).
26 Install the fork spring, with the closer-wound coils at the top. Install the spring seat and spacer.
27 Install the O-ring and fork cap.
28 Install the fork by following the procedure outlined in Section 7. If you won't be installing the fork right away, store it in an upright position.

1987 and 1988 FZR750 models and 1987 through 1990 FZR1000 models

Disassembly

29 Remove the forks following the procedure in Section 7. Work on one fork leg at a time to avoid mixing up the parts.
30 Remove the fork cap and O-ring (it should have been loosened before the forks were removed). Remove the spring washer **(see illustration 6.3c)**, spacer, spring seat and spring **(see illustrations)**.

8.21 Tap the new oil seal into its bore with the same tool used for the guide bushing

8.22 Make sure the retainer is seated securely in its groove

8.23 Tap the dust seal into its bore with the same tool used for the guide bushing

8.30a Remove the spring seat and spring

Frame, suspension and final drive 7•15

1 Fork cap
2 O-ring
3 Spring washer
4 Spacer
5 Spring seat
6 Fork spring
7 Rebound spring
8 Damper rod
9 Inner fork tube
10 Slide bushing
11 Oil lock piece

12 Dust seal
13 Retainer
14 Oil seal
15 Seal spacer
16 Guide bushing
17 Outer fork tube
18 Drain screw
19 Gasket
20 Copper washer
21 Damper rod bolt

8.30b Front fork details (1987 and 1988 FZR750R and 1987 through 1990 FZR1000 models)

31 Invert the fork assembly over a container and allow the oil to drain out **(see illustration)**.
32 Pry the dust seal from the outer tube **(see illustration)**.
33 Pry the retaining ring from its groove in the outer tube **(see illustration)**.
34 Prevent the damper rod from turning using a holding handle (Yamaha tool no. YM-01326, part no. 90890-01326) and adapter **(see illustration)**.
a) For FZR750 models, the adapter is Yamaha tool no. YM-33298. The hex size is 27 mm.
b) For FZR1000 models, the adapter is YM-01327 (part no. 90890-01327). The hex size is 30 mm.
Unscrew the Allen bolt at the bottom of the outer tube and remove the copper washer **(see illustration)**.

8.31 Let the oil drain into a container

8.32 Pry the dust seal out of its bore, taking care not to scratch the fork tube

8.33 Pry the retainer out of its groove

35 Pull out the damper rod and the rebound spring **(see illustration)**. Don't remove the Teflon ring from the damper rod unless a new one will be installed.

8.34a These are the Yamaha special tools used to hold the damper rod from turning

1 Handle   2 Adapter

8.34b Unscrew the damper rod bolt with an Allen bolt bit

8.35 Remove the damper rod and rebound spring from the fork tube

7

7•16 Frame, suspension and final drive

8.36 Pull the fork tubes apart, rapping them against each other like a slide hammer

8.37 Remove the oil lock piece

8.38 Slide the oil seal, spacer and guide bushing off the inner fork tube

1 Oil seal
2 Spacer
3 Guide bushing
4 Slide bushing

36 Hold the outer tube and yank the inner tube away from it, repeatedly (like a slide hammer), until the seal and outer tube guide bushing pop loose **(see illustration)**.
37 Remove the oil lock piece **(see illustration)**.
38 Slide the oil seal, spacer and guide bushing from the inner tube **(see illustration)**.

Inspection

39 Perform Steps 11 through 13 above to inspect the fork components.

Reassembly

40 Always replace the slide bushing (the one that won't come off that's on the bottom of the inner tube) **(see illustration)**. Pry it apart at the slit and slide it off. Make sure the new one seats properly.
41 Install the rebound spring on the damper rod. Install the damper rod in the inner fork tube, then let it slide slowly down until it protrudes from the bottom of the inner fork tube **(see illustration)**.
42 Install the oil lock piece over the end of the damper rod that protrudes from the fork tube **(see illustration)**.
43 Install the inner fork tube in the outer fork tube **(see illustration)**.
44 Apply non-permanent thread locking agent to the damper rod bolt, then install the bolt and tighten it to the torque listed in this Chapter's Specifications **(see illustration)**.

Hold the damper rod from turning with the tool used in Step 34. **Note:** *If you didn't use the tool, tighten the damper rod bolt after the fork spring and cap bolt are installed.*
45 Install the outer guide bushing (see Step 19 above).
46 Slide the oil seal spacer down the inner tube, into position over the guide bushing.
47 Lubricate the lips and the outer diameter of the oil seal with the recommended fork oil (see Chapter 1) and slide it down the inner tube, with the open side of the seal lip facing the spacer **(see illustration)**. Drive the seal into place with the same tools used to drive in the guide bushing (see illustration 8.21). If you

8.40 Replace the slide bushing (arrowed) whenever the fork is overhauled

8.41 Install the damper rod in the inner tube and let it slide down until it emerges from the bottom end

8.42 Install the oil lock piece on the end of the damper rod

8.43 Assemble the inner and outer fork tubes

8.44 Use a new copper washer and non-permanent thread locking agent on the damper rod bolt

8.47 Install the oil seal with the open side down

… Frame, suspension and final drive 7•17

don't have access to these, it is recommended that you take the assembly to a Yamaha dealer service department or other motorcycle repair shop to have the seal driven in. If you are very careful, the seal can be driven in with a hammer and a drift punch. Work around the circumference of the seal, tapping gently on the outer edge of the seal until it's seated. Be careful - if you distort the seal, you'll have to disassemble the fork again and end up taking it to a dealer anyway!

48 Install the retainer, making sure the ring is completely seated in its groove (see illustration 8.33).
49 Install the dust seal, making sure it seats completely (see illustration 8.23).
50 Install the drain screw and a new gasket, if it was removed.
51 Add the recommended type and amount of fork oil (see Chap- ter 1).
52 Install the fork spring, with the closer-wound coils at the top. Install the spring seat and spacer.
53 Refer to Section 6 and install the spring washer, O-ring and fork cap.
54 Install the fork by following the procedure outlined in Section 7. If you won't be installing the fork right away, store it in an upright position.

9 Cartridge forks - disassembly, inspection and reassembly

1989-on FZR750R models

Disassembly

1 Unscrew the cap bolt and pour the fork oil into a container (see illustration).
2 Compress the fork spring and remove the spring seat (it's slotted so it can be slid off the damping adjusting rod).
3 Slip an open-end wrench over the preload adjuster locknut and place another wrench on the preload adjuster hex on the cap bolt. Loosen the cap bolt, then unscrew the adjuster from the damping adjusting rod and unscrew the locknut.
4 Pull out the thin damping force adjusting rod and the fork spring.
5 Prevent the damper rod from turning using a holder (Yamaha tool no. YM-01425, part no. 90890-01425). Unscrew the Allen bolt at the bottom of the outer tube and remove the copper washer.
6 Remove the damper rod and the oil lock piece from the inner fork tube.
7 Pry the dust seal out of the outer fork tube and slide it up the inner fork tube.
Caution: Don't scratch the inner fork tube while you pry the dust seal out.
8 If necessary, pry the retainer out of its groove and remove the front fender stay, ball and spring. Note: The ball and spring are very small. Take care not to lose them.

9 Hold the outer tube and yank the inner tube away from it, repeatedly (like a slide hammer), until the seal and outer tube guide bushing pop loose.
10 Slide the oil seal, spacer and guide bushing off the fork tube, then remove the slide bushing.
11 Carefully note the position of the preload adjuster in the cap bolt, then remove the preload adjuster if necessary.

Inspection

12 Clean all parts in solvent and blow them dry with compressed air, if available. Blow out the passages in the damper rod, but don't try to disassemble it. Check the inner and outer fork tubes, the guide bushings and the damper rod for score marks, scratches, flaking of the chrome and excessive or abnormal wear. Look for dents in the tubes and replace them if any are found. Check the fork seal seat for nicks, gouges and scratches. If damage is evident, leaks will occur around the seal-to-outer tube junction. Replace worn or defective parts with new ones.
13 Have the inner fork tube checked for runout at a dealer service department or other repair shop.

⚠ Warning: If the fork tube is bent, it should not be straightened; replace it with a new one.

14 Measure the overall length of the fork spring and check it for cracks and other damage. Compare the length to the minimum length listed in this Chapter's Specifications. If it's defective or sagged, replace both fork springs with new ones. Never replace only one spring.
15 Check the damping force adjuster rod for bending and replace it if it's bent at all.

Assembly

16 Assembly is the reverse of the disassembly steps. Whenever the forks are overhauled, replace the bushings, oil seal, dust seal and the copper washer that goes on the damper rod bolt. Install the oil seal with its numbered side upward. Lubricate the outer surface of the inner fork tube with fork oil before assembly. Fill the oil to the level listed

1 Cap bolt
2 O-ring
3 Spring seat
4 Preload adjuster locknut
5 Fork spring
6 Rebound spring
7 Damper rod (cartridge)
8 Inner fork tube
9 Slide bushing
10 Oil lock piece
11 Dust seal
12 Retainer
13 Oil seal
14 Seal spacer
15 Guide bushing
16 Outer fork tube

9.1 Front fork details (1989-on FZR750 models)

7•18 Frame, suspension and final drive

9.17 Front fork details (1991 through 1993 FZR1000 models)

1 Cap bolt
2 O-ring
3 Locknut
4 Spacer
5 Fork spring
6 Outer fork tube
7 Guide bushing
8 Damper rod (cartridge)
9 Slide bushing
10 Washer
11 Oil seal
12 Retainer
13 Dust seal
14 Inner fork tube
15 Damper rod bolt

in this Chapter's Specifications (with the fork fully compressed).

1991 through 1993 FZR1000 models

Disassembly

17 Unscrew the fork cap bolt from the outer tube **(see illustration)**.

18 Lift up the fork cap bolt, spacer and fork spring.

19 Install a fork spring compressor (Yamaha tool no. YM-01441) on the spacer and compress the fork spring **(see illustration)**. Slip a rod holder (Yamaha tool no. YM-01434) between the spacer and the locknut **(see illustration)**.

20 Turn the locknut away from the fork cap bolt, then unscrew the cap bolt from the damper rod.

21 Carefully remove the rod holder and spring compressor from the damper rod and spacer.

> **Warning:** *The spring is compressed. Keep your fingers clear of it to prevent injury.*

22 Remove the spacer and spring from the fork tube.

23 Thread the cap bolt back onto the damper rod, then turn the fork upside down over a container. Grasp the cap bolt and use it to pump the damper rod several times to drain the fork oil.

24 Carefully pry the dust seal and retainer out of the outer fork tube with a small standard screwdriver.

25 Hold the outer tube and yank the inner tube away from it, repeatedly (like a slide hammer), until the seal and outer tube guide bushing pop loose.

26 Remove the dust seal, retainer, oil seal, spacer, slide bushing and piston bushing from the inner fork tube.

27 Hold the damper rod from turning with Yamaha tool no. YM-01445, part no. 90890-01445 **(see illustration)** and remove the damper rod bolt. The tool has a 24 mm hex size.

28 Remove the damper rod from the fork tube.

Caution: Keep the damper rod clean. Its internal valves and passages can be contaminated by small bits of foreign material.

Inspection and assembly

29 Perform Steps 12 through 15 above to inspect the fork.

30 Install the damper rod and let it slide slowly into the inner fork tube without scratching the inner fork tube surface.

31 Apply non-permanent thread locking agent to the threads of the damper rod bolt. Hold the damper rod from turning with the tool used in Step 27, install the damper rod bolt and tighten it to the torque listed in this Chapter's Specifications.

32 Coat the outer surface of the inner fork tube with fork oil. Wrap the end of the inner

9.19a This tool is used to compress the fork spring . . .

9.19b . . . and this tool is used to hold the spring down while the locknut is loosened

9.27 This tool is used to hold the damper rod from turning while the bolt is loosened or tightened

Frame, suspension and final drive 7•19

fork tube with plastic wrap to protect the oil seal. Install the new dust seal, retainer, new oil seal (with its numbered or marked side toward the axle holder), washer, slide bushing and guide bushing on the inner fork tube.

33 Assemble the outer tube and inner tube, then press the oil seal into the outer tube with the tool used in Step 21.

34 Install the oil seal retainer securely in its groove.

35 Install the dust seal in the outer fork tube with the tool used in Step 33.

36 Fill the fork with the amount of oil listed in this Chapter's Specifications (before installing the spring and with the damper rod fully compressed). The oil must rise to the top surface of the outer fork tube or it will be impossible to adjust fork oil level correctly. After filling, pump the damper rod slowly up and down at least ten times to distribute the oil. **Note:** *Don't pump rapidly or oil will spray out.*

37 Pump the outer fork tube slowly through a stroke of about 120 mm (4.7 inches) to complete distribution of the fork oil. Don't use too long a stroke or air will be drawn into the oil. If this happens, pump the damper rod and outer tube again as described in Step 36 and the beginning of this step.

38 Wait ten minutes for the oil to settle and air bubbles to leave the fork oil, then check fork oil level, measuring down from the top of the inner fork tube with the damper rod fully compressed and the spring not yet installed.

⚠ **Warning:** *Oil level must be correct and even between the two forks or unstable handling may occur.*

39 Thread the locknut onto the damper rod the distance listed in this Chapter's Specifications.

40 Tighten the spring preload adjuster until there's no play in the stopper inside the adjuster.

41 Thread an internally threaded rod onto the end of the damper rod and pull it up. Install the fork spring (with its small diameter end upward) and the spring spacer.

42 Press down the spacer and fork spring with the fork spring compressor **(see illustration 9.19a)**. Pull the damper rod upward and slip the rod holder between the locknut and spring spacer **(see illustration 9.19b)**.

43 Unscrew the rod puller. Thread the cap bolt onto the rod and tighten it slightly with fingers. Hold the cap bolt from turning and tighten the locknut to the torque listed in this Chapter's Specifications.

44 Carefully remove the rod holder and fork spring compressor.

⚠ **Warning:** *The spring is under pressure.*

45 Thread the cap bolt into the outer fork tube.

1 Steering stem
2 Fork assembly
3 Cap bolt
4 Preload adjuster
5 Outer fork tube
6 Oil seal washer
7 Oil seal
8 Retaining ring
9 Dust seal
10 Damper rod
11 Fork spring
12 Spring guide
13 Spring seat
14 Snap-ring
15 Locknut
16 Copper washer
17 Damper rod bolt
18 Axle pinch bolt

9.47 Front fork details (1994-on FZR1000 models)

46 After installation, adjust the fork spring preload (see Section 19).

1994-on FZR1000 models
Disassembly

47 Hold the outer fork tube and unscrew the cap bolt from the tube **(see illustration)**.

48 Place a wrench over the preload adjuster hex at the top of the fork and hold it so it won't turn. Unscrew the cap bolt from the preload adjuster.

49 Hold the preload adjuster and turn the locknut (beneath the preload adjuster) down away from the preload adjuster.

50 Install the fork spring compressor (US part no. YM-01458, UK part no. 90890-01458) on the fork spring **(see illustrations)**. Hold the preload adjuster with a wrench on its top hex so it won't turn, then thread the tool down to compress the spring.

51 Pry off the snap-ring, then remove the spring compressor. Remove the spring seat and spring guide from the damper rod, then lift the spring out of the fork tube.

52 Point the open end of the outer fork tube into a drain pan. Hold the outer fork tube so it won't fall off the inner tube, then pump the fork tubes several times to force out the oil.

9.50a Fork spring compressor (1994-on FZR1000 models)

9.50b Install the tool like this

7•20 Frame, suspension and final drive

9.55 Damper rod holding tool (1994-on FZR1000 models)

53 Once the fork has drained, carefully pull off the outer fork tube.
Caution: If the dust seal is damaged during this operation, it will have to be replaced. If the bushings inside outer fork tube are damaged, the complete outer fork tube will have to be replaced.
54 Carefully pry out the dust seal, oil seal retaining ring and oil seal, then lift out the oil seal washer.
55 Insert the damper rod holder tool (US part no. YM-01447, UK part no. 90890-01447) into the top of the inner fork tube **(see illustration)**. Use the tool to hold the damper rod so it won't rotate inside the fork tube, then unscrew the damper rod bolt.
56 Pull the damper rod out of the inner fork tube.

Inspection

57 Perform Steps 12 through 15 above to inspect the fork tubes, spring and damper rod.
58 Check the O-rings on the cap bolt and preload adjuster and replace them if they're worn, deteriorated, cut or cracked. It's a good idea to replace them whenever the fork is disassembled.

Assembly

59 Assembly is the reverse of the disassembly steps, with the following additions:
 a) Apply non-permanent thread locking agent to the threads of the damper rod bolt. Hold the bolt with the special tool and tighten it to the torque listed in this Chapter's Specifications.
 b) Use a new snap-ring on the damper rod.
 c) Install the oil seal so its marked side (numbers or manufacturer's mark) will

10.3c . . . and lift the triple clamp off to expose the ring nuts (arrowed)

10.3a Loosen the steering stem nut with a socket . . .

face down when the fork is installed on the bike. Tap the oil seal into its bore with a fork seal driver **(see illustration 8.21)**.
 d) Install the dust seal with the same tool used to install the oil seal.
 e) Tighten the preload adjuster locknut and fork cap bolt to the torques listed in this Chapter's Specifications.

10 Steering head bearings - replacement

1 If the steering head bearing check/adjustment (see Chapter 1) does not remedy excessive play or roughness in the

10.3b . . . unscrew the nut from the steering stem . . .

steering head bearings, the entire front end must be disassembled and the bearings and races replaced with new ones.
2 Refer to Chapter 5 and remove the fuel tank. Refer to Section 7 and remove the front forks.

All except 1989-on FZR750R models

3 If you're working on an FZR600, remove the handlebars (see Section 5) and steering stem nut, then lift off the upper triple clamp (sometimes called the fork bridge or crown) **(see illustrations)**.
4 If you're working on an FZR750/1000, remove the upper triple clamp and handlebars (see Section 5).

1 Steering stem nut
2 Upper triple clamp
3 Lockwasher
4 Upper ring nut
5 Washer
6 Lower ring nut
7 Bearing cover
8 Upper bearing
9 Lower bearing
10 Steering stem

10.6a Steering stem details (except 1989-on FZR750R models)

Frame, suspension and final drive 7•21

10.6b Lift the bearing cover off

10.7a Lift the upper bearing out of its race

5 Unbolt the brake hose junction from the steering head (see Chapter 8).

6 Remove the lockwasher and upper ring nut from the steering stem (see Chapter 1). Remove the lower ring nut and bearing cover **(see illustrations)**.

7 Remove the upper bearing and lower the steering stem and lower triple clamp assembly out of the steering head **(see illustrations)**. If it's stuck, gently tap on the top of the steering stem with a plastic mallet or a hammer and a wood block.

8 Clean all the parts with solvent and dry them thoroughly, using compressed air, if available. If you do use compressed air, don't let the bearings spin as they're dried - it could ruin them. Wipe the old grease out of the frame steering head and bearing races.

9 Examine the races in the steering head for cracks, dents, and pits. If even the slightest amount of wear or damage is evident, the races should be replaced with new ones.

10 To remove the bearing races, drive them out of the steering head with a hammer and long rod **(see illustration)**. A slide hammer with the proper internal-jaw puller will also work.

11 Since the races are an interference fit in the frame, installation will be easier if the new races are left overnight in a refrigerator. This will cause them to contract and slip into place in the frame with very little effort. When installing the races, tap them gently into place with a hammer and punch or a large socket. Do not strike the bearing surface or the race will be damaged.

12 Check the bearings for wear. Look for cracks, dents, and pits in the races and flat spots on the bearings. Replace any defective parts with new ones. If a new bearing is required, replace both of them as a set.

13 Don't remove the lower bearing unless it, or the grease seal underneath, must be replaced **(see illustration 10.7b)**. To remove the bearing from the steering stem, carefully tap between the bearing and steering stem with a hammer and cold chisel **(see illustration)**. You can also use a bearing splitter and puller setup (these can be rented). Tap the lower bearing on with a hammer and piece of pipe the same diameter as the bearing inner race. Don't tap against the rollers or outer race or the bearing will be ruined. As an alternative, take the steering stem to a Yamaha dealer or motorcycle repair shop and have the old bearing pressed off and a new one pressed on.

14 Check the grease seal under the lower bearing and replace it with a new one if necessary.

10.7b Lower the steering stem; remove the bearing and grease seal (arrowed) only if being replaced

15 Inspect the steering stem/lower triple clamp for cracks and other damage. Do not attempt to repair any steering components. Replace them with new parts if defects are found.

16 Pack the bearings with high-quality grease (preferably a moly-based grease) **(see illustration)**. Coat the outer races with grease also.

17 Insert the steering stem/lower triple clamp into the steering head. Install the upper bearing and lower ring nut. refer to Chapter 1 and adjust the bearings.

10.10 Drive the races out with a hammer and long rod

10.13 Gently tap between the lower bearing and clamp to separate the bearing from the steering stem

10.16 Work the grease completely into the rollers

7•22 Frame, suspension and final drive

18 The remainder of installation is the reverse of removal.

1989-on FZR750R models

Removal

19 Loosen the steering stem pinch bolt and remove the steering stem bolt **(see illustration)**.
20 Lift the upper triple clamp off the steering head.
21 Remove the brake hose brackets and disconnect the horn wires.
22 Remove the bearing adjuster ring nut. Remove the bearing cover, the upper bearing race and the upper bearing out of the steering head.
23 Slide the upper dust seal, lower bearing and lower dust seal off the steering stem.

Inspection

24 Check the bearings for wear. Look for cracks, dents, and pits in the races and flat spots, pitting or galling on the bearing balls. Replace any defective parts with new ones. If a new bearing is required, replace both bearings, their races and both dust seals as a set.
25 To remove the bearing races, drive them out of the steering head with a hammer and long rod **(see illustration 10.10)**. A slide hammer with the proper internal-jaw puller will also work.
26 Since the races are an interference fit in the frame, installation will be easier if the new races are left overnight in a refrigerator. This will cause them to contract and slip into place in the frame with very little effort. When installing the races, tap them gently into place with a hammer and punch or a large socket. Do not strike the bearing surface or the race will be damaged.
27 Inspect the steering stem/lower triple clamp for cracks and other damage. Do not attempt to repair any steering components. Replace them with new parts if defects are found.
28 Pack the bearings with high-quality bearing grease (preferably a moly-based grease). Coat the outer races with grease also.

Installation

29 Install the lower dust seal, lower bearing and upper dust seal on the steering stem.
30 Install the steering stem in the steering head. Install the upper bearing and race, the bearing cover and the ring nut (the tapered side of the ring nut must be up).
31 Refer to Chapter 1 and adjust the bearings.
32 The remainder of installation is the reverse of the removal steps.

11 Rear shock absorber - removal, inspection and installation

Removal

1 Support the bike securely so it can't be knocked over during this procedure. Place a jack beneath the frame to lift the rear tire off the ground. Remove the rear wheel (see Chapter 8).

FZR600 models

2 Remove the left and right fairings, the seat and the side covers (see Chapter 9).
3 Support the swingarm so it can't drop. Remove the lower pivot bolt from the relay arm and move the linkage aside **(see illustration)**.
4 Remove the shock absorber lower bolt and nut, washers, collars and grease seals **(see illustration 11.3 and the accompanying illustration)**.

10.19 Steering stem details (1989-on FZR750R models)

1 Steering stem bolt
2 Upper triple clamp
3 Ring nut
4 Bearing cover
5 Upper bearing race
6 Upper bearing
7 Upper dust seal
8 Lower bearing
9 Lower dust seal
10 Lower triple clamp
11 Steering stem pinch bolt

11.3 Remove the nut and take out the suspension linkage lower pivot bolt (arrowed)

1 Shock absorber and spring
2 Bearing
3 Washer
4 Collar
5 Grease seal

11.4 Rear shock absorber details (FZR600 models)

Frame, suspension and final drive 7•23

11.5a Remove the nut from the upper pivot bolt . . .

11.5b . . . then slide out the bolt and remove the shock absorber . . .

11.5c . . . and remove the collar

5 Remove the shock absorber upper nut, washer and bolt **(see illustrations)**.
6 Take the shock absorber out.

FZR750/1000 models (except 1989-on FZR750R)

7 Remove the left, right and lower front fairings, the seat and the side covers (see Chapter 9).
8 Remove the fuel tank (see Chapter 5).
9 Support the swingarm so it can't drop.
10 If you're working on a 1987 or 1988 model, remove the suspension linkage tie rods (see Section 12).
11 If you're working on a 1989 or later model, unbolt the upper ends of the suspension linkage tie rods from the frame and move the linkage aside (see Section 12).
12 Remove the shock absorber lower bolt and nut, spacers and collar **(see illustrations)**. Detach the reservoir (if equipped).
13 Remove the shock absorber upper nut, washer and bolt.
14 Take the shock absorber out.

1989-on FZR750R models

15 Remove the lower fairing (see Chapter 9).
16 Unbolt the spring preload adjuster and remove the retaining bands for the

11.12a Loosen the nut (arrowed) and remove the lower bolt

11.12b Shock absorber details (1987 and 1988 FZR750R models)

1 Shock absorber
2 Bushing
3 Collar
4 Washer
5 Reservoir tank
6 Bearing
7 Grease seal
8 Collar

11.12c Shock absorber details (1987 and 1988 FZR1000 models)

1 Shock absorber
2 Bushing
3 Collar
4 Bearing
5 Grease seal
6 Collar

7•24 Frame, suspension and final drive

11.12d Shock absorber details (1989-on FZR1000 models)

1 Shock absorber
2 Collar
3 Reservoir
4 Reservoir band
5 Reservoir bracket

11.16 Shock absorber details (1989-on FZR750R models)

1 Shock absorber
2 Seat height adjuster
3 Compression damping force adjuster
4 Band
5 Stay
6 Spring preload adjuster

compression damping adjuster **(see illustration)**.
17 Support the swingarm so it can't drop
18 Remove the upper shock absorber bolt.
19 Remove the lower fairing stay.
20 Remove the suspension linkage tie rods (see Section 12).
21 Remove the shock absorber lower bolt. Guide the preload and damping adjusters down through the frame and take the shock absorber out.

11.22 Drill a 2 to 3 mm hole at the specified location (it varies depending on model)

Inspection
22 Check the shock for signs of oil or gas leaks and replace it if you find any. Yamaha specifies releasing the nitrogen gas pressure before throwing away the shock absorber.

> **Warning: Wear eye protection while drilling to prevent injury from flying metal chips.**

To release the gas pressure, drill a hole through the cylinder wall. The hole should be 2 to 3 mm (0.08 to 0.12 inch) in diameter.
a) On all except 1989 and later FZR750R models, the hole should be located 25 to 30 mm (one inch to 1-3/16 inch) beneath the spring seat **(see illustration)**.
b) On 1989 and later FZR750R models, the hole should be 30 to 35 mm (1.2 to 1.4 inch) from the end of the gas-containing portion of the shock absorber.

23 Inspect the pivot hardware at the top and bottom of the shock and replace any worn or damaged parts.

Installation
24 Installation is the reverse of the removal procedure, with the following additions:

a) Lubricate the collars at the top and bottom of the shock absorber with multi-purpose grease. Also grease the washers and seals at the bottom of the shock absorber.
b) Install the upper and lower shock absorber bolts and nuts and the linkage bolts and nuts, then tighten them to the torque values listed in this Chapter's Specifications.

12 Rear suspension linkage - removal, check and installation

1 Support the bike securely so it can't be knocked over during this procedure.
2 Perform the first few steps of the shock absorber procedure to provide access for removal (see Section 11).
3 Disconnect the lower end of the rear shock absorber (see Sec-tion 11).

FZR600 models
4 Remove the nuts and bolts that secure the tie-rods to the swingarm and remove the tie-

Frame, suspension and final drive 7•25

12.4a Loosen the nut and remove the bolt at the upper end of the tie rods . . .

12.4b . . . and at the lower end (left arrow); the bolt and nut (right arrow) secures the muffler/silencer

12.4c Remove the relay arm nut and slide the bolt (arrowed) out of the relay arm and frame

rods **(see illustrations)**. Remove the pivot bolt from the front of the relay arm and remove the relay arm **(see illustration)**.

5 Push the sleeves out of the relay arm **(see illustration)**. Check the sleeves and the bearings in the relay arm for wear **(see illustrations)**.

6 Apply moly-based grease to the bearings and sleeves and install the sleeves in the bearings.

7 Installation is the reverse of removal. Tighten the bolts and nuts to the torque listed in this Chapter's Specifications.

FZR750/1000 models

8 Remove the nuts and bolts that secure the tie-rods to the swingarm and remove the tie-

12.5a Remove the dust cover (arrowed) . . .

12.5b . . . and the grease seal to expose the bearing

12.5c Swingarm and suspension linkage details (FZR600 models)

1 Swingarm	5 Pivot shaft bushing	9 Right tie rod
2 Bearing	6 Pivot shaft	10 Grease seal
3 Thrust washer	7 Chain guard seal	11 Collar
4 Thrust cover	8 Left tie rod	12 Relay arm

7•26 Frame, suspension and final drive

12.8a Remove the nuts from the linkage bolts and the shock absorber lower pivot bolt (arrowed) . . .

12.8b . . . and slide the bolts out

rods **(see illustrations)**. Remove the pivot bolt from the front of the relay arm and remove the relay arm.

9 Push the collars out of the relay arm **(see illustrations)**. Check the collars and the bearings in the relay arm for wear **(see illustrations 12.5b and 12.5c)**. Have them replaced if they're worn.

10 Apply moly-based grease to the bearings and collars and install them in the bearings. Install any grease seals and dust covers.

11 Installation is the reverse of removal. Tighten the bolts and nuts to the torque listed in this Chapter's Specifications.

1 Swingarm
2 Bearing
3 Thrust washer
4 Thrust cover
5 Collar
6 Left tie rod
7 Right tie rod
8 Grease seal
9 Dust cover

12.9a Swingarm and suspension linkage details (1987 and 1988 models)

Frame, suspension and final drive 7•27

13 Swingarm bearings - check

1 Refer to Chapter 8 and remove the rear wheel, then refer to Section 11 and remove the rear shock absorber.
2 Grasp the rear of the swingarm with one hand and place your other hand at the junction of the swingarm and the frame. Try to move the rear of the swingarm from side-to-side. Any wear (play) in the bearings should be felt as movement between the swingarm and the frame at the front. The swingarm will actually be felt to move forward and backward at the front (not from side-to-side). If any play is noted, the bearings should be replaced with new ones (see Section 15).
3 Next, move the swingarm up and down through its full travel. It should move freely, without any binding or rough spots. If it does not move freely, refer to Section 16 for servicing procedures.

14 Swingarm - removal and installation

1 Support the bike securely so it can't be knocked over during this procedure.
2 Remove the rear wheel (see Chapter 8).
3 Remove the chain guard from the swingarm (see illustration 12.5a, 12.9a or 12.9b).
4 Detach the torque link from the swingarm (see illustration). If you're working on a model with an underslung rear caliper, remove the caliper bracket. Support the rear brake caliper and torque link with a piece of rope or wire - don't let them hang by the brake hose.
5 Detach the rear brake hose bracket(s) from the swingarm (if equipped).
6 Detach the shock absorber and rear suspension linkage from the swingarm (see Sections 11 and 12).

12.9b Swingarm and suspension linkage details (1989-on FZR1000 models; 1989-on FZR750R similar)

1 Swingarm
2 Bearing
3 Thrust washer
4 Thrust cover
5 Collar
6 Left tie rod
7 Right tie rod
8 Grease seal
9 Dust cover

14.4 Remove the cotter pin, nut and bolt and detach the torque link from the swingarm (FZR600 shown)

7•28 Frame, suspension and final drive

14.7a Pry the plastic plug out of the recess . . .

14.7b . . . to expose the pivot shaft nut

14.8 Remove the nut

14.9a Support the swingarm, pull out the pivot shaft . . .

14.9b . . . and pull the swingarm back away from the motorcycle

14.10a The chain buffer is attached at the front . . .

14.10b . . . and at the rear on the inside of the swingarm (FZR600 shown)

7 Pry the plastic cover from the swingarm pivot nut **(see illustrations)**.
8 Remove the swingarm pivot nut and washer **(see illustration)**.
9 Support the swingarm and pull the pivot shaft out **(see illustration)**. Remove the swingarm **(see illustration)**.
10 If necessary, detach the chain buffer from the swingarm **(see illustrations 12.4a, 12.9a 12.9b and the accompanying illustrations)**.
11 Check the pivot bearings in the swingarm for dryness or deterioration and lubricate or replace them as necessary (see Section 15).
12 Installation is the reverse of the removal procedure, with the following additions:
a) Be sure the bearing thrust covers and washers are in position before installing the pivot shaft.
b) Be sure the pivot shaft head is seated in its slot before tightening the nut **(see illustration)**.
c) Tighten the pivot shaft nut and the shock absorber and tie-rod lower mounting bolts/nuts to the torque values listed in this Chapter's Specifications.
d) Adjust the chain as described in Chapter 1.

15 Swingarm bearings - inspection and replacement

1 Remove the swingarm (see Section 14).
2 Pry off the thrust cover and remove the thrust washer from each side of the swingarm **(see illustrations)**.

14.12 Be sure the head of the pivot shaft fits into its slot (arrowed)

15.2a Lift off the thrust cover . . .

15.2b . . . and the thrust washer

Frame, suspension and final drive 7•29

15.3 Pull out the pivot shaft collar

15.4 Inspect the bearing in each side of the swingarm

16.3a Remove the bolt and take off the cover (this is an FZR600) . . .

3 Slide the collar out **(see illustration)**.
4 Inspect the bearings **(see illustration)**. If they're dry, lubricate them with lithium-based waterproof wheel bearing grease. If they're worn or damaged, take the swingarm to a Yamaha dealer or motorcycle repair shop for bearing replacement.

16 Drive chain - removal, cleaning and installation

Note: *The original equipment drive chain is of the endless type. If a chain breaking and joining tool is available, the chain can be separated and rejoined without disturbing any components (see Tools and Workshop Tips in the Reference section).*

Removal

1 Disconnect the shift arm from its shaft in the engine (see Chapter 2 or Chapter 3).
2 If the motorcycle is equipped with a hydraulic clutch, remove the clutch release cylinder (see Chapter 3).
3 Remove the bolts securing the engine sprocket cover to the engine case. Take the sprocket cover off and inspect its seals **(see illustrations)**. Replace them if they're worn.
4 Disengage the chain **(see illustration)** and remove the rear wheel (see Chapter 8).
5 Lift the chain off the engine sprocket **(see illustration)**.
6 Detach the swingarm from the frame by following the first few Steps of Section 12. Pull the swingarm back far enough to allow the chain to slip between the frame and the front of the swingarm.

Cleaning

7 Soak the chain in kerosene (paraffin) for approximately five or six minutes. **Caution: *Don't use gasoline (petrol), solvent or other cleaning fluids. Don't use high-pressure water. Remove the chain, wipe it off, then blow it dry with compressed air immediately. The entire process shouldn't take longer than ten minutes - if it does, the O-rings in the chain rollers could be damaged.***

Installation
8 Installation is the reverse of the removal procedure. Make sure the cover dowel is in position **(see illustration)**. Tighten the suspension fasteners and the engine sprocket

16.3b . . . and this is an FZR1000

16.3c Inspect the shift shaft seal in the outside of the cover . . .

16.3d . . . and the one in the inside

16.4 Slip the chain off the rear sprocket

16.5 With slack in the chain, lift it off the engine sprocket

16.8 Be sure the cover dowel (arrowed) is in position

7

17.4 Replace the sprocket if the rubber coating is worn or damaged (arrowed)

17.5a Bend back the lockwasher (arrowed)...

17.5b ...and remove the nut

cover bolts to the torque values listed in this Chapter's Specifications. Adjust the chain (see Chapter 1). Tighten the rear axle nut to the torque listed in the Chapter 8 Specifications.
9 Connect the shift arm to the shift shaft. Be sure to align the punch marks on arm and shaft.
10 Lubricate the chain following the procedure described in Chap- ter 1.
Caution: Use only the recommended engine oil.

17 Sprockets - check and replacement

1 Support the bike securely so it can't be knocked over during this procedure.
2 Whenever the drive chain is inspected, the sprockets should be inspected also. If you are replacing the chain, replace the sprockets as well. Likewise, if the sprockets are in need of replacement, install a new chain also.
3 Remove the engine sprocket cover following the procedure outlined in the previous Section.
4 Check the wear pattern on the sprockets (see Chapter 1). If the sprocket teeth or rubber coating are worn excessively, replace the chain and sprockets **(see illustration)**.
5 To replace the engine sprocket, engage a low transmission gear and have an assistant apply the rear brake. Bend back the lockwasher and remove the nut **(see illustrations)**.
6 With the engine sprocket removed, inspect the transmission output shaft seal **(see illustration)**. If it has been leaking oil, replace it.
7 To remove the rear sprocket, remove the rear wheel (see Chapter 8). Unscrew the nuts holding the sprocket to the wheel coupling and lift it off. Check the condition of the rubber damper under the rear wheel coupling (see Section 18).
8 When installing the rear sprocket, either use new self-locking nuts (models so equipped), or apply a non-hardening thread locking compound to the threads of the studs (standard nuts). Tighten the nuts to the torque listed in this Chapter's Specifications.
9 When installing the engine sprocket, engage it with the chain. Install a new lockwasher, tighten the nut to the torque listed in this Chapter's Specifications and bend a lockwasher tab against the nut.
10 Install the engine sprocket cover (see Section 16) and the shift arm (see Chapter 2 or Chapter 3).

18 Rear wheel coupling/rubber damper - check and replacement

1 Remove the rear wheel (see Chapter 8).
2 Lift the collar and rear sprocket/rear wheel coupling from the wheel **(see illustration)**.
3 Lift the rubber damper segments from the wheel **(see illustration)** and check them for cracks, hardening and general deterioration. Replace the rubber damper with a new one if necessary.
4 Checking and replacement procedures for the coupling bearing are similar to those described for the wheel bearings. Refer to Chapter 8.
5 Installation is the reverse of the removal procedure.

19 Suspension adjustments

1 The front suspension (FZR750/1000 models only) and rear suspension can be made firmer or softer for different riding conditions.

Warning: If you're working on an FZR750/1000, always set both front forks to the same preload setting. Uneven settings can cause unstable handling.
Caution: Turn the adjusters in progressive steps through all of the settings without skipping any of the intermediate settings (for example, don't skip from setting 1 to setting 3).

2 Find the proper settings for your riding conditions in this Chapter's Specifications.

Front forks (1987 and 1988 FZR750R)

3 Spring preload and fork damping can be increased or decreased by turning an adjuster

17.6 If the transmission seal has been leaking (arrowed), replace it

18.2 Lift the sprocket out of the wheel

18.3 Lift the damper segments out of the wheel

Frame, suspension and final drive 7•31

19.4 Turn the adjuster with a wrench to change spring preload

The upper grooves indicate the preload setting and the lower grooves indicate the fork height setting

on the top of each fork. Fork top height can be adjusted by moving the fork up or down in the triple clamps.

4 Adjust spring preload by turning the preload adjuster at the top of the fork **(see illustration)**. The grooves on the adjuster indicate the setting.

5 Adjust fork damping force by turning the damping adjuster at the top of the fork **(see illustration)**. Turning the adjuster toward the no. 4 setting stiffens the fork; turning toward no. 1 setting softens it.

6 To adjust fork top height, remove the side fairings (see Chapter 9). Support the bike securely so it can't be knocked over during this procedure, then raise the front tire off the ground with a jack placed under the engine.

7 Loosen the pinch bolts for the handlebars, upper triple clamp and lower triple clamp (see Sections 5 and 7). Raise or lower the forks,

19.13b . . . the grooves indicate the settings

19.17a The rear spring preload adjuster on FZR600 models is located at the top of the shock absorber . . .

19.5 Turn the damping adjuster on top of the fork cap to increase or decrease damping

using the grooves as a guide (see illustration 19.4). Be sure the settings are even, then tighten the bolts to the torques listed in this Chapter's Specifications.

Front forks (1989-on FZR750)

8 Spring preload, fork compression damping and fork rebound damping can be increased or decreased by turning an adjuster on the top or bottom of each fork. Fork top height can be adjusted by moving the fork up or down in the triple clamps.

9 Perform Steps 4, 6 and 7 above to adjust spring preload and fork height.

10 To set rebound damping, turn the adjuster at the top of the fork all the way in, then back it out the number of clicks necessary to reach the desired setting.

Caution: Don't try to turn the adjuster beyond its minimum or maximum settings.

11 To set compression damping, turn the adjuster at the bottom of the fork all the way

19.14 Turn the preload adjuster (1) clockwise to stiffen the suspension (1989 FZR1000)

19.17b . . . turn it with the special wrench provided in the bike's tool kit

19.13a Place a wrench on the flats at the top of the adjuster (arrowed) and turn the adjuster . . .

in, then back it out the number of clicks necessary to reach the desired setting.

Caution: Don't try to turn the adjuster beyond its minimum or maximum settings.

Front forks (FZR1000)

12 Spring preload is adjustable. Turning the adjuster clockwise makes the suspension firmer and turning it counterclockwise (anti-clockwise) makes it softer.

13 If you're working on a 1987, 1988 or 1990 and later model, turn the adjuster with an open-end wrench **(see illustrations)**.

14 If you're working on a 1989 model, remove the cap from the top of the fork and turn the adjuster with a screwdriver **(see illustration)**.

Rear shock and spring (all models)

15 Adjustments include spring preload (all models) and shock damping (1989 and later FZR750/1000 only).

16 Support the bike securely so it can't be knocked over during this procedure.

FZR600 models

17 Turn the spring adjuster at the top of the shock clockwise to increase spring preload and counterclockwise (anti-clockwise) to decrease it **(see illustration)**. Use the special wrench included in the motorcycle's tool kit or equivalent **(see illustration)**.

1987 and 1988 FZR750R models

18 Loosen the locknut at the bottom of the shock absorber and turn the preload adjuster with the special wrench from the bike's tool kit **(see illustration)**. Measure the length of the

19.18 Loosen the locknut and turn the adjuster to change spring length (and spring preload)

A Spring length   B Adjuster   C Locknut

7•32 Frame, suspension and final drive

19.23a Loosen the locknut and turn the adjusting nut to change spring preload

1 Preload adjusting nut
2 Locknut
3 Damping adjuster

19.23b Measure from between the locknut and adjusting nut to the top of the lower bracket

spring and compare it with the recommended settings listed in this Chapter's Specifications.

19 Set rebound damping force by turning the adjuster all the way in, then turning it out and counting the clicks. Compare the setting to the values listed in this Chapter's Specifications.

1989-on FZR750 models

20 Set spring preload by turning the adjuster in or out. Compare the reading on the adjuster scale to the values listed in this Chapter's Specifications.

Caution: Don't turn any of the adjusters past the specified range.

21 Set rebound damping force by turning the adjuster all the way in, then turning it out and counting the clicks. Compare the setting to the values listed in this Chapter's Specifications.

22 Set compression damping force by turning the adjuster all the way in, then turning it out and counting the clicks. Compare the setting to the values listed in this Chapter's Specifications.

FZR1000 models

23 Loosen the locknut and turn the adjusting nut at the bottom of the shock to set spring preload **(see illustration)**. Measure the distance from the line between the adjusting nut and locknut to the top of the lower mounting bracket **(see illustration)** and compare it with the range listed in this Chapter's Specifications. Spring length changes 1 mm (0.040 inch) for each turn of the adjuster.

Caution: Don't adjust the spring to a length outside the specified range.

24 If you're working on a 1989 or later FZR1000, turn the adjuster at the bottom of the shock to set damping force (see illustration 19.23a).

Caution: Don't turn the adjuster out more than nine clicks from the fully-in position.

Chapter 8
Brakes, wheels and tires

Contents

Brake caliper - removal, overhaul and installation 3	General information 1
Brake check . . . . See Chapter 1	Rear brake master cylinder - removal, overhaul and installation . . . 6
Brake disc(s) - inspection, removal and installation 4	Rear wheel - removal, inspection and installation 12
Brake hoses - inspection and replacement 7	Tires - general information and fitting 14
Brake light switches - check and adjustment . . . . See Chapter 1	Wheel bearings - replacement 13
Brake pads - replacement 2	Wheels - alignment check 10
Brake system bleeding 8	Wheels and tires - general check . . . . See 'Daily (pre-ride) checks
Front brake master cylinder - removal, overhaul and installation . . . 5	Wheels - inspection and repair 9
Front wheel - removal, inspection and installation 11	

Degrees of difficulty

Easy, suitable for novice with little experience	Fairly easy, suitable for beginner with some experience	Fairly difficult, suitable for competent DIY mechanic	Difficult, suitable for experienced DIY mechanic	Very difficult, suitable for expert DIY or professional

Specifications

FZR600/600R brakes

Brake lever free-play and pedal position	See Chapter 1
Brake fluid type	See Chapter 1
Front brake disc thickness	
Standard	4.0 mm (0.16 inch)
Minimum*	3.5 mm (0.14 inch)
Rear brake disc thickness	
Standard	5.0 mm (0.20 inch)
Minimum*	4.5 mm (0.18 inch)
*Refer to marks stamped into the disc (they supersede information printed here)	
Disc runout limit	0.5 mm (0.02 inch)
Pad thickness (front and rear)	
Standard	5 mm (0.2 inch)
Minimum	0.5 mm (0.02 inch)

FZR750R brakes

Brake lever free-play and pedal position	See Chapter 1
Brake fluid type	See Chapter 1
Front brake disc thickness (1987 and 1988)	
Standard	Not specified
Minimum*	4.5 mm (0.18 inch)
Front brake disc thickness (1989-on)	
Standard	5 mm (0.20 inch)
Minimum*	3 mm (0.12 inch)

FZR750R brakes (continued)

Rear brake disc thickness (1987 and 1988)
    Standard .... Not specified
    Minimum* .... 5.5 mm (0.22 inch)
Rear brake disc thickness (1989-on)
    Standard .... 7 mm (0.28 inch)
    Minimum* .... 4 mm (0.16 inch)
*Refer to marks stamped into the disc (they supersede information printed here)
Disc runout limit .... 0.15 mm (0.006 inch)
Pad thickness (front)
  US models
    Standard .... 5.0 mm (0.20 inch)
    Minimum .... 0.5 mm (0.02 inch)
  UK models
    Standard .... 5.3 mm (0.21 inch)
    Minimum .... 1.0 mm (0.04 inch)
Pad thickness (rear)
  All except 1989-on FZR750 models
    Standard .... 5.5 mm (0.22 inch)
    Minimum .... 0.5 mm (0.02 inch)
  1989-on FZR750 models
    Standard .... 5.5 mm (0.22 inch)
    Minimum .... 1.0 mm (0.04 inch)

FZR1000 brakes

Brake lever free-play and pedal position .... See Chapter 1
Brake fluid type .... See Chapter 1
Front brake disc thickness
  1987 and 1988 models
    Standard .... Not specified
    Minimum* .... 3.5 mm (0.14 inch)
  1989-on
    Standard .... 4.0 mm (0.16 inch)
    Minimum* .... 3.0 mm (0.12 inch)
  1989 through 1993 .... 3.0 mm (0.12 inch)
  1994-on .... 3.5 mm (0.14 inch)
Rear brake disc thickness
  1987 and 1988
    Standard .... Not specified
    Minimum* .... 4.5 mm (0.18 inch)
  1989-on
    Standard .... 5.0 mm (0.20 inch)
    Minimum* .... 4.0 mm (0.16 inch)
*Refer to marks stamped into the disc (they supersede information printed here)
Disc runout limit .... 0.15 mm (0.006 inch)
Pad thickness (front and rear)
    Standard .... 5.5 mm (0.22 inch)
    Minimum .... 0.5 mm (0.02 inch)

Wheels and tires

Wheel runout
  FZR600
    Radial (up-and-down) .... 2.0 mm (0.05 inch)
    Axial (side-to-side) .... 2.0 mm (0.05 inch)
  FZR750 (US)
    Radial (up-and-down) .... 1.0 mm (0.04 inch)
    Axial (side-to-side) .... 0.5 mm (0.02 inch)
  FZR750 (UK)
    Radial (up-and-down) .... 2.0 mm (0.05 inch)
    Axial (side-to-side) .... 2.0 mm (0.05 inch)
  FZR1000 (1987 and 1988)
    Radial (up-and-down) .... 1.0 mm (0.04 inch)
    Axial (side-to-side) .... 0.5 mm (0.02 inch)
  FZR1000 (1989-on)
    Radial (up-and-down) .... 2.0 mm (0.05 inch)
    Axial (side-to-side) .... 2.0 mm (0.05 inch)
Tire pressures .... See 'Daily (pre-ride) checks at the beginning of this Manual

Brakes, wheels and tires 8•3

Tire sizes
  FZR600 (1989 US, 1989 and 1990 UK)
    Front 110/70 V17-V240
    Rear 130/70 V18-V240
  FZR600 (1990 US)
    Front 110/70 ZR17
    Rear 140/60 ZR18
  FZR600 (1991-on)
    Front .... 110/70 ZR17 or 110/70 VR-17/V240
    Rear .... 140/60 ZR18 or 140/60 VR18-V240
  FZR750
    1987 (US)
      Front 120/70 VR17/V270
      Rear 160/60 VR18/V270
    1988 (US)
      Front 120/70 ZR17
      Rear 160/60 ZR18
    1989-on (UK)
      Front .... 120/70 ZR17 or 120/70 VR17/V260 or 120/70 VR17/V270
      Rear .... 170/60 ZR17 or 170/70 VR17/V260 or 170/60 VR17/V270
  FZR1000
    1987 (US)
      Front 120/70 VR17/V270
      Rear 160/60 VR18/V270
    1988 (US)
      Front .... 120/70 ZR17 or 120/70 VR17/V270
      Rear .... 160/60 ZR18 or 160/60 VR18/V270
    1987 and 1988 (UK) .... as 1988 US
    1989 and 1990 (US)
      Front 130/60 ZR-17
      Rear 170/60 ZR-17
    1989-on (UK)
      Front .... 130/60 ZR-17 or 130/60 VR17/V280
      Rear .... 170/60 ZR-17 or 170/60 VR17/V280
    1991-on (US)
      Front .... 130/60 ZR-17 or 130/60 VR17/V280
      Rear .... 170/60 ZR-17 or 170/60 VR-17/V280

Torque specifications

Caliper mounting bolts .... 35 Nm (25 ft-lbs)
Front caliper pad retaining bolt (1989-on FZR750) .... 18 Nm (13 ft-lbs)
Caliper bleed valve(s) .... 6 Nm (53 in-lbs)
Front axle
  FZR600, 1987 and 1988 FZR750/1000 .... 52 Nm (42 ft-lbs)
  1989 and 1990 FZR750/1000 .... 75 Nm (54 ft-lbs)
  1991 through 1993 FZR1000 .... 48 Nm (35 ft-lbs)
  1994-on FZR1000 .... 150 Nm (110 ft-lbs)
Front axle clamp bolt
  All except 1989-on FZR750 models .... 20 Nm (14 ft-lbs)
  1989-on FZR750 models .... 35 Nm (25 ft-lbs)
Brake disc mounting bolts .... 20 Nm (14 ft-lbs)*
Union (banjo fitting) bolts
  FZR600 models .... 26 Nm (19 ft-lbs)
  FZR750/1000 models .... 25 Nm (18 ft-lbs)
Master cylinder mounting bolts
  Front
    FZR600, 1987 and 1988 FZR750, 1987 through 1990 FZR1000 .. 9 Nm (6.5 ft-lbs)
    1989-on FZR750 .... 8 Nm (5.8 ft-lbs)
    1991 through 1993 FZR1000 .... 10 Nm (7.2 ft-lbs)
    1994-on FZR1000 .... 13 Nm (9.4 ft-lbs)
  Rear .... 20 Nm (14 ft-lbs)
Rear axle nut
  FZR600 models .... 107 Nm (77 ft-lbs)
  1987 and 1988 FZR750/1000 models .... 110 Nm (80 ft-lbs)
  1989-on FZR750 models .... 75 Nm (54 ft-lbs)
  1989-on FZR1000 models .... 150 Nm (110 ft-lbs)

Apply non-permanent thread locking agent to the threads.

8•4 Brakes, wheels and tires

1 General information

The models covered by this manual are equipped with hydraulic disc brakes on the front and rear. 1989 FZR600 models use a pair of dual-piston calipers at the front. 1994 and later FZR1000 models use a pair of six-piston calipers at the front. All other models use a pair of four-piston calipers at the front. All models use one dual-piston caliper at the rear. The rear caliper on 1988 and later FZR750 models is mounted beneath the disc; on all others it's mounted above the disc.

All models are equipped with cast aluminum wheels, which require very little maintenance and allow tubeless tires to be used.

Caution: Disc brake components rarely require disassembly. Do not disassemble components unless absolutely necessary. If any hydraulic brake line connection in the system is loosened, the entire system should be disassembled, drained, cleaned and then properly filled and bled upon reassembly. Do not use solvents on internal brake components. Solvents will cause seals to swell and distort. Use only clean brake fluid, brake cleaner or alcohol for cleaning. Use care when working with brake fluid as it can injure your eyes and it will damage painted surfaces and plastic parts.

2 Brake pads - replacement

Front calipers

⚠ **Warning:** *When replacing the front brake pads always replace the pads in BOTH calipers - never just on one side. Replace the anti-squeal shims and pad spring whenever the pads are replaced. Also, the dust created by the brake system may contain asbestos, which is harmful to your health. Never blow it out with compressed air and don't inhale any of it. An approved filtering mask should be worn when working on the brakes.*

2.3a Pull out the pad pin retaining clips (all except 1989 and later FZR750 models)

1 Support the bike securely so it can't be knocked over during this procedure.

All except 1989-on FZR750 and 1994-on FZR1000 models

2 Remove the brake pad cover from each caliper (see Chapter 1).
3 Pull the retaining clips out of the pad pins (see illustrations).

2.3b Dual-piston front calipers - exploded view

1 Bleed valve cap
2 Bleed valve
3 Pad pin retaining clip
4 Pad cover
5 Pad pin retaining clip
6 Pad pin
7 Caliper body
8 Pistons
9 Piston seals
10 Dust seals
11 Pads
12 Pad spring
13 Caliper assemblies
14 Brake disc mounting bolts
15 Brake discs

2.3c Four-piston front calipers - exploded view (600 and late 1000 model shown; other models similar)

1 Bleed valve cap
2 Bleed valve
3 Pad cover
4 Pad spring
5 Pad pin retaining clip
6 Pad pin
7 Caliper mounting bolt
8 Pistons
9 Piston seals
10 Dust seals
11 Pads
12 Caliper assembly
13 Caliper mounting bolt
14 Brake disc mounting bolt
15 Brake discs

Brakes, wheels and tires 8•5

2.4 Pull out one of the pad pins (1989 and later FZR750 models use a single pad retaining bolt)

2.5 Remove the pad spring (arrow) and pull out the remaining pad pin

2.6 Pull the pads out of their slots

4 Pull out one of the pad pins **(see illustration)**.

5 Remove the pad spring **(see illustration)**. Note that the longer end of the spring faces forward (in the rotating direction of the brake discs).

6 Pull out the remaining pad pin and lift the pads out of the caliper **(see illustration)**.

1989-on FZR750 and 1994-on FZR1000 models

7 If you're working on a 1989 or later FZR750, unscrew the pad retaining bolt and take off the pad spring **(see illustration)**. Pull the pads out of their slots. If you're working on a 1994 or later FZR1000, remove the caliper mounting bolts and lift the calipers off without disconnecting the brake hoses **(see illustration)**. Remove the retaining pin clips, pad retaining pins, pads and shims.

All models

8 Check the condition of the brake discs (see Section 4). If they are in need of machining or replacement, follow the procedure in that Section to remove them. If they are okay,

2.7a Front calipers (1989-on FZR750 models) - exploded view

1 Bleed valve and cap
2 Pad spring
3 Caliper mounting bolt
4 Pad retaining bolt
5 Caliper body
6 Pistons
7 Piston seals
8 Dust seals
9 Brake pads
10 Brake discs
11 Brake disc mounting bolt
12 Caliper assembly
13 Caliper mounting bolt

2.7b Front calipers (1994-on FZR1000 models)

1 Pad spring
2 Bleed valve
3 Bleed valve cap
4 Pad retaining pin
5 Retaining pin clip
6 Brake hose retainer
7 Pistons
8 Piston seal
9 Dust seal
10 Pad shims
11 Pads
12 Caliper body
13 Brake discs

8•6 Brakes, wheels and tires

2.10a Special lubricants are recommended anywhere salt is used on the roads, to prevent corrosion

A   Apply Duckhams Copper 10 or equivalent to the shaded areas
B   Apply Shin-Etsu G-40M or equivalent silicone grease to the shaded areas

2.10b Apply lubricant to the pad friction areas inside the caliper and to the exposed portion of the caliper pistons

A   Duckhams Copper 10
B   Shin-Etsu G-40M silicone grease

deglaze them with sandpaper or emery cloth, using a swirling motion.

9 Remove the cap from the master cylinder reservoir and siphon out some fluid. Push the pistons into the caliper as far as possible, while checking the master cylinder reservoir to make sure it doesn't overflow. If you can't depress the pistons with thumb pressure, try using a C-clamp (G-clamp). If the piston sticks, remove the caliper and overhaul it as described in Section 3.

⚠️ **Warning: This step is necessary to ensure that the pads move freely in the calipers. Because a large amount of salt is used on roads in the UK, special lubrication of the pads and calipers is required.**

10 Before installing the pads on UK models, apply a thin film of Duckhams Copper 10 or equivalent to the following areas **(see illustrations)**:
a) To the edges of the metal backing on the brake pads
b) To the pad retaining pins or bolt shaft
c) To the areas of the caliper where the pads rub
d) To the threads of the caliper mounting bolts.

Apply a thin film of Shin-Etsu G-40M or equivalent silicone grease to the following:
e) Exposed areas of the caliper pistons
f) The areas of the pad backing plates that contact the pistons.

Caution: Don't use too much Copper 10 and don't apply it to the pad pin retaining clips or the anti-squeal shim(s). Make sure no Copper 10 contacts the brake discs or the pad friction surfaces.

All except 1989-on FZR750 and 1994-on FZR1000 models

11 If you're working on an FZR600 with four-piston calipers, assemble the pads, shims and shim retainers **(see illustration)**.
12 Install the pads in the caliper.
13 Position the pad spring on the pads with its longer end facing forward. Slide the pad pins into their holes, making sure they pass over the fingers on the pad spring.
14 Install the retaining clips in the pad pins.

1989-on FZR750 models

15 Slide the pads into their slots and install the pad spring with its longer tangs forward. Install the pad retaining bolt over the spring and tighten it to the torque listed in this Chapter's Specifications.

1989-on FZR1000 models

16 Slide the pads into their slots and install the pad spring. Push the retaining pins in and secure them with the clips. Install the calipers and tighten their mounting bolts to the torque listed in this Chapter's Specifications.

All models

17 Refill the master cylinder reservoir (see 'Daily (pre-ride) checks at the beginning of this Manual) and install the diaphragm and cap. Operate the brake lever several times to bring the pads into contact with the disc. Check the operation of the brakes carefully before riding the motorcycle.

Rear calipers

⚠️ **Warning: The dust created by the brake system may contain asbestos, which is harmful to your health. Never blow it out with compressed air and don't inhale any of it. An approved filtering mask should be worn when working on the brakes. Replace the anti-squeal shims and pad spring whenever the pads are replaced.**

18 Support the bike securely so it can't be knocked over during this procedure.

1   Brake pads
2   Pad shims
3   Shim retainers

2.11 Pads and shims (FZR600 models with four-piston calipers)

Brakes, wheels and tires 8•7

2.20a High-mount rear caliper - exploded view

1 Bleed valve cap
2 Bleed valve
3 Pad cover
4 Pad pin retaining clip
5 Pad pin
6 Caliper body
7 Piston
8 Piston
9 Piston seals
10 Dust seals
11 Pad spring
12 Pad shims
13 Pads
14 Caliper assembly
15 Torque arm
16 Caliper mounting bolt
17 Brake disc mounting bolt
18 Brake disc

2.20b Low-mount (underslung) rear caliper - exploded view

1 Bleed valve cap
2 Bleed valve
3 Pad cover
4 Pad pin retaining clip
5 Pad pin
6 Caliper body
7 Piston
8 Piston
9 Piston seals
10 Dust seals
11 Pad spring
12 Pad shims
13 Pads
14 Caliper assembly
15 Brake disc mounting bolt
16 Brake disc

19 Remove the pad cover (see Chapter 1).
20 Pull the retaining clips out of the pad pins **(see illustrations)**.
21 Pull one of the pad pins out of the caliper, then lift the pad spring off of the other pad pin and pull it out **(see illustrations)**.
22 Lift the pads out of the caliper **(see illustration)**.
23 Perform Steps 7, 8 and 9 above to inspect the disc and prepare the caliper for pad installation.
24 Note the arrow on each pad shim (see

2.21a Pull out the pad pin . . .

2.21b . . . and remove the pad spring

2.22 Pull the pads out of their slots

8•8 Brakes, wheels and tires

2.24 Be sure the arrows on the pad shims point in the forward rotating direction of the wheel

3.2a Remove the union bolt and two sealing washers - this is a front caliper . . .
1 Union bolt and sealing washers
2 Brake hose fitting locating tab

3.2b . . . and this is a rear caliper
1 Caliper mounting bolts
2 Union bolt and sealing washers
3 Brake hose fitting locating tab

illustration). Be sure it points forward (in the direction of disc rotation) when the pad is installed.

25 Installation is the reverse of the removal steps, with the following additions:
a) Install the pad spring with its longer tangs pointing in the forward rotating direction of the wheel and secure it with the pad pins.
b) Refill the master cylinder reservoir (see 'Daily (pre-ride) checks at the beginning of this Manual).
c) Operate the brake pedal to bring the pads back into contact with the disc. Check the operation of the brakes carefully before riding the motorcycle.

3 Brake caliper - removal, overhaul and installation

Warning: If a front caliper indicates the need for an overhaul (usually due to leaking fluid or sticky operation), BOTH front calipers should be overhauled and all old brake fluid flushed from the system. Also, the dust created by the brake system may contain asbestos, which is harmful to your health. Never blow it out with compressed air and don't inhale any of it. An approved filtering mask should be worn when working on the brakes. Do not, under any circumstances, use petroleum-based solvents to clean brake parts. Use brake cleaner or denatured alcohol only!

Removal

1 Support the bike securely so it can't be knocked over during this procedure.
2 With a clean rag handy to catch spills, remove the brake hose banjo fitting bolt and separate the hose from the caliper **(see illustrations)**. Discard the sealing washers. Place the end of the hose in a container and operate the brake lever to pump out the fluid. Once this is done, wrap a clean shop rag tightly around the hose fitting to soak up any drips and prevent contamination.
3 Unscrew the caliper mounting bolts **(refer to illustrations 2.3a, 2.3c, 2.7, 2.20a, 2.20b and the accompanying illustrations)**.
Caution: Don't remove the bolts that hold the caliper halves together.
4 Lift off the caliper and remove the brake pads (see Section 2).

Overhaul

5 Clean the exterior of the caliper with denatured alcohol or brake system cleaner.
6 Place a few rags between the piston(s) and the caliper frame to act as a cushion, then use compressed air, directed into the fluid inlet, to remove the piston(s) **(see illustrations)**. Use only enough air pressure to ease the piston(s)

3.3a Remove the lower mounting bolt . . .

3.3b . . . and the upper mounting bolt; if the reflector is in the way . . .

3.3c . . . remove its mounting nut (arrowed)

3.6a Blow air into the fluid inlet to force the pistons out; DO NOT get your fingers in the way. This is a front caliper . . .

3.6b . . . the same technique and safety precautions apply to the rear caliper

Brakes, wheels and tires 8•9

3.8a Each caliper bore contains a dust seal and a piston seal (this is a four-piston front caliper) . . .

1 Dust seal   2 Piston seal

3.8b . . . and this is a rear caliper

1 Dust seal   2 Piston seal

3.8c Remove the dust seal from its groove . . .

out of the bore. If a piston is blown out, even with the cushion in place, it may be damaged.

⚠ **Warning: Never place your fingers in front of the piston in an attempt to catch or protect it when applying compressed air, as serious injury could occur.**

7 If compressed air isn't available, reconnect the caliper to the brake hose and pump the brake lever or pedal until the pistons are free.
8 Using a wood or plastic tool, remove the dust seal(s) **(see illustrations)**. Metal tools may cause bore damage.
9 Using a wood or plastic tool, remove the piston seal(s) from the groove in the caliper bore **(see illustration)**.
10 Clean the piston(s) and the bore(s) with denatured alcohol, clean brake fluid or brake system cleaner and blow dry them with filtered, unlubricated compressed air. Inspect the surfaces of the piston(s) for nicks and burrs and loss of plating. Check the caliper bore(s), too. If surface defects are present, the caliper must be replaced. If the caliper is in bad shape, the master cylinder should also be checked.
11 Lubricate new piston seal(s) with clean brake fluid and install it in its groove in the caliper bore. Make sure it isn't twisted and seats completely.
12 Lubricate new dust seal(s) with clean brake fluid and install it in its groove, making sure it seats correctly.

3.9 . . . then remove the piston seal

13 Lubricate the piston(s) with clean brake fluid and install it into the caliper bore. Using your thumbs, push the piston all the way in, making sure it doesn't get cocked in the bore.

Installation

14 Install the caliper, tightening the mounting bolts to the torque listed in this Chapter's Specifications. Install the brake pads.
15 Connect the brake hose to the caliper, using new sealing washers on each side of the fitting. Align the banjo fitting with its tab and tighten the bolt to the torque listed in this Chapter's Specifications.
16 Fill the master cylinder with the recommended brake fluid (see 'Daily (pre-ride) checks at the beginning of this Manual) and bleed the system (see Section 8). Check for leaks.
17 Check the operation of the brakes carefully before riding the motorcycle.

4 Brake disc(s) - inspection, removal and installation

Inspection

1 Support the bike securely so it can't be knocked over during this procedure, with the wheel to be checked off the ground.
2 Visually inspect the surface of the disc(s) for score marks and other damage. Light scratches are normal after use and won't affect brake operation, but deep grooves and heavy score marks will reduce braking efficiency and accelerate pad wear. If the discs are badly grooved they must be machined or replaced.
3 To check disc runout, mount a dial indicator to a fork leg or the swing-arm, with the plunger on the indicator touching the surface of the disc about 1/2-inch from the outer edge **(see illustration)**. Slowly turn the wheel and watch the indicator needle, comparing your reading with the limit listed in this Chapter's Specifications. If the runout is greater than

allowed, check the hub bearings for play (see Section 9). If the bearings are worn, replace them and repeat this check. If the disc runout is still excessive, it will have to be replaced.
4 The disc must not be machined or allowed to wear down to a thickness less than the minimum allowable thickness, stamped on the disc and listed in this Chapter's Specifications. The thickness of the disc can be checked with a micrometer. If the thickness of the disc is less than the minimum allowable, it must be replaced.

Removal

5 Remove the wheel (see Section 11 for front wheel removal or Section 12 for rear wheel removal).

Caution: Don't lay the wheel down and allow it to rest on one of the discs - the disc could become warped. Set the wheel on wood blocks so the disc doesn't support the weight of the wheel.

6 Mark the relationship of the disc to the wheel, so it can be installed in the same position. Remove the Allen head bolts that

4.3 Set up a dial indicator (1) to contact each brake disc, then rotate the wheel to check for runout

8•10 Brakes, wheels and tires

4.6a Brake discs are secured by Allen bolts (arrowed) . . .

4.6b . . . loosen the bolts evenly with an Allen bolt bit . . .

4.6c . . . and lift the disc off the hub

retain the disc to the wheel **(see illustrations)**. Loosen the bolts a little at a time, in a criss-cross pattern, to avoid distorting the disc. Once all the bolts are loose, take the disc off **(see illustration)**.

7 Take note of any paper shims that may be present where the disc mates to the wheel. If there are any, mark their position and be sure to include them when installing the disc.

Installation

8 Position the disc on the wheel, aligning the previously applied matchmarks (if you're reinstalling the original disc). Make sure the arrow (stamped on the disc) marking the direction of rotation is pointing in the proper direction.

4.9a Apply non-permanent thread locking agent to the threads of the disc mounting bolts . . .

4.9b . . . and tighten the bolts evenly to the torque listed in this Chapter's Specifications

9 Apply a non-permanent thread locking compound to the threads of the bolts **(see illustration)**. Install the bolts, tightening them a little at a time, in a criss-cross pattern, until the torque listed in this Chapter's Specifications is reached **(see illustration)**. Thoroughly clean off all grease from the brake disc(s) using acetone or brake system cleaner.

10 Install the wheel.

11 Operate the brake lever or pedal several times to bring the pads into contact with the disc. Check the operation of the brakes carefully before riding the motorcycle.

5 Front brake master cylinder - removal, overhaul and installation

1 If the master cylinder is leaking fluid, or if the lever does not produce a firm feel when the brake is applied, and bleeding the brakes does not help, master cylinder overhaul is recommended.

2 Before disassembling the master cylinder, read through the entire procedure and make sure that you have the correct rebuild kit. Also, you will need some new, clean brake fluid of the recommended type, some clean rags and internal snap-ring pliers. **Note**: *To prevent damage to the paint from spilled brake fluid, always cover the fuel tank when working on the master cylinder.*

Caution: Disassembly, overhaul and reassembly of the brake master cylinder must be done in a spotlessly clean work area to avoid contamination and possible failure of the brake hydraulic system components.

Removal

3 On all except 1989-on FZR750 and 1994-on FZR1000 models, loosen but do not remove the screws holding the reservoir cover in place **(see illustration)**. On 1989-on FZR750 and

1 Reservoir cap
2 Diaphragm
3 Piston assembly and spring
4 Brake hose sealing washers
5 Union bolt
6 Rubber cap
7 Brake hose
8 Master cylinder body
9 Clamp
10 Lockwasher
11 Allen bolt
12 Cover screw

5.3a Front master cylinder (all except 1989-on FZR750 and 1994-on FZR1000 models) - exploded view

Brakes, wheels and tires 8•11

5.3b Front master cylinder (1989-on FZR750 and 1994-on FZR1000) - exploded view

1 Reservoir cover retainer
2 Reservoir cover
3 Diaphragm support
4 Diaphragm
5 Dust boot
6 Snap-ring
7 Master cylinder kit (replace as a set)
8 Master cylinder body

5.5a If there's a rubber boot over the union bolt (arrowed), pull it back (this is an FZR600)

5.5b Remove the union bolt (arrowed) and sealing washers

1994-on FZR1000 models, disconnect the feed hose from the master cylinder body and drain the fluid into a container (see illustration).

4 Disconnect the electrical connectors from the brake light switch (see Chapter 10).

5 Pull back the rubber boot (if equipped), loosen the banjo fitting bolt (see illustrations) and separate the brake hose(s) from the master cylinder. Wrap the end of the hose in a clean rag and suspend the hose in an upright position or bend it down carefully and place the open end in a clean container. The objective is to prevent excessive loss of brake fluid, fluid spills and system contamination.

6 Remove the locknut from the underside of the lever pivot bolt, then unscrew the bolt (see illustration).

7 Remove the master cylinder mounting bolts (see illustrations) and separate the master cylinder from the handlebar. On 1989-on FZR750 and 1994-on FZR1000 models, remove the fluid reservoir if necessary.

Overhaul

8 Detach the cover and the rubber diaphragm, then drain the brake fluid into a suitable container. Remove the splash plate from the bottom of the reservoir (if equipped) (see illustration), then wipe any remaining fluid out of the reservoir with a clean rag.

9 Carefully remove the rubber dust boot from the end of the piston (see illustration).

10 Using snap-ring pliers, remove the snap-ring (see illustration) and slide out the piston

5.6 Remove the locknut (arrowed) and pivot bolt

5.7a The master cylinder is secured by Allen bolts (arrowed) . . .

5.7b . . . or hex bolts (arrowed); be sure the UP mark on the clamp is upright during installation

5.8 Lift the splash plate out of the cylinder body so you can clean the fluid ports in the bottom

5.9 Remove the rubber boot

5.10a Remove the snap-ring from the cylinder bore . . .

8

8•12 Brakes, wheels and tires

5.10b . . . then pull out the piston assembly . . .

5.10c . . . and spring

5.11a Pull the spring out of the lever . . .

assembly and the spring **(see illustrations)**. Lay the parts out in the proper order to prevent confusion during reassembly.

11 Remove the spring and pivot bushing from the lever **(see illustrations)**.

12 Clean all of the parts with brake system cleaner (available at auto parts stores), isopropyl alcohol or clean brake fluid.

Caution: Do not, under any circumstances, use a petroleum-based solvent to clean brake parts. If compressed air is available, use it to dry the parts thoroughly (make sure it's filtered and unlubricated). Check the master cylinder bore for corrosion, scratches, nicks and score marks. If damage is evident, the master cylinder must be replaced with a new one. If the master cylinder is in poor condition, then the calipers should be checked as well.

13 The piston assembly and spring are included in the rebuild kit. Use all of the new parts, regardless of the apparent condition of the old ones.

14 Before reassembling the master cylinder, soak the piston and the rubber cup seals in clean brake fluid for ten or fifteen minutes. Lubricate the master cylinder bore with clean brake fluid, then carefully insert the piston and related parts in the reverse order of disassembly. Make sure the lips on the cup seals do not turn inside out when they are slipped into the bore.

15 Depress the piston, then install the snap-ring (make sure the snap-ring is properly seated in the groove). Install the rubber dust boot (make sure the lip is seated properly in the piston groove).

5.11b . . . and remove the pivot bushing

Installation

16 Attach the master cylinder to the handlebar and tighten the bolts to the torque listed in this Chapter's Specifications.
Caution: If you're working on a model with a hydraulic clutch, don't mix up the clutch master cylinder clamp and the brake master cylinder clamp. The clamps or cylinders may be damaged if the clamps are installed on the wrong cylinders.

17 Connect the brake hose to the master cylinder, using new sealing washers. Tighten the banjo fitting bolt to the torque listed in this Chapter's Specifications. Refer to Section 8 and bleed the air from the system.

6 Rear brake master cylinder - removal, overhaul and installation

1 If the master cylinder is leaking fluid, or if the pedal does not produce a firm feel when the brake is applied, and bleeding the brakes does not help, master cylinder overhaul is recommended.

2 Before disassembling the master cylinder, read through the entire procedure and make sure that you have the correct rebuild kit. Also, you will need some new, clean brake fluid of the recommended type, some clean rags and internal snap-ring pliers.
Caution: Disassembly, overhaul and reassembly of the brake master cylinder must be done in a spotlessly clean work area to avoid contamination and possible failure of the brake hydraulic system components.

Removal

3 Support the bike securely so it can't be knocked over during this procedure. Remove the protective aluminum cover for access to the mounting bolts.

4 Remove the cotter pin from the clevis pin on the master cylinder pushrod **(see illustrations)**. Remove the clevis pin.

1 Reservoir cap
2 Gasket
3 Diaphragm
4 Reservoir
5 Clamp
6 Union bolt
7 Sealing washers
8 Brake line (master cylinder to caliper)
9 Master cylinder assembly
10 Fluid feed hose (reservoir to master cylinder)
11 Master cylinder mounting bolt
12 Feed hose fitting
13 O-ring
14 Master cylinder body
15 Master cylinder kit (replace as a set)
16 Brake pedal
17 Clevis pin
18 Clevis
19 Locknut
20 Washer
21 Cotter pin
22 Brake pedal return spring

6.4a Rear brake master cylinder (1989 FZR600 models) - exploded view

Brakes, wheels and tires 8•13

6.5 Remove the clamp (left arrow) and disconnect the hose; the cylinder body is secured by two bolts (right arrows)

Caution: Do not, under any circumstances, use a petroleum-based solvent to clean brake parts. If compressed air is available, use it to dry the parts thoroughly (make sure it's filtered and unlubricated). Check the master cylinder bore for corrosion, scratches, nicks and score marks. If damage is evident, the master cylinder must be replaced with a new one. If the master cylinder is in poor condition, then the caliper should be checked as well.

12 A new piston and spring are included in the rebuild kit. Use them regardless of the condition of the old ones.

13 Before reassembling the master cylinder, soak the piston and the rubber cup seals in clean brake fluid for ten or fifteen minutes. Lubricate the master cylinder bore with clean brake fluid, then carefully insert the parts in the reverse order of disassembly. Make sure the lips on the cup seals do not turn inside out when they are slipped into the bore.

14 Depress the pushrod, then install the snap-ring (make sure the snap-ring is properly seated in the groove). Install the rubber dust boot (make sure the lip is seated properly in the groove).

15 Install the clevis to the end of the pushrod, then tighten the locknut.

16 Install the feed hose fitting, using a new O-ring.

Installation

17 Install the reservoir (if removed) and engage it with the stay. Connect the banjo fitting to the top of the master cylinder, using a new sealing washer on each side of the fitting. Tighten the union bolt to the torque listed in this Chapter's Specifications.

18 Connect the fluid feed hose to the inlet fitting and install the hose clamp.

19 Connect the clevis to the brake pedal and secure the clevis pin with a new cotter pin.

20 Fill the fluid reservoir with the specified fluid (see 'Daily (pre-ride) checks at the beginning of this Manual) and bleed the system following the procedure in Section 8. Install the aluminum protective cover.

21 Check the position of the brake pedal (see Chapter 1) and adjust it if necessary. Check the operation of the brakes carefully before riding the motorcycle.

6.4b Rear brake master cylinder (all except 1989 FZR600 models) - exploded view

1 Reservoir cap
2 Diaphragm support
3 Diaphragm
4 Reservoir
5 Clamp
6 Union bolt
7 Sealing washers
8 Brake line (master cylinder to caliper)
9 Feed hose fitting screw
10 Fluid feed hose (reservoir to master cylinder)
11 Master cylinder mounting bolt
12 Feed hose fitting
13 O-ring
14 Master cylinder body
15 Master cylinder kit (replace as a set)
16 Brake pedal
17 Clevis pin
18 Clevis
19 Locknut
20 Washer
21 Cotter pin
22 Brake pedal return spring
23 Spring post
24 Sleeve
25 Nut

5 Have a container and some rags ready to catch spilling brake fluid. Using a pair of pliers, slide the clamp up the fluid feed hose and detach the hose from the master cylinder **(see illustration)**. Direct the end of the hose into the container, unscrew the cap on the master cylinder reservoir and allow the fluid to drain.

6 Using a six-point box-end wrench (ring spanner), unscrew the fluid line union bolt from the master cylinder **(see illustration 6.4a or 6.4b)**. Discard the sealing washers on either side of the fitting.

7 Remove the mounting bolts **(see illustration 6.5)** and take the master cylinder off the frame. Remove the reservoir if necessary.

Overhaul

8 Remove the screw, lockwasher and washer and detach the fluid inlet fitting from the master cylinder. Remove the O-ring from the bore.

9 Hold the clevis with a pair of pliers and loosen the locknut. Unscrew the clevis and locknut from the pushrod and carefully remove the rubber dust boot from the pushrod.

10 Depress the pushrod and, using snap-ring pliers, remove the snap-ring. Slide out the piston assembly and spring. Lay the parts out in the proper order to prevent confusion during reassembly.

11 Clean all of the parts with brake system cleaner (available at auto parts stores), isopropyl alcohol or clean brake fluid.

8

8•14 Brakes, wheels and tires

7.2a Front brake hose details (FZR600; US FZR750; 1987 and 1988 FZR1000 models)

1 Union bolts
2 Sealing washers
3 Brake hoses
4 Brake hose junction
5 Junction mounting bolt

7.2b Front brake hose details (1989-on FZR750 and 1994-on FZR1000 models)

1 Sealing washers
2 Union bolts
3 Retainers
4 Retainer bolts
5 Brake hoses

7.2c Front brake hose details (1989 through 1993 FZR1000 models)

1 Sealing washers
2 Union bolts
3 Retainers
4 Retainer bolts
5 Brake hoses

7 Brake hoses - inspection and replacement

Inspection

1 Once a week, or if the motorcycle is used less frequently, before every ride, check the condition of the brake hoses and, on early models, the hoses that feed brake fluid to the anti-dive units on the front forks.

2 Twist and flex the rubber hoses **(see illustrations 6.4a, 6.4b and the accompanying illustrations)** while looking for cracks, bulges and seeping fluid. Check extra carefully around the areas where the hoses connect with the banjo fittings, as these are common areas for hose failure.

3 Inspect the metal banjo fittings connected to brake hoses. If the fittings are rusted, scratched or cracked, replace them.

Replacement

4 Most brake hoses have banjo fittings on each end of the hose. Cover the surrounding area with plenty of rags and unscrew the union bolts on either end of the hose. Detach the hose from any clips that may be present **(see illustration)** and remove the hose.

5 Position the new hose, making sure it isn't twisted or otherwise strained, between the two components. Make sure the metal tube portion of the banjo fitting is located next to the tab on the component it's connected to, if equipped **(see illustrations 3.2a and 3.2b)**. Install the union bolts, using new sealing washers on both sides of the fittings, and tighten them to the torque listed in this Chapter's Specifications.

7.4 There's a hose retainer attached to each front fork

6 Flush the old brake fluid from the system, refill the system with the recommended fluid (see 'Daily (pre-ride) checks at the beginning of this Manual) and bleed the air from the system (see Section 8). Check the operation of the brakes carefully before riding the motorcycle.

8 Brake system bleeding

1 Bleeding the brake is simply the process of removing all the air bubbles from the brake fluid reservoirs, the lines and the brake calipers. Bleeding is necessary whenever a brake system hydraulic connection is loosened, when a component or hose is replaced, or when the master cylinder or caliper is overhauled. Leaks in the system may also allow air to enter, but leaking brake fluid will reveal their presence and warn you of the need for repair.

2 To bleed the brakes, you will need some new, clean brake fluid of the recommended type (see Chapter 1), a length of clear vinyl or plastic tubing, a small container partially filled

Brakes, wheels and tires 8•15

8.5a Each front caliper has a single bleed valve (arrowed) . . .

8.5b . . . and rear calipers have two bleed valves (arrowed); both valves must be bled

with clean brake fluid, some rags and a wrench to fit the brake caliper bleeder valves.
3 Cover the fuel tank and other painted components to prevent damage in the event that brake fluid is spilled.
4 Remove the reservoir cap or cover and slowly pump the brake lever or pedal a few times, until no air bubbles can be seen floating up from the holes at the bottom of the reservoir. Doing this bleeds the air from the master cylinder end of the line. Reinstall the reservoir cap or cover.
5 Slip a box wrench over the caliper bleed valve **(see illustrations)**. Attach one end of the clear vinyl or plastic tubing to the bleeder valve and submerge the other end in the brake fluid in the container.
6 Remove the reservoir cap or cover and check the fluid level. Do not allow the fluid level to drop below the lower mark during the bleeding process.
7 Carefully pump the brake lever or pedal three or four times and hold it while opening the caliper bleeder valve. When the valve is opened, brake fluid will flow out of the caliper into the clear tubing and the lever will move toward the handlebar or the pedal will move down.
8 Retighten the bleeder valve, then release the brake lever or pedal gradually. Repeat the process until no air bubbles are visible in the brake fluid leaving the caliper and the lever or pedal is firm when applied. **Note:** *On rear calipers with two bleeder valves, air must be*

bled from both, one after the other. Remember to add fluid to the reservoir as the level drops. Use only new, clean brake fluid of the recommended type. Never reuse the fluid lost during bleeding.
9 Replace the reservoir cover, wipe up any spilled brake fluid and check the entire system for leaks.

HAYNES HiNT *If bleeding is difficult, it may be necessary to let the brake fluid in the system stabilize for a few hours (it may be aerated). Repeat the bleeding procedure when the tiny bubbles in the system have settled out.*

9 Wheels - inspection and repair

1 Support the motorcycle securely upright, then clean the wheels thoroughly to remove mud and dirt that may interfere with the inspection procedure or mask defects. Make a general check of the wheels and tires as described in 'Daily (pre-ride) checks at the beginning of this Manual.
2 Raise the wheel to be checked off the ground, then attach a dial indicator to the fork slider or the swingarm and position the stem against the side of the rim. Spin the wheel slowly and check the side-to-side (axial) runout of the rim, then compare your readings with the value listed in this Chapter's Specifications **(see illustration)**. In order to accurately check radial runout with the dial indicator, the wheel would have to be removed from the machine and the tire removed from the wheel. With the axle clamped in a vise, the wheel can be rotated to check the runout.
3 An easier, though slightly less accurate, method is to attach a stiff wire pointer to the fork or the swingarm and position the end a fraction of an inch from the wheel (where the wheel and tire join). If the wheel is true, the distance from the pointer to the rim will be constant as the wheel is rotated. **Note:** *If wheel runout is excessive, refer to the appropriate Section in this Chapter and check the wheel bearings very carefully before replacing the wheel.*

4 The wheels should also be visually inspected for cracks, flat spots on the rim and other damage. Since tubeless tires are involved, look very closely for dents in the area where the tire bead contacts the rim. Dents in this area may prevent complete sealing of the tire against the rim, which leads to deflation of the tire over a period of time.
5 If damage is evident, or if runout in either direction is excessive, the wheel will have to be replaced with a new one. Never attempt to repair a damaged cast aluminum wheel.

10 Wheels - alignment check

1 Misalignment of the wheels, which may be due to a cocked rear wheel or a bent frame or triple clamps, can cause strange and possibly serious handling problems. If the frame or triple clamps are at fault, repair by a frame specialist or replacement with new parts are the only alternatives.
2 To check the alignment you will need an assistant, a length of string or a perfectly straight piece of wood and a ruler graduated in 1/64 inch increments. A plumb bob or other suitable weight will also be required.
3 Support the motorcycle in a level position, then measure the width of both tires at their widest points. Subtract the smaller measurement from the larger measurement, then divide the difference by two. The result is the amount of offset that should exist between the front and rear tires on both sides.
4 If a string is used, have your assistant hold one end of it about half way between the floor and the rear axle, touching the rear sidewall of the tire.
5 Run the other end of the string forward and pull it tight so that it is roughly parallel to the floor. Slowly bring the string into contact with the front sidewall of the rear tire, then turn the front wheel until it is parallel with the string. Measure the distance from the front tire sidewall to the string.
6 Repeat the procedure on the other side of the motorcycle. The distance from the front tire sidewall to the string should be equal on both sides.
7 As was previously pointed out, a perfectly straight length of wood may be substituted for the string. The procedure is the same.
8 If the distance between the string and tire is greater on one side, or if the rear wheel appears to be cocked, refer to Chapter 7, Swingarm bearings - check, and make sure the swingarm is tight.
9 If the front-to-back alignment is correct, the wheels still may be out of alignment vertically.
10 Using the plumb bob, or other suitable weight, and a length of string, check the rear wheel to make sure it is vertical. To do this, hold the string against the tire upper sidewall and allow the weight to settle just off the floor. When the string touches both the upper and

9.2 Use a dial indicator to measure wheel runout

A Radial runout   B Axial runout

8

8•16 Brakes, wheels and tires

1 Axle
2 Washer
  (1987 and 1988 models only)
3 Collar
4 Seal
5 Wheel bearing
6 Spacer
7 Speedometer clutch
8 Speedometer clutch retainer
9 Seal
10 Speedometer drive unit

11.5a Front wheel details (all except 1989-on FZR750 models)

11.5b Loosen the pinch bolt . . .

11.5c . . . and unscrew the axle

lower tire sidewalls and is perfectly straight, the wheel is vertical. If it is not, place thin spacers under one leg of the centerstand.

11 Once the rear wheel is vertical, check the front wheel in the same manner. If both wheels are not perfectly vertical, the frame and/or major suspension components are bent.

11 Front wheel - removal, inspection and installation

Removal

1 Support the bike securely so it can't be knocked over during this procedure. Raise the front wheel off the ground by placing a floor jack, with a wood block on the jack head, under the engine.

2 Disconnect the speedometer cable from the drive unit (see Chapter 10).

All except 1989-on FZR750 models

3 If you're working on an FZR600 or a 1989-on FZR1000, remove the left and right fairings (see Chapter 9).

4 Remove the left brake caliper (FZR600) or both brake calipers (all others) and support the caliper(s) with a piece of wire. Don't disconnect the brake hose from the caliper(s).

5 Loosen the axle pinch bolt and unscrew the axle **(see illustrations)**.

6 Support the wheel, then pull out the axle **(see illustration)** and carefully lower the wheel away from the forks.

7 Remove the collar from the right side and the speedometer drive assembly from the left side **(see illustrations)**. Set the wheel aside. *Caution: Don't lay the wheel down and allow it to rest on one of the discs - the disc could become warped. Set the wheel on wood blocks so the disc doesn't support the weight of the wheel.*

Note: Don't operate the front brake lever with the wheel removed.

1989-on FZR750 models

8 Remove the lower fairing (see Chapter 9).

9 Disconnect the speedometer cable from the drive unit at the left fork (see Chapter 10).

10 Unbolt the brake calipers without disconnecting the brake hoses and support them with pieces of wire.

11.6 Pull the axle out of the forks and wheel

11.7a This collar goes between the fork and the right side of the wheel; don't forget to reinstall it

11.7b Pull the speedometer drive out of the wheel; the notch (arrowed) aligns with a protrusion on the fork

Brakes, wheels and tires 8•17

axle into the hub. Slide the wheel into place. Make sure the lugs in the speedometer drive clutch line up with the notches in the speedometer drive gear **(see illustration)**. Make sure the protrusion on the inner side of the left fork fits into the notch in the speedometer gear housing **(see illustration 11.7b)**.

17 Slip the axle into place, then tighten the axle to the torque listed in this Chapter's Specifications. Tighten the axle pinch bolt to the torque listed in this Chapter's Specifications.

18 Apply the front brake, pump the forks up and down several times and check for binding and proper brake operation.

12 Rear wheel - removal, inspection and installation

Removal

1 Support the bike securely so it can't be knocked over during this procedure.

2 If you're working on a model with a low-mount (underslung) rear brake caliper, remove the rear brake caliper (see Section 3). If you're working on a model with a high-mount rear caliper, the caliper can be left in place.

3 Remove the cotter pin from the axle nut and loosen the nut **(see illustrations)**.

---

1 Axle
2 Clip
3 Flange
4 Collar
5 Seal
6 Wheel bearings
7 Spacer
8 Collar
9 Speedometer clutch
10 Speedometer clutch retainer
11 Seal
12 Speedometer drive unit

11.11 Front wheel details - 1989-on FZR750 models

11 Loosen the axle pinch bolt and unscrew the axle **(see illustration)**.

12 Support the wheel, then pull out the axle and carefully lower the wheel away from the forks.

13 Remove the collar from the right side and the speedometer drive assembly and collar from the left side. Set the wheel aside. **Caution: Don't lay the wheel down and allow it to rest on one of the discs - the disc could become warped. Set the wheel on wood blocks so the disc doesn't support the weight of the wheel.**

Note: *Don't operate the front brake lever with the wheel removed.*

Inspection

14 Roll the axle on a flat surface such as a piece of plate glass. If it's bent at all, replace it. If the axle is corroded, remove the corrosion with fine emery cloth.

15 Check the condition of the wheel bearings (see Section 13).

11.16 The tabs on the speedometer clutch (upper arrows) align with the notches in the drive unit (lower arrows)

Installation

16 Installation is the reverse of removal. Apply a thin coat of grease to the seal lip, then slide the

---

1 Axle
2 Washer
3 Cotter pin
4 Nut
5 Bolt
6 Torque link
7 Chain adjuster
8 Adjuster plate
9 Washer
10 Adjusting nut
11 Locknut
12 Caliper bracket
13 Collar
14 Grease seal
15 Wheel bearing
16 Spacer
17 Damper segments (cush drive)
18 Wheel bearings
19 Coupling
20 Sprocket stud
21 Nut
22 Collar
23 Coupling bearing
24 Grease seal
25 Collar
26 Washer
27 Axle nut
28 Cotter pin

12.3a Rear wheel details (FZR600 models)

8•18 Brakes, wheels and tires

12.3b Rear wheel details (1987 and 1988 FZR750 and 1000 models)

1 Axle
2 Cotter pin
3 Washer
4 Brake hose clip
5 Lockwasher
6 Bolt
7 Chain adjuster bolt
8 Chain adjuster block
9 Nut
10 Chain adjuster plate
11 Washer
12 Nut
13 Locknut
14 Torque link bolt
15 Torque link
16 Caliper bracket (high-mount design shown; low-mount design similar)
17 Collar
18 Seal
19 Wheel bearing
20 Spacer
21 Damper segments (cush drive)
22 Wheel bearing
23 Coupling
24 Sprocket stud
25 Nut
26 Sprocket
27 Collar
28 Coupling bearing
29 Seal
30 Collar
31 Chain
32 Washer
33 Axle nut

Brakes, wheels and tires 8•19

12.3c Rear wheel details (1989-on FZR750 models)

1 Cotter pin	9 Collar	17 Cotter pin	25 Sprocket bolt
2 Axle nut	10 Seal	18 Seal	26 Coupling bearing
3 Locknut	11 Wheel bearing	19 Bearing	27 Seal
4 Chain adjuster block	12 Spacer	20 Damper hub	28 Collar
5 Collar	13 Seal	21 Coupling segments	29 Retaining ring
6 Caliper bracket	14 Bearing	22 Wheel bearing	30 Axle
7 Wheel bearing	15 Torque link bolt	23 Collar	31 Chain adjuster block
8 Collar	16 Nut	24 Coupling clutch	32 Bolt

8•20 Brakes, wheels and tires

12.3e Bend back the cotter pin (arrowed) and pull it out, then loosen the axle nut (don't remove it yet)

4 Loosen the chain adjusting bolt locknuts and fully loosen both adjusters (see illustrations).

5 Push the rear wheel as far forward as possible. Lift the top of the chain up off the rear sprocket and pull it to the left while rotating the wheel backwards. This will disengage the chain from the sprocket.

Warning: Don't let your fingers slip between the chain and the sprocket.

6 Unscrew the axle nut (see illustration).

7 Support the wheel and slide the axle and washer out (see illustrations). Lower the

12.3d Rear wheel details (1989-on FZR1000 models)

1 Axle
2 Cotter pin
3 Chain adjuster
4 Nut
5 Brake hose bracket
6 Lockwasher
7 Bolt
8 Nut
9 Torque link bolt
10 Brake hose bracket
11 Caliper bracket
12 Collar
13 Seal
14 Wheel bearing
15 Spacer
16 Damper segments (cush drive)
17 Wheel bearing
18 Coupling
19 Sprocket stud
20 Nut
21 Collar
22 Coupling bearing
23 Seal
24 Collar
25 Sprocket
26 Chain
27 Washer
28 Axle nut

12.4a Loosen the chain adjuster locknut (this is an FZR600; early 750/1000 models similar) . . .

1 Axle nut (remove cotter pin and loosen first)
2 Adjuster nut
3 Locknut

12.4b . . . then create as much slack in the chain as possible (this is a 1989-on FZR1000; later 750 similar)

1 Locknut   2 Adjuster bolt

12.6 Remove the axle nut (this is an FZR1000)

12.7a Pull out the axle (this is an FZR600) . . .

Brakes, wheels and tires 8•21

12.7b ... and this is an FZR1000 (750 models similar)

12.7c Remove the collar from the brake disc side of the wheel ...

12.7d ... and from the sprocket side

wheel and remove it from the swingarm, being careful not to lose the collars on either side of the hub **(see illustrations)**.
Caution: Don't lay the wheel down and allow it to rest on the disc or the sprocket - they could become warped. Set the wheel on wood blocks so the disc or the sprocket doesn't support the weight of the wheel. Do not operate the brake pedal with the wheel removed.

Inspection

8 Before installing the wheel, check the axle for straightness by rolling it on a flat surface such as a piece of plate glass (if the axle is corroded, first remove the corrosion with fine emery cloth). If the axle is bent at all, replace it.
9 Check the condition of the wheel bearings (see Section 13).

Installation

10 Apply a thin coat of grease to the seal lips.
11 Slide the spacers into their proper positions on the sides of the hub **(see illustrations 12.7c and 12.7d)**.
12 Slide the wheel into place **(see illustration)**. If you're working on a model with a high-mount rear brake caliper, slide the brake disc between the pads **(see illustration)**.
13 Lift the chain over the sprocket, raise the wheel, install the axle (pass it through the caliper bracket and all collars) and finger-tighten the axle nut.
14 Adjust the chain slack (see Chapter 1) and tighten the adjuster locknuts.
15 Tighten the axle nut to the torque listed in this Chapter's Specifications. Install a new cotter pin, tightening the axle nut an additional amount, if necessary, to align the hole in the axle with the castellations on the nut. Be sure to bend the cotter pin correctly (see Drive chain and sprockets - check, adjustment and lubrication in Chapter 1).
16 If you're working on a model with a low-mount (underslung) rear brake caliper, install the caliper (see Section 3).

17 Check the operation of the brakes carefully before riding the motorcycle.

13 Wheel bearings - replacement

1 Support the bike securely so it can't be knocked over during this procedure and remove the wheel (see Section 11 (front wheel) or 12 (rear wheel).
2 Set the wheel on blocks so as not to allow the weight of the wheel rest on the brake disc or sprocket.

Front wheel bearings

3 From the right side of the wheel, lift out the collar (if you haven't already done so - **see illustration 11.7a**) and pry out the grease seal **(see illustration 11.5c or 11.11)**.
4 From the left side of the wheel, lift out the speedometer drive unit (if you haven't already done so - **see illustration 11.7b**).
5 From the left side of the wheel, pry out the grease seal, then lift out the speedometer clutch retainer and speedometer clutch **(see illustrations)**.
6 Using a metal rod (preferably a brass drift punch) inserted through the center of the hub bearing, tap evenly around the inner race of the opposite bearing to drive it from the hub

12.12a Position the wheel between the sides of the swingarm with the brake disc on the right ...

12.12b ... and lift it into position; on models with high-mount calipers, slip the disc between the pads

13.5a Pry out the grease seal ...

13.5b ... then lift out the speedometer clutch retainer and the speedometer clutch

8

8•22 Brakes, wheels and tires

13.6a Insert a drift punch through one bearing and tap out the opposite bearing . . .

13.6b . . . then turn the wheel over and lift out the bearing and spacer

13.10a Install the bearing with a socket the same diameter as the outer race (shown) or with a bearing driver

(see illustration). The bearing spacer will also come out (see illustration).
7 Lay the wheel on its other side and remove the remaining bearing using the same technique.
8 Clean the bearings with a high flash-point solvent (one which won't leave any residue) and blow them dry with compressed air (don't let the bearing spin as you dry them). Apply a few drops of oil to the bearing. Hold the outer race of the bearing and rotate the inner race - if the bearing doesn't turn smoothly, has rough spots or is noisy, replace it with a new one.
9 If the bearing checks out okay and will be reused, wash it in solvent once again and dry

it, then pack the bearing with medium-weight multi-purpose lithium-based grease.
10 Thoroughly clean the hub area of the wheel. Install the bearing into the recess in the hub, with the marked or shielded side facing out. Using a bearing driver or a socket large enough to contact the outer race of the bearing, drive it in (see illustration) until it's completely seated (see illustration).
11 Turn the wheel over and install the bearing spacer and bearing, driving the bearing into place as described in Step 10. Install the speedometer clutch and retainer on the left side of the wheel (see illustration).
12 Coat new grease seals with grease (see illustration), then install them. It should be

possible to push the seals in with even finger pressure (see illustration), but if necessary use a seal driver, large socket or a flat piece of wood to drive the seals into place.
13 Install the speedometer drive unit, making sure the lugs in the speedometer clutch align with the notches in the gear (see illustration 11.16).
14 Clean off all grease from the brake disc(s) using acetone or brake system cleaner.
15 Make sure the collar is in place (see illustration 11.7a) and install the wheel.

Rear coupling bearing

16 Lift the collar from the coupling on the sprocket side of the wheel (see illustrations

13.10b The bearing should look like this when it's installed

13.11 Install the speedometer clutch and retainer

13.12a Coat a new seal with grease . . .

13.12b . . . and install it with the closed side outward; evenly-applied thumb pressure should be enough

13.17a Lift out the collar if it's loose enough . . .

13.17b . . . or tap it out with a socket if it's tight

Brakes, wheels and tires 8•23

13.19 Don't forget to install the coupling collar or the bearings will be damaged

13.20 Lift the collar out of the brake disc side of the wheel

13.21 Pry loose the grease seal

12.3a, 12.3b, 12.3d and 12.3e). Pry out the grease seal.

17 Lift the sprocket out of the damper assembly (see Chapter 7). Lift the collar out of the bearing **(see illustration)**. If it's tight, drive it out from the other side with a socket **(see illustration)**. Drive out the coupling bearing with a bearing driver or socket **(see illustrations 12.3a, 12.3b, 12.3d and 12.3e)**.

18 Hold the coupling bearing by the inner race and spin the outer race. If it's rough, loose or noisy, replace the bearing and collar.

19 Drive the bearing and grease seal into the coupling with a bearing driver or socket. Be certain to reinstall the collar **(see illustration)**; if it's left out, the rear wheel bearings will be damaged when the axle nut is tightened.

Rear wheel bearings

20 Lift out the sprocket and damper (see Chapter 7). On the brake disc side of the wheel, lift out the collar **(see illustration)**.

21 Pry out the grease seal on the brake disc side of the wheel **(see illustration)**. Turn the wheel over and pry out the seal on the other side, then turn the wheel back over so the brake disc side is up.

22 Using a metal rod (preferably a brass drift punch) inserted through the center of the hub bearing on the brake disc side, tap evenly around the inner race of the opposite bearing to drive it from the hub **(see illustration)**. Turn the wheel over and remove the bearing and spacer **(see illustration)**.

23 From the sprocket side of the wheel, drive out the remaining bearing in the same manner.

24 Perform Steps 8 and 9 above to inspect the bearings.

25 Install the bearings with their sealed sides facing out. Drive them in with a bearing driver or a socket the same diameter as the bearing outer race. FZR600 models use two wheel bearings on the sprocket side of the wheel **(see illustrations)**.

13.22a Insert a drift punch through one bearing and tap loose the opposite bearing . . .

13.22b . . . then turn the wheel over and take out the bearing and the spacer

13.25a Tap in the bearing with a socket the same diameter as the outer race (shown) or with a bearing driver

13.25b On FZR600, there are two wheel bearings on the coupling side; the first should be installed to this depth . . .

13.25c . . . and the second bearing should be installed next to it like this

13.26a Position the grease seal in its bore . . .

8

8•24 Brakes, wheels and tires

26 On the brake disc side of the wheel, drive in the grease seal **(see illustrations)**.

27 Install the coupling to the wheel, making sure the coupling collar is in position **(see illustration 13.19)**.

14 Tires -
general information and fitting

General information

1 The wheels fitted to all FZR models are designed to take tubeless tires.

2 Refer to *Daily (pre-ride) checks* at the beginning of this manual, and to the scheduled checks in Chapter 1 for tire and wheel maintenance.

Fitting new tires

3 When selecting new tires, refer to the tire information label on the motorcycle and the tire options listed in the owners manual. Ensure that front and rear tire types are compatible, the correct size and correct speed rating; if necessary seek advice from a Yamaha dealer or tire fitting specialist **(see illustration)**.

13.26b ... then tap it into position with a socket, block of wood or bearing driver ...

13.26c ... the seal should be flush with the wheel when installed

4 It is recommended that tires are fitted by a motorcycle tire specialist rather than attempted in the home workshop. The specialist will also be able to balance the wheels after tire fitting.

14.3 Common tire sidewall markings

Chapter 9
Fairing and bodywork

Contents

Fairing - removal and installation	2	Seat - removal and installation	3
Front fender (mudguard) - removal and installation	7	Side covers - removal and installation	4
General information	1	Tailpiece - removal and installation	8
Rear view mirrors - removal and installation	5	Windshield - removal and installation	6

Degrees of difficulty

Easy, suitable for novice with little experience	**Fairly easy,** suitable for beginner with some experience	**Fairly difficult,** suitable for competent DIY mechanic	**Difficult,** suitable for experienced DIY mechanic	**Very difficult,** suitable for expert DIY or professional

1 General information

This Chapter covers the procedures necessary to remove and install the fairings and other body parts. Since many service and repair operations on these motorcycles require removal of the fairings and/or other body parts, the procedures are grouped here and referred to from other Chapters.

In the event of damage to the fairings or other body part, it is usually necessary to remove the broken component and replace it with a new (or used) one. The material that the fairings are composed of doesn't lend itself to conventional repair techniques. There are, however, some shops that specialize in "plastic welding," so it would be advantageous to check around first before throwing the damaged part away.

2 Fairing - removal and installation

1 Support the bike securely so it can't be knocked over during this procedure.

FZR600 models

2 Support the left and right fairings and remove the mounting bolts **(see illustrations)**.

2.2a Remove the Allen bolts beneath the fairing halves at the front . . .

2.2b . . . and at the rear

2.2c Remove the bolts on each side that attach the front fairing to the left and right fairing halves . . .

2.2d . . . and don't forget the bolt inside the air intake

9•2 Fairing and bodywork

2.2e Left and right fairing details (FZR600 dual-headlight models)

1 Left fairing
2 Right fairing
3 Allen bolt
4 Plastic washer
5 Spring nut
6 Special nut
7 Collar
8 Damper

2.2f Left and right fairing details (FZR600 single-headlight models)

1 Left fairing
2 Right fairing
3 Allen bolt
4 Plastic washer
5 Spring nut
6 Special nut
7 Collar
8 Damper

3 Carefully maneuver the fairings away from the bike. If necessary (for access to the EXUP valve, for example), remove the fairing bracket on the left side **(see illustration)**.

4 Disconnect the turn signal wiring connectors and remove the turn signal assemblies (see Chapter 10).

5 Remove the rearview mirrors **(see illustrations)**.

6 Remove the air intake duct covers (if equipped) and air intake ducts, then remove the fasteners and lift off the front fairing **(see illustrations)**.

7 Installation is the reverse of removal. Tighten all fasteners securely, but don't overtighten them and crack the fairing.

2.3 Unbolt the left lower fairing stay for access to the EXUP valve (if equipped)

2.5a ... Pull back the rubber cover to expose the mirror mounting screws ...

2.5b ... hold the mirror mounting nuts with a wrench and remove the mounting screws

2.6a Loosen the clamp at each end of the air duct (left arrow), then remove the fairing mounting nuts (right arrow)

Fairing and bodywork 9•3

2.6b Front fairing details (FZR600 dual-headlight models)

1 Turn signal	4 Mirror mounting	6 Turn signal
2 Mirror	nut	mounting nut
3 Screw	5 Rubber cap	7 Damper

2.6c Fairing stay details (FZR600 dual-headlight models)

| 1 Air duct | 3 Screw | 4 Nut |
| 2 Front fairing | | |

2.6d Front fairing details (FZR600 single-headlight models)

1 Air duct cover	4 Screws	6 Rubber cap
2 Turn signal	5 Turn signal	7 Damper
3 Mirror	mounting nut	

2.6e Fairing stay details (FZR600 single-headlight models)

| 1 Front fairing | 2 Air duct | 3 Nut |

2.8 Fairing details (1987 and 1988 FZR750/1000 models)

1 Allen bolt	5 Side fairing panel
2 Plain washer	6 Collar
3 Spring nut	7 Grommet
4 Front fairing	8 Nut
panel	9 Stay

1987 and 1988 FZR750/1000 models

8 Support the left and right fairings and remove the mounting bolts **(see illustration)**. Carefully maneuver the fairings away from the bike.

9 Disconnect the turn signal wiring connectors and remove the turn signal assemblies (see Chapter 10).

10 Remove the rearview mirrors (see illustrations 2.5a and 2.5b). Disconnect the electrical connectors for the headlights and front position light (if equipped).

11 Remove the air intake ducts.

12 Remove the four mounting nuts and lift off the front fairing together with the headlight assembly.

Caution: Don't drop the headlight assembly as the fairing is removed.

13 Installation is the reverse of removal. Tighten all fasteners securely, but don't overtighten them and crack the fairing.

1989-on FZR750R models

14 Reach through the access hole in each side of the fairing at the rear lower corner and remove the mounting bolt.

15 Turn three quick-release fasteners on each side of the lower fairing counterclockwise, then lower the fairing away from the machine.

16 Disconnect the fuel tank breather pipe from the rollover valve on the tank's top surface.

17 Turn two quick-release fasteners on each side of the small upper fairing panel (over front of fuel tank) counterclockwise. Release the air duct spring bands and remove the fresh air intake.

18 Remove the inner fairing panel on each side of the motorcycle.

19 Disconnect the fuel reserve switch electrical connector on the left side of the motorcycle.

20 Remove the turn signals (see Chapter 10).

21 Remove the rearview mirrors.

22 Disconnect the speedometer cable, remove the upper fairing bolts (one at each

9•4 Fairing and bodywork

2.25a The fairing panels on 1989 and later FZR1000 models are secured by Allen bolts

1 Fairing panel
2 Lower front fairing panel
3 Spring nut
4 Bolt
5 Plastic washer
6 Nut
7 Large bolt
8 Collar
9 Grommet
10 Spring nut

2.25b Fairing details (1989 and 1990 FZR1000, 1991 through 1993 models similar)

rear edge of the upper fairing and another just under the headlights) and take the upper fairing off.

23 Installation is the reverse of removal. Tighten all fasteners securely, but don't overtighten them and crack the fairing.

1989-on FZR1000 models

24 Remove the turn signals (see Chapter 10).
25 Support the left, right and lower front fairings and remove the mounting bolts **(see illustrations)**.

26 Carefully maneuver the fairings away from the bike.
27 Remove the rearview mirrors **(see illustrations 2.5a and 2.5b)**.
28 Remove the air intake ducts **(see illustration)**.

1 Side fairing panels
2 Front fairing panel
3 Side covers
4 Pillion seat cover

2.25c Fairing details (1994-on FZR1000 models)

Fairing and bodywork 9•5

2.28a Remove the air duct bolts . . .

2.28b . . . and disengage the duct from the fitting

2.29a Remove the upper panel screws . . .

29 Remove the inner fairing panels on both sides and disconnect the electrical connector for the fuel reserve switch **(see illustrations)**.

30 Remove the rubber covers from the rear of the headlights and disconnect the headlight electrical connectors (see Chapter 10).

31 Remove the mounting nuts and lift the front fairing off the stay together with the headlight assembly **(see illustration)**.

Caution: Don't let the headlight assembly fall as the fairing is removed. Disconnect the electrical connector for the front position light (if equipped) and take the fairing off the motorcycle.

32 Installation is the reverse of removal. Tighten all fasteners securely, but don't overtighten them and crack the fairing.

2.29b . . . and on the left side, remove two screws above the fuel reserve switch . . .

1 Fairing
2 Inner fairing panels
3 Mirror
4 Front fender

2.29c . . . and disconnect the switch electrical connector

2.31a Front fairing and stay (1987 through 1993 FZR1000 models)

1 Mounting nut   2 Fairing panel

2.31b Front fairing and stay (1994-on FZR1000 models)

9•6 Fairing and bodywork

3.1 Insert the key and turn it clockwise to release the seat

3 Seat - removal and installation

3.2 Pillion seat cover details (1987 and 1988 FZR750)
1. Cover
2. Backrest
3. Grommet
4. Damper
5. Bracket
6. 6 x 10 mm panhead screw and lockwasher

All except 1989-on FZR750 models

1 Release the seat lock with the ignition key **(see illustration)**.
2 If you're working on a 1987 or 1988 FZR750, remove the pillion seat cover **(see illustration)**.
3 Lift the rear of the seat and pull it out toward the rear **(see illustration)**.
4 If the motorcycle has a separate passenger seat, lift it off.
5 Installation is the reverse of removal. Be sure the retaining tabs at the front of the seat engage their slots.

1989-on FZR750 models

6 To remove the seat, unscrew its mounting bolts and lift off (two bolts at front of seat pad and two bolts on each side of tailpiece). The seat pad is held to the tailpiece by four nuts and tow bolts accessed from the underside.
7 Installation is the reverse of removal.

4 Side covers - removal and installation

1 Remove the seat (see Section 3).
2 The side covers are attached by a single screw along the top, molded pins that fit into rubber grommets, as well as molded hooks at the rear that fit into the tailpiece.
3 To detach a side cover, remove the screw, gently pull the cover away from the bike to separate the molded pins from the grommets, then detach the hooks from the tailpiece **(see illustrations)**.

3.3 Lift the seat and remove it toward the rear

4.3a Remove the screw along the top of the side cover (this is an FZR600) . . .

4.3b . . . and this is an FZR1000

4.3c The lower edge of the side cover is secured by a series of rubber grommets (arrowed) . . .

Fairing and bodywork 9•7

4.3d ... and molded pins (upper arrow); the rear is secured by hooks that fit into slots (lower arrows) ...

4.3e ... there's also a hook and slot at the upper rear of the side cover (arrowed)

6.1 The windshield is secured a row of screws along the bottom (arrowed)

Caution: *Do not use force. The pins and hooks can easily be broken.*

4 Installation is the reverse of removal.

5 Rear view mirrors - removal and installation

Mirror removal and installation are part of the fairing removal and installation procedures (see Section 2).

6 Windshield - removal and installation

1 Remove the screws securing the windshield to the fairing **(see illustration)**.
2 Carefully separate the windshield from the fairing. If it sticks, don't attempt to pry it off - just keep applying steady pressure with your fingers.
3 Installation is the reverse of the removal procedure. Be sure each screw has a plastic washer under its head. Tighten the screws securely, but be careful not to overtighten them, as the windshield might crack.

7 Front fender (mudguard) - removal and installation

1 Support the bike securely so it can't be knocked over during this procedure.

7.6a On FZR600 models, remove four bolts (arrowed), the fork brace and the fender

7.6b On 1989 and 1990 FZR1000 models, remove four fender mounting bolts (arrowed)

1987 and 1988 FZR750/1000 models

2 Disconnect the speedometer cable and pull it through the loop attached to the fender.
3 Remove the bolts that hold the front and rear halves of the fender together.
4 Between the forks, remove four bolts and the fork brace. Separate the halves of the fender and remove them from the motorcycle.
5 Installation is the reverse of the removal steps.

All FZR600, 1989-on FZR750 and 1989/1990 FZR1000 models

6 Between the forks, remove the bolts that secure the fork brace (if equipped) and fender **(see illustrations)**. Carefully lift the fender out, taking care not to scratch it.
7 Installation is the reverse of the removal steps.

1991-on FZR1000 models

8 Remove the fasteners and take the fender off the motorcycle **(see illustration)**.

1 Bolt
2 Collar

7.8 Fender (mudguard) mounting details (1991 and later FZR1000 models)

9

9•8 Fairing and bodywork

7.9 Fender components (1991 and later FZR1000 models)

1 Fender
2 Over fender
3 Over fender (installed)
4 Screw
5 Plain washer
6 Spring nut

8.2 Tailpiece mounting screws (arrowed); some models use only the lower screws

9 If necessary, remove the over fenders from the fender **(see illustration)**.

8 Tailpiece - removal and installation

1 Remove the seat (and separate pillion seat on models so equipped).
2 Remove the tailpiece screws and take the tailpiece off **(see illustration)**.
3 Installation is the reverse of removal.

Chapter 10
Electrical system

Contents

Alternator (FZR750/1000) - removal and installation	31
Alternator brushes (FZR750/1000) - inspection and replacement	32
Alternator and regulator/rectifier (FZR600 models) - removal and installation	30
Battery - charging	4
Battery electrolyte level/specific gravity - check	See Chapter 1
Battery - inspection and maintenance	3
Brake light switches - check and replacement	11
Charging system - output test	29
Charging system testing - general information and precautions	28
Clutch switch - check and replacement	22
Electrical fault finding	2
Fuel reserve system	33
Fuses - check and replacement	5
General information	1
Handlebar switches - check	18
Handlebar switches - removal and installation	19
Headlight aim - check and adjustment	8
Headlight bulb - replacement	7
Horn - check and replacement	23
Ignition main (key) switch - check and replacement	17
Instrument and warning light bulbs - replacement	15
Instrument cluster and speedometer cable - removal and installation	12
Instrument cluster - disassembly and reassembly	14
Lighting system - check	6
Meters and gauges - check	13
Neutral switch - check and replacement	20
Oil level sender - removal, check and installation	16
Sidestand switch - check and replacement	21
Starter motor - disassembly, inspection and reassembly	27
Starter motor - removal and installation	26
Starter relay - check and replacement	24
Starting circuit cut-off relay - check and replacement	25
Turn signal circuit - check	10
Turn signals and taillight bulbs - replacement	9
Wiring diagrams	34

Degrees of difficulty

| Easy, suitable for novice with little experience | Fairly easy, suitable for beginner with some experience | Fairly difficult, suitable for competent DIY mechanic | Difficult, suitable for experienced DIY mechanic | Very difficult, suitable for expert DIY or professional |

Specifications

Battery
Capacity/type
- FZR600 .... 12V 12Ah, GM12AZ
- FZR750 .... 12V 8Ah, MF9 (maintenance-free)
- FZR1000 - 1987 through 1990 models 12V 14Ah, YB14L
- FZR1000 - 1991-on .... 12V 12Ah, YTX14-BS (maintenance-free)

Specific gravity .... See Chapter 1

Battery open circuit voltage (1991-on FZR1000 with maintenance-free battery)
- 12.8 volts or more .... No charge needed
- 11.5 to 12.7 volts .... Charge for 5 to 10 hours
- Less than 11.5 volts .... Charge for 15 to 20 hours

Fuse specifications
- Main .... 30 amps
- Headlight
  - 1987 and 1988 .... 15 amps
  - 1989-on .... 20 amps
- Signal, ignition, fan .... 10 amps

Charging system
Output
- FZR600 .... 12V, 21A at 5000 rpm
- FZR750 and 1000 .... 12V, 28A at 5000 rpm

No-load voltage
- FZR600 .... 14.3 to 15.3V at 3000 rpm
- FZR750 and 1000 .... 14.2 to 14.8V at 3000 rpm

Stator coil resistance (FZR600) .... 0.31 to 0.37 ohms
Stator coil resistance (FZR750/1000) .... 0.16 to 0.18 ohms
Field coil resistance (FZR750/1000) .... 3.8 to 4.2 ohms
Brush minimum length (FZR750/1000) .... 4.7 mm (0.19 inch)

Starter motor
Commutator diameter
  Standard .... 28 mm (1.1 inch)
  Minimum .... 27 mm (1.06 inch)
Brush length
  FZR600
    Standard .... 12.5 mm (0.49 inch)
    Minimum .... 4.0 mm (0.16 inch)
  FZR750/1000
    Standard .... 12.0 mm (0.47 inch)
    Minimum .... 5.0 mm (0.20 inch)

Torque specifications
Oil level sender bolts
  FZR600 .... 7 Nm (5.1 ft-lbs)
  FZR750/1000 .... 10 Nm (7.2 ft-lbs)
Alternator rotor bolt (FZR600) .... 80 Nm (58 ft-lbs)
Alternator mounting bolts (FZR750/1000) .... 20 Nm (14 ft-lbs)
Stator coil bolts (FZR600) .... 10 Nm (7.2 ft-lbs)*
  All except UK FZR750 .... 20 Nm (14 ft-lbs)
  UK FZR750 .... 25 Nm (18 ft-lbs)
Starter mounting bolts .... 10 Nm (7.2 ft-lbs)
*Apply non-permanent thread locking agent to the threads.

1 General information

The machines covered by this manual are equipped with a 12-volt electrical system.

The charging system on FZR600 models uses a rotor with permanent magnets that rotates around a stator coil of copper wire. This produces alternating current, which is converted to direct current by the rectifier. The regulator controls the charging system output.

All other models use a three-phase alternator with an integrated circuit regulator built in. The regulator maintains the charging system output within the specified range to prevent overcharging. The alternator diodes (rectifier) convert the AC (alternating current) output of the alternator to DC (direct current) to power the lights and other components and to charge the battery. The alternator is similar to an automotive alternator, with the field current being produced electromagnetically, rather than by permanent magnets.

An electric starter mounted to the engine case behind the cylinders is standard equipment. The starter on early models has four brushes; the starter on later models has two brushes. The starting system includes the motor, the battery, the relay and the various wires and switches. On models equipped with a sidestand switch and clutch switch, if the engine kill switch and the ignition (main key) switch are both in the On position, the circuit relay allows the starter motor to operate only if the transmission is in Neutral (Neutral switch on) or the clutch lever is pulled to the handlebar (clutch switch on) and the sidestand is up (sidestand switch on).

Note: *Keep in mind that electrical parts, once purchased, can't be returned. To avoid unnecessary expense, make very sure the faulty component has been positively identified before buying a replacement part.*

2 Electrical fault finding

A typical electrical circuit consists of an electrical component, the switches, relays, etc. related to that component and the wiring and connectors that hook the component to both the battery and the frame. To aid in locating a problem in any electrical circuit, refer to the wiring diagrams at the end of this Chapter.

Before tackling any troublesome electrical circuit, first study the appropriate diagrams thoroughly to get a complete picture of what makes up that individual circuit. Trouble spots, for instance, can often be narrowed down by noting if other components related to that circuit are operating properly or not. If several components or circuits fail at one time, chances are the fault lies in the fuse or ground/earth connection, as several circuits often are routed through the same fuse and ground/earth connections.

Electrical problems often stem from simple causes, such as loose or corroded connections or a blown fuse. Prior to any electrical troubleshooting, always visually check the condition of the fuse, wires and connections in the problem circuit. Intermittent failures can be especially frustrating, since you can't always duplicate the failure when it's convenient to test. In such situations, a good practice is to clean all connections in the affected circuit, whether or not they appear to be good. All of the connections and wires should also be wiggled to check for looseness which can cause intermittent failure.

If testing instruments are going to be utilized, use the diagrams to plan where you will make the necessary connections in order to accurately pinpoint the trouble spot.

> **HAYNES HiNT** *Full details on the use of test equipment are given in Fault Finding Equipment at the end of this manual.*

Voltage checks should be performed if a circuit is not functioning properly. Connect one lead of a test light or voltmeter to either the negative battery terminal or a known good ground/earth. Connect the other lead to a connector in the circuit being tested, preferably nearest to the battery or fuse. If the bulb lights, voltage is reaching that point, which means the part of the circuit between that connector and the battery is problem-free. Continue checking the remainder of the circuit in the same manner. When you reach a point where no voltage is present, the problem lies between there and the last good test point. Most of the time the problem is due to a loose connection. Keep in mind that some circuits only receive voltage when the ignition key is in the On position.

One method of finding short circuits is to remove the fuse and connect a test light or voltmeter in its place to the fuse terminals. There should be no load in the circuit (it should be switched off). Move the wiring harness from side-to-side while watching the test light. If the bulb lights, there is a short to

Electrical system 10•3

ground/earth somewhere in that area, probably where insulation has rubbed off a wire. The same test can be performed on other components in the circuit, including the switch.

A ground/earth check should be done to see if a component is grounded properly. Disconnect the battery and connect one lead of a self-powered test light (continuity tester) to a known good ground/earth. Connect the other lead to the wire or ground/earth connection being tested. If the bulb lights, the ground/earth is good. If the bulb does not light, the ground/earth is not good.

A continuity check is performed to see if a circuit, section of circuit or individual component is capable of passing electricity through it. Disconnect the battery and connect one lead of a self-powered test light (continuity tester) to one end of the circuit being tested and the other lead to the other end of the circuit. If the bulb lights, there is continuity, which means the circuit is passing electricity through it properly. Switches can be checked in the same way.

Remember that all electrical circuits are designed to conduct electricity from the battery, through the wires, switches, relays, etc. to the electrical component (light bulb, motor, etc.). From there it is directed to the frame (ground/earth) where it is passed back to the battery. Electrical problems are basically an interruption in the flow of electricity from the battery or back to it.

3 Battery - inspection and maintenance

1 Most battery damage is caused by heat, vibration, and/or low electrolyte levels, so keep the battery securely mounted, check the electrolyte level frequently and make sure the charging system is functioning properly.
2 Refer to Chapter 1 for electrolyte level and specific gravity checking procedures.
3 Check around the base inside of the battery for sediment, which is the result of sulfation caused by low electrolyte levels. These deposits will cause internal short circuits, which can quickly discharge the battery. Look for cracks in the case and replace the battery if either of these conditions is found.
4 Check the battery terminals and cable ends for tightness and corrosion. If corrosion is evident, remove the cables from the battery **(see illustration)** and clean the terminals and cable ends with a wire brush or knife and emery paper. Reconnect the cables.

> **HAYNES HiNT** *Apply a thin coat of petroleum jelly to the connections to slow corrosion.*

5 The battery case should be kept clean to prevent current leakage, which can discharge the battery over a period of time (especially when it sits unused). Wash the outside of the case with a solution of baking soda and water. Do not get any baking soda solution in the battery cells. Rinse the battery thoroughly, then dry it.
6 If acid has been spilled on the frame or battery box, neutralize it with the baking soda and water solution, dry it thoroughly, then touch up any damaged paint. Make sure the battery vent tube (if equipped) is directed away from the frame and is not kinked or pinched.
7 If the motorcycle sits unused for long periods of time, disconnect the cables from the battery terminals. Refer to Section 4 and charge the battery approximately once every month.

4 Battery - charging

1 If the machine sits idle for extended periods or if the charging system malfunctions, the battery can be charged from an external source.

Batteries with removable filler caps

2 To properly charge the battery, you will need a charger of the correct rating, a hydrometer, a clean rag and a syringe for adding distilled water to the battery cells.
3 The maximum charging rate for any battery is 1/10 of the rated amp/hour capacity. As an example, the maximum charging rate for a 12 amp/hour battery would be 1.2 amps and the maximum charging rate for a 14 amp/hour battery would be 1.4 amps. If the battery is charged at a higher rate, it could be damaged.
4 Do not allow the battery to be subjected to a so-called quick charge (high rate of charge over a short period of time) unless you are prepared to buy a new battery.

5 When charging the battery, always remove it from the machine and be sure to check the electrolyte level before hooking up the charger. Add distilled water to any cells that are low.
6 Loosen the cell caps, hook up the battery charger leads (red to positive, black to negative), cover the top of the battery with a clean rag, then, and only then, plug in the battery charger.

> ⚠ **Warning:** *Remember, the gas escaping from a charging battery is explosive, so keep open flames and sparks well away from the area. Also, the electrolyte is extremely corrosive and will damage anything it comes in contact with.*

7 Allow the battery to charge until the specific gravity is as specified (refer to Chapter 1 for specific gravity checking procedures). The charger must be unplugged and disconnected from the battery when making specific gravity checks. If the battery overheats or gases excessively, the charging rate is too high. Either disconnect the charger or lower the charging rate to prevent damage to the battery.
8 It's time for a new battery if:
 a) *One or more of the cells is significantly lower in specific gravity than the others after a long slow charge;*
 b) *The battery as a whole doesn't seem to want to take a charge;*
 c) *Battery voltage won't increase;*
 d) *The electrolyte doesn't bubble;*
 e) *The plates are white (indicating sulfation) or debris has accumulated in the bottom of a cell;*
 f) *The plates or insulators are warped or buckled.*

9 When the battery is fully charged, unplug the charger first, then disconnect the leads from the battery. Install the cell caps and wipe any electrolyte off the outside of the battery case.

Maintenance free (sealed) batteries

10 Yamaha recommends different charging techniques, depending on the type of battery charger. Since a hydrometer can't be used to check battery condition (there's no way to insert it into the cells), a voltmeter is used instead to measure the voltage between the positive and negative terminals (open circuit voltage). Before taking the measurement, wait at least 30 minutes after any charging has taken place (including running the engine).
11 To check open circuit voltage, disconnect the negative cable from the battery, then the positive cable. Make sure the battery terminals are clean, then connect the positive terminal of the voltmeter to the battery positive terminal and the negative terminal of the voltmeter to the negative battery terminal. Compare the voltage readings with those listed in this Chapter's Specifications to determine whether, and for how long, the battery needs to be charged.

3.4 Always disconnect the negative battery cable first and reconnect it last to prevent sparks

10•4 Electrical system

4.12 If the charger doesn't have an ammeter built in, connect one in series with the charger like this; DO NOT connect the ammeter between the battery terminals or it will be ruined

4.21 Connect the charger, ammeter and voltmeter to the battery like this; DO NOT connect the ammeter between the battery terminals or it will be ruined

Variable current (adjustable voltage) charger

12 Connect the charger to the battery. If the charger doesn't have an ammeter built in, connect one in series with the charger **(see illustration)**.
13 Plug in the charger, set the voltage at 16 to 17 volts and note the charging current. If it's less than the standard charging current printed on the battery, go to Step 14. If it's more than the standard charging current, skip to Step 15.
14 Set the charging voltage at 20 to 25 volts, then watch the charging current for 3 to 5 minutes. If it reaches one amp or more, reset the voltage at 16 to 17 volts and continue charging. If the current isn't higher than the standard charging current after five minutes, replace the battery.
15 Adjust the voltage so the charging current is at the standard charging level. Set the timer on the charger according to the charging time determined in Step 11.
16 If the required charging time is more than five hours, recheck the charging current after five hours. If necessary, readjust the charging voltage to set the charging current at the standard charging current.
17 After the battery has charged, unplug the charger and disconnect it from the battery. Wait 30 minutes, then connect a voltmeter between the battery terminals and measure open-circuit voltage (the battery needs this time to stabilize).
a) If the reading is 12.8 volts or more, the battery is charged.
b) If the reading is 12.0 to 12.7 volts, continue charging the battery.
c) If the reading is less than 12.0 volts, replace the battery.

Constant current charger

18 Connect the charger and an ammeter to the battery **(see illustration 4.12)**.
19 Plug in the charger. After one hour, make sure that the charger's rated current is flowing.
a) If the current flow is less than the charger's rated current, replace the battery.
b) If the current flow is at the charger's rated current, set charging time according to the charger manufacturer's instructions and go to Step 20.
20 After the battery has charged, unplug the charger and disconnect it from the battery. Refer to Step 17 and check open circuit voltage.

Constant voltage charger

21 Connect the charger, an ammeter and a voltmeter to the battery **(see illustration)**.
22 Plug in the charger and check the ammeter reading.
a) If it's less than the standard charging current printed on the battery, the charger won't work with a maintenance free battery. Use a variable voltage or constant current charger instead.
b) If the current flow is at the standard charging current, set charging time to a maximum of 20 hours and continue charging until charging voltage reaches 16 volts or higher.
23 Once charging voltage has reached 16 volts, unplug the charger. Disconnect the charger from the battery and refer to Step 17 to check open circuit voltage.

5 Fuses - check and replacement

1 FZR600 models have two fuse blocks, one containing a 30-amp main fuse and a spare and the other containing accessory fuses and spares **(see illustrations)**. The main fuse is located on the left side of the motorcycle and the accessory fuses are on the right side. Fuse functions and ratings are listed in this Chapter's Specifications.
2 The fuses on FZR750 and 1987 and 1988 FZR1000 models are located beneath the seat.

5.1a The FZR600 accessory fuses are located in a block on the right side of the motorcycle . . .

5.1b . . . lift the cover for access

5.1c The main fuse and a spare are located in this fuse block on the left side of the motorcycle

Electrical system 10•5

3 All FZR1000 models have two fuse blocks on the left side of the motorcycle **(see illustrations)**. Fuse functions and ratings are listed in this Chapter's Specifications.

4 If you have a test light, all of the fuses can be checked without removing them. Turn the ignition key to the On position, connect one end of the test light to a good ground (earth), then probe each terminal on top of the fuse. If the fuse is good, there will be voltage available at both terminals. If the fuse is blown, there will only be voltage present at one of the terminals.

5 The fuses can also be tested with an ohmmeter or self-powered test light. Remove the fuse and connect the tester to the ends of the fuse. If the ohmmeter shows continuity or the test lamp lights, the fuse is good. If the ohmmeter shows infinite resistance or the test lamp stays out, the fuse is blown.

6 The fuses can be removed and checked visually. If you can't pull the fuse out with your fingertips, use a pair of needle-nose pliers. A blown fuse is easily identified by a break in the element.

7 If a fuse blows, be sure to check the wiring harnesses very carefully for evidence of a short circuit. Look for bare wires and chafed, melted or burned insulation. If a fuse is replaced before the cause is located, the new fuse will blow immediately.

8 Never, under any circumstances, use a higher rated fuse or bridge the fuse block terminals, as damage to the electrical system could result.

9 Occasionally a fuse will blow or cause an open circuit for no obvious reason.

> **HAYNES HINT**
> *Corrosion of the fuse ends and fuse block terminals may occur and cause poor fuse contact. If this happens, remove the corrosion with a wire brush or emery paper, then spray the fuse end and terminals with electrical contact cleaner.*

6 Lighting system - check

1 The battery provides power for operation of the headlight, taillight, brake light, license plate

5.3a On FZR1000 models, the accessory fuse block is on the left side of the motorcycle . . .

light and instrument cluster lights. If none of the lights operate, always check battery voltage before proceeding. Low battery voltage indicates either a faulty battery, low battery electrolyte level or a defective charging system. Refer to Chapter 1 for battery checks and Sections 28 and 29 for charging system tests. Also, check the condition of the fuses and replace any blown fuses with new ones.

Headlight

2 If the headlight is out when the engine is running (US models) or it won't switch on (UK models), check the fuse first with the key On (see Section 5), then unplug the electrical connector for the headlight and use jumper wires to connect the bulb directly to the battery terminals. If the light comes on, the problem lies in the wiring or one of the switches in the circuit. Refer to Section 18 for the switch testing procedures, and also the wiring diagrams at the end of this Chapter.

Taillight/license plate light

3 If the taillight fails to work, check the bulbs and the terminals first, then check for battery voltage at the taillight electrical connector. If voltage is present, check the ground/earth circuit for an open or poor connection.

4 If no voltage is indicated, check the wiring between the taillight and the ignition switch, then check the switch. On UK models, check the lighting switch as well.

Brake light

5 See Section 11 for the brake light switch checking procedure.

5.3b . . . and the main fuse is in this block, also on the left side

Neutral indicator light

6 If the neutral light fails to operate when the transmission is in Neutral, check the fuses and the bulb (see Section 15 for bulb removal procedures). If the bulb and fuses are in good condition, check for battery voltage at the connector attached to the neutral switch on the left side of the engine. If battery voltage is present, refer to Section 20 for the neutral switch check and replacement procedures.

7 If no voltage is indicated, check the wiring between the switch and the bulb for open circuits and poor connections.

Oil level warning light

8 See Section 16 for the oil level sender check.

7 Headlight bulb - replacement

> **Warning:** *If the bulb has just burned out, allow it to cool. It will be hot enough to burn your fingers.*

1 If you're working on an FZR600, remove the left air duct (see Chapter 9). On 1994 FZR600 models, remove the outer cover from the headlight assembly.

2 If you're working on a 1987 or 1988 FZR750 model, remove the left and right fairings, the air ducts and the front fairing together with the headlight assembly (see Chapter 9).

3 Unplug the electrical connector from the headlight. Note the position of any Top, L or R markings for reinstallation and remove the dust cover **(see illustrations)**.

7.3a Lift the cover to expose the electrical connector (on some models, the connector is disconnected first) . . .

7.3b . . . disconnect the electrical connector . . .

7.3c . . . and remove the dust cover

10•6 Electrical system

7.4a Unscrew the retainer or lift the wire ring . . .

7.4b . . . and lift the bulb out; don't touch the glass on the new bulb

8.3a The horizontal adjusters on dual-headlight models are at the lower center (arrowed) . . .

4 Turn the bulb retainer counterclockwise (anti-clockwise) or lift up the retaining clip and swing it out of the way **(see illustration)**. Remove the bulb **(see illustration)**.

5 When installing the new bulb, reverse the removal procedure.

> **HAYNES HiNT** *Be sure not to touch the bulb with your fingers - oil from your skin will cause the bulb to overheat and fail prematurely. If you do touch the bulb, wipe it off with a clean rag dampened with rubbing alcohol.*

8 Headlight aim - check and adjustment

1 An improperly adjusted headlight may cause problems for oncoming traffic or provide poor, unsafe illumination of the road ahead. Before adjusting the headlight, be sure to consult with local traffic laws and regulations. For UK owners, refer to MOT Test Checks in the Reference section of this manual.

2 The headlight beam can be adjusted both vertically and horizontally. Before performing the adjustment, make sure the fuel tank is at least half full, and have an assistant sit on the seat.

3 On dual-headlight models, the horizontal adjusting screws are at the lower center of the headlight assembly **(see illustration)**. The vertical adjusting screws are located at the upper outer corners of the headlight assembly **(see illustration)**.

4 On single-headlight models, the adjusting screws are at the back of the headlight assembly. Models with separate bulbs for high and low beam have two sets of horizontal and vertical screws; models with a single bulb have one set of horizontal and vertical screws.

9 Turn signals and taillight bulbs - replacement

> **HAYNES HiNT** *It is a good idea to use a paper towel or dry cloth when handling the new bulb to prevent injury if the bulb should break and to increase bulb life.*

Turn signal bulbs

1 To replace a turn signal bulb, remove the screw that holds the lens to the turn signal housing **(see illustration)**. Pull out the lens.

2 Push the bulb in and turn it counterclockwise (anti-clockwise) to remove it. Check the socket terminals for corrosion and clean them if necessary. Line up the pins on the new bulb with the slots in the socket, push in and turn the bulb clockwise until it locks in place. **Note:** *The pins on some bulbs are offset so it can only be installed one way.*

8.3b . . . and the vertical adjusters are at the upper corners

3 Position the lens on the reflector and install the screw. Be careful not to overtighten it.

Turn signal housings

4 The turn signal housings are secured to the inside of the fairing (front) or fender/mudguard (rear) by a single nut. To replace a housing, disconnect its electrical connector. Pull back the rubber cap and remove the nut **(see illustration)**. Guide the wiring harness through the nut and the cap and take the housing off the motorcycle. Installation is the reverse of removal.

Taillight bulbs

5 To remove the taillight bulbs, remove the seat (see Chapter 9).

6 Turn the bulb holders counterclockwise (anti-clockwise) **(see illustration)** until they

9.1 Remove the screw from the back of the turn signal housing

9.4 The turn signal housing is secured by a nut (arrowed)

9.6a Turn the bulb socket (arrowed) counterclockwise (anti-clockwise) and take it out of the housing . . .

Electrical system 10•7

9.6b ... then press the bulb into the socket and turn it counterclockwise (anti-clockwise) to remove

10.3a The FZR600 turn signal relay is on the left side of the motorcycle

1 Relay assembly   2 Turn signal relay

10.3b The FZR1000 turn signal relay is on the left side of the motorcycle on 1989-on models

1 Turn signal relay   2 Relay assembly

stop, then pull straight out to remove them from the taillight housing **(see illustration)**. The bulbs can be removed from the holders by turning them counterclockwise (anti-clockwise) and pulling straight out.

7 Check the socket terminals for corrosion and clean them if necessary. Line up the pins on the new bulb with the slots in the socket, push in and turn the bulb clockwise until it locks in place. **Note:** *The pins on the bulb are offset so it can only be installed one way.*

8 Make sure the rubber gaskets are in place and in good condition, then line up the tabs on the holder with the slots in the housing and push the holder into the mounting hole. Turn it clockwise until it stops to lock it in place.

9 Reinstall the seat.

10 Turn signal circuit - check

1 The battery provides power for operation of the signal lights, so if they do not operate, always check the battery voltage and specific gravity first. Low battery voltage indicates either a faulty battery, low electrolyte level or a defective charging system. Refer to Chapter 1 for battery checks and Sections 28 and 29 for charging system tests. Also, check the fuses (see Section 5).

2 Most turn signal problems are the result of a burned out bulb or corroded socket. This is especially true when the turn signals function properly in one direction, but fail to flash in the other direction. Check the bulbs and the sockets (see Section 9).

3 If the bulbs and sockets check out okay, check for power at the turn signal relay with the ignition On. On FZR600 and 1989-on FZR1000 models the relay is located on the left side of the frame at the rear **(see illustrations)**. On 1987 and 1988 FZR1000 and FZR750 models it is under the seat, just

forward of the battery. On UK FZR750 models, it is under the seat next to the starting cut-off relay. Refer to wiring diagrams at the end of the book to identify the power source terminal.

4 If the relay is okay, check the wiring between the turn signal relay and the turn signal lights (see the wiring diagrams at the end of this Chapter).

5 If the wiring checks out okay, replace the turn signal relay.

11 Brake light switches - check and replacement

Circuit check

1 Before checking any electrical circuit, check the fuses (see Section 5).

2 Using a test light connected to a good ground (earth), check for voltage at the brake light switch. If there's no voltage present, check the wire between the switch and the fuse box (see the wiring diagrams at the end of this Chapter).

3 If voltage is available, touch the probe of the test light to the other terminal of the switch, then pull the brake lever or depress

the brake pedal - if the test light doesn't light up, replace the switch.

4 If the test light does light, check the wiring between the switch and the brake lights (see the wiring diagrams at the end of this Chapter).

Switch replacement

Front brake lever switch

5 The switch on some models is secured by a single mounting screw. If you're working on this type, remove the mounting screw and unplug the electrical connectors from the switch **(see illustration)**.

6 The switch on other models slides into the handle pivot and is secured by a prong **(see illustration)**. If you're working on this type, disconnect the electrical connector. Insert a small screwdriver or probe into the release hole on the underside of the lever bracket, press up on the retaining prong and pull out the switch.

7 Installation is the reverse of the removal procedure. The brake lever switch isn't adjustable.

Rear brake pedal switch

8 Unplug the electrical connector in the switch harness.

11.5 To remove this type of switch, disconnect the connectors and remove the mounting screw from below

11.6 To remove this type of switch, insert a tool into the hole under the bracket (arrowed) and release the retainer

10•8 Electrical system

11.9 Disconnect the brake light switch spring (arrowed)

12.2a Unscrew the speedometer cable from the speedometer . . .

12.2b . . . and disconnect the cluster electrical connectors (this is an FZR600)

9 Unhook the switch spring **(see illustration)**.
10 Refer to the switch adjustment procedure in Chapter 1 and remove the switch from its bracket.
11 Install the switch by reversing the removal procedure, then adjust the switch by following the procedure described in Chapter 1.

12 Instrument cluster and speedometer cable - removal and installation

Cluster removal

1 Remove the front fairing (see Chapter 9).
2 Detach the speedometer cable from the speedometer and unplug the electrical connectors from the cluster harness **(see illustrations)**.
3 Remove the instrument cluster mounting nuts **(see illustrations)** and detach the cluster from the front fairing stay.

Speedometer cable removal

4 Disconnect the speedometer cable from the cluster **(see illustration 12.2a)**.
5 Note how it's routed, then disconnect the speedometer cable from the drive gear at the left front fork **(see illustration)**.

Installation

6 Installation is the reverse of the removal procedure. Be sure the speedometer cable is routed so it doesn't cause the steering to bind or interfere with other components. Be sure the squared-off ends of the cable fit into their spindles in the cluster and drive gear **(see illustration)**.

13 Meters and gauges - check

Coolant temperature gauge

1 Refer to Chapter 4 for coolant temperature gauge checking procedures.

Tachometer and speedometer

2 Special instruments are required to properly check the operation of these meters. Take the instrument cluster to a Yamaha dealer service department or other qualified repair shop for diagnosis.

14 Instrument cluster - disassembly and reassembly

1 Remove the cluster (see Section 12).
2 The accompanying photos show the disassembly of a US 1994 FZR600R instrument cluster. Other models are similar. To disassemble the cluster and replace individual gauges, refer to the photos **(see illustrations)**.
3 Reassembly is the reverse of the disassembly procedure.

12.3a Remove the cluster mounting nuts . . .

12.3b . . . and slide the cluster mounting studs out of their brackets

12.5 Disconnect the lower end of the speedometer cable

12.6 Be sure the squared-off ends of the speedometer cable (arrowed) fit into their sockets

14.2a Remove the case screw between the tachometer and speedometer . . .

Electrical system 10•9

14.2b ...and those around the edge of the case

14.2c Lift the lenses off the case

14.2d Remove the tachometer screws...

14.2e ...and disconnect the wires...

14.2f ...the wire colors should be molded into the case, but label the wires if the marks aren't visible

14.2g Lift the tachometer out of the case

14.2h Remove the speedometer gear screws and wires to take the speedometer out

14.2i Disconnect the temperature gauge wires

14.2j If necessary, remove the dampers (upper arrows) and screws that secure the warning light lens (lower arrows)

15 Instrument and warning light bulbs - replacement

1 Remove the front fairing if necessary for access (see Chapter 9).
2 To replace a bulb, pull the appropriate rubber socket out of the back of the instrument cluster housing **(see illustration)**, then pull the bulb out of the socket **(see illustration)**. If the socket contacts are dirty or corroded, they should be scraped clean and sprayed with electrical contact cleaner before new bulbs are installed.
3 Carefully push the new bulb into position, then push the socket into the cluster housing.

15.2a Work the bulb socket free of the cluster...

15.2b ...and pull the bulb out of the socket

10

10•10 Electrical system

16.3a Remove the sender mounting bolts . . .

16.3b . . . and take the sender out of the oil pan; replace the O-ring whenever the sender is removed

16 Oil level sender - removal, check and installation

Removal

1 Drain the engine oil (see Chapter 1).
2 The oil level sender is mounted in the bottom of the oil pan. Note how its wiring harness is routed, then unplug the electrical connector.
3 Remove the sender mounting bolts and remove the sender (see illustrations).

Check

4 Connect an ohmmeter between the terminals of the sender harness. With the sender in its normal installed position (flange and wiring harness at the bottom), the ohmmeter should indicate infinite resistance.
5 Turn the sender upside down. The ohmmeter should now read zero ohms.
6 If the ohmmeter doesn't give the correct indication in Step 4 or 5, replace the sender.

Installation

7 Installation is the reverse of the removal steps. Use a new O-ring and tighten the sender mounting bolts to the torque listed in this Chapter's Specifications.

17 Ignition main (key) switch - check and replacement

Check

1 Remove the front fairing (see Chapter 9). This isn't absolutely necessary, but it makes access to the switch electrical connector easier. Disconnect the electrical connector.
2 Using an ohmmeter, check the continuity of the terminal pairs indicated in the accompanying table (see illustration). Continuity should exist between the terminals connected by a solid line when the switch is in the indicated position.
3 If the switch fails any of the tests, replace it.

Replacement

4 Remove the front fairing, if you haven't already done so (see Chapter 9).
5 Unplug the switch electrical connector.
6 The switch is held to the upper triple clamp with two bolts or Torx screws (see illustration). Unlock the switch with the ignition key and remove the bolts. If necessary, remove the fairing mount for better access to the bolts. Detach the switch from the upper triple clamp.

7 If necessary, remove the Phillips screws and separate the switch from the bracket.
8 Attach the new switch to the bracket with the Phillips screws (if it was removed). Tighten the screws securely. Hold the new switch in position and install the bolts.
9 The remainder of installation is the reverse of the removal procedure.

18 Handlebar switches - check

1 Generally speaking, the switches are reliable and trouble-free. Most troubles, when they do occur, are caused by dirty or corroded contacts, but wear and breakage of internal parts is a possibility that should not be overlooked. If breakage does occur, the entire switch and related wiring harness will have to be replaced with a new one, since individual parts are not usually available.
2 The switches can be checked for continuity with an ohmmeter or a continuity test light. Always disconnect the battery negative cable, which will prevent the possibility of a short circuit, before making the checks.
3 Trace the wiring harness of the switch in question and unplug the electrical connectors.

Switch Position	Wire Color		
	R	Br	L
ON	O——O——O		
OFF			
P	O————————O		

17.2 Continuity table for the ignition switch

17.6 Remove the switch mounting screws or bolts

Electrical system 10•11

4 Using the ohmmeter or test light, check for continuity between the terminals of the switch harness with the switch in the various positions (see illustration). Continuity should exist between the terminals connected by a solid line when the switch is in the indicated position.
5 If the continuity check indicates a problem exists, refer to Sec-tion 11, 19, or 22, remove the switch and spray the switch contacts with electrical contact cleaner. If they are accessible, the contacts can be scraped clean with a knife or polished with crocus cloth. If switch components are damaged or broken, it will be obvious when the switch is disassembled.

19 Handlebar switches - removal and installation

1 The handlebar switches are composed of two halves that clamp around the bars. They are easily removed for cleaning or inspection by taking out the clamp screws and pulling the switch halves away from the handlebars (see illustrations).
2 To completely remove the switches, the electrical connectors in the wiring harness should be unplugged.
3 When installing the switches, make sure the wiring harnesses are properly routed to avoid pinching or stretching the wires.

20 Neutral switch - check and replacement

Check

1 Make sure the transmission is in neutral.
2 Remove the left side of the fairing (lower fairing on 1989 and later FZR750 models) (see Chapter 9). Follow the switch harness (it comes from behind the engine sprocket cover on the left side of the engine) to its connector, then unplug the connector.
3 Locate the sky blue wire's terminal in the harness side of the connector (not the side of the connector that goes to the neutral switch). Connect the terminal to ground/earth (bare metal on the motorcycle frame) with a short length of wire.
a) If the light stays out, check the bulb and the wiring between the ignition switch and neutral switch.
b) If the neutral indicator light comes on, the neutral switch may be bad. Connect an ohmmeter between the sky blue terminal in the switch side of the connector and ground/earth. Shift through the gears. The ohmmeter should indicate continuity in neutral and infinite resistance in all other gears. If not, replace the neutral switch.

"LIGHTING" Switch (UK only)

Switch Position	Wire Color		
	R/Y	L	L/B
OFF			
PO	o—o		
ON	o—o—o		

"START" Switch

Button Position	Wire Color			
	L/W	B	R/Y*	L/B*
OFF				
PUSH	o—o			

* US models only

"TURN" Switch

Switch Position	Wire Color			
	Ch	Br/W	Dg	Y/R	B
L	o———o		o—o	
L → N	o—o			
N → Push				
R → N		o—o		
R		o—o—o		

"CLUTCH" Switch

Clutch lever Position	Wire Color	
	B/Y	L/Y
FREE		
DEPRESS	o—o	

"ENGINE KILL" Switch

Switch Position	Wire Color	
	R/W	R/W
OFF		
ON	o—o	

"DIMMER" Switch

Switch Position	Wire Color		
	Y	L/B	G
HI	o—o		
LO		o—o	

"HORN" Switch

Button Position	Wire Color	
	P	B
PUSH	o—o	
OFF		

"BRAKE" Switch (Front)

Brake lever Position	Wire Color	
	Br	G/Y
FREE		
DEPRESS	o—o	

18.4 Continuity table for the handlebar switches

19.1a Remove the screws that secures the throttle cable (all except 1989 and later FZR750) and hold the switch housing together

19.1b On the clutch side, remove the screws (arrowed) and separate the switch housing

20.6a Remove the neutral switch screws . . .

20.6b . . . and take the switch out of the engine; replace the O-ring (arrowed) with a new one

21.4a Sidestand switch mounting screws (FZR600)

Replacement

4 Remove the engine sprocket cover (see Chapter 7).
5 Unplug the electrical connector (if you haven't already done so). Detach any wiring harness retainers.
6 Remove the switch mounting screws (see illustration) and detach the switch from the crankcase (see illustration). Remove the O-ring and install a new one.
7 Installation is the reverse of the removal steps. Tighten the switch screws securely.

21 Sidestand switch - check and replacement

Check

1 Follow the wiring harness from the switch to the connector, then unplug the connector. Connect the leads of an ohmmeter to the wire terminals on the switch side of the connector. With the sidestand in the up position, there should be continuity through the switch (0 ohms).
2 With the sidestand in the down position, the meter should indicate infinite resistance.
3 If the switch fails either of these tests, replace it.

Replacement

4 With the sidestand in the up position, unscrew the two screws and remove the switch (see illustrations). Disconnect the switch electrical connector.
5 Installation is the reverse of the removal procedure.

22 Clutch switch - check and replacement

Check

1 Disconnect the electrical connector from the clutch switch (see illustration).
2 Connect an ohmmeter between the terminals in the clutch switch. With the clutch lever pulled in, the ohmmeter should show continuity (little or no resistance). With the lever out, the ohmmeter should show infinite resistance.
3 If the switch doesn't check out as described, replace it.

Replacement

4 If you haven't already done so, unplug the wiring connector. Remove the mounting screw and take the switch off (see illustration 22.1).
5 Installation is the reverse of removal.

23 Horn - check and replacement

Check

1 Unplug the electrical connectors from the horn (see illustration). Using two jumper wires, apply battery voltage directly to the terminals on the horn. If the horn sounds, check the switch (see Section 18) and the wiring between the switch and the horn (see the wiring diagrams at the end of this Chapter).
2 If the horn doesn't sound, replace it.

Replacement

3 Unbolt the horn bracket from the frame (see illustration 23.1) and detach the electrical connectors.
4 Unbolt the horn from the bracket and transfer the bracket to the new horn.
5 Installation is the reverse of removal.

24 Starter relay - check and replacement

Check

1 Remove the seat (see Chapter 9).

21.4b Sidestand switch mounting screws (FZR1000)

22.1 Unplug the electrical connector (left arrow) and remove the mounting screw (right arrow)

23.1 Disconnect the connectors and remove the bolt (arrowed) (FZR600 shown; others similar)

Electrical system 10•13

24.3a If necessary for access, lift the relay off its mounting tabs ...

24.3b ... and disconnect the thin wire and ground/earth it to the frame (this is an FZR600) ...

24.3c ... and this is an FZR1000

2 Make sure the battery is fully charged and the relay wiring connections are clean and tight.
3 Disconnect the thin wire from the starter relay and connect it to ground/earth (bare metal on the frame) (see illustrations). The relay should click as the wire is connected and disconnected. If it doesn't, replace the relay.

Replacement

4 Disconnect the cable from the negative terminal of the battery.
5 Detach the battery positive cable, the starter cable and electrical connector from the relay (see illustrations 24.3a, 24.3b and 24.3c).
6 Slide the relay off its mounting tabs.
7 Installation is the reverse of removal. Reconnect the negative battery cable after all the other electrical connections are made.

25 Starting circuit cut-off relay - check and replacement

Check

1 The cut-off relay is part of the relay assembly unit. On 1987 and 1988 FZR1000 models and UK FZR750 models the unit is located under the seat. On FZR600 and 1989-on FZR1000 models it is situated next to the turn signal relay (see illustrations 10.3a and 10.3b) and can be accessed after the left side cover has been removed (see Chapter 9). Use the unit's wire colors as a guide to identification (see the wiring diagrams at the end of this book). Having located the relay, disconnect its wire connector and make the tests directly on the relay terminals as described below.

1987 and 1988 models

2 Connect an ohmmeter between the terminals in the relay that connect to the red-white and black-yellow wires in the wiring harness (see illustration). The ohmmeter should show infinite resistance.
3 Connect a 12-volt battery between the terminals for the black-white wires in the relay (see illustration 25.2) (the motorcycle's battery will work if it's charged). The ohmmeter should now show continuity (little or no resistance).
4 Disconnect and reconnect the battery. The ohmmeter should show continuity whenever the battery is connected and no continuity whenever it's disconnected. If not, replace the relay assembly.

1989-on models (except 1994-on FZR1000)

5 Connect an ohmmeter between the terminals in the relay that connect to the blue-white wires in the wiring harness (see illustration). The ohmmeter should show infinite resistance.
6 Connect the positive terminal of a 12-volt battery (the motorcycle's battery will work if it's charged) to the terminal for the red-white wire in the relay (see illustration 25.5). Connect the battery negative terminal to the relay terminal that connects to the black yellow wire. The ohmmeter should now show continuity (little or no resistance).
7 Move the battery negative terminal's jumper wire from the black-yellow terminal to the sky blue terminal. Again, the ohmmeter should show continuity.
8 If the ohmmeter shows continuity when it should, the cut-off relay is good. If not, replace the relay assembly.

1994-on FZR1000 models

9 Connect the positive terminal of a 12-volt battery (the motorcycle's battery will work if it's charged) to the terminal for the red-black wire in the relay (see illustration). Connect the negative terminal to the black-yellow wire's terminal.

25.2 Starting circuit cut-off relay test (1987 and 1988 models)
1 Ohmmeter
2 Blue-white terminal
3 Blue-white terminal
4 Red-white terminal
5 Black-yellow terminal
6 12-volt battery

25.5 Starting circuit cut-off relay test (all FZR600/750 models; 1987 through 1993 FZR1000 models)
1 Red-white wire terminal
2 Black-yellow wire terminal
3 Sky blue wire terminal
4 Blue-white wire terminal
5 Blue-white wire terminal

25.9 Starting circuit cut-off relay test (1994-on FZR1000 models)
1 Red-black wire terminal
2 Black-yellow wire terminal
3 Blue wire terminal
4 Blue-white wire terminal
5 Sky blue wire terminal
6 Blue-yellow wire terminal

10•14 Electrical system

26.3 Remove the nut (arrowed) and disconnect the cable

26.4a Remove the mounting bolts (arrowed) (this is an FZR600) . . .

26.4b . . . and this is an FZR1000 (FZR750 similar)

10 Connect an ohmmeter in turn between the following pairs of terminals:
a) Blue and blue-white
b) Black-yellow and sky blue
c) Blue-yellow and sky blue

11 The ohmmeter should indicate continuity in each case. If it does not, replace the relay.

Replacement

12 Remove the seat or left side cover (see Chapter 9).

13 Disconnect the relay assembly's wiring connector. Slip the relay assembly off its mounting tab.

14 Installation is the reverse of the removal steps.

26 Starter motor - removal and installation

Removal

1 Remove the seat and side covers (see Chapter 9). Remove the fuel tank (see Chapter 5).

2 Disconnect the cable from the negative terminal of the battery.

3 Pull back the rubber cover, remove the nut retaining the starter cable to the starter and disconnect the cable (see illustration).

4 Remove the starter mounting bolts (see illustrations).

5 Lift the outer end of the starter up a little bit and slide the starter out of the engine case (see illustration).

6 Check the condition of the O-ring on the end of the starter and replace it if necessary. Also check the starter pinion gear and the driven gear inside the engine for chipped or worn teeth (see illustration).

26.5 Slide the starter out; inspect the O-ring and gear teeth . . .

26.6 . . . as well as the teeth on the gear inside the engine (arrowed)

1 Brush assembly
2 Armature
3 O-rings
4 Starter housing
5 O-ring

27.2a Four-brush starter motor - exploded view

Electrical system 10•15

27.2b Remove the two long screws . . .

27.2c . . . and lift off the end covers

27.3 Lower the armature (arrowed) out of the brush plate and starter housing

27.4 Remove the brush plate from the housing

27.5 Push the terminal bolt through the housing and remove the brush holder

1 O-rings
2 Starter housing
3 Bearing
4 Oil seal
5 Armature
6 Bushing
7 Brushes

27.6a Two-brush starter - exploded view

Installation

7 Apply a little engine oil to the O-ring and install the starter by reversing the removal procedure.

27 Starter motor - disassembly, inspection and reassembly

1 Remove the starter motor (see Section 26).

Disassembly

Four-brush starter

2 Mark the position of the housing to each end cover. Remove the two long screws and detach both end covers **(see illustrations)**.
3 Pull the armature out of the housing (toward the pinion gear side) **(see illustration)**.
4 Remove the brush plate from the housing **(see illustration)**.
5 Carefully note how the washers are arranged on the terminal bolt. Remove the nut and push the terminal bolt through the starter housing, then reinstall the washers and nut on the bolt so you don't forget how they go. Remove the two brushes with the plastic holder from the housing **(see illustration)**.

Two-brush starter

6 Mark the position of the housing to each end cover if not already marked. Remove the two long screws and detach both end covers **(see illustrations)**.

27.6b The alignment marks (arrowed) must be aligned when the starter is reassembled

10•16 Electrical system

27.6c Remove the two long screws

27.6d Lift off the brush end cover together with the brushes and shims

27.7a Remove the washers and shims, noting carefully their number and order

7 Remove the shims and brush plate from the brush housing **(see illustrations)**.
8 Pull the armature out of the housing (toward the pinion gear side).

Inspection

9 The parts of the starter motor that most likely will require attention are the brushes. Measure the length of the brushes and compare the results to the brush length listed in this Chapter's Specifications **(see illustration)**. If any of the brushes are worn beyond the specified limits, replace the brush holder assembly with a new one. If the brushes are not worn excessively, cracked, chipped, or otherwise damaged, they may be re-used.
10 Inspect the commutator **(see illustration)** for scoring, scratches and discoloration. The commutator can be cleaned and polished with crocus cloth, but do not use sandpaper or emery paper. After cleaning, wipe away any residue with a cloth soaked in an electrical system cleaner or denatured alcohol. Measure the commutator diameter and compare it to the diameter listed in this Chapter's Specifications. If it is less than the service limit, the motor must be replaced with a new one.
11 Using an ohmmeter or a continuity test light, check for continuity between the commutator bars **(see illustration)**. Continuity should exist between each bar and all of the others. Also, check for continuity between the commutator bars and the armature shaft **(see illustration)**. There should be no continuity between the commutator and the shaft. If the checks indicate otherwise, the armature is defective.
12 Check for continuity between the brush plate and the brushes **(see illustration)**. The meter should read close to 0 ohms. If it doesn't, the brush plate has an open and must be replaced.
13 Using the highest range on the ohmmeter, measure the resistance between the brush holders and the brush plate **(see illustration)**.

27.7b Lift the brush assembly out of the housing so the brushes can be inspected

27.9 Compare the shortest brush length with the Specifications (four-brush starter shown; two-brush model similar)

27.10 Check the commutator for cracks and discoloring, then compare the diameter with the Specifications

27.11a Continuity should exist between the commutator bars

27.11b There should be no continuity between the commutator bars and the armature shaft

27.12 There should be almost no resistance (0 ohms) between the brushes and the brush plate

27.13 There should be no continuity between the brush plate and the brush holders

Electrical system 10•17

27.16 Make sure the leads fit into the notches (arrowed) - and the tongue fits into the notch in the housing (arrowed)

27.17a Install each brush spring on the post in this position . . .

27.17b . . . then pull the end of the spring 1/2 turn clockwise and seat the end of it in the groove in the brush

The reading should be infinite. If there is any reading at all, replace the brush plate.

14 Check the starter pinion gear for worn, cracked, chipped and broken teeth. If the gear is damaged or worn, replace the starter motor.

Reassembly
Four-brush starter

15 Install the plastic brush holder into the housing. Make sure the terminal bolt and washers are assembled in their original order. Tighten the terminal nut securely.

16 Detach the brush springs from the brush plate (this will make armature installation much easier). Install the brush plate into the housing, routing the brush leads into the notches in the plate **(see illustration)**. Make sure the tongue on the brush plate fits into the notch in the housing.

17 Install the brushes into their holders and slide the armature into place. Install the brush springs **(see illustrations)**.

Two-brush starter

18 Reinstall the brush plate in the end housing **(see illustrations 27.7b and 27.6d)**.

All models

19 Install any washers that were present on the end of the armature shaft **(see illustration)**.
20 Install the end covers, aligning the previously applied matchmarks (be sure to install the large O-rings between the starter housing and end covers). Install the O-rings and washers on the two long screws, then install the screws and tighten them securely **(see illustrations)**.

28 Charging system testing - general information and precautions

1 If the performance of the charging system is suspect, the system as a whole should be checked first, followed by testing of the individual components (the alternator and the voltage regulator/rectifier). **Note:** *Before beginning the checks, make sure the battery is fully charged and that all system connections are clean and tight.*

2 Checking the output of the charging system and the performance of the various components within the charging system requires the use of special electrical test equipment. A voltmeter or a multimeter are the absolute minimum tools required. In addition, an ohmmeter is generally required for checking the remainder of the system.

3 When making the checks, follow the procedures carefully to prevent incorrect connections or short circuits, as irreparable damage to electrical system components may result if short circuits occur. Because of the special tools and expertise required, it is recommended that the job of checking the charging system be left to a dealer service department or a reputable motorcycle repair shop.

29 Charging system - output test

Caution: Never disconnect the battery cables from the battery while the engine is running. If the battery is disconnected, the alternator and regulator/rectifier will be damaged.

1 To check the charging system output, you will need a voltmeter or a multimeter with a voltmeter function.

2 The battery must be fully charged (charge it from an external source if necessary) and the engine must be at normal operating temperature to obtain an accurate reading.

3 Attach the positive (red) voltmeter lead to the positive (+) battery terminal and the negative (black) lead to the battery negative (-) terminal. The voltmeter selector switch (if equipped) must be in a DC volt range greater than 15 volts.

4 Start the engine.

5 The charging system no-load voltage should be within the range listed in this Chapter's Specifications. If it's not, refer to the appropriate sub-heading below.

FZR600 models

6 Follow the wiring harness from the upper side of the alternator cover (on the left side of the engine) to the electrical connector and unplug the connector.

27.19 Be sure the shims and washers are in place on both ends of the armature shaft

27.20a Install the washers and O-rings on the long screws (if they were removed)

27.20b Install the screws and be sure to line up the alignment marks on the starter housing and end covers

10•18 Electrical system

29.7 Connect the positive lead of an ohmmeter to terminal 1, and the negative lead in turn to terminals 2 and 3 (FZR600)

7 Connect the positive lead of an ohmmeter to the single terminal of the connector (the side that runs back to the alternator, not the wiring harness side) **(see illustration)**. Connect the negative lead to each of the other terminals in turn and note the reading.
8 If the reading is not within the stator coil resistance range listed in this Chapter's Specifications, replace the stator (see Section 30).
9 If the reading is within the Specifications, refer to the wiring diagrams at the end of the book and check the charging circuit for breaks or poor connections. If the wiring is good, replace the regulator/rectifier unit (see Section 30).

FZR750/1000 models

10 If the no-load voltage is as specified, the alternator is functioning properly. If the voltage is too high, the regulator is at fault and should be replaced. The regulator is located under the cover and is retained by three screws.
11 If the voltage is too low, there may be a fault in the alternator stator or field coils or the brushes may be worn.
12 To check the stator coils, remove the alternator end cover and using an ohmmeter set on the ohms x 1 range, connect one probe to the left white wire terminal and the other first to the center white wire terminal and then to the right wire terminal; in each test the resistance should be as shown in this Chapter's Specifications. If outside of specification, replace the stator coil.
13 Check the brush length as described in Section 32, and replace as a set if worn or damaged.
14 To check the field coil, remove the alternator end cover and using an ohmmeter set on the ohms x 1 range, connect its probes between the field coil terminals. If the resistance is outside of that specified (see Specifications) the alternator field coil should be replaced.

30 Alternator and regulator/rectifier (FZR600 models) - removal and installation

Stator

1 Remove the alternator cover (see Chapter 5).
2 Remove the stator Allen bolts and take the stator out **(see illustration)**.
3 Installation is the reverse of the removal steps. Tighten the Allen bolts securely.

Rotor

4 Remove the alternator cover (see Chapter 5).
5 Shift the transmission into gear and have an assistant apply the rear brake. Remove the rotor bolt and washer **(see illustrations)**.
6 Thread a rotor puller such as Yamaha tool no. YM-01080 (part no. 90890-01080) into the rotor **(see illustration)**. Remove the rotor from the end of the crankshaft and take the Woodruff key out of its slot **(see illustrations)**.
7 Installation is the reverse of the removal steps. Be sure to reinstall the Woodruff key and make sure no metal objects have stuck to the magnets inside the rotor **(see illustrations)**. Align the slot in the rotor with the Woodruff key and install the rotor. Tighten the rotor bolt to the specified torque.

Regulator/rectifier

8 Remove the seat and left side cover (see Chapter 9).
9 Disconnect the electrical connector and remove the unit's mounting screws **(see illustration)**.
10 Installation is the reverse of the removal steps.

31 Alternator (FZR750/1000) - removal and installation

1 Disconnect the cable from the negative terminal of the battery.
2 Remove the seat, side covers and fuel tank (see Chapters 9 and 5).
3 Unplug the alternator electrical connector.
4 Remove the alternator mounting bolts and lift the alternator off the engine **(see illustrations)**. Inspect the alternator O-ring and replace if it's damaged or brittle. If oil has

30.2 Remove the Allen bolts (arrowed) to detach the stator

30.5a Loosen the rotor bolt . . .

30.5b . . . unscrew the bolt and remove the washer

30.6a Use a tool like this one to separate the rotor from the crankshaft . . .

30.6b . . . then take the rotor off . . .

30.6c . . . and lift the Woodruff key out of its slot

Electrical system 10•19

30.7a Remove all objects stuck to the magnets; a small item (arrowed) can ruin the alternator if the engine is run

30.7b Seat the Woodruff key securely in its slot

30.9 The regulator/rectifier is mounted on this bracket on the left side of the motorcycle

31.4a Remove the mounting bolt under the alternator . . .

31.4b . . . and the two on top . . .

31.4c . . . and take the alternator off the engine

been leaking past the alternator drive shaft seal, refer to Chapter 2 and replace it.
5 Installation is the reverse of the removal steps with the following additions:
a) Coat the O-ring with multi-purpose grease **(see illustration)**.
b) Tighten the alternator mounting bolts to the torque listed in this Chapter's Specifications.

32 Alternator brushes (FZR750/1000) - inspection and replacement

1 This check, combined with the charging system output test described in Section 29, should diagnose most charging system problems on 750/1000 models. If the brushes are good and alternator output is low, take the alternator to a dealer service department or other repair shop for further checks, or substitute a known good unit and recheck the charging system output.
2 Remove the alternator (see Section 31).
3 Remove the screws and take the end cover off the alternator.
4 Remove two screws and lift out the brush assembly.
5 Measure the length of the brushes and compare it to the value listed in this Chapter's Specifications **(see illustration)**. If the brushes are worn, replace them.
6 Reverse Steps 2 through 4 to reassemble and install the alternator.

33 Fuel reserve system

Some models are equipped with an electric fuel reserve system activated by a switch on the top left side of the fairing. If the fuel tank won't switch over to Reserve, check the wiring for breaks and bad connections, referring to the Wiring diagrams at the end of the book. To test the switch, disconnect its wiring connector and connect an ohmmeter between the terminals in the switch side of the connector, then turn the switch on and off. The ohmmeter should switch back and forth from infinite resistance to little or no resistance as the switch is operated. If not, replace the switch.

34 Wiring diagrams

Prior to troubleshooting a circuit, check the fuses to make sure they're in good condition. Make sure the battery is fully charged and check the cable connections.
When checking a circuit, make sure all connectors are clean, with no broken or loose terminals or wires. When unplugging a connector, don't pull on the wires - pull only on the connector housings themselves.

31.5 Coat the O-ring with multi-purpose grease

32.5 Measure brush length and replace the brushes if they're worn

10•20 Wiring diagrams

FZR600/600R US models
(dual headlight model shown, single headlight model similar)

Wiring diagrams 10•21

FZR750 1987 and 1988 US models

10•22 Wiring diagrams

FZR1000 1987 and 1988 US models

Wiring diagrams 10•23

FZR1000 1989 and 1990 US models
(UK models similar)

10•24 Wiring diagrams

FZR1000 1991 to 1993 US models

Wiring diagrams 10•25

FZR1000 1994 onwards US models

10•26 Wiring diagrams

FZR600 1989 and 1990 UK models

Wiring diagrams 10•27

FZR600 1991 onwards UK models

Wiring diagrams 10•29

FZR1000 1991-93 UK models

10•30 Wiring diagrams

FZR1000 UK 1994 onwards models
Note: Earth (ground) circuit wiring not shown

Reference   REF•1

Dimensions and Weights ....**REF•1**	Motorcycle Chemicals and Lubricants ....**REF•28**
Conversion Factors ....**REF•3**	Fault Finding ....**REF•29**
Tools and Workshop Tips ....**REF•4**	Fault Finding Equipment ....**REF•37**
MOT Test Checks ....**REF•22**	Technical Terms Explained ....**REF•41**
Storage ....**REF•26**	Index ....**REF•45**

Dimensions and Weights

FZR600 models

Wheelbase
   1989 .... 1420 mm (55.9 inches)
   1991-on .... 1425 mm (56.1 inches)
Overall length .... 2095 mm (82.5 inches)
Overall width .... 700 mm (27.6 inches)
Overall height
   1989 and 1990 .... 1160 mm (45.7 inches)
   1991-on .... 1155 mm (45.5 inches)
Seat height .... 785 mm (30.9 inches)
Ground clearance (minimum) .... 135 mm (5.3 inches)
Weight (with oil and full fuel tank)
   1989 and 1990
      US except California .... 199 kg (439 lbs)
      California .... 204 kg (450 lbs)
      UK .... 201 kg (443 lbs)
   1991-on
      US except California .... 201 kg (443 lbs)
      California .... 206 kg (454 lbs)
      UK .... 203 kg (448 lbs)

REF•2 Dimensions and weights

FZR750R models
	US	UK
Wheelbase	1470 mm (57.9 inches)	1445 mm (56.9 inches)
Overall length	2125 mm (83.7 inches)	2180 mm (85.8 inches)
Overall width	730 mm (28.7 inches)	705 mm (27.8 inches)
Overall height	1215 mm (47.8 inches)	1160 mm (45.7 inches)
Seat height	775 mm (30.5 inches)	775 mm (30.5 inches)
Ground clearance (minimum)	140 mm (5.5 inches)	120 mm (4.7 inches)
Weight (with oil and full fuel tank)	228 kg (503 lbs)	210 kg (463 lbs)

FZR1000 models (US)
Wheelbase .... 1470 mm (57.9 inches)
Overall length
  1987 and 1988 .... 2205 mm (86.8 inches)
  1989 and 1990 .... 2200 mm (86.8 inches)
  1991-on .... 2110 mm (83.1 inches)
Overall width
  1987 through 1990 .... 730 mm (28.7 inches)
  1991 through 1993 .... 745 mm (29.3 inches)
  1994-on .... 755 mm (29.7 inches)
Overall height
  1987 and 1988 .... 1215 mm (47.8 inches)
  1989 and 1990 .... 1160 mm (45.7 inches)
  1991-on .... 1170 mm (46.1 inches)
Seat height
  1987 and 1988 .... 775 mm (30.5 inches)
  1989 and 1990 .... 765 mm (30.1 inches)
  1991 through 1993 .... 775 mm (30.5 inches)
  1994-on .... 780 mm (30.7 inches)
Ground clearance (minimum)
  1987 and 1988 .... 140 mm (5.5 inches)
  1989-on .... 135 mm (5.3 inches)
Weight (with oil and full fuel tank)
  1987 and 1988
    US except California .... 229 kg (505 lbs)
    California .... 230 kg (507 lbs)
  1989 and 1990
    US except California .... 235 kg (518 lbs)
    California .... 236 kg (520 lbs)
  1991-on .... not specified

FZR1000 models (UK)
Wheelbase
  1987 and 1988, 1991-on .... 1470 mm (57.9 inches)
  1989 and 1990 .... 1460 mm (57.5 inches)
Overall length
  1987 and 1988, 1991-on .... 2205 mm (86.8 inches)
  1989 and 1990 .... 2200 mm (86.8 inches)
Overall width
  1987 through 1990 .... 730 mm (28.7 inches)
  1991 through 1993 .... 745 mm (29.3 inches)
  1994-on .... 775 mm (30.5 inches)
Overall height
  1987 and 1988 .... 1215 mm (47.8 inches)
  1989 and 1990 .... 1160 mm (45.7 inches)
  1991 through 1993 .... 1170 mm (46.1 inches)
  1994-on .... 1165 mm (45.9 inches)
Seat height
  1987 and 1988 .... 775 mm (30.5 inches)
  1989 and 1990 .... 765 mm (30.1 inches)
  1991 through 1993 .... 775 mm (30.5 inches)
  1994-on .... 780 mm (30.7 inches)
Ground clearance (minimum)
  1987 and 1988 .... 140 mm (5.5 inches)
  1989-on .... 135 mm (5.3 inches)
Weight (with oil and full fuel tank)
  1987 and 1988 .... 229 kg (505 lbs)
  1989 and 1990 .... 235 kg (518 lbs)
  1991-on .... Not specified

Tools and Workshop Tips REF•3

Buying tools

A toolkit is a fundamental requirement for servicing and repairing a motorcycle. Although there will be an initial expense in building up enough tools for servicing, this will soon be offset by the savings made by doing the job yourself. As experience and confidence grow, additional tools can be added to enable the repair and overhaul of the motorcycle. Many of the specialist tools are expensive and not often used so it may be preferable to hire them, or for a group of friends or motorcycle club to join in the purchase.

As a rule, it is better to buy more expensive, good quality tools. Cheaper tools are likely to wear out faster and need to be renewed more often, nullifying the original saving.

> **Warning:** To avoid the risk of a poor quality tool breaking in use, causing injury or damage to the component being worked on, always aim to purchase tools which meet the relevant national safety standards.

The following lists of tools do not represent the manufacturer's service tools, but serve as a guide to help the owner decide which tools are needed for this level of work. In addition, items such as an electric drill, hacksaw, files, soldering iron and a workbench equipped with a vice, may be needed. Although not classed as tools, a selection of bolts, screws, nuts, washers and pieces of tubing always come in useful.

For more information about tools, refer to the Haynes *Motorcycle Workshop Practice TechBook* (Bk. No. 3470).

Manufacturer's service tools

Inevitably certain tasks require the use of a service tool. Where possible an alternative tool or method of approach is recommended, but sometimes there is no option if personal injury or damage to the component is to be avoided. Where required, service tools are referred to in the relevant procedure.

Service tools can usually only be purchased from a motorcycle dealer and are identified by a part number. Some of the commonly-used tools, such as rotor pullers, are available in aftermarket form from mail-order motorcycle tool and accessory suppliers.

Maintenance and minor repair tools

1. Set of flat-bladed screwdrivers
2. Set of Phillips head screwdrivers
3. Combination open-end and ring spanners
4. Socket set (3/8 inch or 1/2 inch drive)
5. Set of Allen keys or bits
6. Set of Torx keys or bits
7. Pliers, cutters and self-locking grips (Mole grips)
8. Adjustable spanners
9. C-spanners
10. Tread depth gauge and tyre pressure gauge
11. Cable oiler clamp
12. Feeler gauges
13. Spark plug gap measuring tool
14. Spark plug spanner or deep plug sockets
15. Wire brush and emery paper
16. Calibrated syringe, measuring vessel and funnel
17. Oil filter adapters
18. Oil drainer can or tray
19. Pump type oil can
20. Grease gun
21. Straight-edge and steel rule
22. Continuity tester
23. Battery charger
24. Hydrometer (for battery specific gravity check)
25. Anti-freeze tester (for liquid-cooled engines)

REF•4 Tools and Workshop Tips

Repair and overhaul tools

1. Torque wrench (small and mid-ranges)
2. Conventional, plastic or soft-faced hammers
3. Impact driver set
4. Vernier gauge
5. Circlip pliers (internal and external, or combination)
6. Set of cold chisels and punches
7. Selection of pullers
8. Breaker bars
9. Chain breaking/riveting tool set
10. Wire stripper and crimper tool
11. Multimeter (measures amps, volts and ohms)
12. Stroboscope (for dynamic timing checks)
13. Hose clamp (wingnut type shown)
14. Clutch holding tool
15. One-man brake/clutch bleeder kit

Specialist tools

1. Micrometers (external type)
2. Telescoping gauges
3. Dial gauge
4. Cylinder compression gauge
5. Vacuum gauges (left) or manometer (right)
6. Oil pressure gauge
7. Plastigauge kit
8. Valve spring compressor (4-stroke engines)
9. Piston pin drawbolt tool
10. Piston ring removal and installation tool
11. Piston ring clamp
12. Cylinder bore hone (stone type shown)
13. Stud extractor
14. Screw extractor set
15. Bearing driver set

Tools and Workshop Tips REF•5

1 Workshop equipment and facilities

The workbench

● Work is made much easier by raising the bike up on a ramp - components are much more accessible if raised to waist level. The hydraulic or pneumatic types seen in the dealer's workshop are a sound investment if you undertake a lot of repairs or overhauls **(see illustration 1.1)**.

1.1 Hydraulic motorcycle ramp

● If raised off ground level, the bike must be supported on the ramp to avoid it falling. Most ramps incorporate a front wheel locating clamp which can be adjusted to suit different diameter wheels. When tightening the clamp, take care not to mark the wheel rim or damage the tyre - use wood blocks on each side to prevent this.
● Secure the bike to the ramp using tiedowns **(see illustration 1.2)**. If the bike has only a sidestand, and hence leans at a dangerous angle when raised, support the bike on an auxiliary stand.

1.2 Tie-downs are used around the passenger footrests to secure the bike

● Auxiliary (paddock) stands are widely available from mail order companies or motorcycle dealers and attach either to the wheel axle or swingarm pivot **(see illustration 1.3)**. If the motorcycle has a centrestand, you can support it under the crankcase to prevent it toppling whilst either wheel is removed **(see illustration 1.4)**.

1.3 This auxiliary stand attaches to the swingarm pivot

1.4 Always use a block of wood between the engine and jack head when supporting the engine in this way

Fumes and fire

● Refer to the Safety first! page at the beginning of the manual for full details. Make sure your workshop is equipped with a fire extinguisher suitable for fuel-related fires (Class B fire - flammable liquids) - it is not sufficient to have a water-filled extinguisher.
● Always ensure adequate ventilation is available. Unless an exhaust gas extraction system is available for use, ensure that the engine is run outside of the workshop.
● If working on the fuel system, make sure the workshop is ventilated to avoid a build-up of fumes. This applies equally to fume build-up when charging a battery. Do not smoke or allow anyone else to smoke in the workshop.

Fluids

● If you need to drain fuel from the tank, store it in an approved container marked as suitable for the storage of petrol (gasoline) **(see illustration 1.5)**. Do not store fuel in glass jars or bottles.

1.5 Use an approved can only for storing petrol (gasoline)

● Use proprietary engine degreasers or solvents which have a high flash-point, such as paraffin (kerosene), for cleaning off oil, grease and dirt - never use petrol (gasoline) for cleaning. Wear rubber gloves when handling solvent and engine degreaser. The fumes from certain solvents can be dangerous - always work in a well-ventilated area.

Dust, eye and hand protection

● Protect your lungs from inhalation of dust particles by wearing a filtering mask over the nose and mouth. Many frictional materials still contain asbestos which is dangerous to your health. Protect your eyes from spouts of liquid and sprung components by wearing a pair of protective goggles **(see illustration 1.6)**.

1.6 A fire extinguisher, goggles, mask and protective gloves should be at hand in the workshop

● Protect your hands from contact with solvents, fuel and oils by wearing rubber gloves. Alternatively apply a barrier cream to your hands before starting work. If handling hot components or fluids, wear suitable gloves to protect your hands from scalding and burns.

What to do with old fluids

● Old cleaning solvent, fuel, coolant and oils should not be poured down domestic drains or onto the ground. Package the fluid up in old oil containers, label it accordingly, and take it to a garage or disposal facility. Contact your local authority for location of such sites or ring the oil care hotline.

OIL CARE
FOLLOW THE CODE
OIL BANK LINE
0800 66 33 66

Note: It is antisocial and illegal to dump oil down the drain. To find the location of your local oil recycling bank, call this number free.

In the USA, note that any oil supplier must accept used oil for recycling.

REF•6 Tools and Workshop Tips

2 Fasteners -
screws, bolts and nuts

Fastener types and applications

Bolts and screws

● Fastener head types are either of hexagonal, Torx or splined design, with internal and external versions of each type **(see illustrations 2.1 and 2.2)**; splined head fasteners are not in common use on motorcycles. The conventional slotted or Phillips head design is used for certain screws. Bolt or screw length is always measured from the underside of the head to the end of the item **(see illustration 2.11)**.

2.1 Internal hexagon/Allen (A), Torx (B) and splined (C) fasteners, with corresponding bits

2.2 External Torx (A), splined (B) and hexagon (C) fasteners, with corresponding sockets

● Certain fasteners on the motorcycle have a tensile marking on their heads, the higher the marking the stronger the fastener. High tensile fasteners generally carry a 10 or higher marking. Never replace a high tensile fastener with one of a lower tensile strength.

Washers (see illustration 2.3)

● Plain washers are used between a fastener head and a component to prevent damage to the component or to spread the load when torque is applied. Plain washers can also be used as spacers or shims in certain assemblies. Copper or aluminium plain washers are often used as sealing washers on drain plugs.

2.3 Plain washer (A), penny washer (B), spring washer (C) and serrated washer (D)

● The split-ring spring washer works by applying axial tension between the fastener head and component. If flattened, it is fatigued and must be renewed. If a plain (flat) washer is used on the fastener, position the spring washer between the fastener and the plain washer.

● Serrated star type washers dig into the fastener and component faces, preventing loosening. They are often used on electrical earth (ground) connections to the frame.

● Cone type washers (sometimes called Belleville) are conical and when tightened apply axial tension between the fastener head and component. They must be installed with the dished side against the component and often carry an OUTSIDE marking on their outer face. If flattened, they are fatigued and must be renewed.

● Tab washers are used to lock plain nuts or bolts on a shaft. A portion of the tab washer is bent up hard against one flat of the nut or bolt to prevent it loosening. Due to the tab washer being deformed in use, a new tab washer should be used every time it is disturbed.

● Wave washers are used to take up endfloat on a shaft. They provide light springing and prevent excessive side-to-side play of a component. Can be found on rocker arm shafts.

Nuts and split pins

● Conventional plain nuts are usually six-sided **(see illustration 2.4)**. They are sized by thread diameter and pitch. High tensile nuts carry a number on one end to denote their tensile strength.

2.4 Plain nut (A), shouldered locknut (B), nylon insert nut (C) and castellated nut (D)

● Self-locking nuts either have a nylon insert, or two spring metal tabs, or a shoulder which is staked into a groove in the shaft - their advantage over conventional plain nuts is a resistance to loosening due to vibration. The nylon insert type can be used a number of times, but must be renewed when the friction of the nylon insert is reduced, ie when the nut spins freely on the shaft. The spring tab type can be reused unless the tabs are damaged. The shouldered type must be renewed every time it is disturbed.

● Split pins (cotter pins) are used to lock a castellated nut to a shaft or to prevent slackening of a plain nut. Common applications are wheel axles and brake torque arms. Because the split pin arms are deformed to lock around the nut a new split pin must always be used on installation - always fit the correct size split pin which will fit snugly in the shaft hole. Make sure the split pin arms are correctly located around the nut **(see illustrations 2.5 and 2.6)**.

2.5 Bend split pin (cotter pin) arms as shown (arrows) to secure a castellated nut

2.6 Bend split pin (cotter pin) arms as shown to secure a plain nut

Caution: If the castellated nut slots do not align with the shaft hole after tightening to the torque setting, tighten the nut until the next slot aligns with the hole - never slacken the nut to align its slot.

● R-pins (shaped like the letter R), or slip pins as they are sometimes called, are sprung and can be reused if they are otherwise in good condition. Always install R-pins with their closed end facing forwards **(see illustration 2.7)**.

Tools and Workshop Tips REF•7

2.7 Correct fitting of R-pin. Arrow indicates forward direction

Circlips (see illustration 2.8)

● Circlips (sometimes called snap-rings) are used to retain components on a shaft or in a housing and have corresponding external or internal ears to permit removal. Parallel-sided (machined) circlips can be installed either way round in their groove, whereas stamped circlips (which have a chamfered edge on one face) must be installed with the chamfer facing away from the direction of thrust load **(see illustration 2.9)**.

2.8 External stamped circlip (A), internal stamped circlip (B), machined circlip (C) and wire circlip (D)

● Always use circlip pliers to remove and install circlips; expand or compress them just enough to remove them. After installation, rotate the circlip in its groove to ensure it is securely seated. If installing a circlip on a splined shaft, always align its opening with a shaft channel to ensure the circlip ends are well supported and unlikely to catch **(see illustration 2.10)**.

2.9 Correct fitting of a stamped circlip

2.10 Align circlip opening with shaft channel

● Circlips can wear due to the thrust of components and become loose in their grooves, with the subsequent danger of becoming dislodged in operation. For this reason, renewal is advised every time a circlip is disturbed.
● Wire circlips are commonly used as piston pin retaining clips. If a removal tang is provided, long-nosed pliers can be used to dislodge them, otherwise careful use of a small flat-bladed screwdriver is necessary. Wire circlips should be renewed every time they are disturbed.

Thread diameter and pitch

● Diameter of a male thread (screw, bolt or stud) is the outside diameter of the threaded portion **(see illustration 2.11)**. Most motorcycle manufacturers use the ISO (International Standards Organisation) metric system expressed in millimetres, eg M6 refers to a 6 mm diameter thread. Sizing is the same for nuts, except that the thread diameter is measured across the valleys of the nut.
● Pitch is the distance between the peaks of the thread **(see illustration 2.11)**. It is expressed in millimetres, thus a common bolt size may be expressed as 6.0 x 1.0 mm (6 mm thread diameter and 1 mm pitch). Generally pitch increases in proportion to thread diameter, although there are always exceptions.
● Thread diameter and pitch are related for conventional fastener applications and the accompanying table can be used as a guide. Additionally, the AF (Across Flats), spanner or socket size dimension of the bolt or nut **(see illustration 2.11)** is linked to thread and pitch specification. Thread pitch can be measured with a thread gauge **(see illustration 2.12)**.

2.11 Fastener length (L), thread diameter (D), thread pitch (P) and head size (AF)

2.12 Using a thread gauge to measure pitch

AF size	Thread diameter x pitch (mm)
8 mm	M5 x 0.8
8 mm	M6 x 1.0
10 mm	M6 x 1.0
12 mm	M8 x 1.25
14 mm	M10 x 1.25
17 mm	M12 x 1.25

● The threads of most fasteners are of the right-hand type, ie they are turned clockwise to tighten and anti-clockwise to loosen. The reverse situation applies to left-hand thread fasteners, which are turned anti-clockwise to tighten and clockwise to loosen. Left-hand threads are used where rotation of a component might loosen a conventional right-hand thread fastener.

Seized fasteners

● Corrosion of external fasteners due to water or reaction between two dissimilar metals can occur over a period of time. It will build up sooner in wet conditions or in countries where salt is used on the roads during the winter. If a fastener is severely corroded it is likely that normal methods of removal will fail and result in its head being ruined. When you attempt removal, the fastener thread should be heard to crack free and unscrew easily - if it doesn't, stop there before damaging something.
● A smart tap on the head of the fastener will often succeed in breaking free corrosion which has occurred in the threads **(see illustration 2.13)**.
● An aerosol penetrating fluid (such as WD-40) applied the night beforehand may work its way down into the thread and ease removal. Depending on the location, you may be able to make up a Plasticine well around the fastener head and fill it with penetrating fluid.

2.13 A sharp tap on the head of a fastener will often break free a corroded thread

REF•8 Tools and Workshop Tips

● If you are working on an engine internal component, corrosion will most likely not be a problem due to the well lubricated environment. However, components can be very tight and an impact driver is a useful tool in freeing them **(see illustration 2.14)**.

2.14 Using an impact driver to free a fastener

● Where corrosion has occurred between dissimilar metals (eg steel and aluminium alloy), the application of heat to the fastener head will create a disproportionate expansion rate between the two metals and break the seizure caused by the corrosion. Whether heat can be applied depends on the location of the fastener - any surrounding components likely to be damaged must first be removed **(see illustration 2.15)**. Heat can be applied using a paint stripper heat gun or clothes iron, or by immersing the component in boiling water - wear protective gloves to prevent scalding or burns to the hands.

2.15 Using heat to free a seized fastener

● As a last resort, it is possible to use a hammer and cold chisel to work the fastener head unscrewed **(see illustration 2.16)**. This will damage the fastener, but more importantly extreme care must be taken not to damage the surrounding component.

Caution: Remember that the component being secured is generally of more value than the bolt, nut or screw - when the fastener is freed, do not unscrew it with force, instead work the fastener back and forth when resistance is felt to prevent thread damage.

2.16 Using a hammer and chisel to free a seized fastener

Broken fasteners and damaged heads

● If the shank of a broken bolt or screw is accessible you can grip it with self-locking grips. The knurled wheel type stud extractor tool or self-gripping stud puller tool is particularly useful for removing the long studs which screw into the cylinder mouth surface of the crankcase or bolts and screws from which the head has broken off **(see illustration 2.17)**. Studs can also be removed by locking two nuts together on the threaded end of the stud and using a spanner on the lower nut **(see illustration 2.18)**.

2.17 Using a stud extractor tool to remove a broken crankcase stud

2.18 Two nuts can be locked together to unscrew a stud from a component

● A bolt or screw which has broken off below or level with the casing must be extracted using a screw extractor set. Centre punch the fastener to centralise the drill bit, then drill a hole in the fastener **(see illustration 2.19)**. Select a drill bit which is approximately half to three-quarters the

2.19 When using a screw extractor, first drill a hole in the fastener . . .

diameter of the fastener and drill to a depth which will accommodate the extractor. Use the largest size extractor possible, but avoid leaving too small a wall thickness otherwise the extractor will merely force the fastener walls outwards wedging it in the casing thread.

● If a spiral type extractor is used, thread it anti-clockwise into the fastener. As it is screwed in, it will grip the fastener and unscrew it from the casing **(see illustration 2.20)**.

2.20 . . . then thread the extractor anti-clockwise into the fastener

● If a taper type extractor is used, tap it into the fastener so that it is firmly wedged in place. Unscrew the extractor (anti-clockwise) to draw the fastener out.

⚠ *Warning: Stud extractors are very hard and may break off in the fastener if care is not taken - ask an engineer about spark erosion if this happens.*

● Alternatively, the broken bolt/screw can be drilled out and the hole retapped for an oversize bolt/screw or a diamond-section thread insert. It is essential that the drilling is carried out squarely and to the correct depth, otherwise the casing may be ruined - if in doubt, entrust the work to an engineer.

● Bolts and nuts with rounded corners cause the correct size spanner or socket to slip when force is applied. Of the types of spanner/socket available always use a six-point type rather than an eight or twelve-point type - better grip

Tools and Workshop Tips   REF•9

2.21 Comparison of surface drive ring spanner (left) with 12-point type (right)

is obtained. Surface drive spanners grip the middle of the hex flats, rather than the corners, and are thus good in cases of damaged heads **(see illustration 2.21)**.

● Slotted-head or Phillips-head screws are often damaged by the use of the wrong size screwdriver. Allen-head and Torx-head screws are much less likely to sustain damage. If enough of the screw head is exposed you can use a hacksaw to cut a slot in its head and then use a conventional flat-bladed screwdriver to remove it. Alternatively use a hammer and cold chisel to tap the head of the fastener around to slacken it. Always replace damaged fasteners with new ones, preferably Torx or Allen-head type.

> **HAYNES HiNT**
>
> *A dab of valve grinding compound between the screw head and screwdriver tip will often give a good grip.*

Thread repair

● Threads (particularly those in aluminium alloy components) can be damaged by overtightening, being assembled with dirt in the threads, or from a component working loose and vibrating. Eventually the thread will fail completely, and it will be impossible to tighten the fastener.

● If a thread is damaged or clogged with old locking compound it can be renovated with a thread repair tool (thread chaser) **(see illustrations 2.22 and 2.23)**; special thread

2.22 A thread repair tool being used to correct an internal thread

2.23 A thread repair tool being used to correct an external thread

chasers are available for spark plug hole threads. The tool will not cut a new thread, but clean and true the original thread. Make sure that you use the correct diameter and pitch tool. Similarly, external threads can be cleaned up with a die or a thread restorer file **(see illustration 2.24)**.

2.24 Using a thread restorer file

● It is possible to drill out the old thread and retap the component to the next thread size. This will work where there is enough surrounding material and a new bolt or screw can be obtained. Sometimes, however, this is not possible - such as where the bolt/screw passes through another component which must also be suitably modified, also in cases where a spark plug or oil drain plug cannot be obtained in a larger diameter thread size.

● The diamond-section thread insert (often known by its popular trade name of Heli-Coil) is a simple and effective method of renewing the thread and retaining the original size. A kit can be purchased which contains the tap, insert and installing tool **(see illustration 2.25)**. Drill out the damaged thread with the size drill specified **(see illustration 2.26)**. Carefully retap the thread **(see illustration 2.27)**. Install the

2.25 Obtain a thread insert kit to suit the thread diameter and pitch required

2.26 To install a thread insert, first drill out the original thread . . .

2.27 . . . tap a new thread . . .

2.28 . . . fit insert on the installing tool . . .

2.29 . . . and thread into the component . . .

2.30 . . . break off the tang when complete

insert on the installing tool and thread it slowly into place using a light downward pressure **(see illustrations 2.28 and 2.29)**. When positioned between a 1/4 and 1/2 turn below the surface withdraw the installing tool and use the break-off tool to press down on the tang, breaking it off **(see illustration 2.30)**.

● There are epoxy thread repair kits on the market which can rebuild stripped internal threads, although this repair should not be used on high load-bearing components.

Tools and Workshop Tips

Thread locking and sealing compounds

● Locking compounds are used in locations where the fastener is prone to loosening due to vibration or on important safety-related items which might cause loss of control of the motorcycle if they fail. It is also used where important fasteners cannot be secured by other means such as lockwashers or split pins.

● Before applying locking compound, make sure that the threads (internal and external) are clean and dry with all old compound removed. Select a compound to suit the component being secured - a non-permanent general locking and sealing type is suitable for most applications, but a high strength type is needed for permanent fixing of studs in castings. Apply a drop or two of the compound to the first few threads of the fastener, then thread it into place and tighten to the specified torque. Do not apply excessive thread locking compound otherwise the thread may be damaged on subsequent removal.

● Certain fasteners are impregnated with a dry film type coating of locking compound on their threads. Always renew this type of fastener if disturbed.

● Anti-seize compounds, such as copper-based greases, can be applied to protect threads from seizure due to extreme heat and corrosion. A common instance is spark plug threads and exhaust system fasteners.

3 Measuring tools and gauges

Feeler gauges

● Feeler gauges (or blades) are used for measuring small gaps and clearances **(see illustration 3.1)**. They can also be used to measure endfloat (sideplay) of a component on a shaft where access is not possible with a dial gauge.

● Feeler gauge sets should be treated with care and not bent or damaged. They are etched with their size on one face. Keep them clean and very lightly oiled to prevent corrosion build-up.

3.1 Feeler gauges are used for measuring small gaps and clearances - thickness is marked on one face of gauge

● When measuring a clearance, select a gauge which is a light sliding fit between the two components. You may need to use two gauges together to measure the clearance accurately.

Micrometers

● A micrometer is a precision tool capable of measuring to 0.01 or 0.001 of a millimetre. It should always be stored in its case and not in the general toolbox. It must be kept clean and never dropped, otherwise its frame or measuring anvils could be distorted resulting in inaccurate readings.

● External micrometers are used for measuring outside diameters of components and have many more applications than internal micrometers. Micrometers are available in different size ranges, eg 0 to 25 mm, 25 to 50 mm, and upwards in 25 mm steps; some large micrometers have interchangeable anvils to allow a range of measurements to be taken. Generally the largest precision measurement you are likely to take on a motorcycle is the piston diameter.

● Internal micrometers (or bore micrometers) are used for measuring inside diameters, such as valve guides and cylinder bores. Telescoping gauges and small hole gauges are used in conjunction with an external micrometer, whereas the more expensive internal micrometers have their own measuring device.

External micrometer

Note: *The conventional analogue type instrument is described. Although much easier to read, digital micrometers are considerably more expensive.*

● Always check the calibration of the micrometer before use. With the anvils closed (0 to 25 mm type) or set over a test gauge (for

3.2 Check micrometer calibration before use

the larger types) the scale should read zero **(see illustration 3.2)**; make sure that the anvils (and test piece) are clean first. Any discrepancy can be adjusted by referring to the instructions supplied with the tool. Remember that the micrometer is a precision measuring tool - don't force the anvils closed, use the ratchet (4) on the end of the micrometer to close it. In this way, a measured force is always applied.

● To use, first make sure that the item being measured is clean. Place the anvil of the micrometer (1) against the item and use the thimble (2) to bring the spindle (3) lightly into contact with the other side of the item **(see illustration 3.3)**. Don't tighten the thimble down because this will damage the micrometer - instead use the ratchet (4) on the end of the micrometer. The ratchet mechanism applies a measured force preventing damage to the instrument.

● The micrometer is read by referring to the linear scale on the sleeve and the annular scale on the thimble. Read off the sleeve first to obtain the base measurement, then add the fine measurement from the thimble to obtain the overall reading. The linear scale on the sleeve represents the measuring range of the micrometer (eg 0 to 25 mm). The annular scale

3.3 Micrometer component parts

1 Anvil	3 Spindle	5 Frame
2 Thimble	4 Ratchet	6 Locking lever

Tools and Workshop Tips REF•11

on the thimble will be in graduations of 0.01 mm (or as marked on the frame) - one full revolution of the thimble will move 0.5 mm on the linear scale. Take the reading where the datum line on the sleeve intersects the thimble's scale. Always position the eye directly above the scale otherwise an inaccurate reading will result.

In the example shown the item measures 2.95 mm **(see illustration 3.4)**:

Linear scale	2.00 mm
Linear scale	0.50 mm
Annular scale	0.45 mm
Total figure	**2.95 mm**

3.4 Micrometer reading of 2.95 mm

3.5 Micrometer reading of 46.99 mm on linear and annular scales . . .

3.6 . . . and 0.004 mm on vernier scale

3.7 Expand the telescoping gauge in the bore, lock its position . . .

3.8 . . . then measure the gauge with a micrometer

Most micrometers have a locking lever (6) on the frame to hold the setting in place, allowing the item to be removed from the micrometer.
● Some micrometers have a vernier scale on their sleeve, providing an even finer measurement to be taken, in 0.001 increments of a millimetre. Take the sleeve and thimble measurement as described above, then check which graduation on the vernier scale aligns with that of the annular scale on the thimble **Note:** *The eye must be perpendicular to the scale when taking the vernier reading - if necessary rotate the body of the micrometer to ensure this.* Multiply the vernier scale figure by 0.001 and add it to the base and fine measurement figures.

In the example shown the item measures 46.994 mm **(see illustrations 3.5 and 3.6)**:

Linear scale (base)	46.000 mm
Linear scale (base)	00.500 mm
Annular scale (fine)	00.490 mm
Vernier scale	00.004 mm
Total figure	**46.994 mm**

Internal micrometer

● Internal micrometers are available for measuring bore diameters, but are expensive and unlikely to be available for home use. It is suggested that a set of telescoping gauges and small hole gauges, both of which must be used with an external micrometer, will suffice for taking internal measurements on a motorcycle.
● Telescoping gauges can be used to measure internal diameters of components. Select a gauge with the correct size range, make sure its ends are clean and insert it into the bore. Expand the gauge, then lock its position and withdraw it from the bore **(see illustration 3.7)**. Measure across the gauge ends with a micrometer **(see illustration 3.8)**.
● Very small diameter bores (such as valve guides) are measured with a small hole gauge. Once adjusted to a slip-fit inside the component, its position is locked and the gauge withdrawn for measurement with a micrometer **(see illustrations 3.9 and 3.10)**.

Vernier caliper

Note: *The conventional linear and dial gauge type instruments are described. Digital types are easier to read, but are far more expensive.*
● The vernier caliper does not provide the precision of a micrometer, but is versatile in being able to measure internal and external diameters. Some types also incorporate a depth gauge. It is ideal for measuring clutch plate friction material and spring free lengths.
● To use the conventional linear scale vernier, slacken off the vernier clamp screws (1) and set its jaws over (2), or inside (3), the item to be measured **(see illustration 3.11)**. Slide the jaw into contact, using the thumbwheel (4) for fine movement of the sliding scale (5) then tighten the clamp screws (1). Read off the main scale (6) where the zero on the sliding scale (5) intersects it, taking the whole number to the left of the zero; this provides the base measurement. View along the sliding scale and select the division which

3.9 Expand the small hole gauge in the bore, lock its position . . .

3.10 . . . then measure the gauge with a micrometer

lines up exactly with any of the divisions on the main scale, noting that the divisions usually represents 0.02 of a millimetre. Add this fine measurement to the base measurement to obtain the total reading.

REF•12 Tools and Workshop Tips

3.11 Vernier component parts (linear gauge)

1 Clamp screws
2 External jaws
3 Internal jaws
4 Thumbwheel
5 Sliding scale
6 Main scale
7 Depth gauge

In the example shown the item measures 55.92 mm (see illustration 3.12):

Base measurement	55.00 mm
Fine measurement	00.92 mm
Total figure	**55.92 mm**

3.12 Vernier gauge reading of 55.92 mm

- Some vernier calipers are equipped with a dial gauge for fine measurement. Before use, check that the jaws are clean, then close them fully and check that the dial gauge reads zero. If necessary adjust the gauge ring accordingly. Slacken the vernier clamp screw (1) and set its jaws over (2), or inside (3), the item to be measured (see illustration 3.13). Slide the jaws into contact, using the thumbwheel (4) for fine movement. Read off the main scale (5) where the edge of the sliding scale (6) intersects it, taking the whole number to the left of the zero; this provides the base measurement. Read off the needle position on the dial gauge (7) scale to provide the fine measurement; each division represents 0.05 of a millimetre. Add this fine measurement to the base measurement to obtain the total reading.

In the example shown the item measures 55.95 mm (see illustration 3.14):

Base measurement	55.00 mm
Fine measurement	00.95 mm
Total figure	**55.95 mm**

3.13 Vernier component parts (dial gauge)

1 Clamp screw
2 External jaws
3 Internal jaws
4 Thumbwheel
5 Main scale
6 Sliding scale
7 Dial gauge

3.14 Vernier gauge reading of 55.95 mm

Plastigauge

- Plastigauge is a plastic material which can be compressed between two surfaces to measure the oil clearance between them. The width of the compressed Plastigauge is measured against a calibrated scale to determine the clearance.
- Common uses of Plastigauge are for measuring the clearance between crankshaft journal and main bearing inserts, between crankshaft journal and big-end bearing inserts, and between camshaft and bearing surfaces. The following example describes big-end oil clearance measurement.
- Handle the Plastigauge material carefully to prevent distortion. Using a sharp knife, cut a length which corresponds with the width of the bearing being measured and place it carefully across the journal so that it is parallel with the shaft (see illustration 3.15). Carefully install both bearing shells and the connecting rod. Without rotating the rod on the journal tighten its bolts or nuts (as applicable) to the specified torque. The connecting rod and bearings are then disassembled and the crushed Plastigauge examined.

3.15 Plastigauge placed across shaft journal

- Using the scale provided in the Plastigauge kit, measure the width of the material to determine the oil clearance (see illustration 3.16). Always remove all traces of Plastigauge after use using your fingernails.

Caution: Arriving at the correct clearance demands that the assembly is torqued correctly, according to the settings and sequence (where applicable) provided by the motorcycle manufacturer.

3.16 Measuring the width of the crushed Plastigauge

Tools and Workshop Tips REF•13

Dial gauge or DTI (Dial Test Indicator)

● A dial gauge can be used to accurately measure small amounts of movement. Typical uses are measuring shaft runout or shaft endfloat (sideplay) and setting piston position for ignition timing on two-strokes. A dial gauge set usually comes with a range of different probes and adapters and mounting equipment.

● The gauge needle must point to zero when at rest. Rotate the ring around its periphery to zero the gauge.

● Check that the gauge is capable of reading the extent of movement in the work. Most gauges have a small dial set in the face which records whole millimetres of movement as well as the fine scale around the face periphery which is calibrated in 0.01 mm divisions. Read off the small dial first to obtain the base measurement, then add the measurement from the fine scale to obtain the total reading.

In the example shown the gauge reads 1.48 mm **(see illustration 3.17)**:

Base measurement	1.00 mm
Fine measurement	0.48 mm
Total figure	**1.48 mm**

3.17 Dial gauge reading of 1.48 mm

● If measuring shaft runout, the shaft must be supported in vee-blocks and the gauge mounted on a stand perpendicular to the shaft. Rest the tip of the gauge against the centre of the shaft and rotate the shaft slowly whilst watching the gauge reading **(see illustration 3.18)**. Take several measurements along the length of the shaft and record the maximum gauge reading as the amount of runout in the shaft. **Note:** *The reading obtained will be total runout at that point - some manufacturers specify that the runout figure is halved to compare with their specified runout limit.*

● Endfloat (sideplay) measurement requires that the gauge is mounted securely to the surrounding component with its probe touching the end of the shaft. Using hand pressure, push and pull on the shaft noting the maximum endfloat recorded on the gauge **(see illustration 3.19)**.

3.18 Using a dial gauge to measure shaft runout

3.19 Using a dial gauge to measure shaft endfloat

● A dial gauge with suitable adapters can be used to determine piston position BTDC on two-stroke engines for the purposes of ignition timing. The gauge, adapter and suitable length probe are installed in the place of the spark plug and the gauge zeroed at TDC. If the piston position is specified as 1.14 mm BTDC, rotate the engine back to 2.00 mm BTDC, then slowly forwards to 1.14 mm BTDC.

Cylinder compression gauges

● A compression gauge is used for measuring cylinder compression. Either the rubber-cone type or the threaded adapter type can be used. The latter is preferred to ensure a perfect seal against the cylinder head. A 0 to 300 psi (0 to 20 Bar) type gauge (for petrol/gasoline engines) will be suitable for motorcycles.

● The spark plug is removed and the gauge either held hard against the cylinder head (cone type) or the gauge adapter screwed into the cylinder head (threaded type) **(see illustration 3.20)**. Cylinder compression is measured with the engine turning over, but not running - carry out the compression test as described in *Fault Finding Equipment*. The gauge will hold the reading until manually released.

Oil pressure gauge

● An oil pressure gauge is used for measuring engine oil pressure. Most gauges come with a set of adapters to fit the thread of the take-off point **(see illustration 3.21)**. If the take-off point specified by the motorcycle manufacturer is an external oil pipe union, make sure that the specified replacement union is used to prevent oil starvation.

3.20 Using a rubber-cone type cylinder compression gauge

3.21 Oil pressure gauge and take-off point adapter (arrow)

● Oil pressure is measured with the engine running (at a specific rpm) and often the manufacturer will specify pressure limits for a cold and hot engine.

Straight-edge and surface plate

● If checking the gasket face of a component for warpage, place a steel rule or precision straight-edge across the gasket face and measure any gap between the straight-edge and component with feeler gauges **(see illustration 3.22)**. Check diagonally across the component and between mounting holes **(see illustration 3.23)**.

3.22 Use a straight-edge and feeler gauges to check for warpage

3.23 Check for warpage in these directions

REF•14 Tools and Workshop Tips

- Checking individual components for warpage, such as clutch plain (metal) plates, requires a perfectly flat plate or piece or plate glass and feeler gauges.

4 Torque and leverage

What is torque?

- Torque describes the twisting force about a shaft. The amount of torque applied is determined by the distance from the centre of the shaft to the end of the lever and the amount of force being applied to the end of the lever; distance multiplied by force equals torque.
- The manufacturer applies a measured torque to a bolt or nut to ensure that it will not slacken in use and to hold two components securely together without movement in the joint. The actual torque setting depends on the thread size, bolt or nut material and the composition of the components being held.
- Too little torque may cause the fastener to loosen due to vibration, whereas too much torque will distort the joint faces of the component or cause the fastener to shear off. Always stick to the specified torque setting.

Using a torque wrench

- Check the calibration of the torque wrench and make sure it has a suitable range for the job. Torque wrenches are available in Nm (Newton-metres), kgf m (kilograms-force metre), lbf ft (pounds-feet), lbf in (inch-pounds). Do not confuse lbf ft with lbf in.
- Adjust the tool to the desired torque on the scale (see illustration 4.1). If your torque wrench is not calibrated in the units specified, carefully convert the figure (see *Conversion Factors*). A manufacturer sometimes gives a torque setting as a range (8 to 10 Nm) rather than a single figure - in this case set the tool midway between the two settings. The same torque may be expressed as 9 Nm ± 1 Nm. Some torque wrenches have a method of locking the setting so that it isn't inadvertently altered during use.

- Install the bolts/nuts in their correct location and secure them lightly. Their threads must be clean and free of any old locking compound. Unless specified the threads and flange should be dry - oiled threads are necessary in certain circumstances and the manufacturer will take this into account in the specified torque figure. Similarly, the manufacturer may also specify the application of thread-locking compound.
- Tighten the fasteners in the specified sequence until the torque wrench clicks, indicating that the torque setting has been reached. Apply the torque again to double-check the setting. Where different thread diameter fasteners secure the component, as a rule tighten the larger diameter ones first.
- When the torque wrench has been finished with, release the lock (where applicable) and fully back off its setting to zero - do not leave the torque wrench tensioned. Also, do not use a torque wrench for slackening a fastener.

Angle-tightening

- Manufacturers often specify a figure in degrees for final tightening of a fastener. This usually follows tightening to a specific torque setting.
- A degree disc can be set and attached to the socket (see illustration 4.2) or a protractor can be used to mark the angle of movement on the bolt/nut head and the surrounding casting (see illustration 4.3).

4.2 Angle tightening can be accomplished with a torque-angle gauge . . .

4.1 Set the torque wrench index mark to the setting required, in this case 12 Nm

4.3 . . . or by marking the angle on the surrounding component

Loosening sequences

- Where more than one bolt/nut secures a component, loosen each fastener evenly a little at a time. In this way, not all the stress of the joint is held by one fastener and the components are not likely to distort.
- If a tightening sequence is provided, work in the REVERSE of this, but if not, work from the outside in, in a criss-cross sequence (see illustration 4.4).

4.4 When slackening, work from the outside inwards

Tightening sequences

- If a component is held by more than one fastener it is important that the retaining bolts/nuts are tightened evenly to prevent uneven stress build-up and distortion of sealing faces. This is especially important on high-compression joints such as the cylinder head.
- A sequence is usually provided by the manufacturer, either in a diagram or actually marked in the casting. If not, always start in the centre and work outwards in a criss-cross pattern (see illustration 4.5). Start off by securing all bolts/nuts finger-tight, then set the torque wrench and tighten each fastener by a small amount in sequence until the final torque is reached. By following this practice,

4.5 When tightening, work from the inside outwards

Tools and Workshop Tips REF•15

the joint will be held evenly and will not be distorted. Important joints, such as the cylinder head and big-end fasteners often have two- or three-stage torque settings.

Applying leverage

● Use tools at the correct angle. Position a socket wrench or spanner on the bolt/nut so that you pull it towards you when loosening. If this can't be done, push the spanner without curling your fingers around it **(see illustration 4.6)** - the spanner may slip or the fastener loosen suddenly, resulting in your fingers being crushed against a component.

4.6 If you can't pull on the spanner to loosen a fastener, push with your hand open

● Additional leverage is gained by extending the length of the lever. The best way to do this is to use a breaker bar instead of the regular length tool, or to slip a length of tubing over the end of the spanner or socket wrench.
● If additional leverage will not work, the fastener head is either damaged or firmly corroded in place (see *Fasteners*).

5 Bearings

Bearing removal and installation

Drivers and sockets

● Before removing a bearing, always inspect the casing to see which way it must be driven out - some casings will have retaining plates or a cast step. Also check for any identifying markings on the bearing and if installed to a certain depth, measure this at this stage. Some roller bearings are sealed on one side - take note of the original fitted position.
● Bearings can be driven out of a casing using a bearing driver tool (with the correct size head) or a socket of the correct diameter. Select the driver head or socket so that it contacts the outer race of the bearing, not the balls/rollers or inner race. Always support the casing around the bearing housing with wood blocks, otherwise there is a risk of fracture. The bearing is driven out with a few blows on the driver or socket from a heavy mallet. Unless access is severely restricted (as with wheel bearings), a pin-punch is not recommended unless it is moved around the bearing to keep it square in its housing.

● The same equipment can be used to install bearings. Make sure the bearing housing is supported on wood blocks and line up the bearing in its housing. Fit the bearing as noted on removal - generally they are installed with their marked side facing outwards. Tap the bearing squarely into its housing using a driver or socket which bears only on the bearing's outer race - contact with the bearing balls/rollers or inner race will destroy it **(see illustrations 5.1 and 5.2)**.
● Check that the bearing inner race and balls/rollers rotate freely.

5.1 Using a bearing driver against the bearing's outer race

5.2 Using a large socket against the bearing's outer race

Pullers and slide-hammers

● Where a bearing is pressed on a shaft a puller will be required to extract it **(see illustration 5.3)**. Make sure that the puller clamp or legs fit securely behind the bearing and are unlikely to slip out. If pulling a bearing off a gear shaft for example, you may have to locate the puller behind a gear pinion if there is no access to the race and draw the gear pinion off the shaft as well **(see illustration 5.4)**.

Caution: Ensure that the puller's centre bolt locates securely against the end of the shaft and will not slip when pressure is applied. Also ensure that puller does not damage the shaft end.

5.4 Where no access is available to the rear of the bearing, it is sometimes possible to draw off the adjacent component

● Operate the puller so that its centre bolt exerts pressure on the shaft end and draws the bearing off the shaft.
● When installing the bearing on the shaft, tap only on the bearing's inner race - contact with the balls/rollers or outer race with destroy the bearing. Use a socket or length of tubing as a drift which fits over the shaft end **(see illustration 5.5)**.

5.5 When installing a bearing on a shaft use a piece of tubing which bears only on the bearing's inner race

● Where a bearing locates in a blind hole in a casing, it cannot be driven or pulled out as described above. A slide-hammer with knife-edged bearing puller attachment will be required. The puller attachment passes through the bearing and when tightened expands to fit firmly behind the bearing **(see illustration 5.6)**. By operating the slide-hammer part of the tool the bearing is jarred out of its housing **(see illustration 5.7)**.
● It is possible, if the bearing is of reasonable weight, for it to drop out of its housing if the casing is heated as described opposite. If this

5.3 This bearing puller clamps behind the bearing and pressure is applied to the shaft end to draw the bearing off

Tools and Workshop Tips

5.6 Expand the bearing puller so that it locks behind the bearing . . .

5.7 . . . attach the slide hammer to the bearing puller

method is attempted, first prepare a work surface which will enable the casing to be tapped face down to help dislodge the bearing - a wood surface is ideal since it will not damage the casing's gasket surface. Wearing protective gloves, tap the heated casing several times against the work surface to dislodge the bearing under its own weight **(see illustration 5.8)**.

5.8 Tapping a casing face down on wood blocks can often dislodge a bearing

- Bearings can be installed in blind holes using the driver or socket method described above.

Drawbolts

- Where a bearing or bush is set in the eye of a component, such as a suspension linkage arm or connecting rod small-end, removal by drift may damage the component. Furthermore, a rubber bushing in a shock absorber eye cannot successfully be driven out of position. If access is available to a engineering press, the task is straightforward. If not, a drawbolt can be fabricated to extract the bearing or bush.

5.9 Drawbolt component parts assembled on a suspension arm

1. Bolt or length of threaded bar
2. Nuts
3. Washer (external diameter greater than tubing internal diameter)
4. Tubing (internal diameter sufficient to accommodate bearing)
5. Suspension arm with bearing
6. Tubing (external diameter slightly smaller than bearing)
7. Washer (external diameter slightly smaller than bearing)

5.10 Drawing the bearing out of the suspension arm

- To extract the bearing/bush you will need a long bolt with nut (or piece of threaded bar with two nuts), a piece of tubing which has an internal diameter larger than the bearing/bush, another piece of tubing which has an external diameter slightly smaller than the bearing/bush, and a selection of washers **(see illustrations 5.9 and 5.10)**. Note that the pieces of tubing must be of the same length, or longer, than the bearing/bush.
- The same kit (without the pieces of tubing) can be used to draw the new bearing/bush back into place **(see illustration 5.11)**.

5.11 Installing a new bearing (1) in the suspension arm

Temperature change

- If the bearing's outer race is a tight fit in the casing, the aluminium casing can be heated to release its grip on the bearing. Aluminium will expand at a greater rate than the steel bearing outer race. There are several ways to do this, but avoid any localised extreme heat (such as a blow torch) - aluminium alloy has a low melting point.
- Approved methods of heating a casing are using a domestic oven (heated to 100°C) or immersing the casing in boiling water **(see illustration 5.12)**. Low temperature range localised heat sources such as a paint stripper heat gun or clothes iron can also be used **(see illustration 5.13)**. Alternatively, soak a rag in boiling water, wring it out and wrap it around the bearing housing.

> **Warning: All of these methods require care in use to prevent scalding and burns to the hands. Wear protective gloves when handling hot components.**

5.12 A casing can be immersed in a sink of boiling water to aid bearing removal

5.13 Using a localised heat source to aid bearing removal

- If heating the whole casing note that plastic components, such as the neutral switch, may suffer - remove them beforehand.
- After heating, remove the bearing as described above. You may find that the expansion is sufficient for the bearing to fall out of the casing under its own weight or with a light tap on the driver or socket.
- If necessary, the casing can be heated to aid bearing installation, and this is sometimes the recommended procedure if the motorcycle manufacturer has designed the housing and bearing fit with this intention.

Tools and Workshop Tips REF•17

- Installation of bearings can be eased by placing them in a freezer the night before installation. The steel bearing will contract slightly, allowing easy insertion in its housing. This is often useful when installing steering head outer races in the frame.

Bearing types and markings

- Plain shell bearings, ball bearings, needle roller bearings and tapered roller bearings will all be found on motorcycles (see illustrations 5.14 and 5.15). The ball and roller types are usually caged between an inner and outer race, but uncaged variations may be found.

5.14 Shell bearings are either plain or grooved. They are usually identified by colour code (arrow)

5.15 Tapered roller bearing (A), needle roller bearing (B) and ball journal bearing (C)

- Shell bearings (often called inserts) are usually found at the crankshaft main and connecting rod big-end where they are good at coping with high loads. They are made of a phosphor-bronze material and are impregnated with self-lubricating properties.
- Ball bearings and needle roller bearings consist of a steel inner and outer race with the balls or rollers between the races. They require constant lubrication by oil or grease and are good at coping with axial loads. Taper roller bearings consist of rollers set in a tapered cage set on the inner race; the outer race is separate. They are good at coping with axial loads and prevent movement along the shaft - a typical application is in the steering head.
- Bearing manufacturers produce bearings to ISO size standards and stamp one face of the bearing to indicate its internal and external diameter, load capacity and type (see illustration 5.16).
- Metal bushes are usually of phosphor-bronze material. Rubber bushes are used in suspension mounting eyes. Fibre bushes have also been used in suspension pivots.

5.16 Typical bearing marking

Bearing fault finding

- If a bearing outer race has spun in its housing, the housing material will be damaged. You can use a bearing locking compound to bond the outer race in place if damage is not too severe.
- Shell bearings will fail due to damage of their working surface, as a result of lack of lubrication, corrosion or abrasive particles in the oil (see illustration 5.17). Small particles of dirt in the oil may embed in the bearing material whereas larger particles will score the bearing and shaft journal. If a number of short journeys are made, insufficient heat will be generated to drive off condensation which has built up on the bearings.

5.17 Typical bearing failures

- Ball and roller bearings will fail due to lack of lubrication or damage to the balls or rollers. Tapered-roller bearings can be damaged by overloading them. Unless the bearing is sealed on both sides, wash it in paraffin (kerosene) to remove all old grease then allow it to dry. Make a visual inspection looking to dented balls or rollers, damaged cages and worn or pitted races (see illustration 5.18).
- A ball bearing can be checked for wear by listening to it when spun. Apply a film of light oil to the bearing and hold it close to the ear - hold the outer race with one hand and spin the inner race with the other hand (see illustration 5.19). The bearing should be almost silent when spun; if it grates or rattles it is worn.

5.18 Example of ball journal bearing with damaged balls and cages

5.19 Hold outer race and listen to inner race when spun

6 Oil seals

Oil seal removal and installation

- Oil seals should be renewed every time a component is dismantled. This is because the seal lips will become set to the sealing surface and will not necessarily reseal.
- Oil seals can be prised out of position using a large flat-bladed screwdriver (see illustration 6.1). In the case of crankcase seals, check first that the seal is not lipped on the inside, preventing its removal with the crankcases joined.

6.1 Prise out oil seals with a large flat-bladed screwdriver

- New seals are usually installed with their marked face (containing the seal reference code) outwards and the spring side towards the fluid being retained. In certain cases, such as a two-stroke engine crankshaft seal, a double lipped seal may be used due to there being fluid or gas on each side of the joint.

Tools and Workshop Tips

● Use a bearing driver or socket which bears only on the outer hard edge of the seal to install it in the casing - tapping on the inner edge will damage the sealing lip.

Oil seal types and markings

● Oil seals are usually of the single-lipped type. Double-lipped seals are found where a liquid or gas is on both sides of the joint.
● Oil seals can harden and lose their sealing ability if the motorcycle has been in storage for a long period - renewal is the only solution.
● Oil seal manufacturers also conform to the ISO markings for seal size - these are moulded into the outer face of the seal **(see illustration 6.2)**.

6.2 These oil seal markings indicate inside diameter, outside diameter and seal thickness

7 Gaskets and sealants

Types of gasket and sealant

● Gaskets are used to seal the mating surfaces between components and keep lubricants, fluids, vacuum or pressure contained within the assembly. Aluminium gaskets are sometimes found at the cylinder joints, but most gaskets are paper-based. If the mating surfaces of the components being joined are undamaged the gasket can be installed dry, although a dab of sealant or grease will be useful to hold it in place during assembly.
● RTV (Room Temperature Vulcanising) silicone rubber sealants cure when exposed to moisture in the atmosphere. These sealants are good at filling pits or irregular gasket faces, but will tend to be forced out of the joint under very high torque. They can be used to replace a paper gasket, but first make sure that the width of the paper gasket is not essential to the shimming of internal components. RTV sealants should not be used on components containing petrol (gasoline).
● Non-hardening, semi-hardening and hard setting liquid gasket compounds can be used with a gasket or between a metal-to-metal joint. Select the sealant to suit the application: universal non-hardening sealant can be used on virtually all joints; semi-hardening on joint faces which are rough or damaged; hard setting sealant on joints which require a permanent bond and are subjected to high temperature and pressure. **Note:** *Check first if the paper gasket has a bead of sealant impregnated in its surface before applying additional sealant.*
● When choosing a sealant, make sure it is suitable for the application, particularly if being applied in a high-temperature area or in the vicinity of fuel. Certain manufacturers produce sealants in either clear, silver or black colours to match the finish of the engine. This has a particular application on motorcycles where much of the engine is exposed.
● Do not over-apply sealant. That which is squeezed out on the outside of the joint can be wiped off, whereas an excess of sealant on the inside can break off and clog oilways.

Breaking a sealed joint

● Age, heat, pressure and the use of hard setting sealant can cause two components to stick together so tightly that they are difficult to separate using finger pressure alone. Do not resort to using levers unless there is a pry point provided for this purpose **(see illustration 7.1)** or else the gasket surfaces will be damaged.
● Use a soft-faced hammer **(see illustration 7.2)** or a wood block and conventional hammer to strike the component near the mating surface. Avoid hammering against cast extremities since they may break off. If this method fails, try using a wood wedge between the two components.

Caution: If the joint will not separate, double-check that you have removed all the fasteners.

7.1 If a pry point is provided, apply gently pressure with a flat-bladed screwdriver

7.2 Tap around the joint with a soft-faced mallet if necessary - don't strike cooling fins

Removal of old gasket and sealant

● Paper gaskets will most likely come away complete, leaving only a few traces stuck on

> **HAYNES HiNT**
>
> *Most components have one or two hollow locating dowels between the two gasket faces. If a dowel cannot be removed, do not resort to gripping it with pliers - it will almost certainly be distorted. Install a close-fitting socket or Phillips screwdriver into the dowel and then grip the outer edge of the dowel to free it.*

the sealing faces of the components. It is imperative that all traces are removed to ensure correct sealing of the new gasket.
● Very carefully scrape all traces of gasket away making sure that the sealing surfaces are not gouged or scored by the scraper **(see illustrations 7.3, 7.4 and 7.5)**. Stubborn deposits can be removed by spraying with an aerosol gasket remover. Final preparation of

7.3 Paper gaskets can be scraped off with a gasket scraper tool . . .

7.4 . . . a knife blade . . .

7.5 . . . or a household scraper

Tools and Workshop Tips REF•19

7.6 Fine abrasive paper is wrapped around a flat file to clean up the gasket face

7.7 A kitchen scourer can be used on stubborn deposits

8.1 Tighten the chain breaker to push the pin out of the link . . .

8.2 . . . withdraw the pin, remove the tool . . .

8.3 . . . and separate the chain link

8.4 Insert the new soft link, with O-rings, through the chain ends . . .

8.5 . . . install the O-rings over the pin ends . . .

8.6 . . . followed by the sideplate

8.7 Push the sideplate into position using a clamp

the gasket surface can be made with very fine abrasive paper or a plastic kitchen scourer **(see illustrations 7.6 and 7.7)**.

● Old sealant can be scraped or peeled off components, depending on the type originally used. Note that gasket removal compounds are available to avoid scraping the components clean; make sure the gasket remover suits the type of sealant used.

8 Chains

Breaking and joining final drive chains

● Drive chains for all but small bikes are continuous and do not have a clip-type connecting link. The chain must be broken using a chain breaker tool and the new chain securely riveted together using a new soft rivet-type link. Never use a clip-type connecting link instead of a rivet-type link, except in an emergency. Various chain breaking and riveting tools are available, either as separate tools or combined as illustrated in the accompanying photographs - read the instructions supplied with the tool carefully.

> **Warning: The need to rivet the new link pins correctly cannot be overstressed - loss of control of the motorcycle is very likely to result if the chain breaks in use.**

● Rotate the chain and look for the soft link. The soft link pins look like they have been deeply centre-punched instead of peened over like all the other pins **(see illustration 8.9)** and its sideplate may be a different colour. Position the soft link midway between the sprockets and assemble the chain breaker tool over one of the soft link pins **(see illustration 8.1)**. Operate the tool to push the pin out through the chain **(see illustration 8.2)**. On an O-ring chain, remove the O-rings **(see illustration 8.3)**. Carry out the same procedure on the other soft link pin.

> **Caution: Certain soft link pins (particularly on the larger chains) may require their ends to be filed or ground off before they can be pressed out using the tool.**

● Check that you have the correct size and strength (standard or heavy duty) new soft link - do not reuse the old link. Look for the size marking on the chain sideplates **(see illustration 8.10)**.

● Position the chain ends so that they are engaged over the rear sprocket. On an O-ring chain, install a new O-ring over each pin of the link and insert the link through the two chain ends **(see illustration 8.4)**. Install a new O-ring over the end of each pin, followed by the sideplate (with the chain manufacturer's marking facing outwards) **(see illustrations 8.5 and 8.6)**. On an unsealed chain, insert the link through the two chain ends, then install the sideplate with the chain manufacturer's marking facing outwards.

● Note that it may not be possible to install the sideplate using finger pressure alone. If using a joining tool, assemble it so that the plates of the tool clamp the link and press the sideplate over the pins **(see illustration 8.7)**. Otherwise, use two small sockets placed over

REF•20 Tools and Workshop Tips

8.8 Assemble the chain riveting tool over one pin at a time and tighten it fully

8.9 Pin end correctly riveted (A), pin end unriveted (B)

the rivet ends and two pieces of the wood between a G-clamp. Operate the clamp to press the sideplate over the pins.

● Assemble the joining tool over one pin (following the maker's instructions) and tighten the tool down to spread the pin end securely **(see illustrations 8.8 and 8.9)**. Do the same on the other pin.

> ⚠ **Warning: Check that the pin ends are secure and that there is no danger of the sideplate coming loose. If the pin ends are cracked the soft link must be renewed.**

Final drive chain sizing

● Chains are sized using a three digit number, followed by a suffix to denote the chain type **(see illustration 8.10)**. Chain type is either standard or heavy duty (thicker sideplates), and also unsealed or O-ring/X-ring type.

● The first digit of the number relates to the pitch of the chain, ie the distance from the centre of one pin to the centre of the next pin **(see illustration 8.11)**. Pitch is expressed in eighths of an inch, as follows:

8.10 Typical chain size and type marking

8.11 Chain dimensions

Sizes commencing with a 4 (eg 428) have a pitch of 1/2 inch (12.7 mm)

Sizes commencing with a 5 (eg 520) have a pitch of 5/8 inch (15.9 mm)

Sizes commencing with a 6 (eg 630) have a pitch of 3/4 inch (19.1 mm)

● The second and third digits of the chain size relate to the width of the rollers, again in imperial units, eg the 525 shown has 5/16 inch (7.94 mm) rollers **(see illustration 8.11)**.

9 Hoses

Clamping to prevent flow

● Small-bore flexible hoses can be clamped to prevent fluid flow whilst a component is worked on. Whichever method is used, ensure that the hose material is not permanently distorted or damaged by the clamp.

a) A brake hose clamp available from auto accessory shops **(see illustration 9.1)**.
b) A wingnut type hose clamp **(see illustration 9.2)**.
c) Two sockets placed each side of the hose and held with straight-jawed self-locking grips **(see illustration 9.3)**.
d) Thick card each side of the hose held between straight-jawed self-locking grips **(see illustration 9.4)**.

9.1 Hoses can be clamped with an automotive brake hose clamp . . .

9.2 . . . a wingnut type hose clamp . . .

9.3 . . . two sockets and a pair of self-locking grips . . .

9.4 . . . or thick card and self-locking grips

Freeing and fitting hoses

● Always make sure the hose clamp is moved well clear of the hose end. Grip the hose with your hand and rotate it whilst pulling it off the union. If the hose has hardened due to age and will not move, slit it with a sharp knife and peel its ends off the union **(see illustration 9.5)**.

● Resist the temptation to use grease or soap on the unions to aid installation; although it helps the hose slip over the union it will equally aid the escape of fluid from the joint. It is preferable to soften the hose ends in hot water and wet the inside surface of the hose with water or a fluid which will evaporate.

9.5 Cutting a coolant hose free with a sharp knife

Conversion Factors REF•21

Length (distance)
Inches (in)	x 25.4	= Millimetres (mm)	x 0.0394	=	Inches (in)
Feet (ft)	x 0.305	= Metres (m)	x 3.281	=	Feet (ft)
Miles	x 1.609	= Kilometres (km)	x 0.621	=	Miles

Volume (capacity)
Cubic inches (cu in; in^3)	x 16.387	= Cubic centimetres (cc; cm^3)	x 0.061	=	Cubic inches (cu in; in^3)
Imperial pints (Imp pt)	x 0.568	= Litres (l)	x 1.76	=	Imperial pints (Imp pt)
Imperial quarts (Imp qt)	x 1.137	= Litres (l)	x 0.88	=	Imperial quarts (Imp qt)
Imperial quarts (Imp qt)	x 1.201	= US quarts (US qt)	x 0.833	=	Imperial quarts (Imp qt)
US quarts (US qt)	x 0.946	= Litres (l)	x 1.057	=	US quarts (US qt)
Imperial gallons (Imp gal)	x 4.546	= Litres (l)	x 0.22	=	Imperial gallons (Imp gal)
Imperial gallons (Imp gal)	x 1.201	= US gallons (US gal)	x 0.833	=	Imperial gallons (Imp gal)
US gallons (US gal)	x 3.785	= Litres (l)	x 0.264	=	US gallons (US gal)

Mass (weight)
Ounces (oz)	x 28.35	= Grams (g)	x 0.035	=	Ounces (oz)
Pounds (lb)	x 0.454	= Kilograms (kg)	x 2.205	=	Pounds (lb)

Force
Ounces-force (ozf; oz)	x 0.278	= Newtons (N)	x 3.6	=	Ounces-force (ozf; oz)
Pounds-force (lbf; lb)	x 4.448	= Newtons (N)	x 0.225	=	Pounds-force (lbf; lb)
Newtons (N)	x 0.1	= Kilograms-force (kgf; kg)	x 9.81	=	Newtons (N)

Pressure
Pounds-force per square inch (psi; lbf/in^2; lb/in^2)	x 0.070	= Kilograms-force per square centimetre (kgf/cm^2; kg/cm^2)	x 14.223	=	Pounds-force per square inch (psi; lbf/in^2; lb/in^2)
Pounds-force per square inch (psi; lbf/in^2; lb/in^2)	x 0.068	= Atmospheres (atm)	x 14.696	=	Pounds-force per square inch (psi; lbf/in^2; lb/in^2)
Pounds-force per square inch (psi; lbf/in^2; lb/in^2)	x 0.069	= Bars	x 14.5	=	Pounds-force per square inch (psi; lbf/in^2; lb/in^2)
Pounds-force per square inch (psi; lbf/in^2; lb/in^2)	x 6.895	= Kilopascals (kPa)	x 0.145	=	Pounds-force per square inch (psi; lbf/in^2; lb/in^2)
Kilopascals (kPa)	x 0.01	= Kilograms-force per square centimetre (kgf/cm^2; kg/cm^2)	x 98.1	=	Kilopascals (kPa)
Millibar (mbar)	x 100	= Pascals (Pa)	x 0.01	=	Millibar (mbar)
Millibar (mbar)	x 0.0145	= Pounds-force per square inch (psi; lbf/in^2; lb/in^2)	x 68.947	=	Millibar (mbar)
Millibar (mbar)	x 0.75	= Millimetres of mercury (mmHg)	x 1.333	=	Millibar (mbar)
Millibar (mbar)	x 0.401	= Inches of water (inH$_2$O)	x 2.491	=	Millibar (mbar)
Millimetres of mercury (mmHg)	x 0.535	= Inches of water (inH$_2$O)	x 1.868	=	Millimetres of mercury (mmHg)
Inches of water (inH$_2$O)	x 0.036	= Pounds-force per square inch (psi; lbf/in^2; lb/in^2)	x 27.68	=	Inches of water (inH$_2$O)

Torque (moment of force)
Pounds-force inches (lbf in; lb in)	x 1.152	= Kilograms-force centimetre (kgf cm; kg cm)	x 0.868	–	Pounds-force inches (lbf in; lb in)
Pounds-force inches (lbf in; lb in)	x 0.113	= Newton metres (Nm)	x 8.85	=	Pounds-force inches (lbf in; lb in)
Pounds-force inches (lbf in; lb in)	x 0.083	= Pounds-force feet (lbf ft; lb ft)	x 12	=	Pounds-force inches (lbf in; lb in)
Pounds-force feet (lbf ft; lb ft)	x 0.138	= Kilograms-force metres (kgf m; kg m)	x 7.233	=	Pounds-force feet (lbf ft; lb ft)
Pounds-force feet (lbf ft; lb ft)	x 1.356	= Newton metres (Nm)	x 0.738	=	Pounds-force feet (lbf ft; lb ft)
Newton metres (Nm)	x 0.102	= Kilograms-force metres (kgf m; kg m)	x 9.804	=	Newton metres (Nm)

Power
Horsepower (hp)	x 745.7	= Watts (W)	x 0.0013	=	Horsepower (hp)

Velocity (speed)
Miles per hour (miles/hr; mph)	x 1.609	= Kilometres per hour (km/hr; kph)	x 0.621	=	Miles per hour (miles/hr; mph)

Fuel consumption*
Miles per gallon (mpg)	x 0.354	= Kilometres per litre (km/l)	x 2.825	=	Miles per gallon (mpg)

Temperature
Degrees Fahrenheit = (°C x 1.8) + 32   Degrees Celsius (Degrees Centigrade; °C) = (°F - 32) x 0.56

*It is common practice to convert from miles per gallon (mpg) to litres/100 kilometres (l/100km), where mpg x l/100 km = 282

REF•22 MOT Test Checks

About the MOT Test

In the UK, all vehicles more than three years old are subject to an annual test to ensure that they meet minimum safety requirements. A current test certificate must be issued before a machine can be used on public roads, and is required before a road fund licence can be issued. Riding without a current test certificate will also invalidate your insurance.

For most owners, the MOT test is an annual cause for anxiety, and this is largely due to owners not being sure what needs to be checked prior to submitting the motorcycle for testing. The simple answer is that a fully roadworthy motorcycle will have no difficulty in passing the test.

This is a guide to getting your motorcycle through the MOT test. Obviously it will not be possible to examine the motorcycle to the same standard as the professional MOT tester, particularly in view of the equipment required for some of the checks. However, working through the following procedures will enable you to identify any problem areas before submitting the motorcycle for the test.

It has only been possible to summarise the test requirements here, based on the regulations in force at the time of printing. Test standards are becoming increasingly stringent, although there are some exemptions for older vehicles. More information about the MOT test can be obtained from the TSO publications, *How Safe is your Motorcycle* and *The MOT Inspection Manual for Motorcycle Testing*.

Many of the checks require that one of the wheels is raised off the ground. If the motorcycle doesn't have a centre stand, note that an auxiliary stand will be required. Additionally, the help of an assistant may prove useful.

Certain exceptions apply to machines under 50 cc, machines without a lighting system, and Classic bikes - if in doubt about any of the requirements listed below seek confirmation from an MOT tester prior to submitting the motorcycle for the test.

Check that the frame number is clearly visible.

> **HAYNES HINT** *If a component is in borderline condition, the tester has discretion in deciding whether to pass or fail it. If the motorcycle presented is clean and evidently well cared for, the tester may be more inclined to pass a borderline component than if the motorcycle is scruffy and apparently neglected.*

Electrical System

Lights, turn signals, horn and reflector

✔ With the ignition on, check the operation of the following electrical components. **Note:** *The electrical components on certain small-capacity machines are powered by the generator, requiring that the engine is run for this check.*

a) Headlight and tail light. Check that both illuminate in the low and high beam switch positions.
b) Position lights. Check that the front position (or sidelight) and tail light illuminate in this switch position.
c) Turn signals. Check that all flash at the correct rate, and that the warning light(s) function correctly. Check that the turn signal switch works correctly.
d) Hazard warning system (where fitted). Check that all four turn signals flash in this switch position.
e) Brake stop light. Check that the light comes on when the front and rear brakes are independently applied. Models first used on or after 1st April 1986 must have a brake light switch on each brake.
f) Horn. Check that the sound is continuous and of reasonable volume.

✔ Check that there is a red reflector on the rear of the machine, either mounted separately or as part of the tail light lens.
✔ Check the condition of the headlight, tail light and turn signal lenses.

Headlight beam height

✔ The MOT tester will perform a headlight beam height check using specialised beam setting equipment **(see illustration 1)**. This equipment will not be available to the home mechanic, but if you suspect that the headlight is incorrectly set or may have been maladjusted in the past, you can perform a rough test as follows.

✔ Position the bike in a straight line facing a brick wall. The bike must be off its stand, upright and with a rider seated. Measure the height from the ground to the centre of the headlight and mark a horizontal line on the wall at this height. Position the motorcycle 3.8 metres from the wall and draw a vertical line up the wall central to the centreline of the motorcycle. Switch to dipped beam and check that the beam pattern falls slightly lower than the horizontal line and to the left of the vertical line **(see illustration 2)**.

Headlight beam height checking equipment

Home workshop beam alignment check

MOT Test Checks REF•23

Exhaust System and Final Drive

Exhaust

✔ Check that the exhaust mountings are secure and that the system does not foul any of the rear suspension components.
✔ Start the motorcycle. When the revs are increased, check that the exhaust is neither holed nor leaking from any of its joints. On a linked system, check that the collector box is not leaking due to corrosion.
✔ Note that the exhaust decibel level ("loudness" of the exhaust) is assessed at the discretion of the tester. If the motorcycle was first used on or after 1st January 1985 the silencer must carry the BSAU 193 stamp, or a marking relating to its make and model, or be of OE (original equipment) manufacture. If the silencer is marked NOT FOR ROAD USE, RACING USE ONLY or similar, it will fail the MOT.

Final drive

✔ On chain or belt drive machines, check that the chain/belt is in good condition and does not have excessive slack. Also check that the sprocket is securely mounted on the rear wheel hub. Check that the chain/belt guard is in place.
✔ On shaft drive bikes, check for oil leaking from the drive unit and fouling the rear tyre.

Steering and Suspension

Steering

✔ With the front wheel raised off the ground, rotate the steering from lock to lock. The handlebar or switches must not contact the fuel tank or be close enough to trap the rider's hand. Problems can be caused by damaged lock stops on the lower yoke and frame, or by the fitting of non-standard handlebars.
✔ When performing the lock to lock check, also ensure that the steering moves freely without drag or notchiness. Steering movement can be impaired by poorly routed cables, or by overtight head bearings or worn bearings. The tester will perform a check of the steering head bearing lower race by mounting the front wheel on a surface plate, then performing a lock to lock check with the weight of the machine on the lower bearing (see illustration 3).
✔ Grasp the fork sliders (lower legs) and attempt to push and pull on the forks (see illustration 4). Any play in the steering head bearings will be felt. Note that in extreme cases, wear of the front fork bushes can be misinterpreted for head bearing play.
✔ Check that the handlebars are securely mounted.
✔ Check that the handlebar grip rubbers are secure. They should by bonded to the bar left end and to the throttle cable pulley on the right end.

Front suspension

✔ With the motorcycle off the stand, hold the front brake on and pump the front forks up and down (see illustration 5). Check that they are adequately damped.

Front wheel mounted on a surface plate for steering head bearing lower race check

Checking the steering head bearings for freeplay

Hold the front brake on and pump the front forks up and down to check operation

REF•24 MOT Test Checks

Inspect the area around the fork dust seal for oil leakage (arrow)

Bounce the rear of the motorcycle to check rear suspension operation

Checking for rear suspension linkage play

✔ Inspect the area above and around the front fork oil seals **(see illustration 6)**. There should be no sign of oil on the fork tube (stanchion) nor leaking down the slider (lower leg). On models so equipped, check that there is no oil leaking from the anti-dive units.

✔ On models with swingarm front suspension, check that there is no freeplay in the linkage when moved from side to side.

Rear suspension

✔ With the motorcycle off the stand and an assistant supporting the motorcycle by its handlebars, bounce the rear suspension **(see illustration 7)**. Check that the suspension components do not foul on any of the cycle parts and check that the shock absorber(s) provide adequate damping.

✔ Visually inspect the shock absorber(s) and check that there is no sign of oil leakage from its damper. This is somewhat restricted on certain single shock models due to the location of the shock absorber.

✔ With the rear wheel raised off the ground, grasp the wheel at the highest point and attempt to pull it up **(see illustration 8)**. Any play in the swingarm pivot or suspension linkage bearings will be felt as movement.

Note: *Do not confuse play with actual suspension movement.* Failure to lubricate suspension linkage bearings can lead to bearing failure **(see illustration 9)**.

✔ With the rear wheel raised off the ground, grasp the swingarm ends and attempt to move the swingarm from side to side and forwards and backwards - any play indicates wear of the swingarm pivot bearings **(see illustration 10)**.

Worn suspension linkage pivots (arrows) are usually the cause of play in the rear suspension

Grasp the swingarm at the ends to check for play in its pivot bearings

MOT Test Checks REF•25

Brake pad wear can usually be viewed without removing the caliper. Most pads have wear indicator grooves (1) and some also have indicator tangs (2)

On drum brakes, check the angle of the operating lever with the brake fully applied. Most drum brakes have a wear indicator pointer and scale.

Brakes, Wheels and Tyres

Brakes

✔ With the wheel raised off the ground, apply the brake then free it off, and check that the wheel is about to revolve freely without brake drag.

✔ On disc brakes, examine the disc itself. Check that it is securely mounted and not cracked.

✔ On disc brakes, view the pad material through the caliper mouth and check that the pads are not worn down beyond the limit **(see illustration 11)**.

✔ On drum brakes, check that when the brake is applied the angle between the operating lever and cable or rod is not too great **(see illustration 12)**. Check also that the operating lever doesn't foul any other components.

✔ On disc brakes, examine the flexible hoses from top to bottom. Have an assistant hold the brake on so that the fluid in the hose is under pressure, and check that there is no sign of fluid leakage, bulges or cracking. If there are any metal brake pipes or unions, check that these are free from corrosion and damage. Where a brake-linked anti-dive system is fitted, check the hoses to the anti-dive in a similar manner.

✔ Check that the rear brake torque arm is secure and that its fasteners are secured by self-locking nuts or castellated nuts with split-pins or R-pins **(see illustration 13)**.

✔ On models with ABS, check that the self-check warning light in the instrument panel works.

✔ The MOT tester will perform a test of the motorcycle's braking efficiency based on a calculation of rider and motorcycle weight. Although this cannot be carried out at home, you can at least ensure that the braking systems are properly maintained. For hydraulic disc brakes, check the fluid level, lever/pedal feel (bleed of air if its spongy) and pad material. For drum brakes, check adjustment, cable or rod operation and shoe lining thickness.

Wheels and tyres

✔ Check the wheel condition. Cast wheels should be free from cracks and if of the built-up design, all fasteners should be secure. Spoked wheels should be checked for broken, corroded, loose or bent spokes.

✔ With the wheel raised off the ground, spin the wheel and visually check that the tyre and wheel run true. Check that the tyre does not foul the suspension or mudguards.

✔ With the wheel raised off the ground, grasp the wheel and attempt to move it about the axle (spindle) **(see illustration 14)**. Any play felt here indicates wheel bearing failure.

Brake torque arm must be properly secured at both ends

Check for wheel bearing play by trying to move the wheel about the axle (spindle)

REF•26 MOT Test Checks

Checking the tyre tread depth

Tyre direction of rotation arrow can be found on tyre sidewall

Castellated type wheel axle (spindle) nut must be secured by a split pin or R-pin

Two straightedges are used to check wheel alignment

✔ Check the tyre tread depth, tread condition and sidewall condition **(see illustration 15)**.
✔ Check the tyre type. Front and rear tyre types must be compatible and be suitable for road use. Tyres marked NOT FOR ROAD USE, COMPETITION USE ONLY or similar, will fail the MOT.

✔ If the tyre sidewall carries a direction of rotation arrow, this must be pointing in the direction of normal wheel rotation **(see illustration 16)**.
✔ Check that the wheel axle (spindle) nuts (where applicable) are properly secured. A self-locking nut or castellated nut with a split-pin or R-pin can be used **(see illustration 17)**.
✔ Wheel alignment is checked with the motorcycle off the stand and a rider seated. With the front wheel pointing straight ahead, two perfectly straight lengths of metal or wood and placed against the sidewalls of both tyres **(see illustration 18)**. The gap each side of the front tyre must be equidistant on both sides. Incorrect wheel alignment may be due to a cocked rear wheel (often as the result of poor chain adjustment) or in extreme cases, a bent frame.

General checks and condition

✔ Check the security of all major fasteners, bodypanels, seat, fairings (where fitted) and mudguards.

✔ Check that the rider and pillion footrests, handlebar levers and brake pedal are securely mounted.

✔ Check for corrosion on the frame or any load-bearing components. If severe, this may affect the structure, particularly under stress.

Sidecars

A motorcycle fitted with a sidecar requires additional checks relating to the stability of the machine and security of attachment and swivel joints, plus specific wheel alignment (toe-in) requirements. Additionally, tyre and lighting requirements differ from conventional motorcycle use. Owners are advised to check MOT test requirements with an official test centre.

Storage REF•27

Preparing for storage

Before you start

If repairs or an overhaul is needed, see that this is carried out now rather than left until you want to ride the bike again.

Give the bike a good wash and scrub all dirt from its underside. Make sure the bike dries completely before preparing for storage.

Engine

● Remove the spark plug(s) and lubricate the cylinder bores with approximately a teaspoon of motor oil using a spout-type oil can **(see illustration 1)**. Reinstall the spark plug(s). Crank the engine over a couple of times to coat the piston rings and bores with oil. If the bike has a kickstart, use this to turn the engine over. If not, flick the kill switch to the OFF position and crank the engine over on the starter **(see illustration 2)**. If the nature on the ignition system prevents the starter operating with the kill switch in the OFF position, remove the spark plugs and fit them back in their caps; ensure that the plugs are earthed (grounded) against the cylinder head when the starter is operated **(see illustration 3)**.

⚠ **Warning: It is important that the plugs are earthed (grounded) away from the spark plug holes otherwise there is a risk of atomised fuel from the cylinders igniting.**

HAYNES HiNT *On a single cylinder four-stroke engine, you can seal the combustion chamber completely by positioning the piston at TDC on the compression stroke.*

● Drain the carburettor(s) otherwise there is a risk of jets becoming blocked by gum deposits from the fuel **(see illustration 4)**.

● If the bike is going into long-term storage, consider adding a fuel stabiliser to the fuel in the tank. If the tank is drained completely, corrosion of its internal surfaces may occur if left unprotected for a long period. The tank can be treated with a rust preventative especially for this purpose. Alternatively, remove the tank and pour half a litre of motor oil into it, install the filler cap and shake the tank to coat its internals with oil before draining off the excess. The same effect can also be achieved by spraying WD40 or a similar water-dispersant around the inside of the tank via its flexible nozzle.

● Make sure the cooling system contains the correct mix of antifreeze. Antifreeze also contains important corrosion inhibitors.

● The air intakes and exhaust can be sealed off by covering or plugging the openings. Ensure that you do not seal in any condensation; run the engine until it is hot,

1 Squirt a drop of motor oil into each cylinder

2 Flick the kill switch to OFF . . .

3 . . . and ensure that the metal bodies of the plugs (arrows) are earthed against the cylinder head

4 Connect a hose to the carburettor float chamber drain stub (arrow) and unscrew the drain screw

REF•28 Storage

Exhausts can be sealed off with a plastic bag

Disconnect the negative lead (A) first, followed by the positive lead (B)

Use a suitable battery charger - this kit also assess battery condition

then switch off and allow to cool. Tape a piece of thick plastic over the silencer end(s) **(see illustration 5)**. Note that some advocate pouring a tablespoon of motor oil into the silencer(s) before sealing them off.

Battery

● Remove it from the bike - in extreme cases of cold the battery may freeze and crack its case **(see illustration 6)**.

● Check the electrolyte level and top up if necessary (conventional refillable batteries). Clean the terminals.
● Store the battery off the motorcycle and away from any sources of fire. Position a wooden block under the battery if it is to sit on the ground.
● Give the battery a trickle charge for a few hours every month **(see illustration 7)**.

Tyres

● Place the bike on its centrestand or an auxiliary stand which will support the motorcycle in an upright position. Position wood blocks under the tyres to keep them off the ground and to provide insulation from damp. If the bike is being put into long-term storage, ideally both tyres should be off the ground; not only will this protect the tyres, but will also ensure that no load is placed on the steering head or wheel bearings.
● Deflate each tyre by 5 to 10 psi, no more or the beads may unseat from the rim, making subsequent inflation difficult on tubeless tyres.

Pivots and controls

● Lubricate all lever, pedal, stand and footrest pivot points. If grease nipples are fitted to the rear suspension components, apply lubricant to the pivots.
● Lubricate all control cables.

Cycle components

● Apply a wax protectant to all painted and plastic components. Wipe off any excess, but don't polish to a shine. Where fitted, clean the screen with soap and water.
● Coat metal parts with Vaseline (petroleum jelly). When applying this to the fork tubes, do not compress the forks otherwise the seals will rot from contact with the Vaseline.
● Apply a vinyl cleaner to the seat.

Storage conditions

● Aim to store the bike in a shed or garage which does not leak and is free from damp.
● Drape an old blanket or bedspread over the bike to protect it from dust and direct contact with sunlight (which will fade paint). This also hides the bike from prying eyes. Beware of tight-fitting plastic covers which may allow condensation to form and settle on the bike.

Getting back on the road

Engine and transmission

● Change the oil and replace the oil filter. If this was done prior to storage, check that the oil hasn't emulsified - a thick whitish substance which occurs through condensation.
● Remove the spark plugs. Using a spout-type oil can, squirt a few drops of oil into the cylinder(s). This will provide initial lubrication as the piston rings and bores comes back into contact. Service the spark plugs, or fit new ones, and install them in the engine.

● Check that the clutch isn't stuck on. The plates can stick together if left standing for some time, preventing clutch operation. Engage a gear and try rocking the bike back and forth with the clutch lever held against the handlebar. If this doesn't work on cable-operated clutches, hold the clutch lever back against the handlebar with a strong elastic band or cable tie for a couple of hours **(see illustration 8)**.
● If the air intakes or silencer end(s) were blocked off, remove the bung or cover used.
● If the fuel tank was coated with a rust

Hold clutch lever back against the handlebar with elastic bands or a cable tie

Storage

preventative, oil or a stabiliser added to the fuel, drain and flush the tank and dispose of the fuel sensibly. If no action was taken with the fuel tank prior to storage, it is advised that the old fuel is disposed of since it will go off over a period of time. Refill the fuel tank with fresh fuel.

Frame and running gear

● Oil all pivot points and cables.
● Check the tyre pressures. They will definitely need inflating if pressures were reduced for storage.
● Lubricate the final drive chain (where applicable).
● Remove any protective coating applied to the fork tubes (stanchions) since this may well destroy the fork seals. If the fork tubes weren't protected and have picked up rust spots, remove them with very fine abrasive paper and refinish with metal polish.
● Check that both brakes operate correctly. Apply each brake hard and check that it's not possible to move the motorcycle forwards, then check that the brake frees off again once released. Brake caliper pistons can stick due to corrosion around the piston head, or on the sliding caliper types, due to corrosion of the slider pins. If the brake doesn't free after repeated operation, take the caliper off for examination. Similarly drum brakes can stick due to a seized operating cam, cable or rod linkage.
● If the motorcycle has been in long-term storage, renew the brake fluid and clutch fluid (where applicable).
● Depending on where the bike has been stored, the wiring, cables and hoses may have been nibbled by rodents. Make a visual check and investigate disturbed wiring loom tape.

Battery

● If the battery has been previously removal and given top up charges it can simply be reconnected. Remember to connect the positive cable first and the negative cable last.
● On conventional refillable batteries, if the battery has not received any attention, remove it from the motorcycle and check its electrolyte level. Top up if necessary then charge the battery. If the battery fails to hold a charge and a visual checks show heavy white sulphation of the plates, the battery is probably defective and must be renewed. This is particularly likely if the battery is old. Confirm battery condition with a specific gravity check.
● On sealed (MF) batteries, if the battery has not received any attention, remove it from the motorcycle and charge it according to the information on the battery case - if the battery fails to hold a charge it must be renewed.

Starting procedure

● If a kickstart is fitted, turn the engine over a couple of times with the ignition OFF to distribute oil around the engine. If no kickstart is fitted, flick the engine kill switch OFF and the ignition ON and crank the engine over a couple of times to work oil around the upper cylinder components. If the nature of the ignition system is such that the starter won't work with the kill switch OFF, remove the spark plugs, fit them back into their caps and earth (ground) their bodies on the cylinder head. Reinstall the spark plugs afterwards.
● Switch the kill switch to RUN, operate the choke and start the engine. If the engine won't start don't continue cranking the engine - not only will this flatten the battery, but the starter motor will overheat. Switch the ignition off and try again later. If the engine refuses to start, go through the fault finding procedures in this manual. **Note:** *If the bike has been in storage for a long time, old fuel or a carburettor blockage may be the problem. Gum deposits in carburettors can block jets - if a carburettor cleaner doesn't prove successful the carburettors must be dismantled for cleaning.*
● Once the engine has started, check that the lights, turn signals and horn work properly.
● Treat the bike gently for the first ride and check all fluid levels on completion. Settle the bike back into the maintenance schedule.

Motorcycle Chemicals and Lubricants

A number of chemicals and lubricants are available for use in motorcycle maintenance and repair. They include a wide variety of products ranging from cleaning solvents and degreasers to lubricants and protective sprays for rubber, plastic and vinyl.

● **Contact point/spark plug cleaner** is a solvent used to clean oily film and dirt from points, grime from electrical connectors and oil deposits from spark plugs. It is oil free and leaves no residue. It can also be used to remove gum and varnish from carburettor jets and other orifices.

● **Carburettor cleaner** is similar to contact point/spark plug cleaner but it usually has a stronger solvent and may leave a slight oily reside. It is not recommended for cleaning electrical components or connections.

● **Brake system cleaner** is used to remove grease or brake fluid from brake system components (where clean surfaces are absolutely necessary and petroleum-based solvents cannot be used); it also leaves no residue.

● **Silicone-based lubricants** are used to protect rubber parts such as hoses and grommets, and are used as lubricants for hinges and locks.

● **Multi-purpose grease** is an all purpose lubricant used wherever grease is more practical than a liquid lubricant such as oil. Some multi-purpose grease is coloured white and specially formulated to be more resistant to water than ordinary grease.

● **Gear oil** (sometimes called gear lube) is a specially designed oil used in transmissions and final drive units, as well as other areas where high friction, high temperature lubrication is required. It is available in a number of viscosities (weights) for various applications.

● **Motor oil**, of course, is the lubricant specially formulated for use in the engine. It normally contains a wide variety of additives to prevent corrosion and reduce foaming and wear. Motor oil comes in various weights (viscosity ratings) of from 5 to 80. The recommended weight of the oil depends on the seasonal temperature and the demands on the engine. Light oil is used in cold climates and under light load conditions; heavy oil is used in hot climates and where high loads are encountered. Multi-viscosity oils are designed to have characteristics of both light and heavy oils and are available in a number of weights from 5W-20 to 20W-50.

● **Petrol additives** perform several functions, depending on their chemical makeup. They usually contain solvents that help dissolve gum and varnish that build up on carburettor and inlet parts. They also serve to break down carbon deposits that form on the inside surfaces of the combustion chambers. Some additives contain upper cylinder lubricants for valves and piston rings.

● **Brake and clutch fluid** is a specially formulated hydraulic fluid that can withstand the heat and pressure encountered in brake/clutch systems. Care must be taken that this fluid does not come in contact with painted surfaces or plastics. An opened container should always be resealed to prevent contamination by water or dirt.

● **Chain lubricants** are formulated especially for use on motorcycle final drive chains. A good chain lube should adhere well and have good penetrating qualities to be effective as a lubricant inside the chain and on the side plates, pins and rollers. Most chain lubes are either the foaming type or quick drying type and are usually marketed as sprays. Take care to use a lubricant marked as being suitable for O-ring chains.

● **Degreasers** are heavy duty solvents used to remove grease and grime that may accumulate on engine and frame components. They can be sprayed or brushed on and, depending on the type, are rinsed with either water or solvent.

● **Solvents** are used alone or in combination with degreasers to clean parts and assemblies during repair and overhaul. The home mechanic should use only solvents that are non-flammable and that do not produce irritating fumes.

● **Gasket sealing compounds** may be used in conjunction with gaskets, to improve their sealing capabilities, or alone, to seal metal-to-metal joints. Many gasket sealers can withstand extreme heat, some are impervious to petrol and lubricants, while others are capable of filling and sealing large cavities. Depending on the intended use, gasket sealers either dry hard or stay relatively soft and pliable. They are usually applied by hand, with a brush, or are sprayed on the gasket sealing surfaces.

● **Thread locking compound** is an adhesive locking compound that prevents threaded fasteners from loosening because of vibration. It is available in a variety of types for different applications.

● **Moisture dispersants** are usually sprays that can be used to dry out electrical components such as the fuse block and wiring connectors. Some types can also be used as treatment for rubber and as a lubricant for hinges, cables and locks.

● **Waxes and polishes** are used to help protect painted and plated surfaces from the weather. Different types of paint may require the use of different types of wax polish. Some polishes utilise a chemical or abrasive cleaner to help remove the top layer of oxidised (dull) paint on older vehicles. In recent years, many non-wax polishes (that contain a wide variety of chemicals such as polymers and silicones) have been introduced. These non-wax polishes are usually easier to apply and last longer than conventional waxes and polishes.

Fault Finding   REF•31

This Section provides an easy reference-guide to the more common faults that are likely to afflict your machine. Obviously, the opportunities are almost limitless for faults to occur as a result of obscure failures, and to try and cover all eventualities would require a book. Indeed, a number have been written on the subject.

Successful troubleshooting is not a mysterious 'black art' but the application of a bit of knowledge combined with a systematic and logical approach to the problem. Approach any troubleshooting by first accurately identifying the symptom and then checking through the list of possible causes, starting with the simplest or most obvious and progressing in stages to the most complex.

Take nothing for granted, but above all apply liberal quantities of common sense.

The main symptom of a fault is given in the text as a major heading below which are listed the various systems or areas which may contain the fault. Details of each possible cause for a fault and the remedial action to be taken are given, in brief, in the paragraphs below each heading. Further information should be sought in the relevant Chapter.

1 Engine doesn't start or is difficult to start
- [ ] Starter motor doesn't rotate
- [ ] Starter motor rotates but engine does not turn over
- [ ] Starter works but engine won't turn over (seized)
- [ ] No fuel flow
- [ ] Engine flooded
- [ ] No spark or weak spark
- [ ] Compression low
- [ ] Stalls after starting
- [ ] Rough idle

2 Poor running at low speed
- [ ] Spark weak
- [ ] Fuel/air mixture incorrect
- [ ] Compression low
- [ ] Poor acceleration

3 Poor running or no power at high speed
- [ ] Firing incorrect
- [ ] Fuel/air mixture incorrect
- [ ] Compression low
- [ ] Knocking or pinging
- [ ] Miscellaneous causes

4 Overheating
- [ ] Engine overheats
- [ ] Firing incorrect
- [ ] Fuel/air mixture incorrect
- [ ] Compression too high
- [ ] Engine load excessive
- [ ] Lubrication inadequate
- [ ] Miscellaneous causes

5 Clutch problems
- [ ] Clutch slipping
- [ ] Clutch not disengaging completely

6 Gear shifting problems
- [ ] Doesn't go into gear, or lever doesn't return
- [ ] Jumps out of gear
- [ ] Overshifts

7 Abnormal engine noise
- [ ] Knocking or pinging
- [ ] Piston slap or rattling
- [ ] Valve noise
- [ ] Other noise

8 Abnormal driveline noise
- [ ] Clutch noise
- [ ] Transmission noise
- [ ] Chain or final drive noise

9 Abnormal frame and suspension noise
- [ ] Front end noise
- [ ] Shock absorber noise
- [ ] Brake noise

10 Oil level indicator light comes on
- [ ] Engine lubrication system
- [ ] Electrical system

11 Excessive exhaust smoke
- [ ] White smoke
- [ ] Black smoke
- [ ] Brown smoke

12 Poor handling or stability
- [ ] Handlebar hard to turn
- [ ] Handlebar shakes or vibrates excessively
- [ ] Handlebar pulls to one side
- [ ] Poor shock absorbing qualities

13 Braking problems
- [ ] Brakes are spongy, don't hold
- [ ] Brake lever or pedal pulsates
- [ ] Brakes drag

14 Electrical problems
- [ ] Battery dead or weak
- [ ] Battery overcharged

REF•32 Fault Finding

1 Engine doesn't start or is difficult to start

Starter motor does not rotate

- [ ] Engine kill switch Off.
- [ ] Fuse blown. Check fuse block (Chapter 10).
- [ ] Battery voltage low. Check and recharge battery (Chapter 10).
- [ ] Starter motor defective. Make sure the wiring to the starter is secure. Make sure the starter relay clicks when the start button is pushed. If the relay clicks, then the fault is in the wiring or motor.
- [ ] Starter relay faulty. Check it according to the procedure in Chapter 10.
- [ ] Starter button not contacting. The contacts could be wet, corroded or dirty. Disassemble and clean the switch (Chapter 10).
- [ ] Wiring open or shorted. Check all wiring connections and harnesses to make sure that they are dry, tight and not corroded. Also check for broken or frayed wires that can cause a short to ground (see wiring diagram, Chapter 10).
- [ ] Ignition switch defective. Check the switch according to the procedure in Chapter 10. Replace the switch with a new one if it is defective.
- [ ] Engine kill switch defective. Check for wet, dirty or corroded contacts. Clean or replace the switch as necessary (Chapter 10).
- [ ] Faulty starter lockout circuit. Check the wiring and the switch itself according to the procedures in Chapter 10.

Starter motor rotates but engine does not turn over

- [ ] Starter motor clutch defective. Inspect and repair or replace (Chapter 2 or Chapter 3).
- [ ] Damaged idler or starter gears. Inspect and replace the damaged parts (Chapter 2 or Chapter 3).

Starter works but engine won't turn over (seized)

- [ ] Seized engine caused by one or more internally damaged components. Failure due to wear, abuse or lack of lubrication. Damage can include seized valves, valve lifters, camshaft, pistons, crankshaft, connecting rod bearings, or transmission gears or bearings. Refer to Chapter 2 or Chapter 3 for engine disassembly.

No fuel flow

- [ ] No fuel in tank.
- [ ] Fuel tap in off position.
- [ ] Tank cap air vent obstructed. Usually caused by dirt or water. Remove it and clean the cap vent hole.
- [ ] Inline fuel filter clogged. Replace the filter (Chapter 1).
- [ ] Electric fuel pump not working. Test it according to the procedures in Chapter 5.
- [ ] Fuel line clogged. Pull the fuel line loose and carefully blow through it.
- [ ] Inlet needle valve clogged. For all of the valves to be clogged, either a very bad batch of fuel with an unusual additive has been used, or some other foreign material has entered the tank. Many times after a machine has been stored for many months without running, the fuel turns to a varnish-like liquid and forms deposits on the inlet needle valves and jets. The carburetors should be removed and overhauled if draining the float bowls doesn't solve the problem.

Engine flooded

- [ ] Float level too high. Check and adjust as described in Chapter 5.
- [ ] Inlet needle valve worn or stuck open. A piece of dirt, rust or other debris can cause the inlet needle to seat improperly, causing excess fuel to be admitted to the float bowl. In this case, the float chamber should be cleaned and the needle and seat inspected. If the needle and seat are worn, then the leaking will persist and the parts should be replaced with new ones (Chapter 5).
- [ ] Starting technique incorrect. Under normal circumstances (i.e., if all the carburetor functions are sound) the machine should start with little or no throttle. When the engine is cold, the choke should be operated and the engine started without opening the throttle. When the engine is at operating temperature, only a very slight amount of throttle should be necessary. If the engine is flooded, turn the fuel tap off and hold the throttle open while cranking the engine. This will allow additional air to reach the cylinders. Remember to turn the fuel tap back on after the engine starts.

No spark or weak spark

- [ ] Ignition switch Off.
- [ ] Engine kill switch turned to the Off position.
- [ ] Battery voltage low. Check and recharge battery as necessary (Chapter 10).
- [ ] Spark plug dirty, defective or worn out. Locate reason for fouled plug(s) using spark plug condition chart and follow the plug maintenance procedures in Chapter 1.
- [ ] Spark plug cap or secondary (HT) wiring faulty. Check condition. Replace either or both components if cracks or deterioration are evident (Chapter 6).
- [ ] Spark plug cap not making good contact. Make sure that the plug cap fits snugly over the plug end.
- [ ] Igniter defective. Check the unit, referring to Chapter 6 for details.
- [ ] Signal generator defective. Check the unit, referring to Chapter 6 for details.
- [ ] Ignition coil(s) defective. Check the coils, referring to Chapter 6.
- [ ] Ignition or kill switch shorted. This is usually caused by water, corrosion, damage or excessive wear. The switches can be disassembled and cleaned with electrical contact cleaner. If cleaning does not help, replace the switches (Chapter 10).
- [ ] Wiring shorted or broken between:
  Ignition switch and engine kill switch (or blown fuse)
  Igniter and engine kill switch
  Igniter and ignition coil
  Ignition coil and plug
  Igniter and signal generator
- [ ] Make sure that all wiring connections are clean, dry and tight. Look for chafed and broken wires (Chapters 6 and 10).

Compression low

- [ ] Spark plug loose. Remove the plug and inspect the threads. Reinstall and tighten to the specified torque (Chapter 1).
- [ ] Cylinder head not sufficiently tightened down. If the cylinder head is suspected of being loose, then there's a chance that the gasket or head is damaged if the problem has persisted for any length of time. The head nuts should be tightened to the proper torque in the correct sequence (Chapter 2 or Chapter 3).
- [ ] Improper valve clearance. This means that the valve is not closing completely and compression pressure is leaking past the valve. Check and adjust the valve clearances (Chapter 1).
- [ ] Cylinder and/or piston worn. Excessive wear will cause compression pressure to leak past the rings. This is usually accompanied by worn rings as well. A top end overhaul is necessary (Chapter 2 or Chapter 3).
- [ ] Piston rings worn, weak, broken, or sticking. Broken or sticking piston rings usually indicate a lubrication or carburetion problem that causes excess carbon deposits or seizures to form on the pistons and rings. Top end overhaul is necessary (Chapter 2 or Chapter 3).
- [ ] Piston ring-to-groove clearance excessive. This is caused by excessive wear of the piston ring lands. Piston replacement is necessary (Chapter 2 or Chapter 3).
- [ ] Cylinder head gasket damaged. If the head is allowed to become loose, or if excessive carbon build-up on the piston crown and combustion chamber causes extremely high compression, the head gasket may leak. Retorquing the head is not always sufficient to restore the seal, so gasket replacement is necessary (Chapter 2 or Chapter 3).

Fault Finding REF•33

- [ ] Cylinder head warped. This is caused by overheating or improperly tightened head nuts. Machine shop resurfacing or head replacement is necessary (Chapter 2 or Chapter 3).
- [ ] Valve spring broken or weak. Caused by component failure or wear; the spring(s) must be replaced (Chapter 2 or Chapter 3).
- [ ] Valve not seating properly. This is caused by a bent valve (from over-revving or improper valve adjustment), burned valve or seat (improper carburetion) or an accumulation of carbon deposits on the seat (from carburetion or lubrication problems). The valves must be cleaned and/or replaced and the seats serviced if possible (Chapter 2 or Chapter 3).

Stalls after starting

- [ ] Improper choke action. Make sure the choke rod is getting a full stroke and staying in the out position.
- [ ] Ignition malfunction. See Chapter 6.
- [ ] Carburetor malfunction. See Chapter 5.
- [ ] Fuel contaminated. The fuel can be contaminated with either dirt or water, or can change chemically if the machine is allowed to sit for several months or more. Drain the tank and float bowls (Chapter 5).
- [ ] Intake air leak. Check for loose carburetor-to-intake manifold connections, loose or missing vacuum gauge access port cap or hose, or loose carburetor top (Chapter 5).
- [ ] Engine idle speed incorrect. Turn throttle stop screw until the engine idles at the specified rpm (Chapter 1).

Rough idle

- [ ] Ignition malfunction. See Chapter 6.
- [ ] Idle speed incorrect. See Chapter 1.
- [ ] Carburetors not synchronized. Adjust carburetors with vacuum gauge or manometer set as described in Chapter 1.
- [ ] Carburetor malfunction. See Chapter 5.
- [ ] Fuel contaminated. The fuel can be contaminated with either dirt or water, or can change chemically if the machine is allowed to sit for several months or more. Drain the tank and float bowls (Chapter 5).
- [ ] Intake air leak. Check for loose carburetor-to-intake manifold connections, loose or missing vacuum gauge access port cap or hose, or loose carburetor top (Chapter 5).
- [ ] Air cleaner clogged. Service or replace air filter element (Chapter 1).

2 Poor running at low speed

Spark weak

- [ ] Battery voltage low. Check and recharge battery (Chapter 10).
- [ ] Spark plug fouled, defective or worn out. Refer to Chapter 1 for spark plug maintenance.
- [ ] Spark plug cap or high tension wiring defective. Refer to Chapters 1 and 6 for details on the ignition system.
- [ ] Spark plug cap not making contact.
- [ ] Incorrect spark plug. Wrong type, heat range or cap configuration. Check and install correct plugs listed in Chapter 1. A cold plug or one with a recessed firing electrode will not operate at low speeds without fouling.
- [ ] Igniter defective. See Chapter 6.
- [ ] Signal generator defective. See Chapter 6.
- [ ] Ignition coil(s) defective. See Chapter 6.

Fuel/air mixture incorrect

- [ ] Pilot screw(s) out of adjustment (Chapters 1 and 5).
- [ ] Pilot jet or air passage clogged. Remove and overhaul the carburetors (Chapter 5).
- [ ] Air bleed holes clogged. Remove carburetor and blow out all passages (Chapter 5).
- [ ] Air cleaner clogged, poorly sealed or missing.
- [ ] Air cleaner-to-carburetor boot poorly sealed. Look for cracks, holes or loose clamps and replace or repair defective parts.
- [ ] Fuel level too high or too low. Adjust the floats (Chapter 5).
- [ ] Fuel tank air vent obstructed. Make sure that the air vent passage in the filler cap is open.
- [ ] Carburetor intake manifolds loose. Check for cracks, breaks, tears or loose clamps or bolts. Repair or replace the rubber boots.

Compression low

- [ ] Spark plug loose. Remove the plug and inspect the threads. Reinstall and tighten to the specified torque (Chapter 1).
- [ ] Cylinder head not sufficiently tightened down. If the cylinder head is suspected of being loose, then there's a chance that the gasket and head are damaged if the problem has persisted for any length of time. The head nuts should be tightened to the proper torque in the correct sequence (Chapter 2 or Chapter 3).
- [ ] Improper valve clearance. This means that the valve is not closing completely and compression pressure is leaking past the valve. Check and adjust the valve clearances (Chapter 1).
- [ ] Cylinder and/or piston worn. Excessive wear will cause compression pressure to leak past the rings. This is usually accompanied by worn rings as well. A top end overhaul is necessary (Chapter 2 or Chapter 3).
- [ ] Piston rings worn, weak, broken, or sticking. Broken or sticking piston rings usually indicate a lubrication or carburetion problem that causes excess carbon deposits or seizures to form on the pistons and rings. Top end overhaul is necessary (Chapter 2 or Chapter 3).
- [ ] Piston ring-to-groove clearance excessive. This is caused by excessive wear of the piston ring lands. Piston replacement is necessary (Chapter 2 or Chapter 3).
- [ ] Cylinder head gasket damaged. If the head is allowed to become loose, or if excessive carbon build-up on the piston crown and combustion chamber causes extremely high compression, the head gasket may leak. Retorquing the head is not always sufficient to restore the seal, so gasket replacement is necessary (Chapter 2 or Chapter 3).
- [ ] Cylinder head warped. This is caused by overheating or improperly tightened head nuts. Machine shop resurfacing or head replacement is necessary (Chapter 2 or Chapter 3).
- [ ] Valve spring broken or weak. Caused by component failure or wear; the spring(s) must be replaced (Chapter 2 or Chapter 3).
- [ ] Valve not seating properly. This is caused by a bent valve (from over-revving or improper valve adjustment), burned valve or seat (improper carburetion) or an accumulation of carbon deposits on the seat (from carburetion, lubrication problems). The valves must be cleaned and/or replaced and the seats serviced if possible (Chapter 2 or Chapter 3).

Poor acceleration

- [ ] Carburetors leaking or dirty. Overhaul the carburetors (Chapter 5).
- [ ] Timing not advancing. The signal generator or the igniter may be defective. If so, they must be replaced with new ones, as they can't be repaired.
- [ ] Carburetors not synchronized. Adjust them with a vacuum gauge set or manometer (Chapter 1).
- [ ] Engine oil viscosity too high. Using a heavier oil than that recommended in Chapter 1 can damage the oil pump or lubrication system and cause drag on the engine.
- [ ] Brakes dragging. Usually caused by debris which has entered the brake piston sealing boot, or from a warped disc or bent axle. Repair as necessary (Chapter 8).

REF•34 Fault Finding

3 Poor running or no power at high speed

Firing incorrect

- ☐ Air filter restricted. Clean or replace filter (Chapter 1).
- ☐ Spark plug fouled, defective or worn out. See Chapter 1 for spark plug maintenance.
- ☐ Spark plug cap or secondary (HT) wiring defective. See Chapters 1 and 6 for details of the ignition system.
- ☐ Spark plug cap not in good contact. See Chapter 6.
- ☐ Incorrect spark plug. Wrong type, heat range or cap configuration. Check and install correct plugs listed in Chapter 1. A cold plug or one with a recessed firing electrode will not operate at low speeds without fouling.
- ☐ Igniter defective. See Chapter 6.
- ☐ Ignition coil(s) defective. See Chapter 6.

Fuel/air mixture incorrect

- ☐ Main jet clogged. Dirt, water or other contaminants can clog the main jets. Replace the fuel filter and clean the float bowl area, and the jets and carburetor orifices (Chapter 5).
- ☐ Main jet wrong size. The standard jetting is for sea level atmospheric pressure and oxygen content.
- ☐ Throttle shaft-to-carburetor body clearance excessive. Refer to Chapter 5 for inspection and part replacement procedures.
- ☐ Air bleed holes clogged. Remove and overhaul carburetors (Chapter 5).
- ☐ Air filter clogged, poorly sealed, or missing.
- ☐ Air filter-to-carburetor boot poorly sealed. Look for cracks, holes or loose clamps, and replace or repair defective parts.
- ☐ Fuel level too high or too low. Adjust the float(s) (Chapter 5).
- ☐ Fuel tank air vent obstructed. Make sure the air vent passage in the filler cap is open.
- ☐ Carburetor intake manifolds loose. Check for cracks, breaks, tears or loose clamps or bolts. Repair or replace the rubber boots (Chapter 5).
- ☐ Fuel tap clogged. Remove the tap and clean it (Chapter 5).
- ☐ Fuel line clogged. Pull the fuel line loose and carefully blow through it.
- ☐ Fuel Filter clogged. Replace it.

Compression low

- ☐ Spark plug loose. Remove the plug and inspect the threads. Reinstall and tighten to the specified torque (Chapter 1).
- ☐ Cylinder head not sufficiently tightened down. If the cylinder head is suspected of being loose, then there's a chance that the gasket and head are damaged if the problem has persisted for any length of time. The head nuts should be tightened to the proper torque in the correct sequence (Chapter 2 or Chapter 3).
- ☐ Improper valve clearance. This means that the valve is not closing completely and compression pressure is leaking past the valve. Check and adjust the valve clearances (Chapter 1).
- ☐ Cylinder and/or piston worn. Excessive wear will cause compression pressure to leak past the rings. This is usually accompanied by worn rings as well. A top end overhaul is necessary (Chapter 2 or Chapter 3).
- ☐ Piston rings worn, weak, broken, or sticking. Broken or sticking piston rings usually indicate a lubrication or carburetion problem that causes excess carbon deposits or seizures to form on the pistons and rings. Top end overhaul is necessary (Chapter 2 or Chapter 3).
- ☐ Piston ring-to-groove clearance excessive. This is caused by excessive wear of the piston ring lands. Piston replacement is necessary (Chapter 2 or Chapter 3).
- ☐ Cylinder head gasket damaged. If the head is allowed to become loose, or if excessive carbon build-up on the piston crown and combustion chamber causes extremely high compression, the head gasket may leak. Retorquing the head is not always sufficient to restore the seal, so gasket replacement is necessary (Chapter 2 or Chapter 3).
- ☐ Cylinder head warped. This is caused by overheating or improperly tightened head nuts. Machine shop resurfacing or head replacement is necessary (Chapter 2 or Chapter 3).
- ☐ Valve spring broken or weak. Caused by component failure or wear; the spring(s) must be replaced (Chapter 2 or Chapter 3).
- ☐ Valve not seating properly. This is caused by a bent valve (from over-revving or improper valve adjustment), burned valve or seat (improper carburetion) or an accumulation of carbon deposits on the seat (from carburetion or lubrication problems). The valves must be cleaned and/or replaced and the seats serviced if possible (Chapter 2 or Chapter 3).

Knocking or pinging

- ☐ Carbon build-up in combustion chamber. Use of a fuel additive that will dissolve the adhesive bonding the carbon particles to the crown and chamber is the easiest way to remove the build-up. Otherwise, the cylinder head will have to be removed and decarbonized (Chapter 2 or Chapter 3).
- ☐ Incorrect or poor quality fuel. Old or improper grades of fuel can cause detonation. This causes the piston to rattle, thus the knocking or pinging sound. Drain old fuel and always use the recommended fuel grade.
- ☐ Spark plug heat range incorrect. Uncontrolled detonation indicates the plug heat range is too hot. The plug in effect becomes a glow plug, raising cylinder temperatures. Install the proper heat range plug (Chapter 1).
- ☐ Improper air/fuel mixture. This will cause the cylinder to run hot, which leads to detonation. Clogged jets or an air leak can cause this imbalance. See Chapter 5.

Miscellaneous causes

- ☐ Throttle valve doesn't open fully. Adjust the cable slack (Chapter 1).
- ☐ Clutch slipping. May be caused by a cable that is improperly adjusted (FZR600 and UK F2R750 models) or loose or worn clutch components. Refer to Chapter 1 for cable adjustment and Chapter 2 or Chapter 3 for clutch component replacement.
- ☐ Timing not advancing.
- ☐ Engine oil viscosity too high. Using a heavier oil than the one recommended in Chapter 1 can damage the oil pump or lubrication system and cause drag on the engine.
- ☐ Brakes dragging. Usually caused by debris which has entered the brake piston sealing boot, or from a warped disc or bent axle. Repair as necessary.

Fault Finding REF•35

4 Overheating

Engine overheats

- [ ] Coolant level low. Check coolant level as described in Chapter 1. If coolant level is low, the engine will overheat.
- [ ] Leak in cooling system. Check cooling system hoses and radiator for leaks and other damage. Repair or replace parts as necessary (Chapter 4).
- [ ] Thermostat stuck closed. Check and replace as described in Chapter 5.
- [ ] Faulty radiator cap. Remove the cap and have it pressure checked.
- [ ] Coolant passages clogged. Drain and flush the entire system, then refill with new coolant.
- [ ] Water pump defective. Remove the pump and check the components.
- [ ] Clogged radiator fins. Clean them by blowing compressed air through the fins from the back side.
- [ ] Engine oil level low. Check and add oil ('Daily (pre-ride) checks').
- [ ] Wrong type of oil. If you're not sure what type of oil is in the engine, drain it and fill with the correct type (Chapter 1).
- [ ] Air leak at carburetor intake boots. Check and tighten or replace as necessary (Chapter 5).
- [ ] Float level low. Check and adjust if necessary (Chapter 5).
- [ ] Worn oil pump or clogged oil passages. Check oil pressure (Chapter 2 or Chapter 3). Replace pump or clean passages as necessary.
- [ ] Clogged oil cooler or lines (if equipped). Remove and check for foreign material (see Chapter 2 or Chapter 3).
- [ ] Carbon build-up in combustion chambers. Use of a fuel additive that will dissolve the adhesive bonding the carbon particles to the piston crowns and chambers is the easiest way to remove the build-up. Otherwise, the cylinder head will have to be removed and decarbonized (Chapter 2 or Chapter 3).

Firing incorrect

- [ ] Spark plug fouled, defective or worn out. See Chapter 1 for spark plug maintenance.
- [ ] Incorrect spark plug (see Chapter 1).
- [ ] Faulty ignition coil(s) (Chapter 6).

Fuel/air mixture incorrect

- [ ] Main jet clogged. Dirt, water and other contaminants can clog the main jets. Clean the fuel tap filter, the float bowl area and the jets and carburetor orifices (Chapter 5).
- [ ] Main jet wrong size. The standard jetting is for sea level atmospheric pressure and oxygen content.
- [ ] Air filter poorly sealed or missing.
- [ ] Air filter-to-carburetor boot poorly sealed. Look for cracks, holes or loose clamps and replace or repair.
- [ ] Fuel level too low. Adjust the float(s) (Chapter 5).
- [ ] Fuel tank air vent obstructed. Make sure that the air vent passage in the filler cap is open.
- [ ] Carburetor intake manifolds loose. Check for cracks, breaks, tears or loose clamps or bolts. Repair or replace the rubber boots (Chapter 5).

Compression too high

- [ ] Carbon build-up in combustion chamber. Use of a fuel additive that will dissolve the adhesive bonding the carbon particles to the piston crown and chamber is the easiest way to remove the build-up. Otherwise, the cylinder head will have to be removed and decarbonized (Chapter 2 or Chapter 3).
- [ ] Improperly machined head surface or installation of incorrect gasket during engine assembly.

Engine load excessive

- [ ] Clutch slipping. Can be caused by damaged, loose or worn clutch components. Refer to Chapter 2 or Chapter 3 for overhaul procedures.
- [ ] Engine oil level too high. The addition of too much oil will cause pressurization of the crankcase and inefficient engine operation. Check Specifications and drain to proper level (Chapter 1).
- [ ] Engine oil viscosity too high. Using a heavier oil than the one recommended in Chapter 1 can damage the oil pump or lubrication system as well as cause drag on the engine.
- [ ] Brakes dragging. Usually caused by debris which has entered the brake piston sealing boot, or from a warped disc or bent axle. Repair as necessary.

Lubrication inadequate

- [ ] Engine oil level too low. Friction caused by intermittent lack of lubrication or from oil that is overworked can cause overheating. The oil provides a definite cooling function in the engine. Check the oil level ('Daily (pre-ride) checks').
- [ ] Poor quality engine oil or incorrect viscosity or type. Oil is rated not only according to viscosity but also according to type. Some oils are not rated high enough for use in this engine. Check the Specifications section and change to the correct oil (Chapter 1).
- [ ] Camshaft or journals worn. Excessive wear causing drop in oil pressure. Replace cam and/or cylinder head. Abnormal wear could be caused by oil starvation at high rpm from low oil level or improper weight or type of oil (Chapter 1).
- [ ] Crankshaft and/or bearings worn. Same problems as paragraph 3. Check and replace crankshaft and/or bearings (Chapter 2 or Chapter 3).

Miscellaneous causes

- [ ] Modification to exhaust system. Most aftermarket exhaust systems cause the engine to run leaner, which make them run hotter. When installing an accessory exhaust system, always rejet the carburetors.

5 Clutch problems

Clutch slipping
- ☐ Friction plates worn or warped. Overhaul the clutch assembly (Chapter 2 or Chapter 3).
- ☐ Steel plates worn or warped (Chapter 2 or Chapter 3).
- ☐ Clutch springs broken or weak. Old or heat-damaged springs (from slipping clutch) should be replaced with new ones (Chapter 2 or Chapter 3).
- ☐ Worn or warped clutch plates. Replace (Chapter 2 or Chapter 3).
- ☐ Clutch release mechanism defective. Replace any defective parts (Chapter 2 or Chapter 3).
- ☐ Clutch boss or housing unevenly worn. This causes improper engagement of the plates. Replace the damaged or worn parts (Chapter 2 or Chapter 3).

Clutch not disengaging completely
- ☐ Clutch lever play excessive (see Chapter 1). Clutch cable improperly adjusted or hydraulic components worn. Adjust cable (Chapter 1) or repair hydraulic components (Chapter 3).
- ☐ Clutch plates warped or damaged. This will cause clutch drag, which in turn will cause the machine to creep. Overhaul the clutch assembly (Chapter 2 or Chapter 3).
- ☐ Clutch spring tension uneven. Usually caused by a sagged or broken spring. Check and replace the springs (Chapter 2 or Chapter 3).
- ☐ Engine oil deteriorated. Old, thin, worn out oil will not provide proper lubrication for the plates, causing the clutch to drag. Replace the oil and filter (Chapter 1).
- ☐ Engine oil viscosity too high. Using a heavier oil than recommended in Chapter 1 can cause the plates to stick together, putting a drag on the engine. Change to the correct weight oil (Chapter 1).
- ☐ Clutch housing seized on shaft. Lack of lubrication, severe wear or damage can cause the housing to seize on the shaft. Overhaul of the clutch, and perhaps transmission, may be necessary to repair the damage (Chapter 2 or Chapter 3).
- ☐ Clutch release mechanism defective. Worn or damaged release mechanism parts can stick and fail to apply force to the pressure plate. Overhaul the release mechanism (Chapter 2 or Chapter 3).
- ☐ Loose clutch hub nut. Causes housing and boss misalignment putting a drag on the engine. Engagement adjustment continually varies. Overhaul the clutch assembly (Chapter 2 or Chapter 3).

6 Gear shifting problems

Doesn't go into gear or lever doesn't return
- ☐ Clutch not disengaging. See above.
- ☐ Shift fork(s) bent or seized. Often caused by dropping the machine or from lack of lubrication. Overhaul the transmission (Chapter 2 or Chapter 3).
- ☐ Gear(s) stuck on shaft. Most often caused by a lack of lubrication or excessive wear in transmission bearings and bushings. Overhaul the transmission (Chapter 2 or Chapter 3).
- ☐ Shift cam binding. Caused by lubrication failure or excessive wear. Replace the cam and bearing (Chapter 2 or Chapter 3).
- ☐ Shift lever return spring weak or broken (Chapter 2 or Chapter 3).
- ☐ Shift lever broken. Splines stripped out of lever or shaft, caused by allowing the lever to get loose or from dropping the machine. Replace necessary parts (Chapter 2 or Chapter 3).
- ☐ Shift mechanism pawl broken or worn. Full engagement and rotary movement of shift drum results. Replace shaft assembly (Chapter 2 or Chapter 3).
- ☐ Pawl spring broken. Allows pawl to float, causing sporadic shift operation. Replace spring (Chapter 2 or Chapter 3).

Jumps out of gear
- ☐ Shift fork(s) worn. Overhaul the transmission (Chapter 2 or Chapter 3).
- ☐ Gear groove(s) worn. Overhaul the transmission (Chapter 2 or Chapter 3).
- ☐ Gear dogs or dog slots worn or damaged. The gears should be inspected and replaced. No attempt should be made to service the worn parts.

Overshifts
- ☐ Pawl spring weak or broken (Chapter 2 or Chapter 3).
- ☐ Shift drum stopper lever not functioning (Chapter 2 or Chapter 3).
- ☐ Overshift limiter broken or distorted (Chapter 2 or Chapter 3).

7 Abnormal engine noise

Knocking or pinging
- ☐ Carbon build-up in combustion chamber. Use of a fuel additive that will dissolve the adhesive bonding the carbon particles to the piston crown and chamber is the easiest way to remove the build-up. Otherwise, the cylinder head will have to be removed and decarbonized (Chapter 2 or Chapter 3).
- ☐ Incorrect or poor quality fuel. Old or improper fuel can cause detonation. This causes the pistons to rattle, thus the knocking or pinging sound. Drain the old fuel and always use the recommended grade fuel (Chapter 5).
- ☐ Spark plug heat range incorrect. Uncontrolled detonation indicates that the plug heat range is too hot. The plug in effect becomes a glow plug, raising cylinder temperatures. Install the proper heat range plug (Chapter 1).
- ☐ Improper air/fuel mixture. This will cause the cylinders to run hot and lead to detonation. Clogged jets or an air leak can cause this imbalance. See Chapter 5.

Piston slap or rattling
- ☐ Cylinder-to-piston clearance excessive. Caused by improper assembly. Inspect and overhaul top end parts (Chapter 2 or Chapter 3).
- ☐ Connecting rod bent. Caused by over-revving, trying to start a badly flooded engine or from ingesting a foreign object into the combustion chamber. Replace the damaged parts (Chapter 2 or Chapter 3).
- ☐ Piston pin or piston pin bore worn or seized from wear or lack of lubrication. Replace damaged parts (Chapter 2 or Chapter 3).

Fault Finding   REF•37

7 Abnormal engine noise (continued)

- ☐ Piston ring(s) worn, broken or sticking. Overhaul the top end (Chapter 2 or Chapter 3).
- ☐ Piston seizure damage. Usually from lack of lubrication or overheating. Replace the pistons and bore the cylinders, as necessary (Chapter 2 or Chapter 3).
- ☐ Connecting rod upper or lower end clearance excessive. Caused by excessive wear or lack of lubrication. Replace worn parts.

Valve noise

- ☐ Incorrect valve clearances. Adjust the clearances by referring to Chapter 1.
- ☐ Valve spring broken or weak. Check and replace weak valve springs (Chapter 2 or Chapter 3).
- ☐ Camshaft or cylinder head worn or damaged. Lack of lubrication at high rpm is usually the cause of damage. Insufficient oil or failure to change the oil at the recommended intervals are the chief causes. Since there are no replaceable bearings in the head, the head itself will have to be replaced if there is excessive wear or damage (Chapter 2 or Chapter 3).

Other noise

- ☐ Cylinder head gasket leaking.
- ☐ Exhaust pipe leaking at cylinder head connection. Caused by improper fit of pipe(s) or loose exhaust flange. All exhaust fasteners should be tightened evenly and carefully. Failure to do this will lead to a leak.
- ☐ Crankshaft runout excessive. Caused by a bent crankshaft (from over-revving) or damage from an upper cylinder component failure. Can also be attributed to dropping the machine on either of the crankshaft ends.
- ☐ Engine mounting bolts loose. Tighten all engine mount bolts to the specified torque (Chapter 2 or Chapter 3).
- ☐ Crankshaft bearings worn (Chapter 2 or Chapter 3).
- ☐ Camshaft chain tensioner defective. Replace according to the procedure in Chapter 2 or Chapter 3.
- ☐ Camshaft chain, sprockets or guides worn (Chapter 2 or Chapter 3).

8 Abnormal driveline noise

Clutch noise

- ☐ Clutch housing/friction plate clearance excessive (Chapter 2 or Chapter 3).
- ☐ Loose or damaged clutch pressure plate and/or bolts (Chapter 2 or Chapter 3).

Transmission noise

- ☐ Bearings worn. Also includes the possibility that the shafts are worn. Overhaul the transmission (Chapter 2 or Chapter 3).
- ☐ Gears worn or chipped (Chapter 2 or Chapter 3).
- ☐ Metal chips jammed in gear teeth. Probably pieces from a broken clutch, gear or shift mechanism that were picked up by the gears. This will cause early bearing failure (Chapter 2 or Chapter 3).

- ☐ Engine oil level too low. Causes a howl from transmission. Also affects engine power and clutch operation ('Daily (pre-ride) checks').

Chain or final drive noise

- ☐ Chain not adjusted properly (Chapter 1).
- ☐ Engine sprocket or rear sprocket loose. Tighten fasteners (Chapter 7).
- ☐ Sprocket(s) worn. Replace sprocket(s). (Chapter 7).
- ☐ Rear sprocket warped. Replace (Chapter 7).
- ☐ Wheel coupling worn. Replace coupling (Chapter 7).

9 Abnormal frame and suspension noise

Front end noise

- ☐ Low fluid level or improper viscosity oil in forks. This can sound like spurting and is usually accompanied by irregular fork action (Chapter 7).
- ☐ Spring weak or broken. Makes a clicking or scraping sound. Fork oil, when drained, will have a lot of metal particles in it (Chapter 7).
- ☐ Steering head bearings loose or damaged. Clicks when braking. Check and adjust or replace as necessary (Chapter 7).
- ☐ Fork clamps loose. Make sure all fork clamp pinch bolts are tight (Chapter 7).
- ☐ Fork tube bent. Good possibility if machine has been dropped. Replace tube with a new one (Chapter 7).
- ☐ Front axle or axle clamp bolt loose. Tighten them to the specified torque (Chapter 8).

Shock absorber noise

- ☐ Fluid level incorrect. Indicates a leak caused by defective seal. Shock will be covered with oil. Replace shock (Chapter 7).
- ☐ Defective shock absorber with internal damage. This is in the body of the shock and can't be remedied. The shock must be replaced with a new one (Chapter 7).
- ☐ Bent or damaged shock body. Replace the shock with a new one (Chapter 7).

Brake noise

- ☐ Squeal caused by pad shim not installed or positioned correctly (Chapter 8).
- ☐ Squeal caused by dust on brake pads. Usually found in combination with glazed pads. Clean using brake cleaning solvent (Chapter 8).
- ☐ Contamination of brake pads. Oil, brake fluid or dirt causing brake to chatter or squeal. Clean or replace pads (Chapter 8).
- ☐ Pads glazed. Caused by excessive heat from prolonged use or from contamination. Do not use sandpaper, emery cloth, carborundum cloth or any other abrasive to roughen the pad surfaces as abrasives will stay in the pad material and damage the disc. A very fine flat file can be used, but pad replacement is suggested as a cure (Chapter 8).
- ☐ Disc warped. Can cause a chattering, clicking or intermittent squeal. Usually accompanied by a pulsating lever and uneven braking. Replace the disc (Chapter 8).
- ☐ Loose or worn wheel bearings. Check and replace as needed (Chapter 8).

REF•38 Fault Finding

10 Oil level indicator light comes on

Engine lubrication system
- [ ] Yamaha FZR models use an oil level light rather than an oil pressure light.
- [ ] Engine oil level low. Inspect for leak or other problem causing low oil level and add recommended oil (Chapters 1, 2 and 3).

Electrical system
- [ ] Oil level switch defective. Check the switch according to the procedure in Chapter 10. Replace it if it's defective.
- [ ] Oil level indicator light circuit defective. Check for pinched, shorted, disconnected or damaged wiring (Chapter 1).

11 Excessive exhaust smoke

White smoke
- [ ] Piston oil ring worn. The ring may be broken or damaged, causing oil from the crankcase to be pulled past the piston into the combustion chamber. Replace the rings with new ones (Chapter 2 or Chapter 3).
- [ ] Cylinders worn, cracked, or scored. Caused by overheating or oil starvation. If worn or scored, the cylinders will have to be rebored and new pistons installed. If cracked, the cylinder block will have to be replaced (see Chapter 2 or Chapter 3).
- [ ] Valve oil seal damaged or worn. Replace oil seals with new ones (Chapter 2 or Chapter 3).
- [ ] Valve guide worn. Perform a complete valve job (Chapter 2 or Chapter 3).
- [ ] Engine oil level too high, which causes the oil to be forced past the rings. Drain oil to the proper level (Chapter 1).
- [ ] Head gasket broken between oil return and cylinder. Causes oil to be pulled into the combustion chamber. Replace the head gasket and check the head for warpage (Chapter 2 or Chapter 3).
- [ ] Abnormal crankcase pressurization, which forces oil past the rings. Clogged breather or hoses usually the cause (Chapter 2 or Chapter 3).

Black smoke
- [ ] Air filter clogged. Clean or replace the element (Chapter 1).
- [ ] Main jet too large or loose. Compare the jet size to the Specifications (Chapter 5).
- [ ] Choke stuck, causing fuel to be pulled through choke circuit (Chapter 5).
- [ ] Fuel level too high. Check and adjust the float level as necessary (Chapter 5).
- [ ] Inlet needle held off needle seat. Clean the float bowls and fuel line and replace the needles and seats if necessary (Chapter 5).

Brown smoke
- [ ] Main jet too small or clogged. Lean condition caused by wrong size main jet or by a restricted orifice. Clean float bowl and jets and compare jet size to Specifications (Chapter 5).
- [ ] Fuel flow insufficient. Fuel inlet needle valve stuck closed due to chemical reaction with old fuel. Float level incorrect. Restricted fuel line. Clean line and float bowl and adjust floats if necessary.
- [ ] Carburetor intake manifolds loose (Chapter 5).
- [ ] Air filter poorly sealed or not installed (Chapter 1).

12 Poor handling or stability

Handlebar hard to turn
- [ ] Steering stem locknut too tight (Chapter 7).
- [ ] Bearings damaged. Roughness can be felt as the bars are turned from side-to-side. Replace bearings and races (Chapter 7).
- [ ] Races dented or worn. Denting results from wear in only one position (e.g., straight ahead), from a collision or hitting a pothole or from dropping the machine. Replace races and bearings (Chapter 7).
- [ ] Steering stem lubrication inadequate. Causes are grease getting hard from age or being washed out by high pressure car washes. Disassemble steering head and repack bearings (Chapter 7).
- [ ] Steering stem bent. Caused by a collision, hitting a pothole or by dropping the machine. Replace damaged part. Don't try to straighten the steering stem (Chapter 7).
- [ ] Front tire air pressure too low ('Daily (pre-ride) checks').

Handlebar shakes or vibrates excessively
- [ ] Tires worn or out of balance (Chapter 8).
- [ ] Swingarm bearings worn. Replace worn bearings by referring to Chapter 7.
- [ ] Rim(s) warped or damaged. Inspect wheels for runout (Chapter 8).
- [ ] Wheel bearings worn. Worn front or rear wheel bearings can cause poor tracking. Worn front bearings will cause wobble (Chapter 8).
- [ ] Handlebar clamp bolts loose (Chapter 7).
- [ ] Steering stem or fork clamps loose. Tighten them to the specified torque (Chapter 7).
- [ ] Engine mount bolts loose. Will cause excessive vibration with increased engine rpm (Chapter 2 or Chapter 3).

Handlebar pulls to one side
- [ ] Frame bent. Definitely suspect this if the machine has been dropped. May or may not be accompanied by cracking near the bend. Replace the frame (Chapter 7).
- [ ] Wheel out of alignment. Caused by improper location of axle spacers or from bent steering stem or frame (Chapter 7).
- [ ] Swingarm bent or twisted. Caused by age (metal fatigue) or impact damage. Replace the arm (Chapter 7).
- [ ] Steering stem bent. Caused by impact damage or by dropping the motorcycle. Replace the steering stem (Chapter 7).
- [ ] Fork leg bent. Disassemble the forks and replace the damaged parts (Chapter 8).
- [ ] Fork oil level uneven. Check and add or drain as necessary (Chapter 7).

Poor shock absorbing qualities
Too hard:
   Fork oil level excessive (Chapter 7).
   Fork oil viscosity too high. Use a lighter oil (see the Specifications in Chapter 1).
   Fork tube bent. Causes a harsh, sticking feeling (Chapter 7).
   Shock shaft or body bent or damaged (Chapter 7).
   Fork internal damage (Chapter 7).
   Shock internal damage.
   Tire pressure too high (Daily (pre-ride) checks).
Too soft:
   Fork or shock oil insufficient and/or leaking (Chapter 7).
   Fork oil level too low (Chapter 7).
   Fork oil viscosity too light (Chapter 7).
   Fork springs weak or broken (Chapter 7).

Fault Finding REF•39

13 Braking problems

Brakes are spongy, don't hold
- [ ] Air in brake line. Caused by inattention to master cylinder fluid level or by leakage. Locate problem and bleed brakes (Chapter 8).
- [ ] Pad or disc worn (Chapters 1 and 8).
- [ ] Brake fluid leak. See paragraph 1.
- [ ] Contaminated pads. Caused by contamination with oil, grease, brake fluid, etc. Clean or replace pads. Clean disc thoroughly with brake cleaner (Chapter 8).
- [ ] Brake fluid deteriorated. Fluid is old or contaminated. Drain system, replenish with new fluid and bleed the system (Chapter 8).
- [ ] Master cylinder internal parts worn or damaged causing fluid to bypass (Chapter 8).
- [ ] Master cylinder bore scratched by foreign material or broken spring. Repair or replace master cylinder (Chapter 8).
- [ ] Disc warped. Replace disc (Chapter 8).

Brake lever or pedal pulsates
- [ ] Disc warped. Replace disc (Chapter 8).
- [ ] Axle bent. Replace axle (Chapter 8).
- [ ] Brake caliper bolts loose (Chapter 8).
- [ ] Brake caliper shafts damaged or sticking, causing caliper to bind. Lube the shafts or replace them if they are corroded or bent (Chapter 8).
- [ ] Wheel warped or otherwise damaged (Chapter 8).
- [ ] Wheel bearings damaged or worn (Chapter 8).

Brakes drag
- [ ] Master cylinder piston seized. Caused by wear or damage to piston or cylinder bore (Chapter 8).
- [ ] Lever balky or stuck. Check pivot and lubricate (Chapter 8).
- [ ] Brake caliper binds. Caused by inadequate lubrication or damage to caliper shafts (Chapter 8).
- [ ] Brake caliper piston seized in bore. Caused by wear or ingestion of dirt past deteriorated seal (Chapter 8).
- [ ] Brake pad damaged. Pad material separated from backing plate. Usually caused by faulty manufacturing process or from contact with chemicals. Replace pads (Chapter 8).
- [ ] Pads improperly installed (Chapter 8).
- [ ] Front brake lever or rear brake pedal freeplay insufficient (Chapter 1).

14 Electrical problems

Battery dead or weak
- [ ] Battery faulty. Caused by sulfated plates which are shorted through sedimentation or low electrolyte level. Also, broken battery terminal making only occasional contact (Chapter 10).
- [ ] Battery cables making poor contact (Chapter 10).
- [ ] Load excessive. Caused by addition of high wattage lights or other electrical accessories.
- [ ] Ignition switch defective. Switch either grounds internally or fails to shut off system. Replace the switch (Chapter 10).
- [ ] Regulator/rectifier defective (Chapter 10).
- [ ] Stator coil open or shorted (Chapter 10).
- [ ] Wiring faulty. Wiring grounded or connections loose in ignition, charging or lighting circuits (Chapter 10).

Battery overcharged
- [ ] Regulator/rectifier defective. Overcharging is noticed when battery gets excessively warm or boils over (Chapter 10).
- [ ] Battery defective. Replace battery with a new one (Chapter 10).
- [ ] Battery amperage too low, wrong type or size. Install manufacturer's specified amp-hour battery to handle charging load (Chapter 10).

REF•40 Fault Finding Equipment

Checking engine compression

- Low compression will result in exhaust smoke, heavy oil consumption, poor starting and poor performance. A compression test will provide useful information about an engine's condition and if performed regularly, can give warning of trouble before any other symptoms become apparent.
- A compression gauge will be required, along with an adapter to suit the spark plug hole thread size. Note that the screw-in type gauge/adapter set up is preferable to the rubber cone type.
- Before carrying out the test, first check the valve clearances as described in Chapter 1.

1 Run the engine until it reaches normal operating temperature, then stop it and remove the spark plug(s), taking care not to scald your hands on the hot components.
2 Install the gauge adapter and compression gauge in No. 1 cylinder spark plug hole **(see illustration 1)**.

Screw the compression gauge adapter into the spark plug hole, then screw the gauge into the adapter

3 On kickstart-equipped motorcycles, make sure the ignition switch is OFF, then open the throttle fully and kick the engine over a couple of times until the gauge reading stabilises.
4 On motorcycles with electric start only, the procedure will differ depending on the nature of the ignition system. Flick the engine kill switch (engine stop switch) to OFF and turn the ignition switch ON; open the throttle fully and crank the engine over on the starter motor for a couple of revolutions until the gauge reading stabilises. If the starter will not operate with the kill switch OFF, turn the ignition switch OFF and refer to the next paragraph.
5 Install the spark plugs back into their suppressor caps and arrange the plug electrodes so that their metal bodies are earthed (grounded) against the cylinder head; this is essential to prevent damage to the ignition system as the engine is spun over **(see illustration 2)**. Position the plugs well

All spark plugs must be earthed (grounded) against the cylinder head

away from the plug holes otherwise there is a risk of atomised fuel escaping from the combustion chambers and igniting. As a safety precaution, cover the top of the valve cover with rag. Now turn the ignition switch ON and kill switch ON, open the throttle fully and crank the engine over on the starter motor for a couple of revolutions until the gauge reading stabilises.
6 After one or two revolutions the pressure should build up to a maximum figure and then stabilise. Take a note of this reading and on multi-cylinder engines repeat the test on the remaining cylinders.
7 The correct pressures are given in Chapter 2 Specifications. If the results fall within the specified range and on multi-cylinder engines all are relatively equal, the engine is in good condition. If there is a marked difference between the readings, or if the readings are lower than specified, inspection of the top-end components will be required.
8 Low compression pressure may be due to worn cylinder bores, pistons or rings, failure of the cylinder head gasket, worn valve seals, or poor valve seating.
9 To distinguish between cylinder/piston wear and valve leakage, pour a small quantity of oil into the bore to temporarily seal the piston rings, then repeat the compression tests **(see illustration 3)**. If the readings show

Bores can be temporarily sealed with a squirt of motor oil

a noticeable increase in pressure this confirms that the cylinder bore, piston, or rings are worn. If, however, no change is indicated, the cylinder head gasket or valves should be examined.
10 High compression pressure indicates excessive carbon build-up in the combustion chamber and on the piston crown. If this is the case the cylinder head should be removed and the deposits removed. Note that excessive carbon build-up is less likely with the used on modern fuels.

Checking battery open-circuit voltage

⚠ *Warning: The gases produced by the battery are explosive - never smoke or create any sparks in the vicinity of the battery. Never allow the electrolyte to contact your skin or clothing - if it does, wash it off and seek immediate medical attention.*

Fault Finding Equipment REF•41

Measuring open-circuit battery voltage

Float-type hydrometer for measuring battery specific gravity

- Before any electrical fault is investigated the battery should be checked.
- You'll need a dc voltmeter or multimeter to check battery voltage. Check that the leads are inserted in the correct terminals on the meter, red lead to positive (+ve), black lead to negative (-ve). Incorrect connections can damage the meter.
- A sound fully-charged 12 volt battery should produce between 12.3 and 12.6 volts across its terminals (12.8 volts for a maintenance-free battery). On machines with a 6 volt battery, voltage should be between 6.1 and 6.3 volts.

1 Set a multimeter to the 0 to 20 volts dc range and connect its probes across the battery terminals. Connect the meter's positive (+ve) probe, usually red, to the battery positive (+ve) terminal, followed by the meter's negative (-ve) probe, usually black, to the battery negative terminal (-ve) **(see illustration 4)**.

2 If battery voltage is low (below 10 volts on a 12 volt battery or below 4 volts on a six volt battery), charge the battery and test the voltage again. If the battery repeatedly goes flat, investigate the motorcycle's charging system.

Checking battery specific gravity (SG)

⚠️ *Warning: The gases produced by the battery are explosive - never smoke or create any sparks in the vicinity of the battery. Never allow the electrolyte to contact your skin or clothing - if it does, wash it off and seek immediate medical attention.*

- The specific gravity check gives an indication of a battery's state of charge.
- A hydrometer is used for measuring specific gravity. Make sure you purchase one which has a small enough hose to insert in the aperture of a motorcycle battery.
- Specific gravity is simply a measure of the electrolyte's density compared with that of water. Water has an SG of 1.000 and fully-charged battery electrolyte is about 26% heavier, at 1.260.
- Specific gravity checks are not possible on maintenance-free batteries. Testing the open-circuit voltage is the only means of determining their state of charge.

1 To measure SG, remove the battery from the motorcycle and remove the first cell cap. Draw some electrolyte into the hydrometer and note the reading **(see illustration 5)**. Return the electrolyte to the cell and install the cap.

2 The reading should be in the region of 1.260 to 1.280. If SG is below 1.200 the battery needs charging. Note that SG will vary with temperature; it should be measured at 20°C (68°F). Add 0.007 to the reading for every 10°C above 20°C, and subtract 0.007 from the reading for every 10°C below 20°C. Add 0.004 to the reading for every 10°F above 68°F, and subtract 0.004 from the reading for every 10°F below 68°F.

3 When the check is complete, rinse the hydrometer thoroughly with clean water.

Checking for continuity

- The term continuity describes the uninterrupted flow of electricity through an electrical circuit. A continuity check will determine whether an **open-circuit** situation exists.
- Continuity can be checked with an ohmmeter, multimeter, continuity tester or battery and bulb test circuit **(see illustrations 6, 7 and 8)**.

Digital multimeter can be used for all electrical tests

Battery-powered continuity tester

Battery and bulb test circuit

REF•42 Fault Finding Equipment

Continuity check of front brake light switch using a meter - note split pins used to access connector terminals

Continuity check of rear brake light switch using a continuity tester

- All of these instruments are self-powered by a battery, therefore the checks are made with the ignition OFF.
- As a safety precaution, always disconnect the battery negative (-ve) lead before making checks, particularly if ignition switch checks are being made.
- If using a meter, select the appropriate ohms scale and check that the meter reads infinity (∞). Touch the meter probes together and check that meter reads zero; where necessary adjust the meter so that it reads zero.
- After using a meter, always switch it OFF to conserve its battery.

Switch checks

1 If a switch is at fault, trace its wiring up to the wiring connectors. Separate the wire connectors and inspect them for security and condition. A build-up of dirt or corrosion here will most likely be the cause of the problem - clean up and apply a water dispersant such as WD40.

2 If using a test meter, set the meter to the ohms x 10 scale and connect its probes across the wires from the switch **(see illustration 9)**. Simple ON/OFF type switches, such as brake light switches, only have two wires whereas combination switches, like the ignition switch, have many internal links. Study the wiring diagram to ensure that you are connecting across the correct pair of wires. Continuity (low or no measurable resistance - 0 ohms) should be indicated with the switch ON and no continuity (high resistance) with it OFF.

3 Note that the polarity of the test probes doesn't matter for continuity checks, although care should be taken to follow specific test procedures if a diode or solid-state component is being checked.

4 A continuity tester or battery and bulb circuit can be used in the same way. Connect its probes as described above **(see illustration 10)**. The light should come on to indicate continuity in the ON switch position, but should extinguish in the OFF position.

Wiring checks

- Many electrical faults are caused by damaged wiring, often due to incorrect routing or chaffing on frame components.
- Loose, wet or corroded wire connectors can also be the cause of electrical problems, especially in exposed locations.

1 A continuity check can be made on a single length of wire by disconnecting it at each end and connecting a meter or continuity tester across both ends of the wire **(see illustration 11)**.

2 Continuity (low or no resistance - 0 ohms) should be indicated if the wire is good. If no continuity (high resistance) is shown, suspect a broken wire.

Checking for voltage

- A voltage check can determine whether current is reaching a component.
- Voltage can be checked with a dc voltmeter, multimeter set on the dc volts scale, test light or buzzer **(see illustrations 12 and 13)**. A meter has the advantage of being able to measure actual voltage.
- When using a meter, check that its leads are inserted in the correct terminals on the meter, red to positive (+ve), black to negative (-ve). Incorrect connections can damage the meter.
- A voltmeter (or multimeter set to the dc volts scale) should always be connected in parallel (across the load). Connecting it in series will destroy the meter.
- Voltage checks are made with the ignition ON.

Continuity check of front brake light switch sub-harness

A simple test light can be used for voltage checks

A buzzer is useful for voltage checks

Fault Finding Equipment REF•43

Checking for voltage at the rear brake light power supply wire using a meter . . .

1 First identify the relevant wiring circuit by referring to the wiring diagram at the end of this manual. If other electrical components share the same power supply (ie are fed from the same fuse), take note whether they are working correctly - this is useful information in deciding where to start checking the circuit.

2 If using a meter, check first that the meter leads are plugged into the correct terminals on the meter (see above). Set the meter to the dc volts function, at a range suitable for the battery voltage. Connect the meter red probe (+ve) to the power supply wire and the black probe to a good metal earth (ground) on the motorcycle's frame or directly to the battery negative (-ve) terminal **(see illustration 14)**. Battery voltage should be shown on the meter

. . . or a test light - note the earth connection to the frame (arrow)

with the ignition switched ON.

3 If using a test light or buzzer, connect its positive (+ve) probe to the power supply terminal and its negative (-ve) probe to a good earth (ground) on the motorcycle's frame or directly to the battery negative (-ve) terminal **(see illustration 15)**. With the ignition ON, the test light should illuminate or the buzzer sound.

4 If no voltage is indicated, work back towards the fuse continuing to check for voltage. When you reach a point where there is voltage, you know the problem lies between that point and your last check point.

Checking the earth (ground)

- Earth connections are made either directly to the engine or frame (such as sensors, neutral switch etc. which only have a positive feed) or by a separate wire into the earth circuit of the wiring harness. Alternatively a short earth wire is sometimes run directly from the component to the motorcycle's frame.
- Corrosion is often the cause of a poor earth connection.
- If total failure is experienced, check the security of the main earth lead from the negative (-ve) terminal of the battery and also the main earth (ground) point on the wiring harness. If corroded, dismantle the connection and clean all surfaces back to bare metal.

1 To check the earth on a component, use an insulated jumper wire to temporarily bypass its earth connection **(see illustration 16)**. Connect one end of the jumper wire between the earth terminal or metal body of the component and the other end to the motorcycle's frame.

2 If the circuit works with the jumper wire installed, the original earth circuit is faulty. Check the wiring for open-circuits or poor connections. Clean up direct earth connections, removing all traces of corrosion and remake the joint. Apply petroleum jelly to the joint to prevent future corrosion.

Tracing a short-circuit

- A short-circuit occurs where current shorts to earth (ground) bypassing the circuit components. This usually results in a blown fuse.

- A short-circuit is most likely to occur where the insulation has worn through due to wiring chafing on a component, allowing a direct path to earth (ground) on the frame.

1 Remove any bodypanels necessary to access the circuit wiring.

2 Check that all electrical switches in the circuit are OFF, then remove the circuit fuse and connect a test light, buzzer or voltmeter (set to the dc scale) across the fuse terminals. No voltage should be shown.

3 Move the wiring from side to side whilst observing the test light or meter. When the test light comes on, buzzer sounds or meter shows voltage, you have found the cause of the short. It will usually shown up as damaged or burned insulation.

4 Note that the same test can be performed on each component in the circuit, even the switch.

A selection of jumper wires for making earth (ground) checks

Technical Terms Explained

A

ABS (Anti-lock braking system) A system, usually electronically controlled, that senses incipient wheel lockup during braking and relieves hydraulic pressure at wheel which is about to skid.

Aftermarket Components suitable for the motorcycle, but not produced by the motorcycle manufacturer.

Allen key A hexagonal wrench which fits into a recessed hexagonal hole.

Alternating current (ac) Current produced by an alternator. Requires converting to direct current by a rectifier for charging purposes.

Alternator Converts mechanical energy from the engine into electrical energy to charge the battery and power the electrical system.

Ampere (amp) A unit of measurement for the flow of electrical current. Current = Volts ÷ Ohms.

Ampere-hour (Ah) Measure of battery capacity.

Angle-tightening A torque expressed in degrees. Often follows a conventional tightening torque for cylinder head or main bearing fasteners **(see illustration)**.

Angle-tightening cylinder head bolts

Antifreeze A substance (usually ethylene glycol) mixed with water, and added to the cooling system, to prevent freezing of the coolant in winter. Antifreeze also contains chemicals to inhibit corrosion and the formation of rust and other deposits that would tend to clog the radiator and coolant passages and reduce cooling efficiency.

Anti-dive System attached to the fork lower leg (slider) to prevent fork dive when braking hard.

Anti-seize compound A coating that reduces the risk of seizing on fasteners that are subjected to high temperatures, such as exhaust clamp bolts and nuts.

API American Petroleum Institute. A quality standard for 4-stroke motor oils.

Asbestos A natural fibrous mineral with great heat resistance, commonly used in the composition of brake friction materials. Asbestos is a health hazard and the dust created by brake systems should never be inhaled or ingested.

ATF Automatic Transmission Fluid. Often used in front forks.

ATU Automatic Timing Unit. Mechanical device for advancing the ignition timing on early engines.

ATV All Terrain Vehicle. Often called a Quad.

Axial play Side-to-side movement.

Axle A shaft on which a wheel revolves. Also known as a spindle.

B

Backlash The amount of movement between meshed components when one component is held still. Usually applies to gear teeth.

Ball bearing A bearing consisting of a hardened inner and outer race with hardened steel balls between the two races.

Bearings Used between two working surfaces to prevent wear of the components and a build-up of heat. Four types of bearing are commonly used on motorcycles: plain shell bearings, ball bearings, tapered roller bearings and needle roller bearings.

Bevel gears Used to turn the drive through 90°. Typical applications are shaft final drive and camshaft drive **(see illustration)**.

Bevel gears are used to turn the drive through 90°

BHP Brake Horsepower. The British measurement for engine power output. Power output is now usually expressed in kilowatts (kW).

Bias-belted tyre Similar construction to radial tyre, but with outer belt running at an angle to the wheel rim.

Big-end bearing The bearing in the end of the connecting rod that's attached to the crankshaft.

Bleeding The process of removing air from an hydraulic system via a bleed nipple or bleed screw.

Bottom-end A description of an engine's crankcase components and all components contained there-in.

BTDC Before Top Dead Centre in terms of piston position. Ignition timing is often expressed in terms of degrees or millimetres BTDC.

Bush A cylindrical metal or rubber component used between two moving parts.

Burr Rough edge left on a component after machining or as a result of excessive wear.

C

Cam chain The chain which takes drive from the crankshaft to the camshaft(s).

Canister The main component in an evaporative emission control system (California market only); contains activated charcoal granules to trap vapours from the fuel system rather than allowing them to vent to the atmosphere.

Castellated Resembling the parapets along the top of a castle wall. For example, a castellated wheel axle or spindle nut.

Catalytic converter A device in the exhaust system of some machines which converts certain pollutants in the exhaust gases into less harmful substances.

Charging system Description of the components which charge the battery, ie the alternator, rectifer and regulator.

Circlip A ring-shaped clip used to prevent endwise movement of cylindrical parts and shafts. An internal circlip is installed in a groove in a housing; an external circlip fits into a groove on the outside of a cylindrical piece such as a shaft. Also known as a snap-ring.

Clearance The amount of space between two parts. For example, between a piston and a cylinder, between a bearing and a journal, etc.

Coil spring A spiral of elastic steel found in various sizes throughout a vehicle, for example as a springing medium in the suspension and in the valve train.

Compression Reduction in volume, and increase in pressure and temperature, of a gas, caused by squeezing it into a smaller space.

Compression damping Controls the speed the suspension compresses when hitting a bump.

Compression ratio The relationship between cylinder volume when the piston is at top dead centre and cylinder volume when the piston is at bottom dead centre.

Continuity The uninterrupted path in the flow of electricity. Little or no measurable resistance.

Continuity tester Self-powered bleeper or test light which indicates continuity.

Cp Candlepower. Bulb rating commonly found on US motorcycles.

Crossply tyre Tyre plies arranged in a criss-cross pattern. Usually four or six plies used, hence 4PR or 6PR in tyre size codes.

Cush drive Rubber damper segments fitted between the rear wheel and final drive sprocket to absorb transmission shocks **(see illustration)**.

Cush drive rubbers dampen out transmission shocks

D

Degree disc Calibrated disc for measuring piston position. Expressed in degrees.

Dial gauge Clock-type gauge with adapters for measuring runout and piston position. Expressed in mm or inches.

Diaphragm The rubber membrane in a master cylinder or carburettor which seals the upper chamber.

Diaphragm spring A single sprung plate often used in clutches.

Direct current (dc) Current produced by a dc generator.

Technical Terms Explained

Decarbonisation The process of removing carbon deposits - typically from the combustion chamber, valves and exhaust port/system.
Detonation Destructive and damaging explosion of fuel/air mixture in combustion chamber instead of controlled burning.
Diode An electrical valve which only allows current to flow in one direction. Commonly used in rectifiers and starter interlock systems.
Disc valve (or rotary valve) A induction system used on some two-stroke engines.
Double-overhead camshaft (DOHC) An engine that uses two overhead camshafts, one for the intake valves and one for the exhaust valves.
Drivebelt A toothed belt used to transmit drive to the rear wheel on some motorcycles. A drivebelt has also been used to drive the camshafts. Drivebelts are usually made of Kevlar.
Driveshaft Any shaft used to transmit motion. Commonly used when referring to the final driveshaft on shaft drive motorcycles.

E

Earth return The return path of an electrical circuit, utilising the motorcycle's frame.
ECU (Electronic Control Unit) A computer which controls (for instance) an ignition system, or an anti-lock braking system.
EGO Exhaust Gas Oxygen sensor. Sometimes called a Lambda sensor.
Electrolyte The fluid in a lead-acid battery.
EMS (Engine Management System) A computer controlled system which manages the fuel injection and the ignition systems in an integrated fashion.
Endfloat The amount of lengthways movement between two parts. As applied to a crankshaft, the distance that the crankshaft can move side-to-side in the crankcase.
Endless chain A chain having no joining link. Common use for cam chains and final drive chains.
EP (Extreme Pressure) Oil type used in locations where high loads are applied, such as between gear teeth.
Evaporative emission control system Describes a charcoal filled canister which stores fuel vapours from the tank rather than allowing them to vent to the atmosphere. Usually only fitted to California models and referred to as an EVAP system.
Expansion chamber Section of two-stroke engine exhaust system so designed to improve engine efficiency and boost power.

F

Feeler blade or gauge A thin strip or blade of hardened steel, ground to an exact thickness, used to check or measure clearances between parts.
Final drive Description of the drive from the transmission to the rear wheel. Usually by chain or shaft, but sometimes by belt.
Firing order The order in which the engine cylinders fire, or deliver their power strokes, beginning with the number one cylinder.
Flooding Term used to describe a high fuel level in the carburettor float chambers, leading to fuel overflow. Also refers to excess fuel in the combustion chamber due to incorrect starting technique.

Free length The no-load state of a component when measured. Clutch, valve and fork spring lengths are measured at rest, without any preload.
Freeplay The amount of travel before any action takes place. The looseness in a linkage, or an assembly of parts, between the initial application of force and actual movement. For example, the distance the rear brake pedal moves before the rear brake is actuated.
Fuel injection The fuel/air mixture is metered electronically and directed into the engine intake ports (indirect injection) or into the cylinders (direct injection). Sensors supply information on engine speed and conditions.
Fuel/air mixture The charge of fuel and air going into the engine. See **Stoichiometric ratio**.
Fuse An electrical device which protects a circuit against accidental overload. The typical fuse contains a soft piece of metal which is calibrated to melt at a predetermined current flow (expressed as amps) and break the circuit.

G

Gap The distance the spark must travel in jumping from the centre electrode to the side electrode in a spark plug. Also refers to the distance between the ignition rotor and the pickup coil in an electronic ignition system.
Gasket Any thin, soft material - usually cork, cardboard, asbestos or soft metal - installed between two metal surfaces to ensure a good seal. For instance, the cylinder head gasket seals the joint between the block and the cylinder head.
Gauge An instrument panel display used to monitor engine conditions. A gauge with a movable pointer on a dial or a fixed scale is an analogue gauge. A gauge with a numerical readout is called a digital gauge.
Gear ratios The drive ratio of a pair of gears in a gearbox, calculated on their number of teeth.
Glaze-busting see **Honing**
Grinding Process for renovating the valve face and valve seat contact area in the cylinder head.
Gudgeon pin The shaft which connects the connecting rod small-end with the piston. Often called a piston pin or wrist pin.

H

Helical gears Gear teeth are slightly curved and produce less gear noise that straight-cut gears. Often used for primary drives.

Installing a Helicoil thread insert in a cylinder head

Helicoil A thread insert repair system. Commonly used as a repair for stripped spark plug threads (see illustration).
Honing A process used to break down the glaze on a cylinder bore (also called glaze-busting). Can also be carried out to roughen a rebored cylinder to aid ring bedding-in.
HT (High Tension) Description of the electrical circuit from the secondary winding of the ignition coil to the spark plug.
Hydraulic A liquid filled system used to transmit pressure from one component to another. Common uses on motorcycles are brakes and clutches.
Hydrometer An instrument for measuring the specific gravity of a lead-acid battery.
Hygroscopic Water absorbing. In motorcycle applications, braking efficiency will be reduced if DOT 3 or 4 hydraulic fluid absorbs water from the air - care must be taken to keep new brake fluid in tightly sealed containers.

I

lbf ft Pounds-force feet. An imperial unit of torque. Sometimes written as ft-lbs.
lbf in Pound-force inch. An imperial unit of torque, applied to components where a very low torque is required. Sometimes written as in-lbs.
IC Abbreviation for Integrated Circuit.
Ignition advance Means of increasing the timing of the spark at higher engine speeds. Done by mechanical means (ATU) on early engines or electronically by the ignition control unit on later engines.
Ignition timing The moment at which the spark plug fires, expressed in the number of crankshaft degrees before the piston reaches the top of its stroke, or in the number of millimetres before the piston reaches the top of its stroke.
Infinity (∞) Description of an open-circuit electrical state, where no continuity exists.
Inverted forks (upside down forks) The sliders or lower legs are held in the yokes and the fork tubes or stanchions are connected to the wheel axle (spindle). Less unsprung weight and stiffer construction than conventional forks.

J

JASO Quality standard for 2-stroke oils.
Joule The unit of electrical energy.
Journal The bearing surface of a shaft.

K

Kickstart Mechanical means of turning the engine over for starting purposes. Only usually fitted to mopeds, small capacity motorcycles and off-road motorcycles.
Kill switch Handebar-mounted switch for emergency ignition cut-out. Cuts the ignition circuit on all models, and additionally prevent starter motor operation on others.
km Symbol for kilometre.
kmh Abbreviation for kilometres per hour.

L

Lambda (λ) sensor A sensor fitted in the exhaust system to measure the exhaust gas oxygen content (excess air factor).

Technical Terms Explained

Lapping see Grinding.
LCD Abbreviation for Liquid Crystal Display.
LED Abbreviation for Light Emitting Diode.
Liner A steel cylinder liner inserted in a aluminium alloy cylinder block.
Locknut A nut used to lock an adjustment nut, or other threaded component, in place.
Lockstops The lugs on the lower triple clamp (yoke) which abut those on the frame, preventing handlebar-to-fuel tank contact.
Lockwasher A form of washer designed to prevent an attaching nut from working loose.
LT Low Tension Description of the electrical circuit from the power supply to the primary winding of the ignition coil.

M

Main bearings The bearings between the crankshaft and crankcase.
Maintenance-free (MF) battery A sealed battery which cannot be topped up.
Manometer Mercury-filled calibrated tubes used to measure intake tract vacuum. Used to synchronise carburettors on multi-cylinder engines.
Micrometer A precision measuring instrument that measures component outside diameters (see illustration).

Tappet shims are measured with a micrometer

MON (Motor Octane Number) A measure of a fuel's resistance to knock.
Monograde oil An oil with a single viscosity, eg SAE80W.
Monoshock A single suspension unit linking the swingarm or suspension linkage to the frame.
mph Abbreviation for miles per hour.
Multigrade oil Having a wide viscosity range (eg 10W40). The W stands for Winter, thus the viscosity ranges from SAE10 when cold to SAE40 when hot.
Multimeter An electrical test instrument with the capability to measure voltage, current and resistance. Some meters also incorporate a continuity tester and buzzer.

N

Needle roller bearing Inner race of caged needle rollers and hardened outer race. Examples of uncaged needle rollers can be found on some engines. Commonly used in rear suspension applications and in two-stroke engines.
Nm Newton metres.
NOx Oxides of Nitrogen. A common toxic pollutant emitted by petrol engines at higher temperatures.

O

Octane The measure of a fuel's resistance to knock.
OE (Original Equipment) Relates to components fitted to a motorcycle as standard or replacement parts supplied by the motorcycle manufacturer.
Ohm The unit of electrical resistance. Ohms = Volts ÷ Current.
Ohmmeter An instrument for measuring electrical resistance.
Oil cooler System for diverting engine oil outside of the engine to a radiator for cooling purposes.
Oil injection A system of two-stroke engine lubrication where oil is pump-fed to the engine in accordance with throttle position.
Open-circuit An electrical condition where there is a break in the flow of electricity - no continuity (high resistance).
O-ring A type of sealing ring made of a special rubber-like material; in use, the O-ring is compressed into a groove to provide the sealing action.
Oversize (OS) Term used for piston and ring size options fitted to a rebored cylinder.
Overhead cam (sohc) engine An engine with single camshaft located on top of the cylinder head.
Overhead valve (ohv) engine An engine with the valves located in the cylinder head, but with the camshaft located in the engine block or crankcase.
Oxygen sensor A device installed in the exhaust system which senses the oxygen content in the exhaust and converts this information into an electric current. Also called a Lambda sensor.

P

Plastigauge A thin strip of plastic thread, available in different sizes, used for measuring clearances. For example, a strip of Plastigauge is laid across a bearing journal. The parts are assembled and dismantled; the width of the crushed strip indicates the clearance between journal and bearing.
Polarity Either negative or positive earth (ground), determined by which battery lead is connected to the frame (earth return). Modern motorcycles are usually negative earth.
Pre-ignition A situation where the fuel/air mixture ignites before the spark plug fires. Often due to a hot spot in the combustion chamber caused by carbon build-up. Engine has a tendency to 'run-on'.
Pre-load (suspension) The amount a spring is compressed when in the unloaded state. Preload can be applied by gas, spacer or mechanical adjuster.
Premix The method of engine lubrication on older two-stroke engines. Engine oil is mixed with the petrol in the fuel tank in a specific ratio. The fuel/oil mix is sometimes referred to as "petroil".
Primary drive Description of the drive from the crankshaft to the clutch. Usually by gear or chain.
PS Pfedestärke - a German interpretation of BHP.
PSI Pounds-force per square inch. Imperial measurement of tyre pressure and cylinder pressure measurement.
PTFE Polytetrafluoroethylene. A low friction substance.
Pulse secondary air injection system A process of promoting the burning of excess fuel present in the exhaust gases by routing fresh air into the exhaust ports.

Q

Quartz halogen bulb Tungsten filament surrounded by a halogen gas. Typically used for the headlight (see illustration).

Quartz halogen headlight bulb construction

R

Rack-and-pinion A pinion gear on the end of a shaft that mates with a rack (think of a geared wheel opened up and laid flat). Sometimes used in clutch operating systems.
Radial play Up and down movement about a shaft.
Radial ply tyres Tyre plies run across the tyre (from bead to bead) and around the circumference of the tyre. Less resistant to tread distortion than other tyre types.
Radiator A liquid-to-air heat transfer device designed to reduce the temperature of the coolant in a liquid cooled engine.
Rake A feature of steering geometry - the angle of the steering head in relation to the vertical (see illustration).

Steering geometry

Technical Terms Explained

Rebore Providing a new working surface to the cylinder bore by boring out the old surface. Necessitates the use of oversize piston and rings.
Rebound damping A means of controlling the oscillation of a suspension unit spring after it has been compressed. Resists the spring's natural tendency to bounce back after being compressed.
Rectifier Device for converting the ac output of an alternator into dc for battery charging.
Reed valve An induction system commonly used on two-stroke engines.
Regulator Device for maintaining the charging voltage from the generator or alternator within a specified range.
Relay A electrical device used to switch heavy current on and off by using a low current auxiliary circuit.
Resistance Measured in ohms. An electrical component's ability to pass electrical current.
RON (Research Octane Number) A measure of a fuel's resistance to knock.
rpm revolutions per minute.
Runout The amount of wobble (in-and-out movement) of a wheel or shaft as it's rotated. The amount a shaft rotates 'out-of-true'. The out-of-round condition of a rotating part.

S

SAE (Society of Automotive Engineers) A standard for the viscosity of a fluid.
Sealant A liquid or paste used to prevent leakage at a joint. Sometimes used in conjunction with a gasket.
Service limit Term for the point where a component is no longer useable and must be renewed.
Shaft drive A method of transmitting drive from the transmission to the rear wheel.
Shell bearings Plain bearings consisting of two shell halves. Most often used as big-end and main bearings in a four-stroke engine. Often called bearing inserts.
Shim Thin spacer, commonly used to adjust the clearance or relative positions between two parts. For example, shims inserted into or under tappets or followers to control valve clearances. Clearance is adjusted by changing the thickness of the shim.
Short-circuit An electrical condition where current shorts to earth (ground) bypassing the circuit components.
Skimming Process to correct warpage or repair a damaged surface, eg on brake discs or drums.
Slide-hammer A special puller that screws into or hooks onto a component such as a shaft or bearing; a heavy sliding handle on the shaft bottoms against the end of the shaft to knock the component free.
Small-end bearing The bearing in the upper end of the connecting rod at its joint with the gudgeon pin.
Spalling Damage to camshaft lobes or bearing journals shown as pitting of the working surface.
Specific gravity (SG) The state of charge of the electrolyte in a lead-acid battery. A measure of the electrolyte's density compared with water.
Straight-cut gears Common type gear used on gearbox shafts and for oil pump and water pump drives.
Stanchion The inner sliding part of the front forks, held by the yokes. Often called a fork tube.

Stoichiometric ratio The optimum chemical air/fuel ratio for a petrol engine, said to be 14.7 parts of air to 1 part of fuel.
Sulphuric acid The liquid (electrolyte) used in a lead-acid battery. Poisonous and extremely corrosive.
Surface grinding (lapping) Process to correct a warped gasket face, commonly used on cylinder heads.

T

Tapered-roller bearing Tapered inner race of caged needle rollers and separate tapered outer race. Examples of taper roller bearings can be found on steering heads.
Tappet A cylindrical component which transmits motion from the cam to the valve stem, either directly or via a pushrod and rocker arm. Also called a cam follower.
TCS Traction Control System. An electronically-controlled system which senses wheel spin and reduces engine speed accordingly.
TDC Top Dead Centre denotes that the piston is at its highest point in the cylinder.
Thread-locking compound Solution applied to fastener threads to prevent slackening. Select type to suit application.
Thrust washer A washer positioned between two moving components on a shaft. For example, between gear pinions on gearshaft.
Timing chain See **Cam Chain**.
Timing light Stroboscopic lamp for carrying out ignition timing checks with the engine running.
Top-end A description of an engine's cylinder block, head and valve gear components.
Torque Turning or twisting force about a shaft.
Torque setting A prescribed tightness specified by the motorcycle manufacturer to ensure that the bolt or nut is secured correctly. Undertightening can result in the bolt or nut coming loose or a surface not being sealed. Overtightening can result in stripped threads, distortion or damage to the component being retained.
Torx key A six-point wrench.
Tracer A stripe of a second colour applied to a wire insulator to distinguish that wire from another one with the same colour insulator. For example, Br/W is often used to denote a brown insulator with a white tracer.
Trail A feature of steering geometry. Distance from the steering head axis to the tyre's central contact point.
Triple clamps The cast components which extend from the steering head and support the fork stanchions or tubes. Often called fork yokes.
Turbocharger A centrifugal device, driven by exhaust gases, that pressurises the intake air. Normally used to increase the power output from a given engine displacement.
TWI Abbreviation for Tyre Wear Indicator. Indicates the location of the tread depth indicator bars on tyres.

U

Universal joint or U-joint (UJ) A double-pivoted connection for transmitting power from a driving to a driven shaft through an angle. Typically found in shaft drive assemblies.
Unsprung weight Anything not supported by the bike's suspension (ie the wheel, tyres, brakes, final drive and bottom (moving) part of the suspension).

V

Vacuum gauges Clock-type gauges for measuring intake tract vacuum. Used for carburettor synchronisation on multi-cylinder engines.
Valve A device through which the flow of liquid, gas or vacuum may be stopped, started or regulated by a moveable part that opens, shuts or partially obstructs one or more ports or passageways. The intake and exhaust valves in the cylinder head are of the poppet type.
Valve clearance The clearance between the valve tip (the end of the valve stem) and the rocker arm or tappet/follower. The valve clearance is measured when the valve is closed. The correct clearance is important - if too small the valve won't close fully and will burn out, whereas if too large noisy operation will result.
Valve lift The amount a valve is lifted off its seat by the camshaft lobe.
Valve timing The exact setting for the opening and closing of the valves in relation to piston position.
Vernier caliper A precision measuring instrument that measures inside and outside dimensions. Not quite as accurate as a micrometer, but more convenient.
VIN Vehicle Identification Number. Term for the bike's engine and frame numbers.
Viscosity The thickness of a liquid or its resistance to flow.
Volt A unit for expressing electrical "pressure" in a circuit. Volts = current x ohms.

W

Water pump A mechanically-driven device for moving coolant around the engine.
Watt A unit for expressing electrical power. Watts = volts x current.
Wear limit see **Service limit**
Wet liner A liquid-cooled engine design where the pistons run in liners which are directly surrounded by coolant **(see illustration)**.

Wet liner arrangement

Wheelbase Distance from the centre of the front wheel to the centre of the rear wheel.
Wiring harness or loom Describes the electrical wires running the length of the motorcycle and enclosed in tape or plastic sheathing. Wiring coming off the main harness is usually referred to as a sub harness.
Woodruff key A key of semi-circular or square section used to locate a gear to a shaft. Often used to locate the alternator rotor on the crankshaft.
Wrist pin Another name for gudgeon or piston pin.

REF•48 Index

Note: *References throughout this index are in the form - "Chapter number" • "page number"*

A

Air filter
  element - 1•12
  housing - 5•7
Air induction system - 5•23
Alternator - 10•18, 10•19
  brushes - 1•26, 10•19
Antifreeze - 0•10, 1•2, 1•4

B

Battery - 10•3
  electrolyte level/specific gravity - 1•19, REF•41
  open-circuit voltage - REF•40
Bearings - REF•15
  connecting rod - 2•32, 2•35, 3•35, 3•37
  main - 2•32, 2•33, 3•35, 3•36, 3•37
  steering head - 1•18, 1•25, 7•20
  swingarm - 1•25, 7•28
  wheel - 1•19, 8•21
Bleeding the brakes - 8•14
Bodywork - 9•1 et seq
Brakes - 8•1 et seq
  bleeding - 8•14
  caliper - 8•8
  check - 1•16
  disc - 8•9
  fluid - 0•11, 1•2, 1•4, 1•25
  hoses - 1•27, 8•14
  light switches - 10•7
  master cylinder - 8•10, 8•12
  pads - 8•4
  seals - 1•27

Braking problems - REF•39
Bulbs - 10•5, 10•6, 10•9

C

Cables
  choke - 5•19
  clutch - 0•10, 2•28
  speedometer - 10•8
  throttle - 5•18
Caliper - 8•8
Camshaft - 2•8, 3•12
  chain and guides - 2•37, 3•37
  chain tensioner - 2•7, 3•12
Capacity - 1•2, 1•3
Carburetor - 1•14, 5•8, 5•9, 5•10, 5•16, 5•17
Cartridge forks - 7•17
Chains - REF•19
Charging system - 10•17
Chemicals - REF•30
Choke cable - 5•19
Clutch - 2•1 et seq, 3•1 et seq
  cable - 0•10, 2•28
  check - 1•15
  fluid - 0•11, 1•2, 1•4, 1•25
  problems - REF•36
  release mechanism - 3•27
  removal - 2•24, 3•23
  switch - 10•12
Component locations - 1•6
Connecting rods - 2•35, 3•37
  bearings - 2•32, 2•35, 3•35, 3•37
Continuity - REF•41

Conventional forks - 7•12
Conversion factors - REF•21
Coolant - 0•10, 1•2, 1•4
  pump - 4•10
  reservoir - 4•3
  temperature gauge and sender unit - 4•6
Cooling fan - 4•3
Cooling system - 4•1 et seq
  draining, flushing and refilling - 1•26
  inspection - 1•12
Crankcase - 2•30, 2•32, 3•31, 3•35
  ventilation system - 1•21
Crankshaft - 2•33, 3•36
Cylinder block - 2•15, 3•18
Cylinder compression - 1•21
Cylinder head - 2•10, 2•12, 3•15, 3•17

D

Daily (pre-ride) checks - 0•10
Dimensions - REF•1
Disc - 8•9
Draining the cooling system - 1•26
Drive chain - 0•11, 1•9, 7•29
Driveline noise - REF•37

E

Earth - REF•43
Electrical fault finding - 10•2
Electrical problems - REF•39
Electrical system - 10•1 et seq

Index

Engine
- camshaft - 2•8, 3•12
- camshaft chain and guides - 2•37, 3•37
- camshaft chain tensioner - 2•7, 3•12
- compression - REF•40
- connecting rods - 2•35, 3•37
- crankcase - 2•30, 2•32, 3•31, 3•35
- crankshaft - 2•33, 3•36
- cylinder block - 2•15, 3•18
- cylinder head - 2•10, 2•12, 3•15, 3•17
- disassembly and reassembly - 2•5, 3•10
- doesn't start - REF•32
- fault finding - REF•32
- main and connecting rod bearings - 2•32, 2•33, 2•35, 3•35, 3•36, 3•37
- noise - REF•36
- oil - 0•10, 1•2, 1•3, 1•10, 1•21
- oil filter - 1•10, 1•21
- oil pan and relief valve - 2•20, 3•20
- oil pump - 2•21, 3•22
- piston rings - 2•19, 3•20
- pistons - 2•16, 3•20
- removal and installation - 2•4, 3•8
- valve cover - 2•6, 3•10
- valves/valve seats/valve guides - 2•12, 3•17

Evaporation control system - 5•24
Excessive exhaust smoke - REF•38
Exhaust system - 5•1 et seq
- check - 1•20
- fault finding - REF•38
- removal - 5•19

F
Fairing - 9•1 et seq
Fasteners - 1•21, REF•7
Fault finding - REF•31
- equipment - REF•40
Final drive - 7•1 et seq
Fluids - 1•2, 1•3
Flushing the cooling system - 1•26
Footpegs and pads - 7•7
Forks - 7•11, 7•12, 7•17
- oil change - 7•10
Frame - 7•1 et seq
- noise - REF•37
Front fender - 9•7
Fuel filter - 1•20, 1•26
Fuel pump - 5•21, 5•23
Fuel reserve system - 10•19
Fuel system - 5•1 et seq
- check - 1•20
Fuel tank - 5•4, 5•7
Fuses - 10•4
FZR600 engine - 2•1 et seq
FZR750/1000 engine - 3•1 et seq

G
Gaskets - REF•18
Gauges - 10•8, REF•10
Gear shifting problems - REF•36
Getting back on the road - REF•28

H
Handlebars - 7•8
- switches -10•10, 10•11
Headlight
- aim - 10•6
- bulb - 10•5
Horn - 10•12
Hoses - 1•27, 8•14, REF•20
Hydraulic clutch fluid - 0•11, 1•2, 1•4, 1•25

I
Identification numbers - 0•9
Idle fuel/air mixture adjustment - 5•8
Igniter - 6•4
Ignition - 6•1 et seq
- coils - 6•2
- main (key) switch - 10•10
Instrument
- bulbs - 10•9
- cluster - 10•8
Intake manifolds - 5•9
Introduction - 0•4

L
Legal checks - 0•11
Leverage - REF•14
Lighting system - 10•5
Lubricants - 1•2, 1•3, REF•30
Lubrication - 1•17

M
Main bearings - 2•32, 2•33, 3•35, 3•36, 3•37
Maintenance schedule - 1•8
Major engine repair - 2•4, 3•8
Master cylinder - 8•10, 8•12
Measuring tools - REF•10
Meters - 10•8
Mirrors - 9•7
MOT - REF•22
Mudguard - 9•7

N
Neutral switch - 10•11

O
Oil
- cooler - 2•43, 3•45
- filter - 1•10, 1•21
- level indicator light comes on - REF•38
- level sender - 10•10
- lines - 3•23, 3•45
- pan and relief valve - 2•20, 3•20
- pump - 2•21, 3•22
- seals - REF•17

Oil, engine - 0•10, 1•2, 1•3, 1•10, 1•21
Oil, transmission - 0•10, 1•2, 1•3
Overheating - REF•35

P
Pads - 8•4
Pickup coil - 6•3
Piston - 2•16, 3•20
- rings - 2•19, 3•20
Pivot points - 1•25

R
Radiator - 4•9
- cap - 4•3
Rear suspension pivot points - 1•25
Rear view mirrors - 9•7
Rear wheel coupling/rubber damper - 7•30
Reference - REF•1 et seq
Refilling the cooling system - 1•26
Regulator/rectifier - 10•18
Routine maintenance and servicing - 1•1 et seq

S
Safety checks - 0•11
Safety first - 0•8
Sealants - REF•18
Seals - 1•27
Seat - 9•6
Shift cam and forks - 2•41, 3•43
Shift mechanism - 2•29, 3•29
Shock absorber - 7•22
Short-circuit - REF•43
Side covers - 9•6
Sidestand - 7•8
- switch - 1•21, 10•12
Spark plugs - 1•13, 1•21
Speedometer cable - 10•8
Sprockets - 7•30
Starter clutch - 2•22, 3•43
Starter motor - 10•14, 10•15
Starter relay - 10•12
Starting circuit cut-off relay - 10•13
Starting problems - REF•32
Steering - 0•11
- head bearings - 1•18, 1•25, 7•20
Storage - REF•27
Suspension - 7•1 et seq
- adjustments - 7•30
- check - 0•11, 1•19, 1•21
- linkage - 7•24
- noise - REF•37
Swingarm - 7•27
- bearings - 1•25, 7•28
- play - 1•21
Switches - 1•21, 4•3, 10•7, 10•10, 10•11, 10•12

Index

T

Taillight bulb - 10•6
Tailpiece - 9•8
Technical terms explained - REF•44
Thermostat - 4•6
Thermostatic switch - 4•3
Throttle
  cables - 5•18
  operation/grip freeplay - 1•14
Tires - 0•12, 1•19, 8•24
Tools - REF•3
Torque - REF•14

Transmission - 2•1 et seq, 3•1 et seq
  oil - 0•10, 1•2, 1•3
  shafts - 2•37, 2•38, 3•38
Turn signal circuit - 10•7
  bulb - 10•6

V

Valves - 2•12, 3•17
  clearances - 1•22, 1•26
  cover - 2•6, 3•10
Voltage - REF•42

W

Warning light bulbs - 10•9
Water jacket joint - 4•12, 4•13
Water pump - 4•10
Weights - REF•1
Wheels - 1•19, 8•15, 8•16, 8•17
  bearings - 1•19, 8•21
Windshield - 9•7
Wiring diagrams - 10•19 et seq
Workshop tips - REF•3

Haynes Motorcycle Manuals – The Complete List

Title	Book No
BMW	
BMW 2-valve Twins (70 - 96)	0249
BMW K100 & 75 2-valve Models (83 - 96)	1373
BMW R850 & R1100 4-valve Twins (93 - 97)	3466
BSA	
BSA Bantam (48 - 71)	0117
BSA Unit Singles (58 - 72)	0127
BSA Pre-unit Singles (54 - 61)	0326
BSA A7 & A10 Twins (47 - 62)	0121
BSA A50 & A65 Twins (62 - 73)	0155
DUCATI	
Ducati MK III & Desmo Singles (69 - 76)	0445
Ducati 600, 750 & 900 2-valve V-Twins (91 - 96)	3290
Ducati 748, 916 & 996 4-valve V-Twins (94 - 01)	3756
HARLEY-DAVIDSON	
Harley-Davidson Sportsters (70 - 01)	0702
Harley-Davidson Big Twins (70 - 99)	0703
HONDA	
Honda NB, ND, NP & NS50 Melody (81 - 85)	◊ 0622
Honda NE/NB50 Vision & SA50 Vision Met-in (85 - 95)	◊ 1278
Honda MB, MBX, MT & MTX50 (80 - 93)	0731
Honda C50, C70 & C90 (67 - 99)	0324
Honda XR80R & XR100R (85 - 96)	2218
Honda XL/XR 80, 100, 125, 185 & 200 2-valve Models (78 - 87)	0566
Honda H100 & H100S Singles (80 - 92)	◊ 0734
Honda CB/CD125T & CM125C Twins (77 - 88)	◊ 0571
Honda CG125 (76 - 00)	◊ 0433
Honda NS125 (86 - 93)	◊ 3056
Honda MBX/MTX125 & MTX200 (83 - 93)	◊ 1132
Honda CD/CM185 200T & CM250C 2-valve Twins (77 - 85)	0572
Honda XL/XR 250 & 500 (78 - 84)	0567
Honda XR250L, XR250R & XR400R (86 - 01)	2219
Honda CB250 & CB400N Super Dreams (78 - 84)	◊ 0540
Honda CR Motocross Bikes (86 - 01)	2222
Honda Elsinore 250 (73 - 75)	0217
Honda CBR400RR Fours (88 - 99)	3552
Honda VFR400 (NC30) & RVF400 (NC35) V-Fours (89 - 98)	3496
Honda CB500 (93 - 01)	3753
Honda CB400 & CB550 Fours (73 - 77)	0262
Honda CX/GL500 & 650 V-Twins (78 - 84)	0442
Honda CBX550 Four (82 - 86)	◊ 0940
Honda XL600R & XR600R (83 - 00)	2183
Honda XL600/650V Transalp & XRV750 Africa Twin (87 - 02)	3919
Honda CBR600F1 & 1000F Fours (87 - 96)	1730
Honda CBR600F2 & F3 Fours (91 - 98)	2070
Honda CBR600F4 (99 - 02)	3911
Honda CB600F Hornet (98 - 02)	3915
Honda CB650 sohc Fours (78 - 84)	0665
Honda NTV600/650/Deauville V-Twins (88 - 01)	3243
Honda Shadow VT600 & 750 (USA) (88 - 00)	2312
Honda CB750 sohc Four (69 - 79)	0131
Honda V45/65 Sabre & Magna (82 - 88)	0820
Honda VFR750 & 700 V-Fours (86 - 97)	2101
Honda VFR800 V-Fours (97 - 01)	3703
Honda VTR1000 (FireStorm, Super Hawk) & XL1000V (Varadero) (97 - 00)	3744
Honda CB750 & CB900 dohc Fours (78 - 84)	0535
Honda CBR900RR FireBlade (92 - 99)	2161
Honda CBR900RR FireBlade (00 - 03)	4060
Honda CBR1100XX Super Blackbird (97 - 02)	3901
Honda ST1100 Pan European V-Fours (90 - 01)	3384
Honda Shadow VT1100 (USA) (85 - 98)	2313
Honda GL1000 Gold Wing (75 - 79)	0309
Honda GL1100 Gold Wing (79 - 81)	0669
Honda Gold Wing 1200 (USA) (84 - 87)	2199
Honda Gold Wing 1500 (USA) (88 - 00)	2225
KAWASAKI	
Kawasaki AE/AR 50 & 80 (81 - 95)	1007
Kawasaki KC, KE & KH100 (75 - 99)	1371
Kawasaki KMX125 & 200 (86 - 02)	◊ 3046
Kawasaki 250, 350 & 400 Triples (72 - 79)	0134
Kawasaki 400 & 440 Twins (74 - 81)	0281
Kawasaki 400, 500 & 550 Fours (79 - 91)	0910
Kawasaki EN450 & 500 Twins (Ltd/Vulcan) (85 - 93)	2053
Kawasaki EX & ER500 (GPZ500S & ER-5) Twins (87 - 99)	2052
Kawasaki ZX600 (Ninja ZX-6, ZZ-R600) Fours (90 - 00)	2146
Kawasaki ZX-6R Ninja Fours (95 - 98)	3541
Kawasaki ZX600 (GPZ600R, GPX600R, Ninja 600R & RX) & ZX750 (GPX750R, Ninja 750R) Fours (85 - 97)	1780
Kawasaki 650 Four (76 - 78)	0373
Kawasaki Vulcan 700/750 & 800 (85 - 01)	2457
Kawasaki 750 Air-cooled Fours (80 - 91)	0574
Kawasaki ZR550 & 750 Zephyr Fours (90 - 97)	3382
Kawasaki ZX750 (Ninja ZX-7 & ZXR750) Fours (89 - 96)	2054
Kawasaki Ninja ZX-7R & ZX-9R (ZX750P, ZX900B/C/D/E) (94 - 00)	3721
Kawasaki 900 & 1000 Fours (73 - 77)	0222
Kawasaki ZX900, 1000 & 1100 Liquid-cooled Fours (83 - 97)	1681
MOTO GUZZI	
Moto Guzzi 750, 850 & 1000 V-Twins (74 - 78)	0339
MZ	
MZ ETZ Models (81 - 95)	◊ 1680
NORTON	
Norton 500, 600, 650 & 750 Twins (57 - 70)	0187
Norton Commando (68 - 77)	0125
PEUGEOT	
Peugeot Speedfight, Trekker & Vivacity Scooters (96 - 02)	3920
PIAGGIO	
Piaggio (Vespa) Scooters (91 - 98)	3492
SUZUKI	
Suzuki GT, ZR & TS50 (77 - 90)	◊ 0799
Suzuki TS50X (84 - 00)	◊ 1599
Suzuki 100, 125, 185 & 250 Air-cooled Trail bikes (79 - 89)	0797
Suzuki GP100 & 125 Singles (78 - 93)	◊ 0576
Suzuki GS, GN, GZ & DR125 Singles (82 - 99)	◊ 0888
Suzuki 250 & 350 Twins (68 - 78)	0120
Suzuki GT250X7, GT200X5 & SB200 Twins (78 - 83)	◊ 0469
Suzuki GS/GSX250, 400 & 450 Twins (79 - 85)	0736
Suzuki GS500 Twin (89 - 02)	3238
Suzuki GS550 (77 - 82) & GS750 Fours (76 - 79)	0363
Suzuki GS/GSX550 4-valve Fours (83 - 88)	1133
Suzuki SV650 (99 - 02)	3912
Suzuki GSX-R600 & 750 (96 - 99)	3553
Suzuki GSX-R600 (01 - 02), GSX-R750 (00 - 02) & GSX-R1000 (01 - 02)	3986
Suzuki GSF600 & 1200 Bandit Fours (95 - 01)	3367
Suzuki GS850 Fours (78 - 88)	0536
Suzuki GS1000 Four (77 - 79)	0484
Suzuki GSX-R750, GSX-R1100 (85 - 92), GSX600F, GSX750F, GSX1100F (Katana) Fours (88 - 96)	2055
Suzuki GSX600/750F & GSX750 (98 - 02)	3987
Suzuki GS/GSX1000, 1100 & 1150 4-valve Fours (79 - 88)	0737
TRIUMPH	
Triumph Tiger Cub & Terrier (52 - 68)	0414
Triumph 350 & 500 Unit Twins (58 - 73)	0137
Triumph Pre-Unit Twins (47 - 62)	0251
Triumph 650 & 750 2-valve Unit Twins (63 - 83)	0122
Triumph Trident & BSA Rocket 3 (69 - 75)	0136
Triumph Fuel Injected Triples (97 - 00)	3755
Triumph Triples & Fours (carburettor engines) (91 - 99)	2162
VESPA	
Vespa P/PX125, 150 & 200 Scooters (78 - 95)	0707
Vespa Scooters (59 - 78)	0126
YAMAHA	
Yamaha DT50 & 80 Trail Bikes (78 - 95)	◊ 0800
Yamaha T50 & 80 Townmate (83 - 95)	◊ 1247
Yamaha YB100 Singles (73 - 91)	◊ 0474
Yamaha RS/RXS100 & 125 Singles (74 - 95)	0331
Yamaha RD & DT125LC (82 - 87)	◊ 0887
Yamaha TZR125 (87 - 93) & DT125R (88 - 02)	◊ 1655
Yamaha TY50, 80, 125 & 175 (74 - 84)	◊ 0464
Yamaha XT & SR125 (82 - 02)	1021
Yamaha Trail Bikes (81 - 00)	2350
Yamaha 250 & 350 Twins (70 - 79)	0040
Yamaha XS250, 360 & 400 sohc Twins (75 - 84)	0378
Yamaha RD250 & 350LC Twins (80 - 82)	0803
Yamaha RD350 YPVS Twins (83 - 95)	1158
Yamaha RD400 Twin (75 - 79)	0333
Yamaha XT, TT & SR500 Singles (75 - 83)	0342
Yamaha XZ550 Vision V-Twins (82 - 85)	0821
Yamaha FJ, FZ, XJ & YX600 Radian (84 - 92)	2100
Yamaha XJ600S (Diversion, Seca II) & XJ600N Fours (92 - 99)	2145
Yamaha YZF600R Thundercat & FZS600 Fazer (96 - 01)	3702
Yamaha YZF-R6 (98 - 02)	3900
Yamaha 650 Twins (70 - 83)	0341
Yamaha XJ650 & 750 Fours (80 - 84)	0738
Yamaha XS750 & 850 Triples (76 - 85)	0340
Yamaha TDM850, TRX850 & XTZ750 (89 - 99)	3540
Yamaha YZF750R & YZF1000R Thunderace (93 - 00)	3720
Yamaha FZR600, 750 & 1000 Fours (87 - 96)	2056
Yamaha XV V-Twins (81 - 96)	0802
Yamaha XJ900F Fours (83 - 94)	3239
Yamaha XJ900S Diversion (94 - 01)	3739
Yamaha YZF-R1 (98 - 01)	3754
Yamaha FJ1100 & 1200 Fours (84 - 96)	2057
Yamaha XJR1200 & 1300 (95 - 03)	3981
ATVs	
Honda ATC70, 90, 110, 185 & 200 (71 - 85)	0565
Honda TRX300 Shaft Drive ATVs (88 - 00)	2125
Honda TRX300EX & TRX400EX ATVs (93 - 99)	2318
Honda Foreman 400 and 450 ATVs (95 - 02)	2465
Kawasaki Bayou 220/300 & Prairie 300 ATVs (86 - 01)	2351
Polaris ATVs (85 to 97)	2302
Yamaha YT, YFM, YTM & YTZ ATVs (80 - 85)	1154
Yamaha YFS200 Blaster ATV (88 - 98)	2317
Yamaha YFB250 Timberwolf ATV (92 - 96)	2217
Yamaha YFM350 (ER and Big Bear) ATVs (87 - 99)	2126
Yamaha Warrior and Banshee ATVs (87 - 99)	2314
ATV Basics	10450
MOTORCYCLE TECHBOOKS	
Motorcycle Basics TechBook (2nd Edition)	3515
Motorcycle Electrical TechBook (3rd Edition)	3471
Motorcycle Fuel Systems TechBook	3514
Motorcycle Workshop Practice TechBook (2nd Edition)	3470

◊ = not available in the USA   **Bold type** = Superbike

The manuals on this page are available through good motorcycle dealers and accessory shops. In case of difficulty, contact: **Haynes Publishing**
(UK) +44 1963 442030   (USA) +1 805 498 6703
(FR) +33 1 47 17 66 29   (SV) +46 18 124016
(Australia/New Zealand) +61 3 9763 8100

MCL14.4/03

Preserving Our Motoring Heritage

The Model J Duesenberg Derham Tourster. Only eight of these magnificent cars were ever built – this is the only example to be found outside the United States of America

Almost every car you've ever loved, loathed or desired is gathered under one roof at the Haynes Motor Museum. Over 300 immaculately presented cars and motorbikes represent every aspect of our motoring heritage, from elegant reminders of bygone days, such as the superb Model J Duesenberg to curiosities like the bug-eyed BMW Isetta. There are also many old friends and flames. Perhaps you remember the 1959 Ford Popular that you did your courting in? The magnificent 'Red Collection' is a spectacle of classic sports cars including AC, Alfa Romeo, Austin Healey, Ferrari, Lamborghini, Maserati, MG, Riley, Porsche and Triumph.

A Perfect Day Out

Each and every vehicle at the Haynes Motor Museum has played its part in the history and culture of Motoring. Today, they make a wonderful spectacle and a great day out for all the family. Bring the kids, bring Mum and Dad, but above all bring your camera to capture those golden memories for ever. You will also find an impressive array of motoring memorabilia, a comfortable 70 seat video cinema and one of the most extensive transport book shops in Britain. The Pit Stop Cafe serves everything from a cup of tea to wholesome, home-made meals or, if you prefer, you can enjoy the large picnic area nestled in the beautiful rural surroundings of Somerset.

John Haynes O.B.E., Founder and Chairman of the museum at the wheel of a Haynes Light 12.

The 1936 490cc sohc-engined International Norton – well known for its racing success

The Museum is situated on the A359 Yeovil to Frome road at Sparkford, just off the A303 in Somerset. It is about 40 miles south of Bristol, and 25 minutes drive from the M5 intersection at Taunton.
Open 9.30am - 5.30pm (10.00am - 4.00pm Winter) 7 days a week, *except Christmas Day, Boxing Day and New Years Day*
Special rates available for schools, coach parties and outings Charitable Trust No. 292048